THE wallflower

YAMATONADESHIKO SHICHIHENGE

♥ 2 ♥

Tomoko Hayakawa

TRANSLATED AND ADAPTED BY
David Ury

LETTERED BY
Dana Hayward

DEL
REY

BALLANTINE BOOKS • NEW YORK

The Wallflower 2 is a work of fiction. Names, characters, places, and incidents are the products of the author's imagination or are used fictitiously. Any resemblance to actual events, locales, or persons, living or dead, is entirely coincidental.

2005 Del Rey® Books Trade Paperback Edition

Published in the United States by Del Rey® Books, an imprint of Random House Publishing Group, a division of Random House Inc., New York.

Del Rey is a registered trademark and the Del Rey colophon is a trademark of Random House, Inc.

Originally published in Japan in 2001 by Kodansha Ltd., Tokyo as *Yamatonadeshiko Shichihenge*, in 2003.
This publication rights arranged through Kodansha Ltd.

Library of Congress Control Number: 2004095918

ISBN 0-345-47949-1

Printed in the United States of America

www.delreymanga.com

9 8 7 6 5

First Edition: January, 2005

Translator and adapter—David Ury

Lettering—Dana Hayward

Contents

A Note from the Author

I'M A "BEE"

PEOPLE KEEP SAYING THEY WANT TO SEE MY PICTURE.

♥ Lately, my life has been really hectic. Everybody was so worked up about Y2K*, but now, several months have already passed. I was all excited about Volume 1, and now, suddenly, Volume 2 is coming out. I'm gonna keep working hard, so please keep following the adventures of Sunako and the "Creatures of the Light."

—Tomoko Hayakawa

*Editor's note: This volume was originally published in Japan in March 2001, hence the reference to Y2K. . . .

Honorifics

Throughout the Del Rey Manga books, you will find Japanese honorifics left intact in the translations. For those not familiar with how the Japanese use honorifics, and more important, how they differ from American honorifics, we present this brief overview.

Politeness has always been a critical facet of Japanese culture. Ever since the feudal era, when Japan was a highly stratified society, use of honorifics—which can be defined as polite speech that indicates relationship or status—has played an essential role in the Japanese language. When addressing someone in Japanese, an honorific usually takes the form of a suffix attached to one's name (example: "Asuna-san"), or as a title at the end of one's name or in place of the name itself (example: "Negi-sensei," or simply "Sensei!").

Honorifics can be expressions of respect or endearment. In the context of manga and anime, honorifics give insight into the nature of the relationship between characters. Many translations into English leave out these important honorifics, and therefore distort the "feel" of the original Japanese. Because Japanese honorifics contain nuances that English honorifics lack, it is our policy at Del Rey not to translate them. Here, instead, is a guide to some of the honorifics you may encounter in Del Rey Manga.

-san: This is the most common honorific, and is equivalent to Mr., Miss, Ms., Mrs., etc. It is the all-purpose honorific and can be used in any situation where politeness is required.

-sama: This is one level higher than "-san." It is used to confer great respect.

-dono: This comes from the word "tono," which means "lord." It is an even higher level than "-sama," and confers utmost respect.

-kun: This suffix is used at the end of boys' names to express familiarity or endearment. It is also sometimes used by men among friends, or when addressing someone younger or of a lower station.

-chan: This is used to express endearment, mostly toward girls. It is also used for little boys, pets, and even among lovers. It gives a sense of childish cuteness.

Bozu: This is an informal way to refer to a boy, similar to the English term "kid" or "squirt."

Sempai: This title suggests that the addressee is one's "senior" in a group or organization. It is most often used in a school setting, where underclassmen refer to their upperclassmen as "sempai." It can also be used in the workplace, such as when a newer employee addresses an employee who has seniority in the company.

Kohai: This is the opposite of "sempai," and is used toward underclassmen in school or newcomers in the workplace. It connotes that the addressee is of lower station.

Sensei: Literally meaning "one who has come before," this title is used for teachers, doctors, or masters of any profession or art.

[blank]: Usually forgotten in these lists, but perhaps the most significant difference between Japanese and English. The lack of honorific means that the speaker has permission to address the person in a very intimate way. Usually, only family, spouses, or very close friends have this kind of permission. Known as *yobisute*, it can be gratifying when someone who has earned the intimacy starts to call one by one's name without an honorific. But when that intimacy hasn't been earned, it can also be very insulting.

THE wallflower

YAMATONADESHIKO SHICHIHENGE

ヤマトナデシコ七変化♡

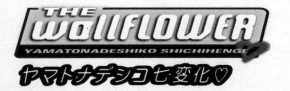

Chapter 6
Sunako, They're Calling You.

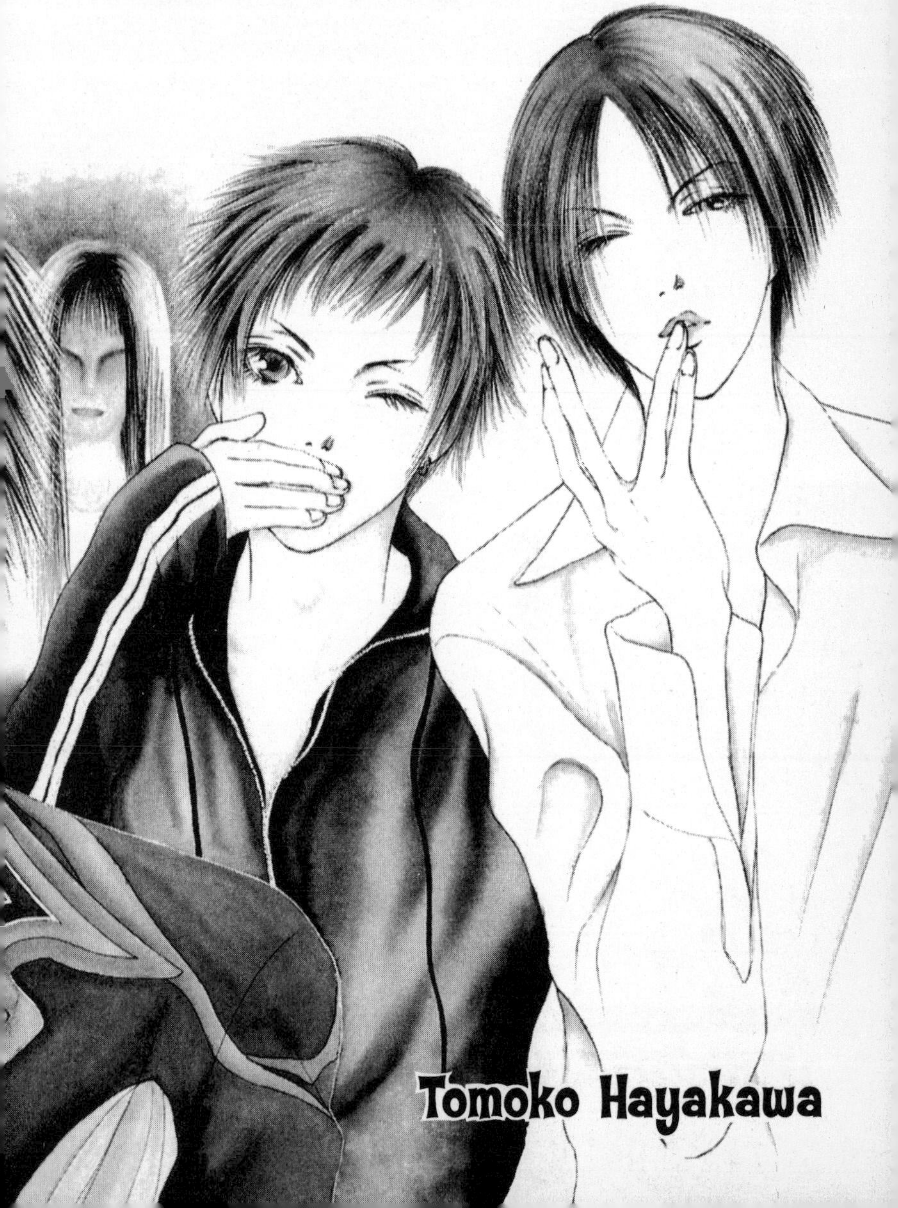
Tomoko Hayakawa

THE wallflower

YAMATONADESHIKO SHICHIHENGE

♥ BOOK 2 ♥

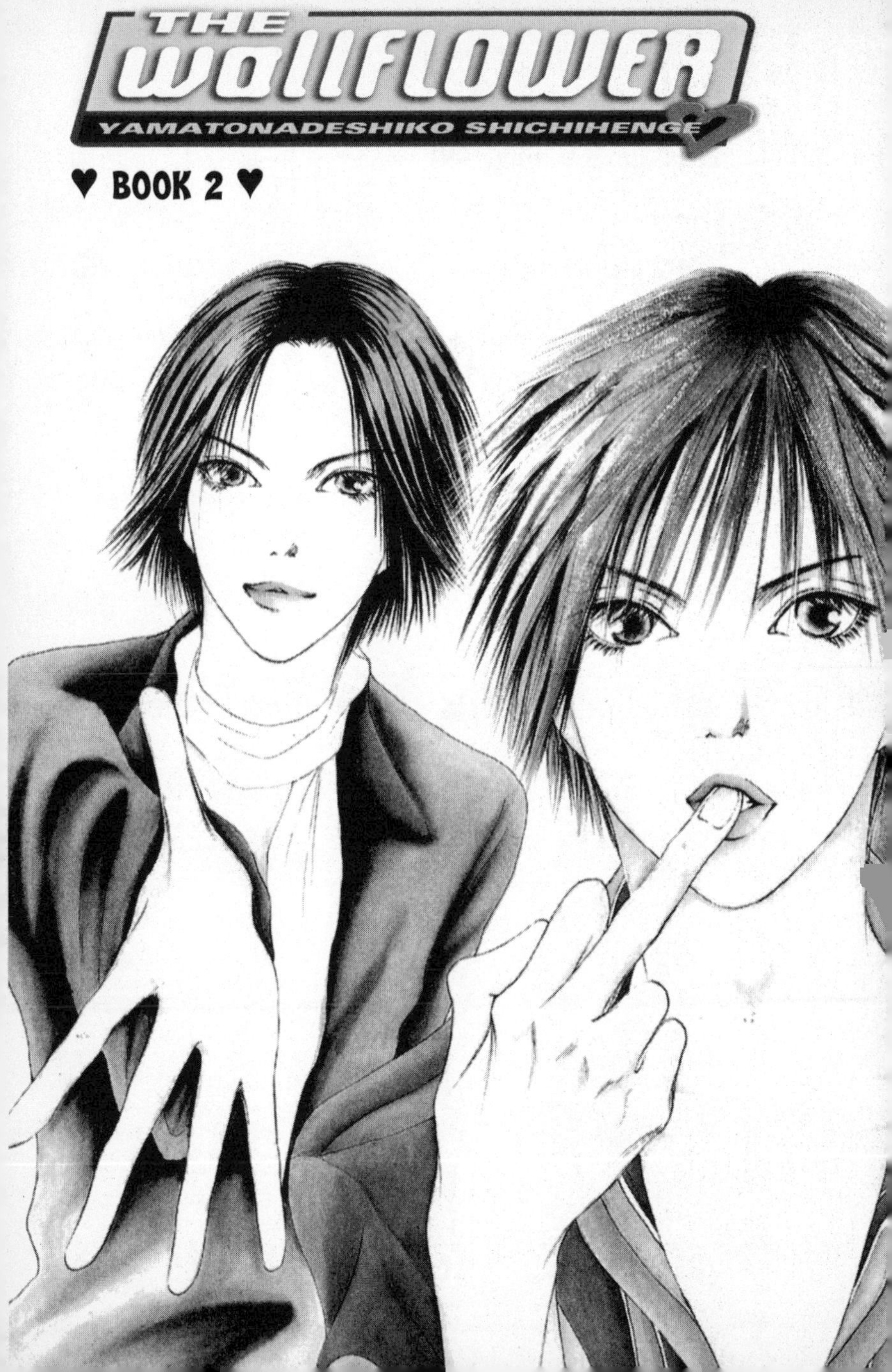

CONTENTS

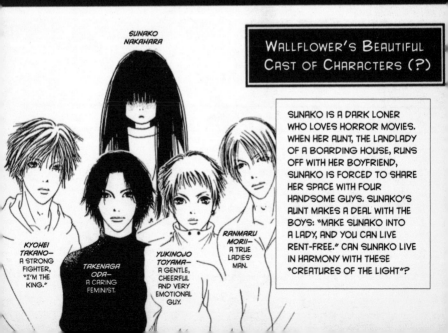

WALLFLOWER'S BEAUTIFUL CAST OF CHARACTERS (?)

SUNAKO NAKAHARA
RANMARU MORII— A TRUE LADIES' MAN.
YUKINOJO TOYAMA— A GENTLE, CHEERFUL AND VERY EMOTIONAL GUY.
TAKENAGA ODA— A CARING FEMINIST.
KYOHEI TAKANO— A STRONG FIGHTER, "I'M THE KING."

SUNAKO IS A DARK LONER WHO LOVES HORROR MOVIES. WHEN HER AUNT, THE LANDLADY OF A BOARDING HOUSE, RUNS OFF WITH HER BOYFRIEND, SUNAKO IS FORCED TO SHARE HER SPACE WITH FOUR HANDSOME GUYS. SUNAKO'S AUNT MAKES A DEAL WITH THE BOYS: "MAKE SUNAKO INTO A LADY, AND YOU CAN LIVE RENT-FREE." CAN SUNAKO LIVE IN HARMONY WITH THESE "CREATURES OF THE LIGHT"?

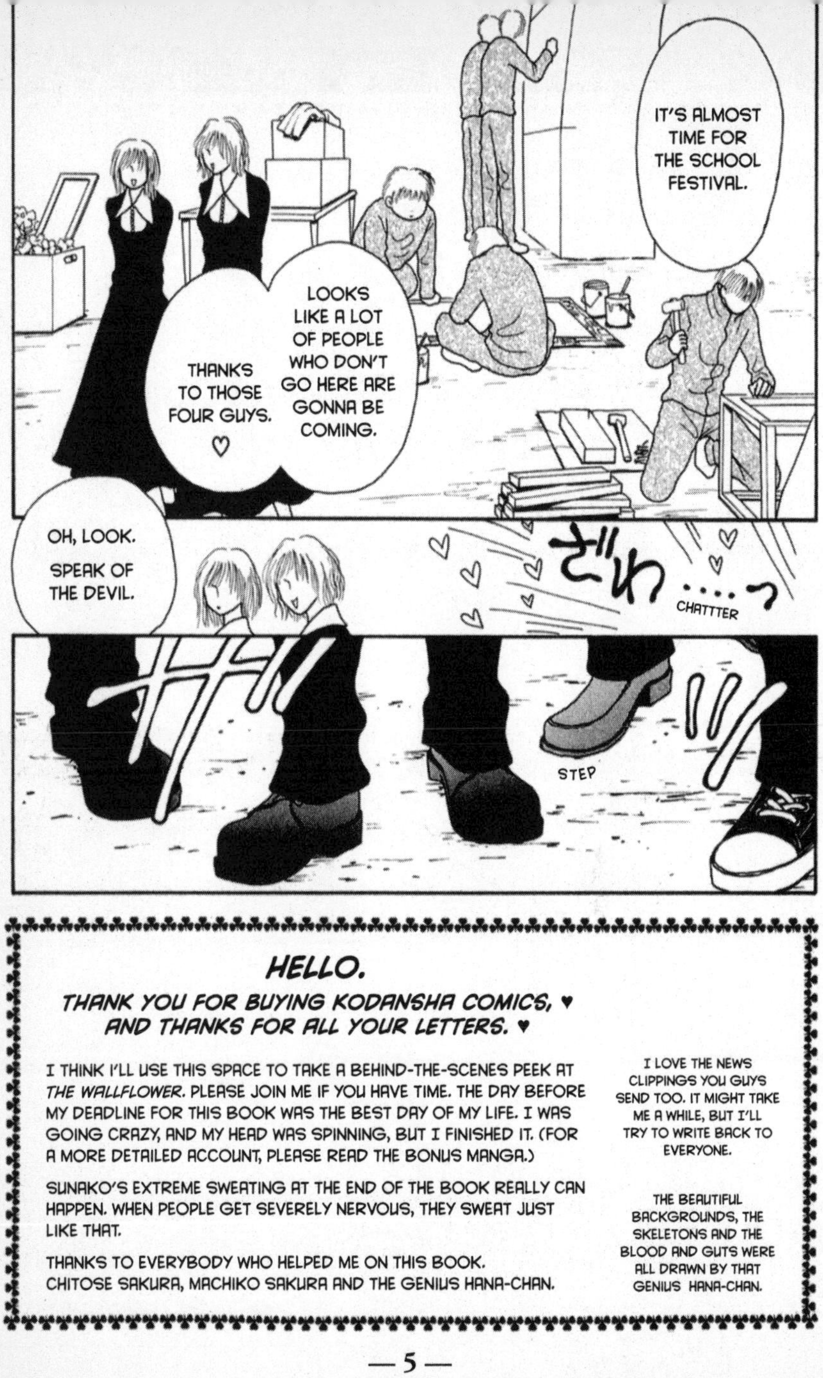

IT'S ALMOST TIME FOR THE SCHOOL FESTIVAL.
LOOKS LIKE A LOT OF PEOPLE WHO DON'T GO HERE ARE GONNA BE COMING.
THANKS TO THOSE FOUR GUYS. ♡
ざわ……
CHATTER
OH, LOOK.
SPEAK OF THE DEVIL.
STEP

HELLO.

THANK YOU FOR BUYING KODANSHA COMICS, ♥ AND THANKS FOR ALL YOUR LETTERS. ♥

I THINK I'LL USE THIS SPACE TO TAKE A BEHIND-THE-SCENES PEEK AT *THE WALLFLOWER*. PLEASE JOIN ME IF YOU HAVE TIME. THE DAY BEFORE MY DEADLINE FOR THIS BOOK WAS THE BEST DAY OF MY LIFE. I WAS GOING CRAZY, AND MY HEAD WAS SPINNING, BUT I FINISHED IT. (FOR A MORE DETAILED ACCOUNT, PLEASE READ THE BONUS MANGA.)

SUNAKO'S EXTREME SWEATING AT THE END OF THE BOOK REALLY CAN HAPPEN. WHEN PEOPLE GET SEVERELY NERVOUS, THEY SWEAT JUST LIKE THAT.

THANKS TO EVERYBODY WHO HELPED ME ON THIS BOOK.
CHITOSE SAKURA, MACHIKO SAKURA AND THE GENIUS HANA-CHAN.

I LOVE THE NEWS CLIPPINGS YOU GUYS SEND TOO. IT MIGHT TAKE ME A WHILE, BUT I'LL TRY TO WRITE BACK TO EVERYONE.

THE BEAUTIFUL BACKGROUNDS, THE SKELETONS AND THE BLOOD AND GUTS WERE ALL DRAWN BY THAT GENIUS HANA-CHAN.

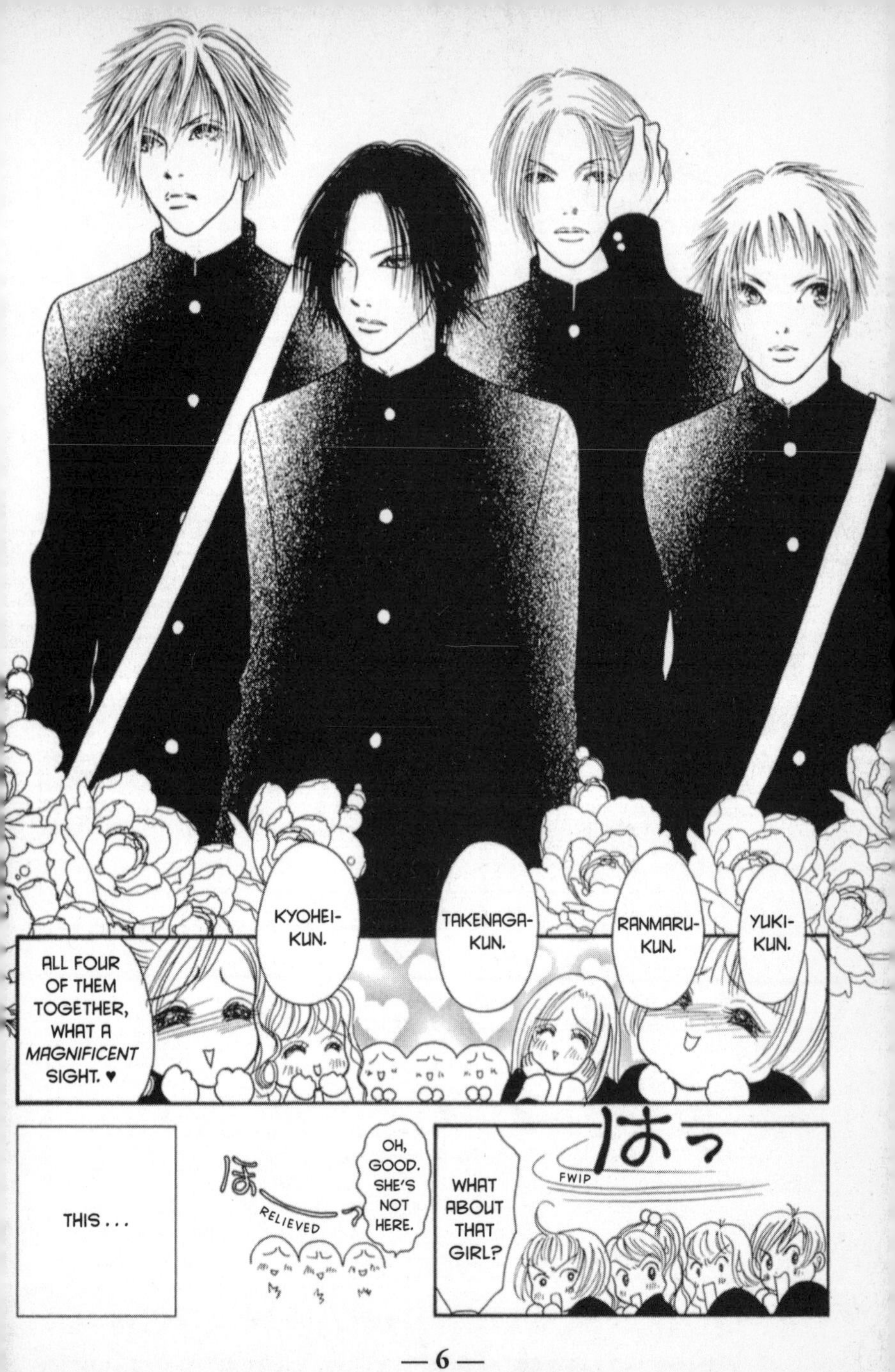
YUKI-KUN.
RANMARU-KUN.
TAKENAGA-KUN.
KYOHEI-KUN.
ALL FOUR OF THEM TOGETHER, WHAT A *MAGNIFICENT* SIGHT. ♥
はっ
FWIP
WHAT ABOUT THAT GIRL?
ほーっ
RELIEVED
OH, GOOD. SHE'S NOT HERE.
THIS . . .

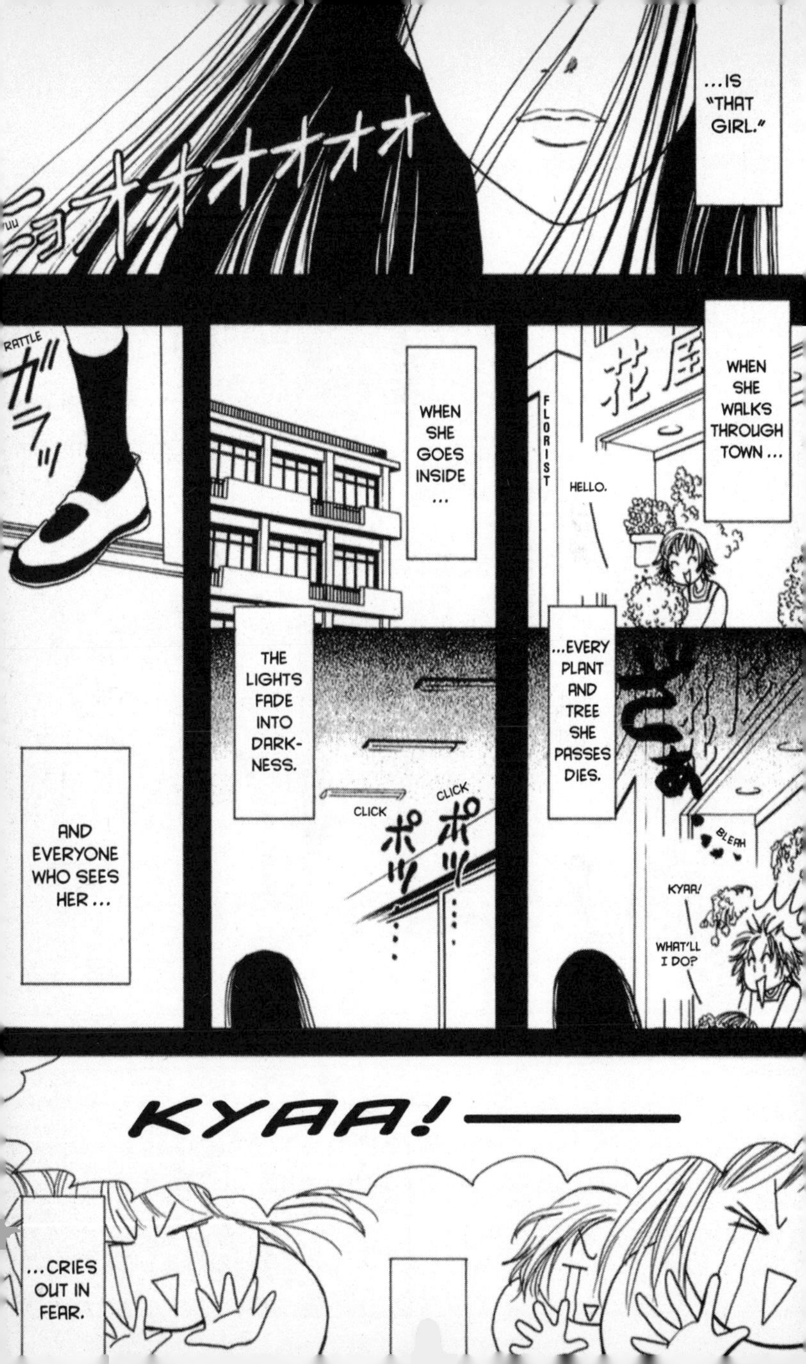
...IS "THAT GIRL."
YUU
WHEN SHE WALKS THROUGH TOWN ...
FLORIST
HELLO.
...EVERY PLANT AND TREE SHE PASSES DIES.
BLEAH
KYAA!
WHAT'LL I DO?
WHEN SHE GOES INSIDE ...
THE LIGHTS FADE INTO DARKNESS.
CLICK
CLICK
RATTLE
AND EVERYONE WHO SEES HER ...
KYAA!——
...CRIES OUT IN FEAR.

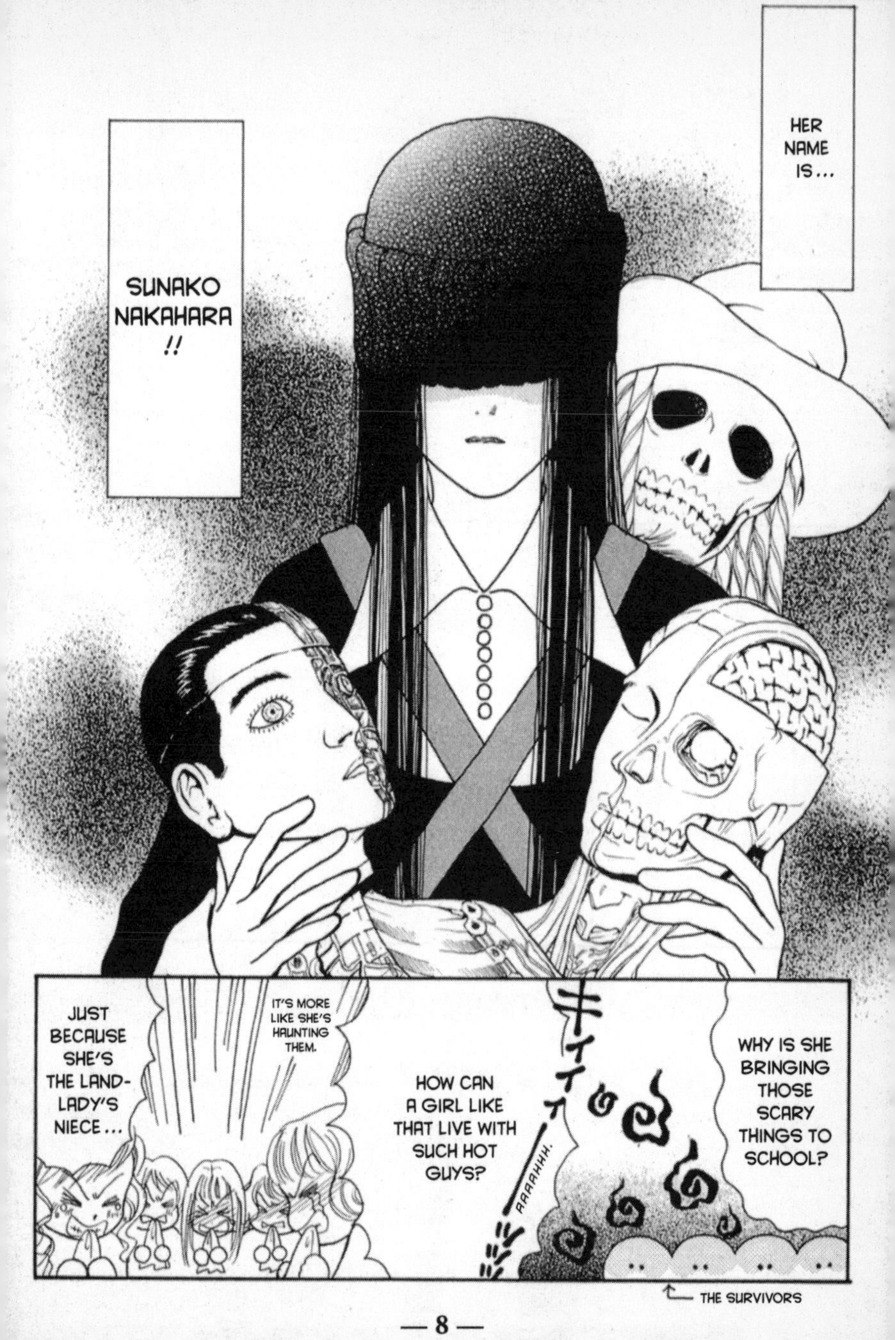
HER NAME IS…
SUNAKO NAKAHARA !!
WHY IS SHE BRINGING THOSE SCARY THINGS TO SCHOOL?
AAAAHHH.
HOW CAN A GIRL LIKE THAT LIVE WITH SUCH HOT GUYS?
IT'S MORE LIKE SHE'S HAUNTING THEM.
JUST BECAUSE SHE'S THE LAND-LADY'S NIECE…
THE SURVIVORS

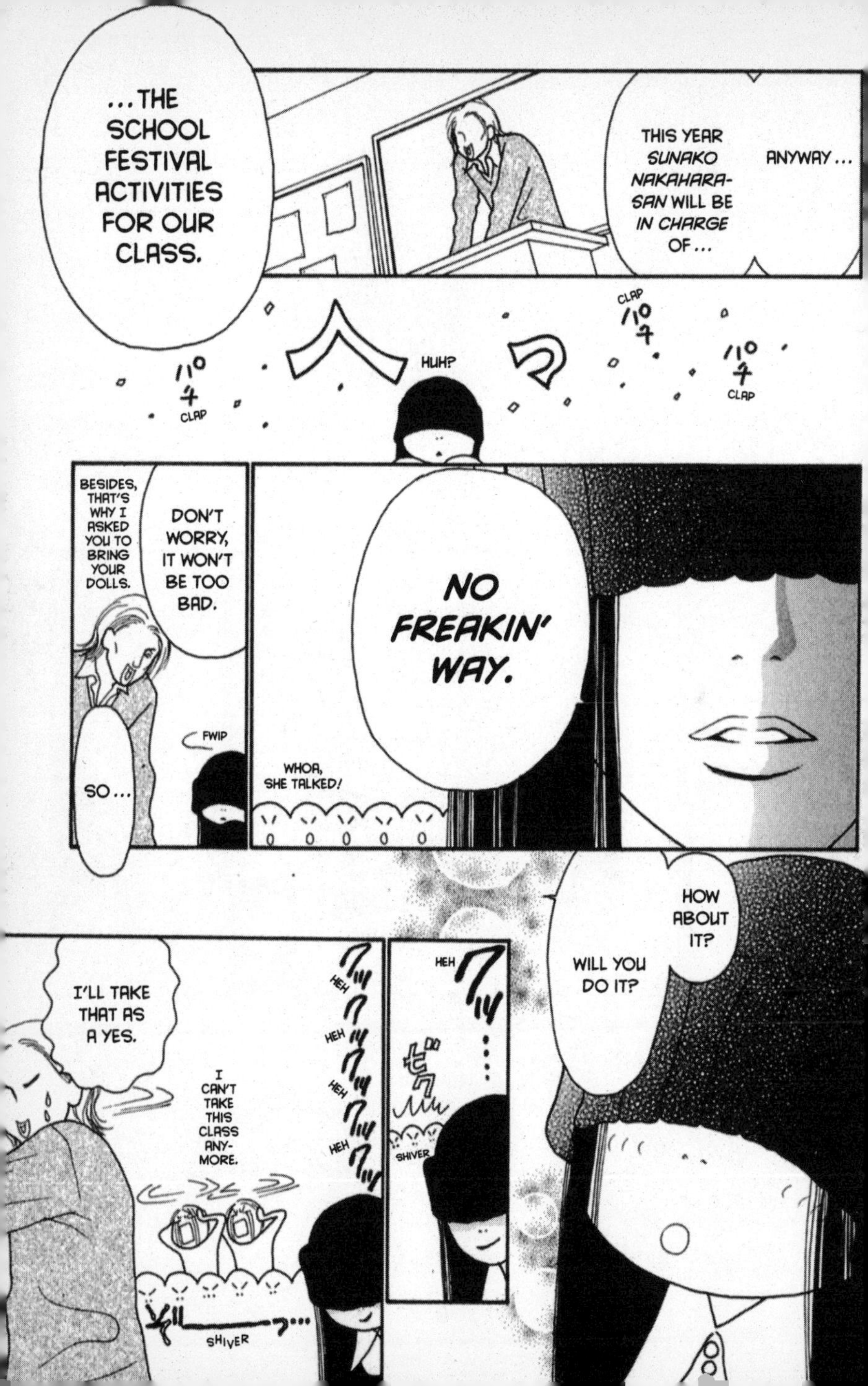
ANYWAY...
THIS YEAR SUNAKO NAKAHARA-SAN WILL BE IN CHARGE OF...
...THE SCHOOL FESTIVAL ACTIVITIES FOR OUR CLASS.
CLAP
CLAP
HUH?
CLAP
NO FREAKIN' WAY.
WHOA, SHE TALKED!
DON'T WORRY, IT WON'T BE TOO BAD.
BESIDES, THAT'S WHY I ASKED YOU TO BRING YOUR DOLLS.
FWIP
SO...
HOW ABOUT IT?
WILL YOU DO IT?
HEH
SHIVER
HEH
HEH
HEH
HEH
I'LL TAKE THAT AS A YES.
I CAN'T TAKE THIS CLASS ANYMORE.
SHIVER

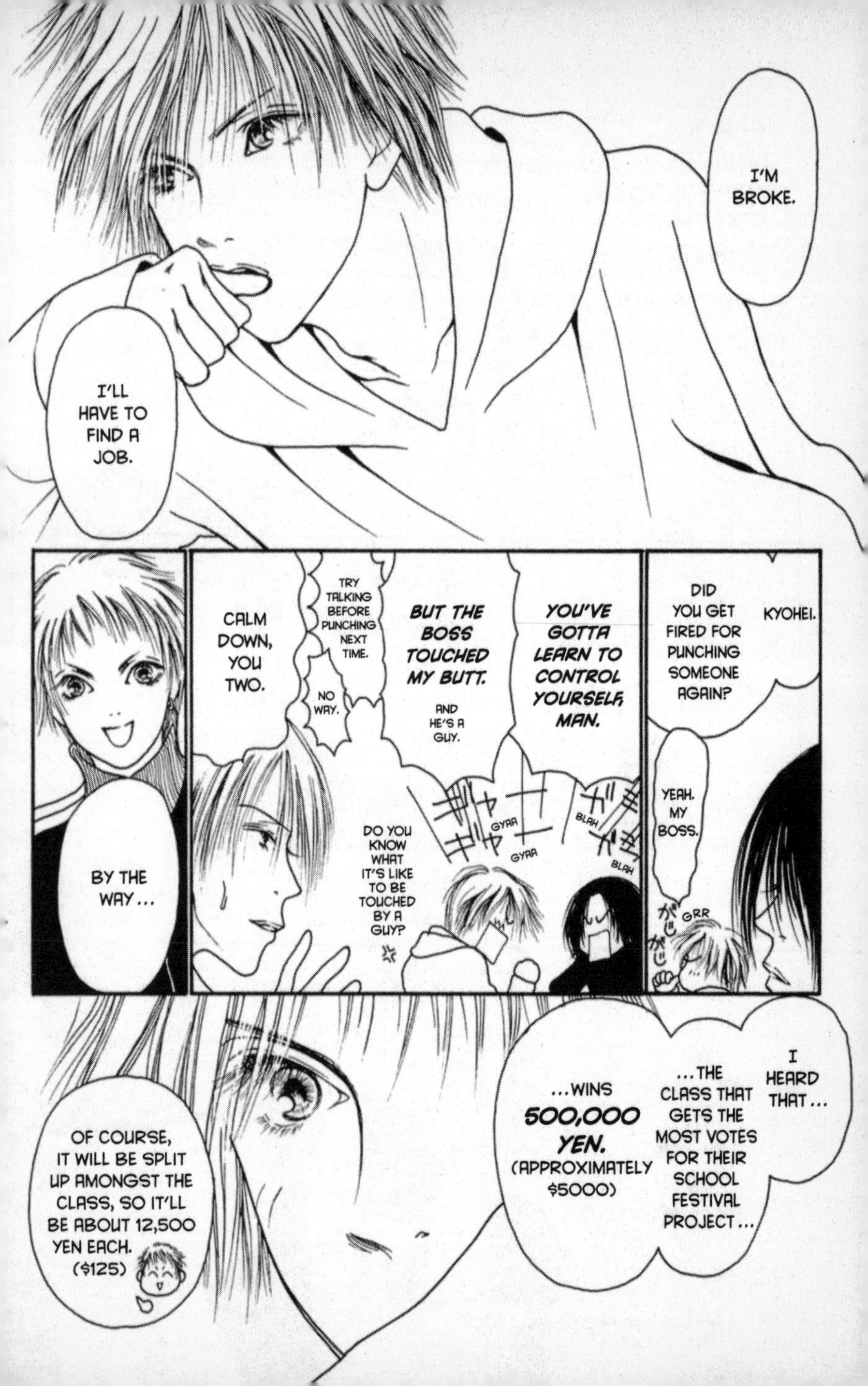
I'M BROKE.
I'LL HAVE TO FIND A JOB.
KYOHEI.
DID YOU GET FIRED FOR PUNCHING SOMEONE AGAIN?
YEAH. MY BOSS.
GRR
YOU'VE GOTTA LEARN TO CONTROL YOURSELF, MAN.
BUT THE BOSS TOUCHED MY BUTT.
AND HE'S A GUY.
TRY TALKING BEFORE PUNCHING NEXT TIME.
NO WAY.
BLAH
BLAH
GYAA
GYAA
DO YOU KNOW WHAT IT'S LIKE TO BE TOUCHED BY A GUY?
CALM DOWN, YOU TWO.
BY THE WAY...
I HEARD THAT...
...THE CLASS THAT GETS THE MOST VOTES FOR THEIR SCHOOL FESTIVAL PROJECT...
...WINS 500,000 YEN. (APPROXIMATELY $5000)
OF COURSE, IT WILL BE SPLIT UP AMONGST THE CLASS, SO IT'LL BE ABOUT 12,500 YEN EACH. ($125)

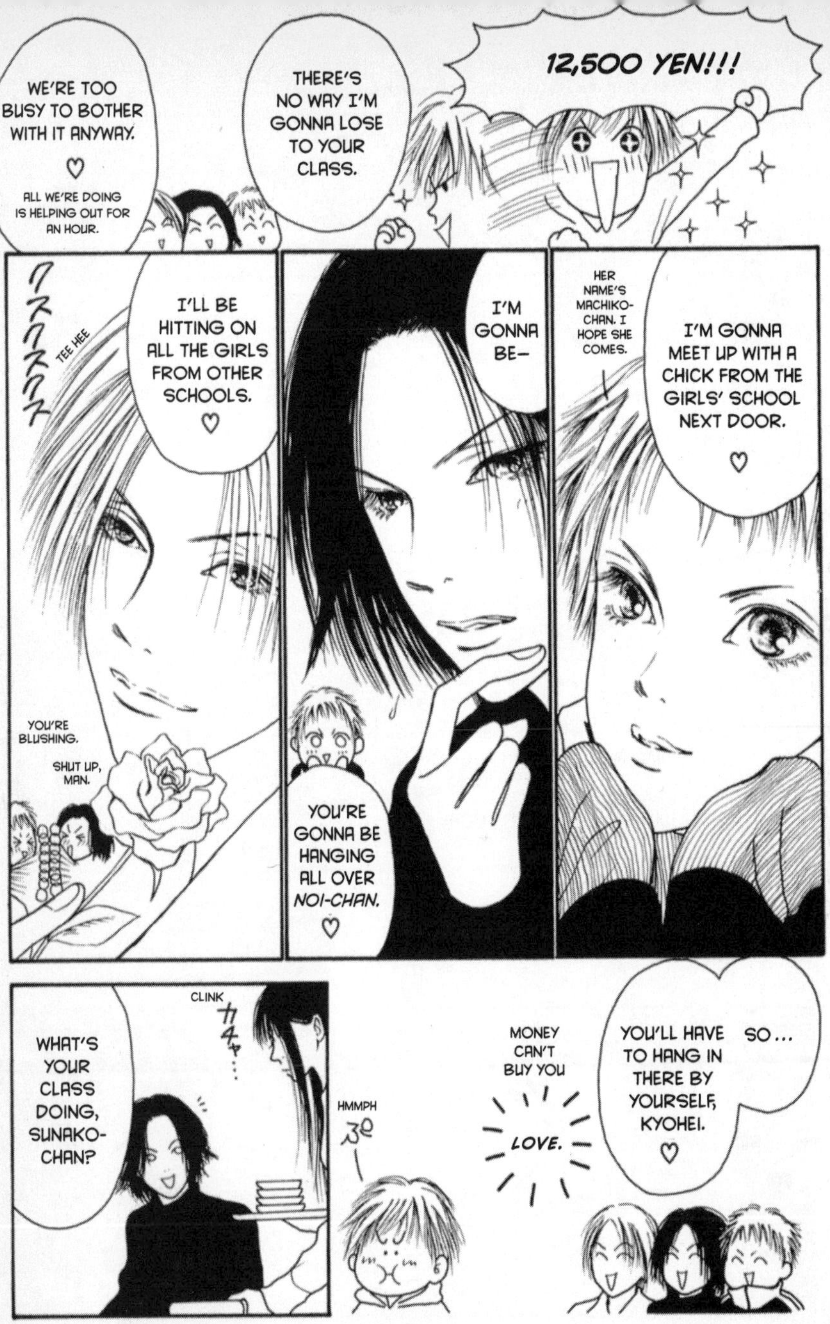
12,500 YEN!!!
THERE'S NO WAY I'M GONNA LOSE TO YOUR CLASS.
WE'RE TOO BUSY TO BOTHER WITH IT ANYWAY. ♡
ALL WE'RE DOING IS HELPING OUT FOR AN HOUR.
I'M GONNA MEET UP WITH A CHICK FROM THE GIRLS' SCHOOL NEXT DOOR. ♡
HER NAME'S MACHIKO-CHAN. I HOPE SHE COMES.
I'M GONNA BE—
YOU'RE GONNA BE HANGING ALL OVER NOI-CHAN. ♡
I'LL BE HITTING ON ALL THE GIRLS FROM OTHER SCHOOLS. ♡
クスクスクス
TEE HEE
YOU'RE BLUSHING.
SHUT UP, MAN.
SO... YOU'LL HAVE TO HANG IN THERE BY YOURSELF, KYOHEI. ♡
MONEY CAN'T BUY YOU LOVE.
HMMPH
ぷぅ
CLINK
カチャ…
WHAT'S YOUR CLASS DOING, SUNAKO-CHAN?

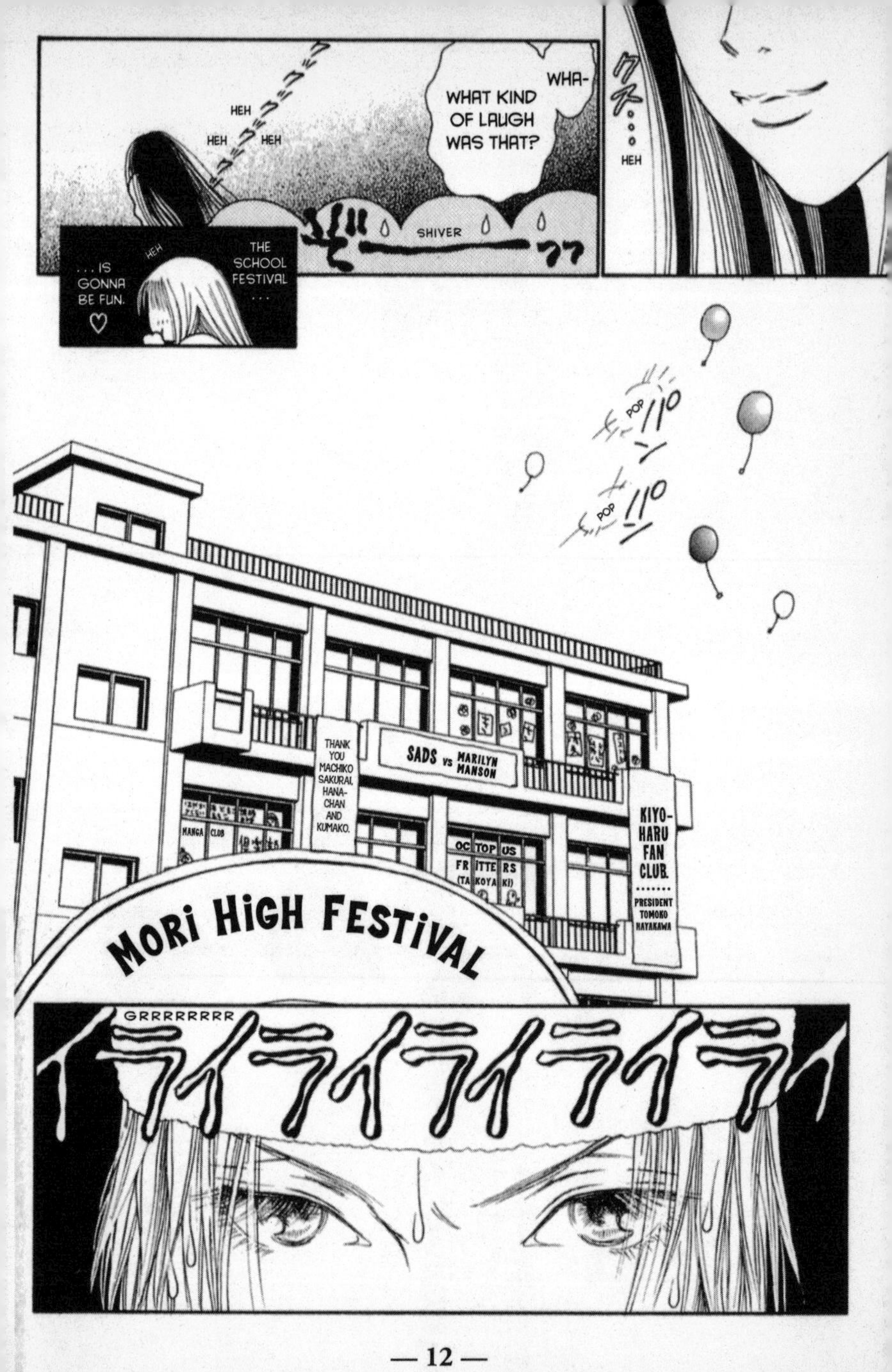
HEH
WHA-
WHAT KIND OF LAUGH WAS THAT?
HEH HEH HEH
SHIVER
THE SCHOOL FESTIVAL . . .
. . . IS GONNA BE FUN. ♡
HEH
POP
POP
KIYO-HARU FAN CLUB. .... PRESIDENT TOMOKO HAYAKAWA
SADS VS MARILYN MANSON
THANK YOU MACHIKO SAKURAI, HANA-CHAN AND KUMAKO.
OCTOPUS FRITTERS (TAKOYAKI)
MANGA CLUB
MORI HIGH FESTIVAL
GRRRRRRRR

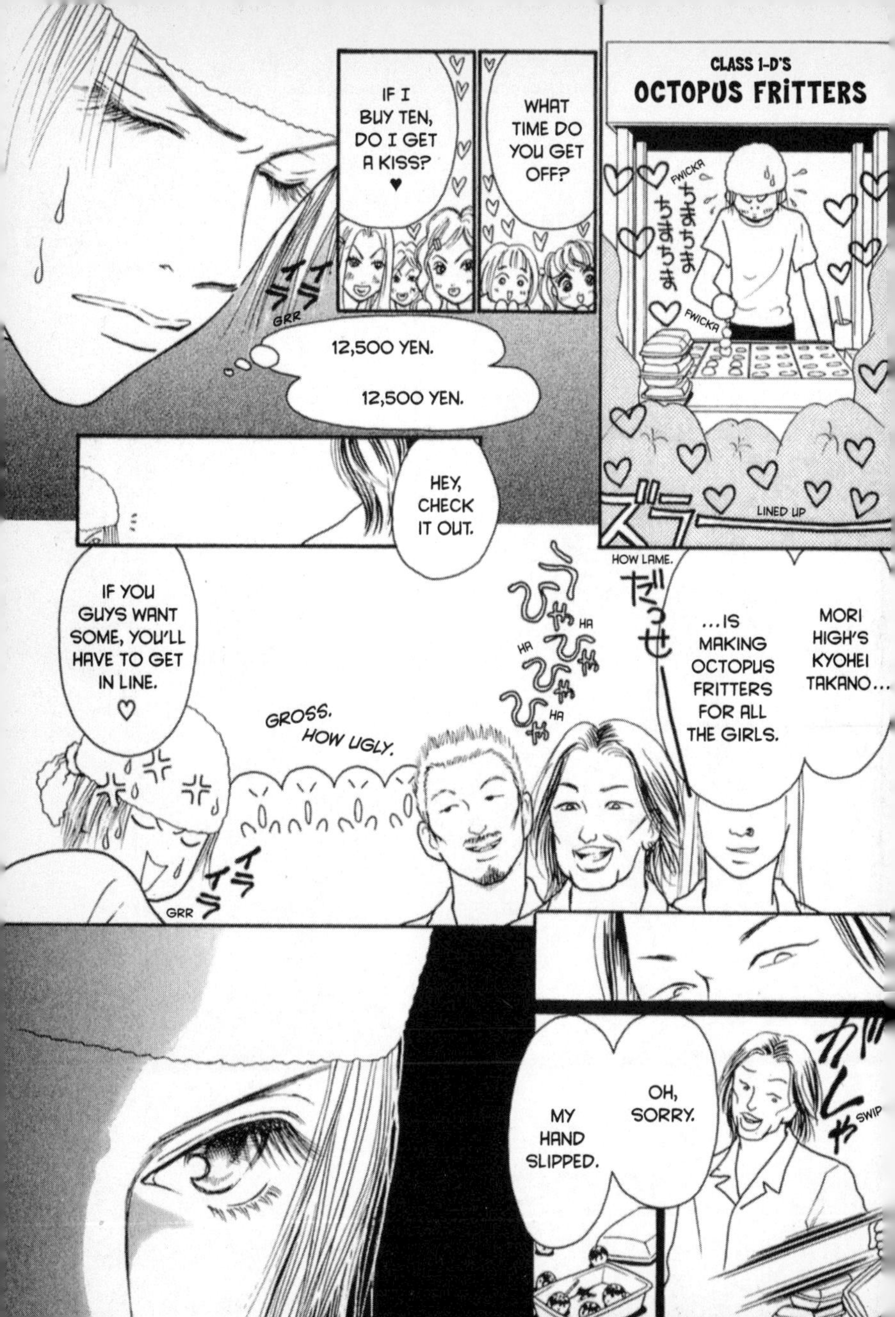
CLASS 1-D'S
OCTOPUS FRITTERS
FWICKA
FWICKA
LINED UP
WHAT TIME DO YOU GET OFF?
IF I BUY TEN, DO I GET A KISS? ♥
GRR
12,500 YEN.
12,500 YEN.
HEY, CHECK IT OUT.
MORI HIGH'S KYOHEI TAKANO...
...IS MAKING OCTOPUS FRITTERS FOR ALL THE GIRLS.
HOW LAME.
HA
HA
HA
GROSS. HOW UGLY.
IF YOU GUYS WANT SOME, YOU'LL HAVE TO GET IN LINE. ♡
GRR
OH, SORRY.
MY HAND SLIPPED.
SWIP

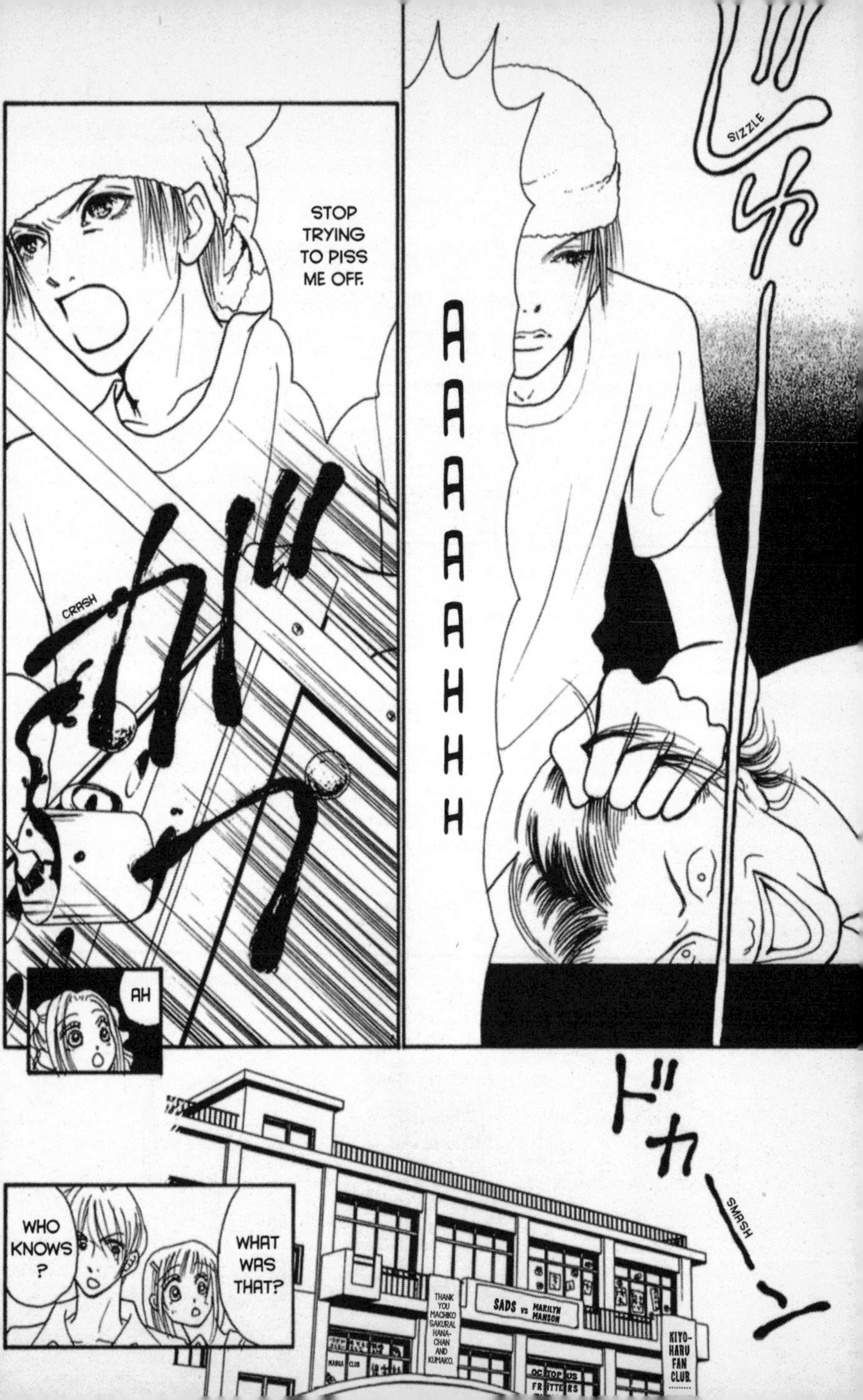
SIZZLE
AAAAAHHH
STOP TRYING TO PISS ME OFF.
CRASH
AH
SMASH
WHAT WAS THAT?
WHO KNOWS?
THANK YOU MACHIKO SAKURAI, HANA-CHAN AND KUMAKO.
SADS VS MARILYN MANSON
KIYO-HARU FAN CLUB.
MANGA CLUB
OCTOPUS FRITTERS

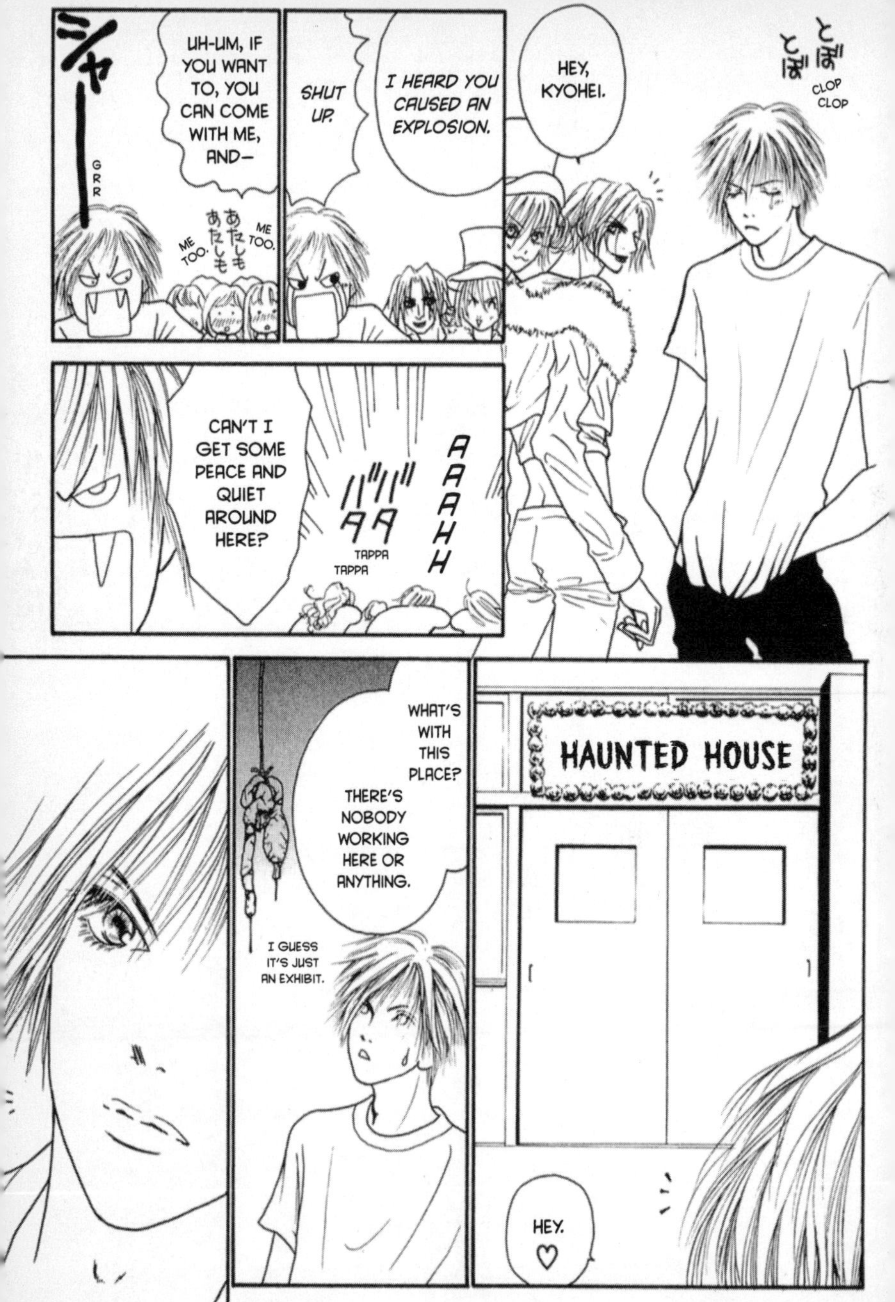

とぼとぼ
CLOP CLOP
HEY, KYOHEI.
I HEARD YOU CAUSED AN EXPLOSION.
SHUT UP.
あたしも あたしも
ME TOO. ME TOO.
UH-UM, IF YOU WANT TO, YOU CAN COME WITH ME, AND—
シャー
GRR
CAN'T I GET SOME PEACE AND QUIET AROUND HERE?
AAAAHH
バタバタ
TAPPA TAPPA
HAUNTED HOUSE
HEY. ♡
WHAT'S WITH THIS PLACE?
THERE'S NOBODY WORKING HERE OR ANYTHING.
I GUESS IT'S JUST AN EXHIBIT.

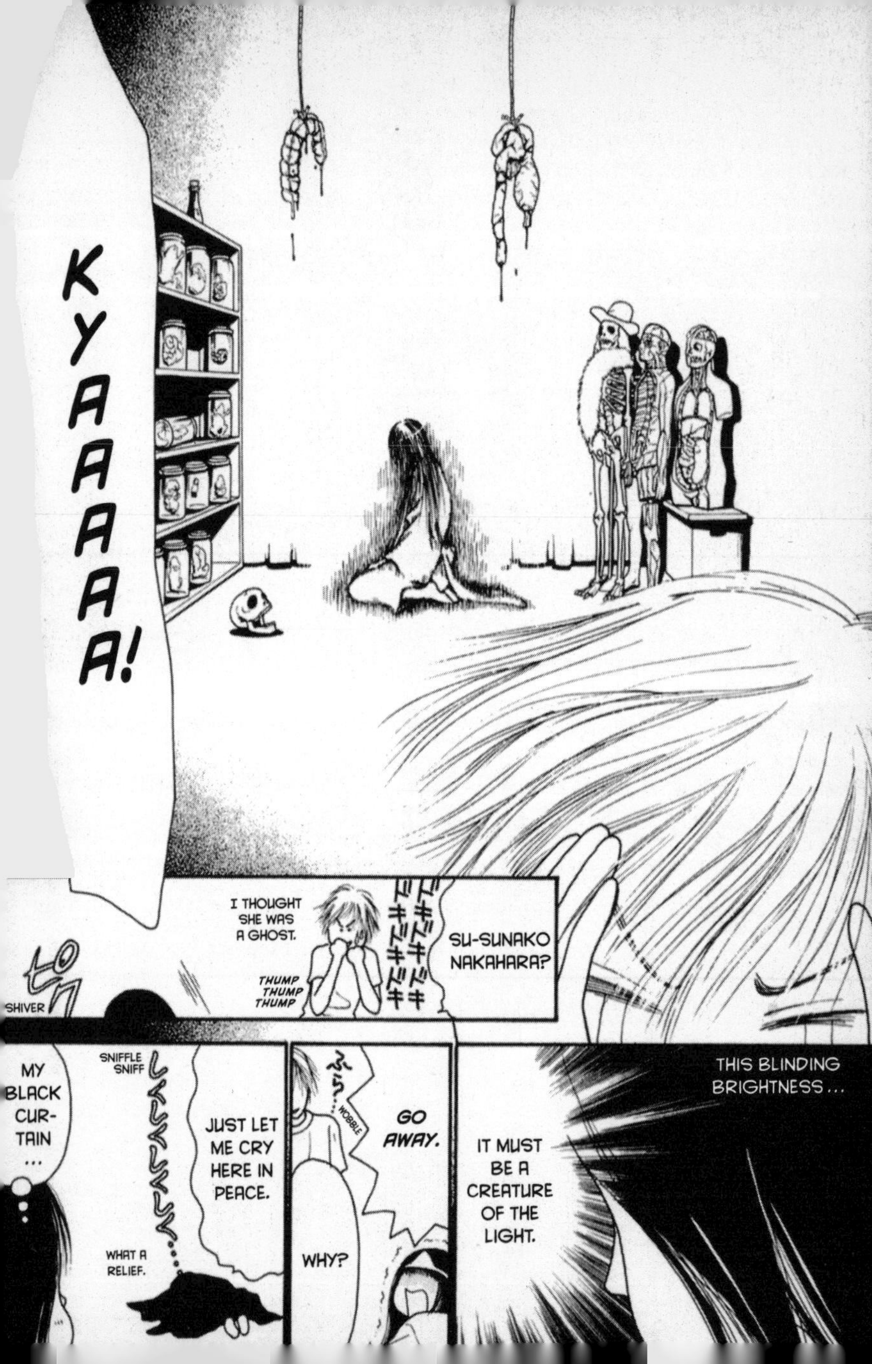
KYAAAAA!
SU-SUNAKO NAKAHARA?
ドキドキドキ
THUMP THUMP THUMP
I THOUGHT SHE WAS A GHOST.
ピク
SHIVER
THIS BLINDING BRIGHTNESS…
IT MUST BE A CREATURE OF THE LIGHT.
GO AWAY.
ふら…
WOBBLE
WHY?
JUST LET ME CRY HERE IN PEACE.
しくしくしくしく
SNIFFLE SNIFF
MY BLACK CUR-TAIN …
WHAT A RELIEF.

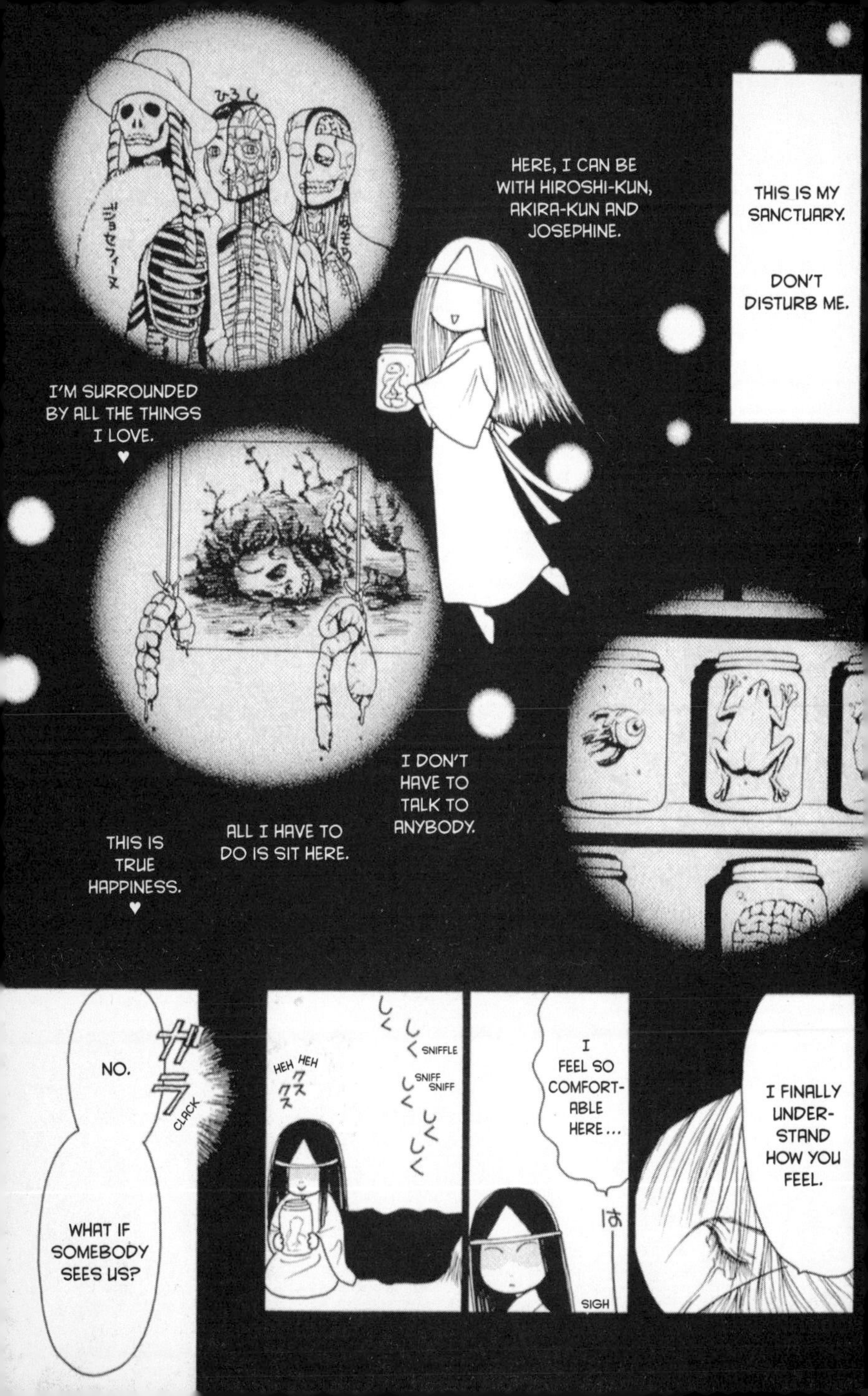
THIS IS MY SANCTUARY.
DON'T DISTURB ME.
HERE, I CAN BE WITH HIROSHI-KUN, AKIRA-KUN AND JOSEPHINE.
ひろし
ジョセフィーヌ
I'M SURROUNDED BY ALL THE THINGS I LOVE. ♥
I DON'T HAVE TO TALK TO ANYBODY.
ALL I HAVE TO DO IS SIT HERE.
THIS IS TRUE HAPPINESS. ♥
I FINALLY UNDERSTAND HOW YOU FEEL.
I FEEL SO COMFORTABLE HERE...
は
SIGH
しくしく
SNIFFLE
しくしくしく
SNIFF SNIFF
クスクス
HEH HEH
ガラ
CLACK
NO.
WHAT IF SOMEBODY SEES US?

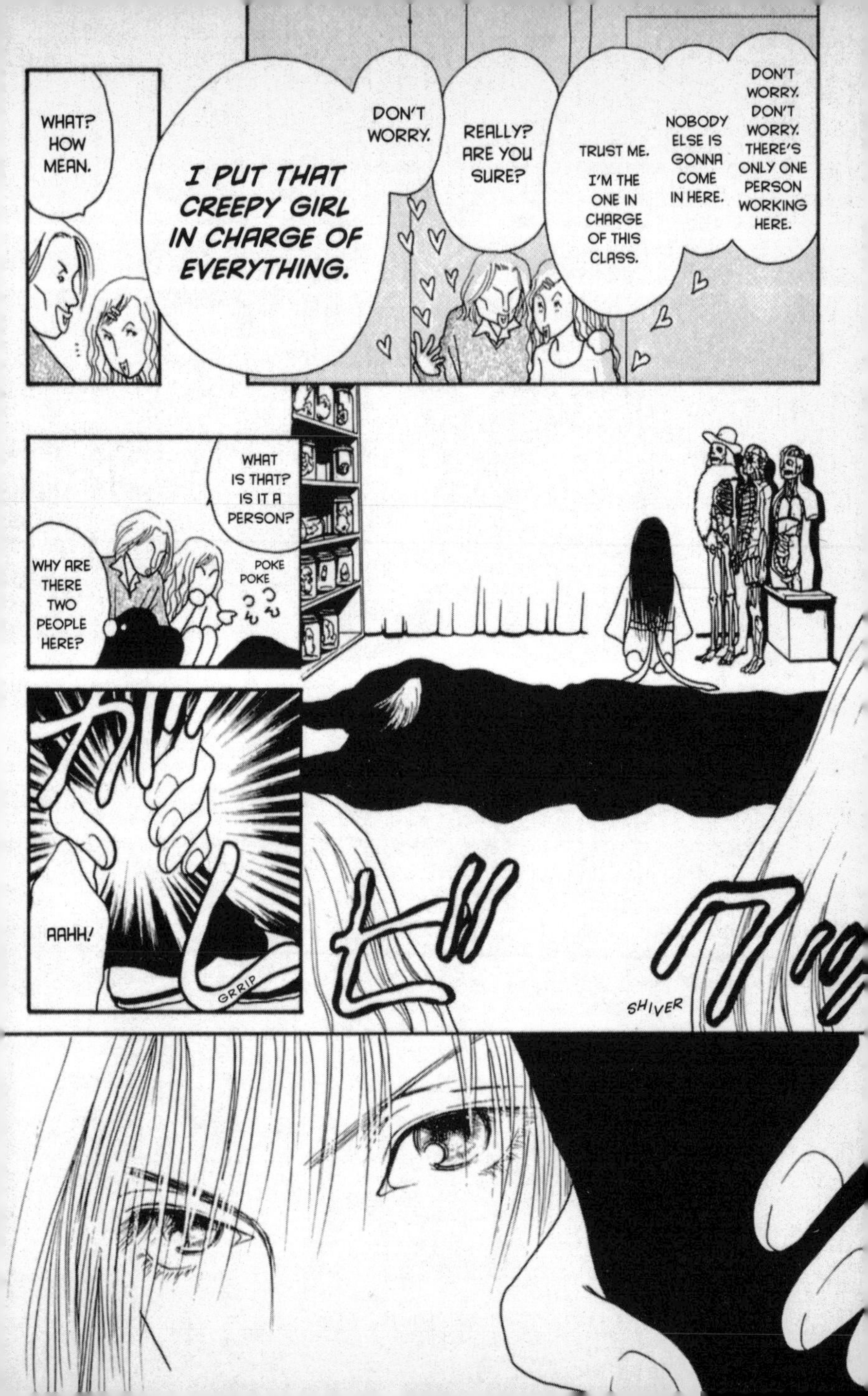
DON'T WORRY. DON'T WORRY. THERE'S ONLY ONE PERSON WORKING HERE.
NOBODY ELSE IS GONNA COME IN HERE.
TRUST ME. I'M THE ONE IN CHARGE OF THIS CLASS.
REALLY? ARE YOU SURE?
DON'T WORRY.
I PUT THAT CREEPY GIRL IN CHARGE OF EVERYTHING.
WHAT? HOW MEAN.
SHIVER
WHAT IS THAT? IS IT A PERSON?
POKE POKE
WHY ARE THERE TWO PEOPLE HERE?
AAHH!
GRRIP

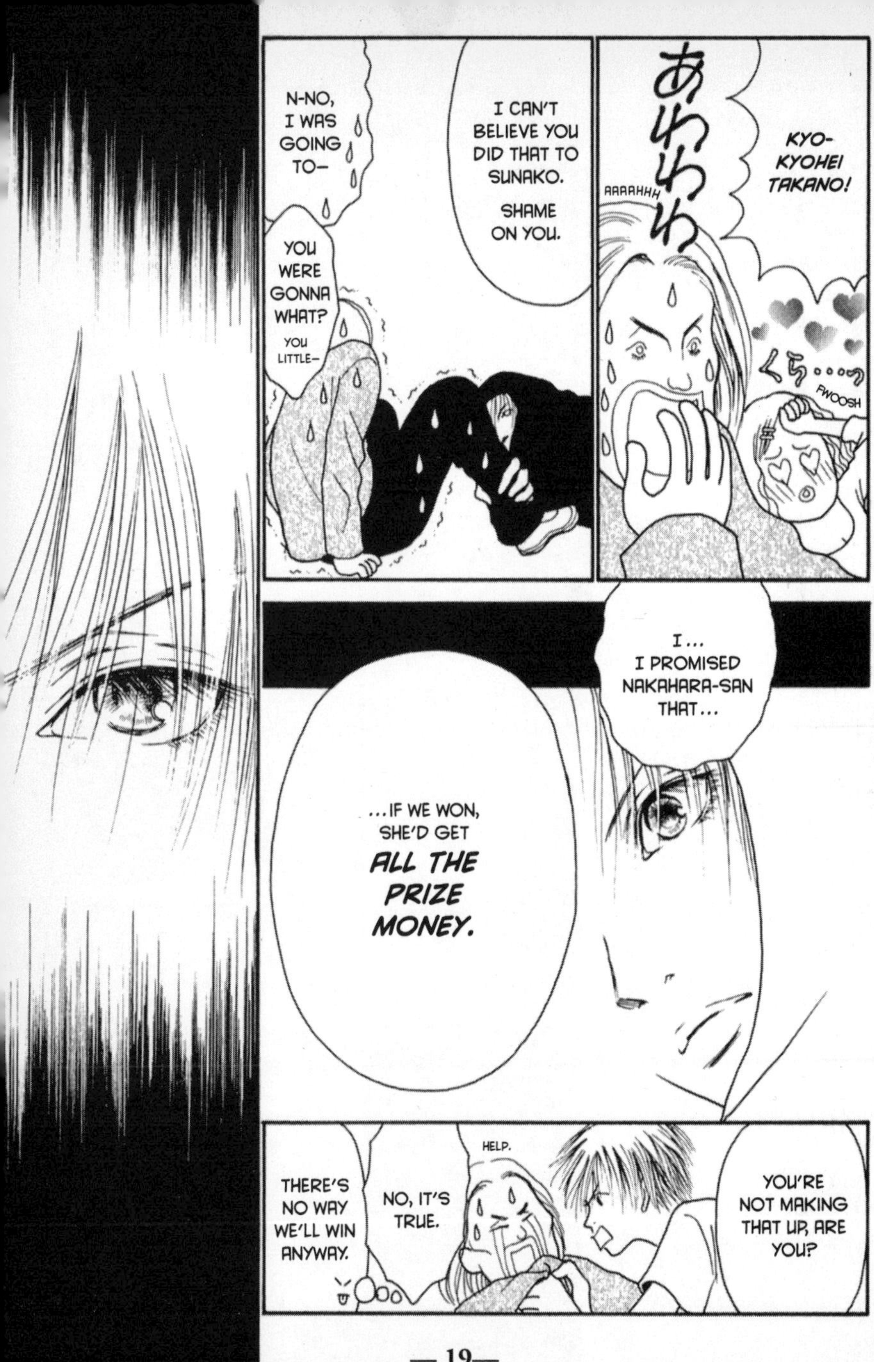
KYO-KYOHEI TAKANO!
あわわわ
AAAAHHH
くら・・・っ
FWOOSH
I CAN'T BELIEVE YOU DID THAT TO SUNAKO.
SHAME ON YOU.
N-NO, I WAS GOING TO—
YOU WERE GONNA WHAT?
YOU LITTLE—
I... I PROMISED NAKAHARA-SAN THAT...
...IF WE WON, SHE'D GET ALL THE PRIZE MONEY.
YOU'RE NOT MAKING THAT UP, ARE YOU?
HELP.
NO, IT'S TRUE.
THERE'S NO WAY WE'LL WIN ANYWAY.

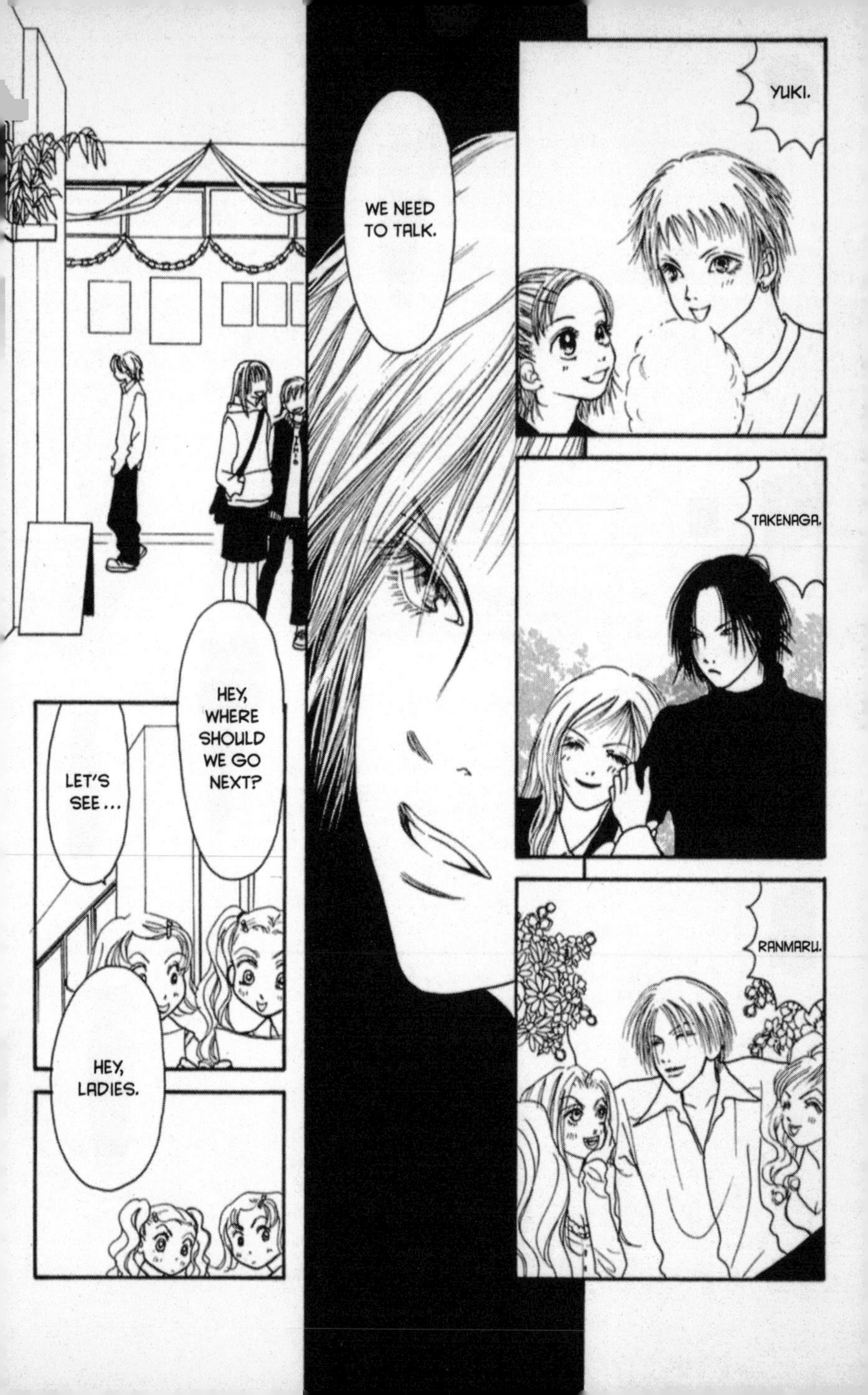
YUKI.
TAKENAGA.
RANMARU.
WE NEED TO TALK.
HEY, WHERE SHOULD WE GO NEXT?
LET'S SEE...
HEY, LADIES.

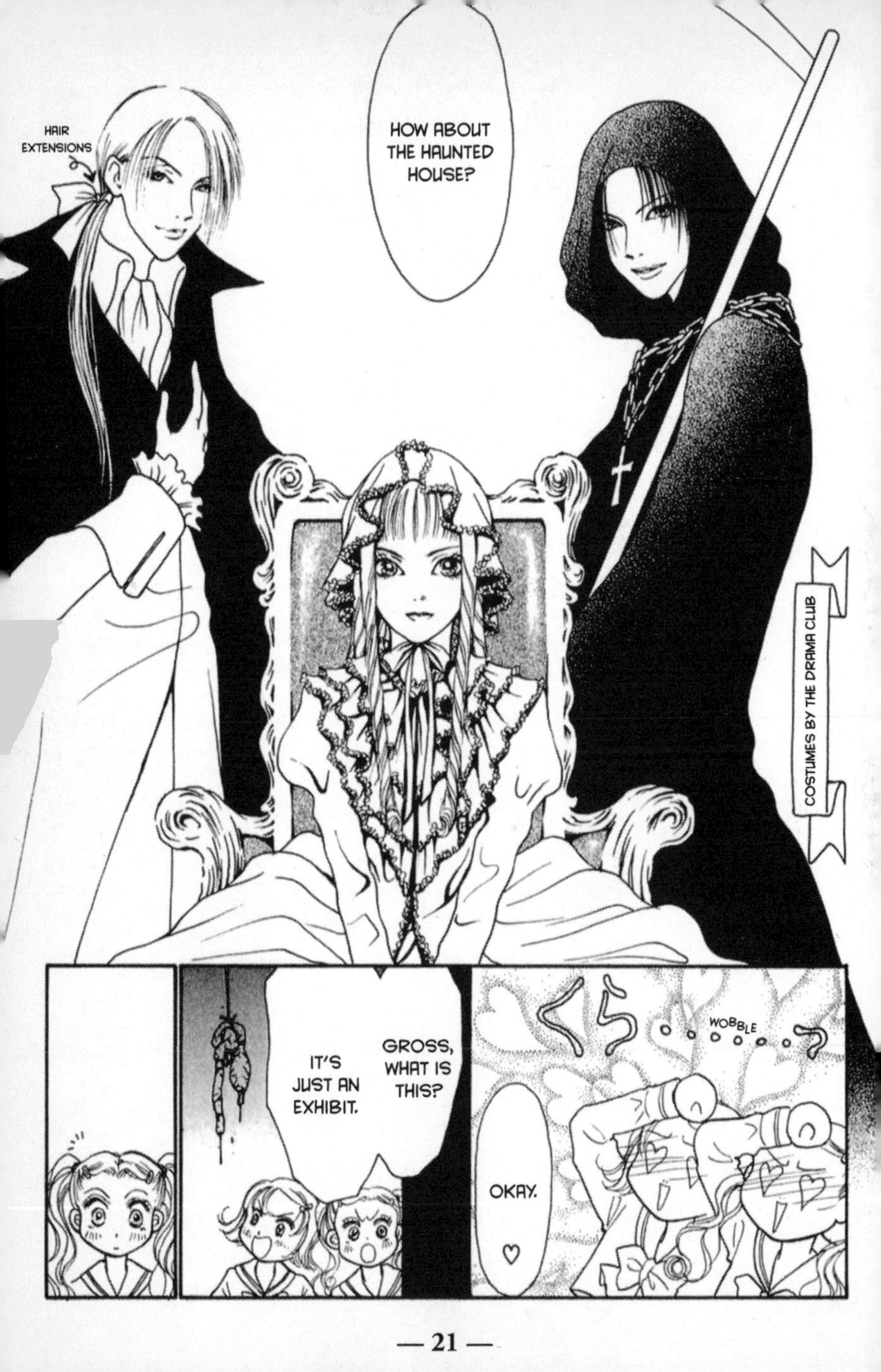
HOW ABOUT THE HAUNTED HOUSE?
COSTUMES BY THE DRAMA CLUB
HAIR EXTENSIONS
くら……っ
WOBBLE
OKAY. ♡
GROSS, WHAT IS THIS?
IT'S JUST AN EXHIBIT.

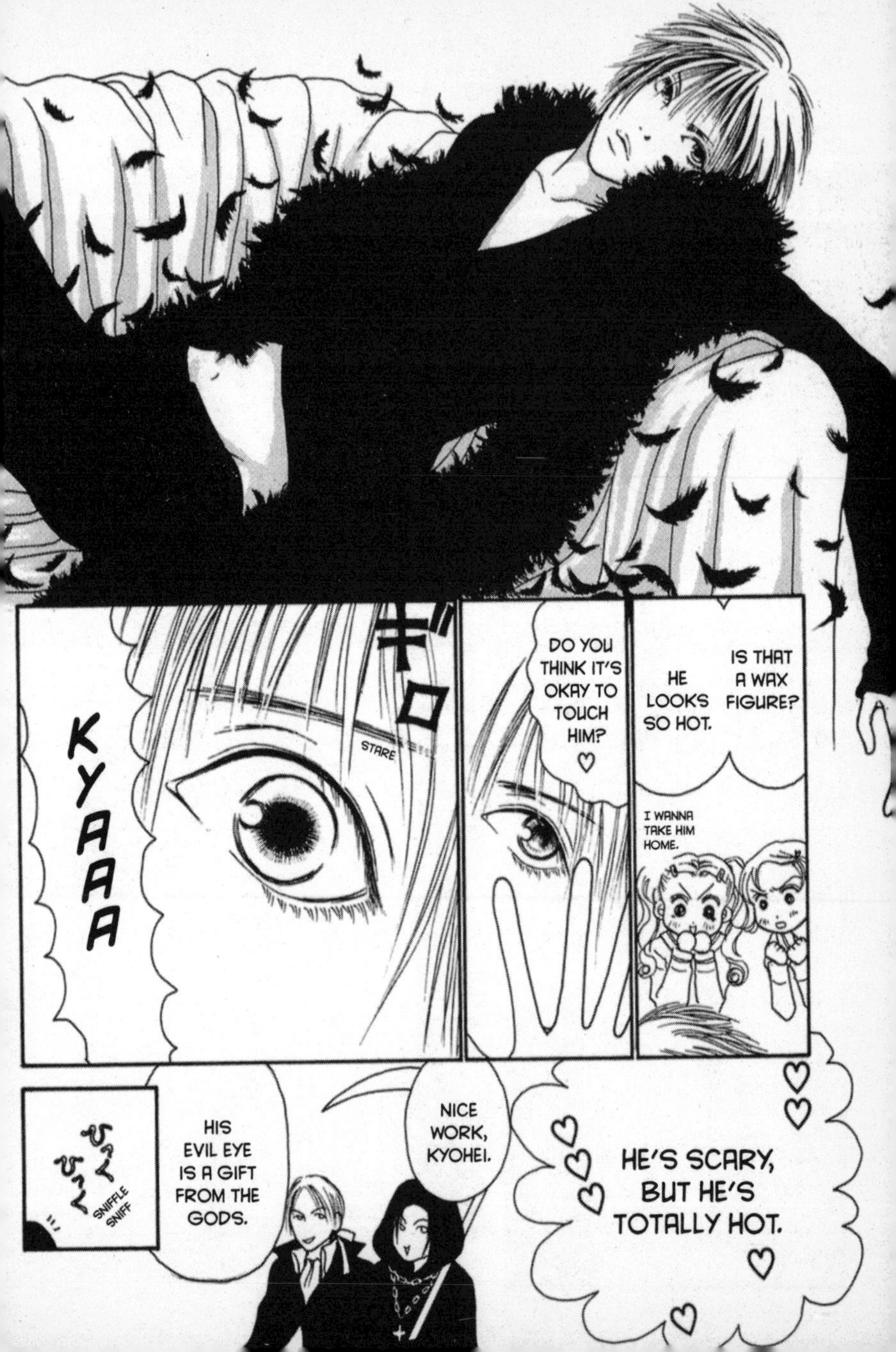
IS THAT A WAX FIGURE?
HE LOOKS SO HOT.
I WANNA TAKE HIM HOME.
DO YOU THINK IT'S OKAY TO TOUCH HIM? ♡
ギロ
STARE
KYAAAA
HE'S SCARY, BUT HE'S TOTALLY HOT.
NICE WORK, KYOHEI.
HIS EVIL EYE IS A GIFT FROM THE GODS.
ひっく ひっく
SNIFFLE SNIFF

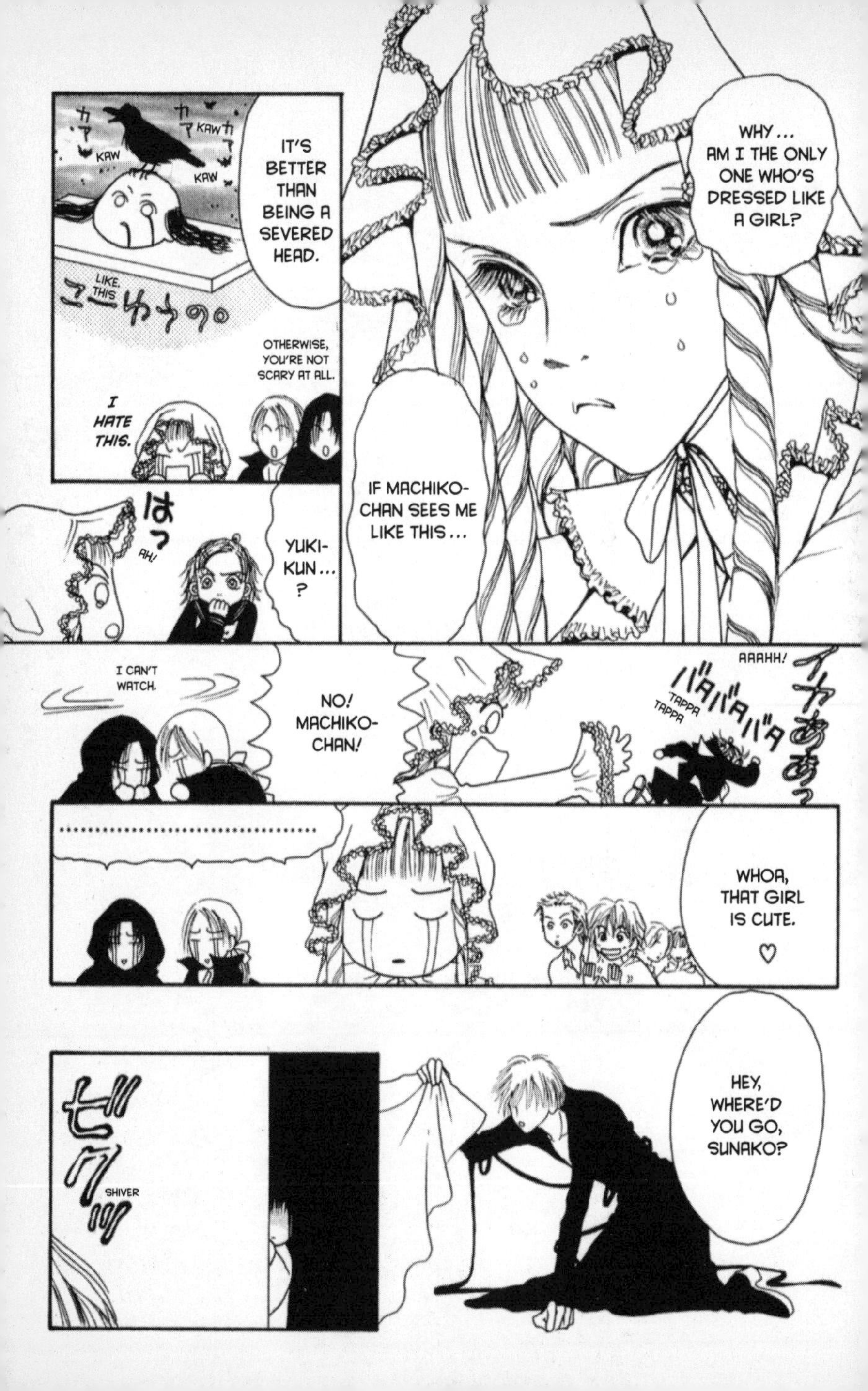
WHY... AM I THE ONLY ONE WHO'S DRESSED LIKE A GIRL?
IF MACHIKO-CHAN SEES ME LIKE THIS...
IT'S BETTER THAN BEING A SEVERED HEAD.
KAW
KAW
KAW
LIKE THIS
OTHERWISE, YOU'RE NOT SCARY AT ALL.
I HATE THIS.
AH!
YUKI-KUN...?
AAAHH!
TAPPA TAPPA
NO! MACHIKO-CHAN!
I CAN'T WATCH.
WHOA, THAT GIRL IS CUTE. ♡
....
HEY, WHERE'D YOU GO, SUNAKO?
SHIVER

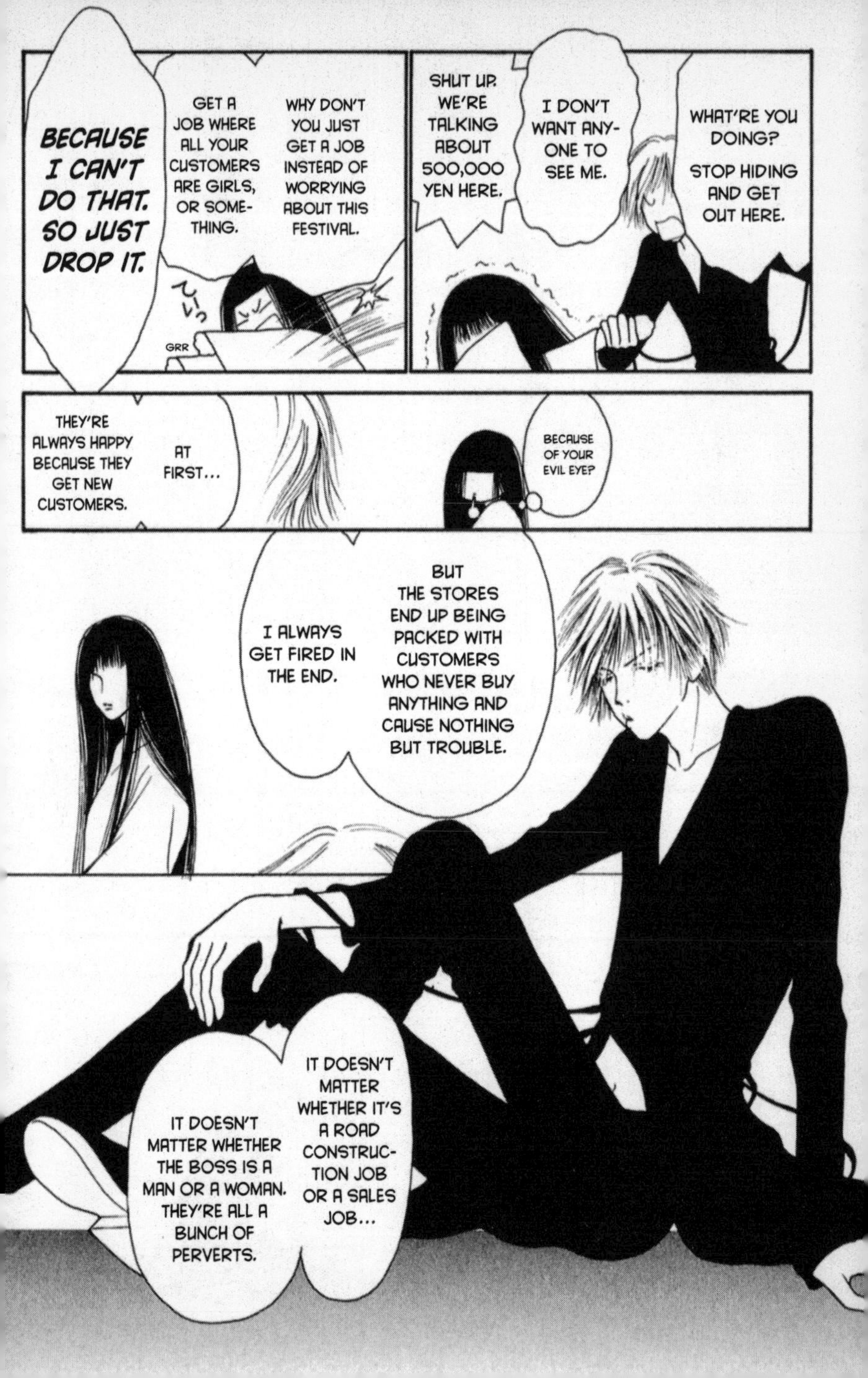
WHAT'RE YOU DOING?
STOP HIDING AND GET OUT HERE.
I DON'T WANT ANY-ONE TO SEE ME.
SHUT UP. WE'RE TALKING ABOUT 500,000 YEN HERE.
WHY DON'T YOU JUST GET A JOB INSTEAD OF WORRYING ABOUT THIS FESTIVAL.
GET A JOB WHERE ALL YOUR CUSTOMERS ARE GIRLS, OR SOME-THING.
GRR
BECAUSE I CAN'T DO THAT. SO JUST DROP IT.
BECAUSE OF YOUR EVIL EYE?
AT FIRST…
THEY'RE ALWAYS HAPPY BECAUSE THEY GET NEW CUSTOMERS.
BUT THE STORES END UP BEING PACKED WITH CUSTOMERS WHO NEVER BUY ANYTHING AND CAUSE NOTHING BUT TROUBLE.
I ALWAYS GET FIRED IN THE END.
IT DOESN'T MATTER WHETHER IT'S A ROAD CONSTRUC-TION JOB OR A SALES JOB…
IT DOESN'T MATTER WHETHER THE BOSS IS A MAN OR A WOMAN. THEY'RE ALL A BUNCH OF PERVERTS.

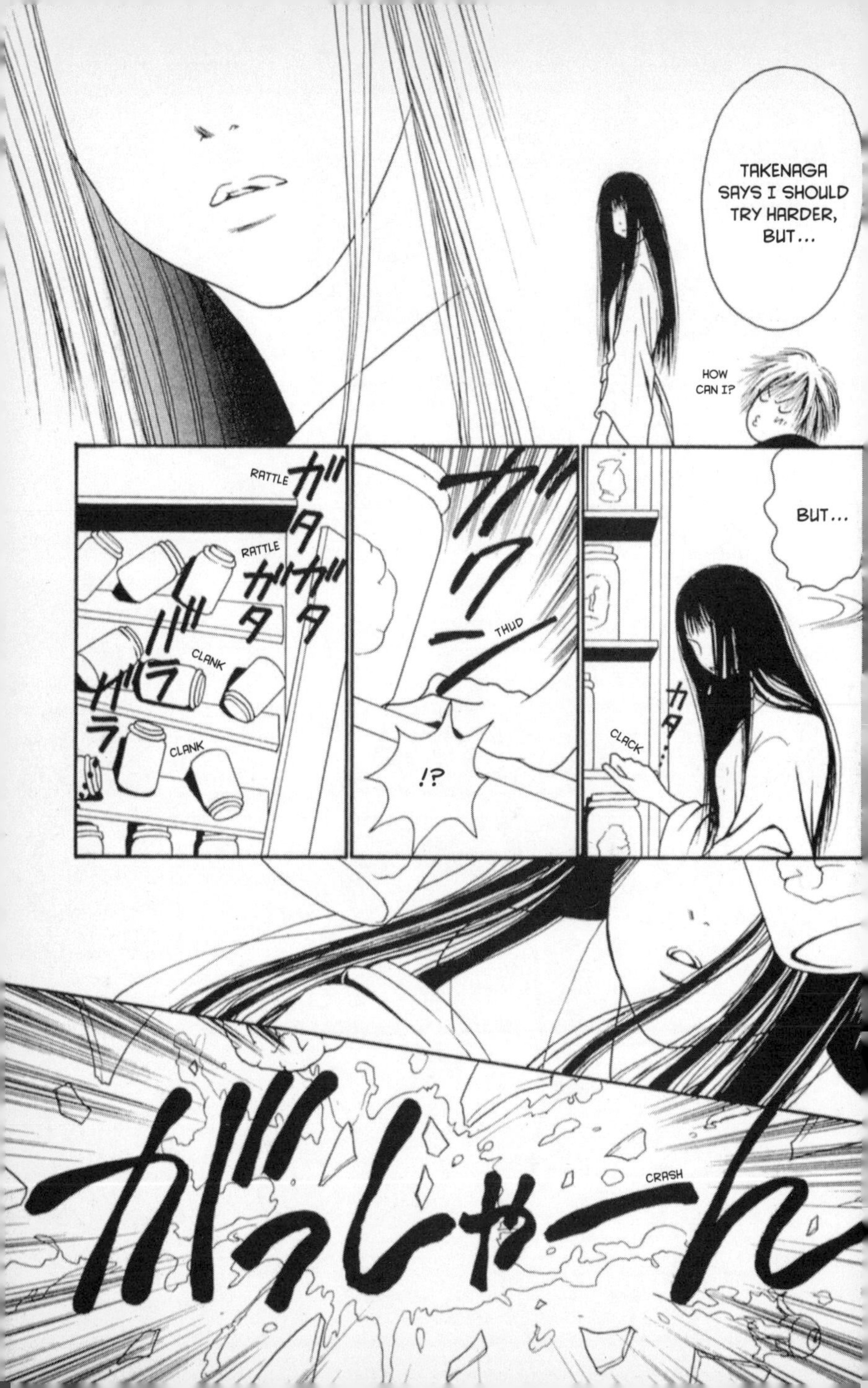
TAKENAGA SAYS I SHOULD TRY HARDER, BUT...
HOW CAN I?
BUT...
カタ...
CLACK
ガクーン
THUD
!?
ガタ
RATTLE
ガタ
RATTLE
ガタ
ガラ
CLANK
ガラ
CLANK
がっしゃーん
CRASH

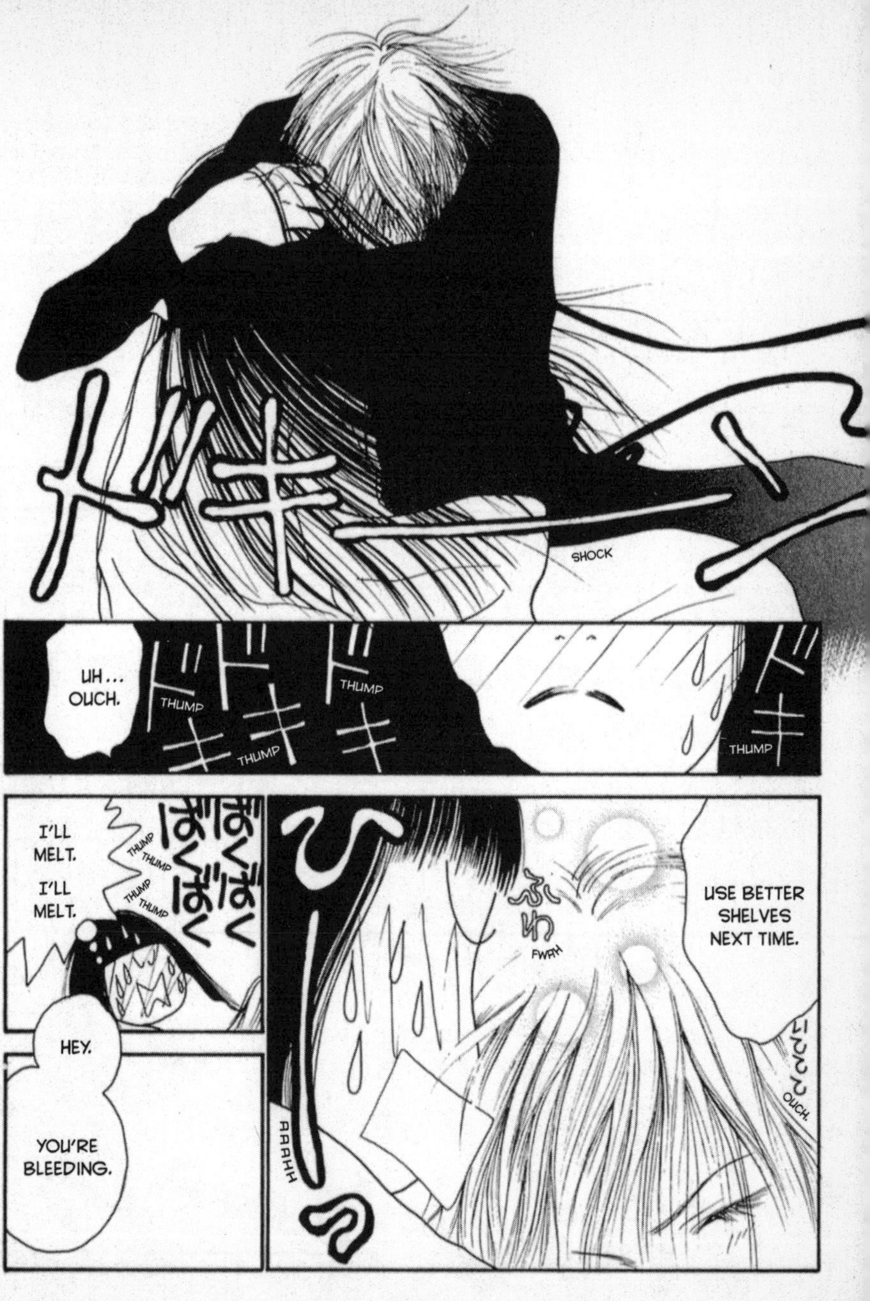
SHOCK
THUMP
THUMP
THUMP
THUMP
UH... OUCH.
USE BETTER SHELVES NEXT TIME.
OUCH.
FWAH
AAAHH
I'LL MELT.
I'LL MELT.
THUMP THUMP
THUMP THUMP
HEY.
YOU'RE BLEEDING.

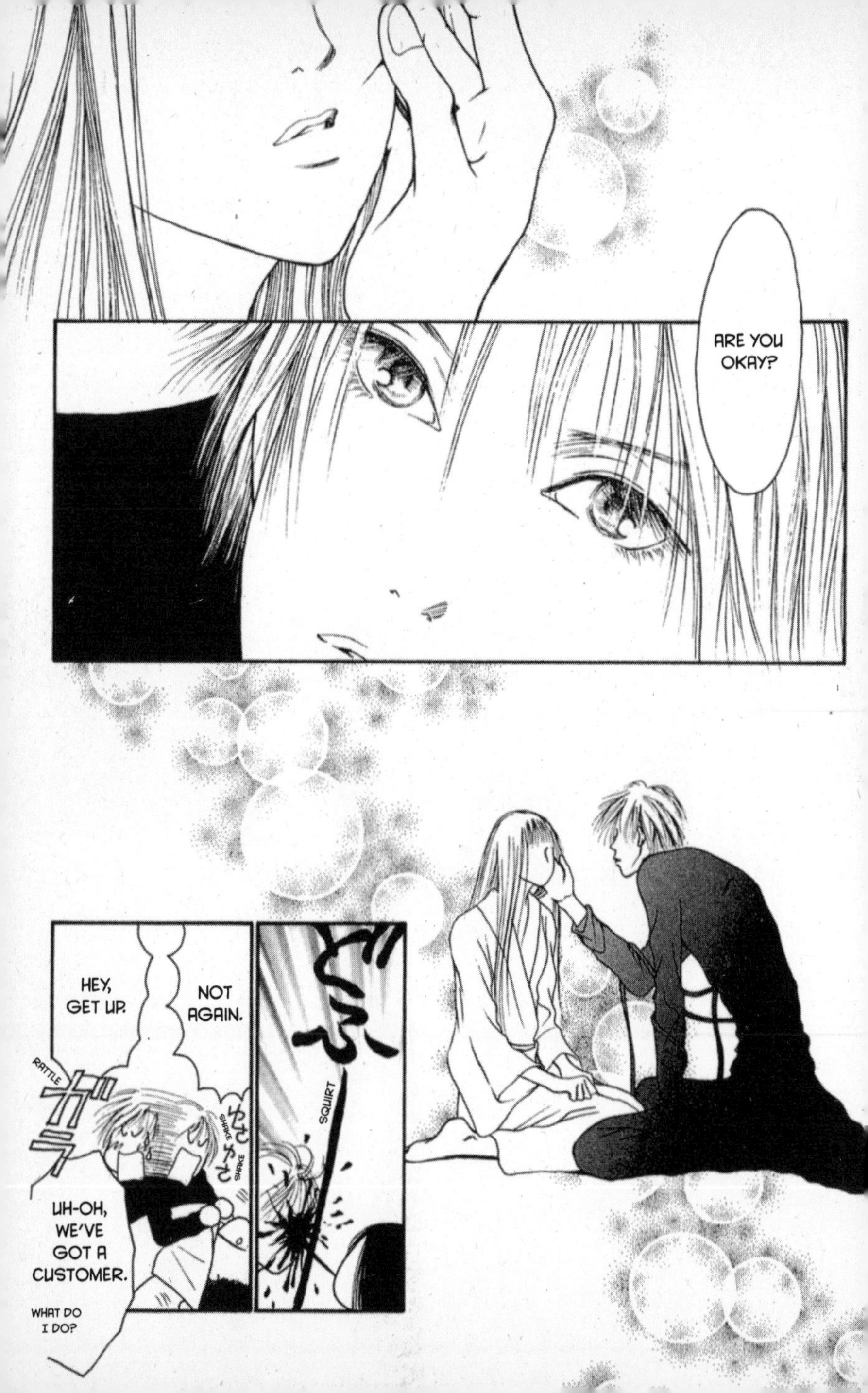
ARE YOU OKAY?
SQUIRT
NOT AGAIN.
HEY, GET UP.
SHAKE SHAKE
RATTLE
UH-OH, WE'VE GOT A CUSTOMER.
WHAT DO I DO?

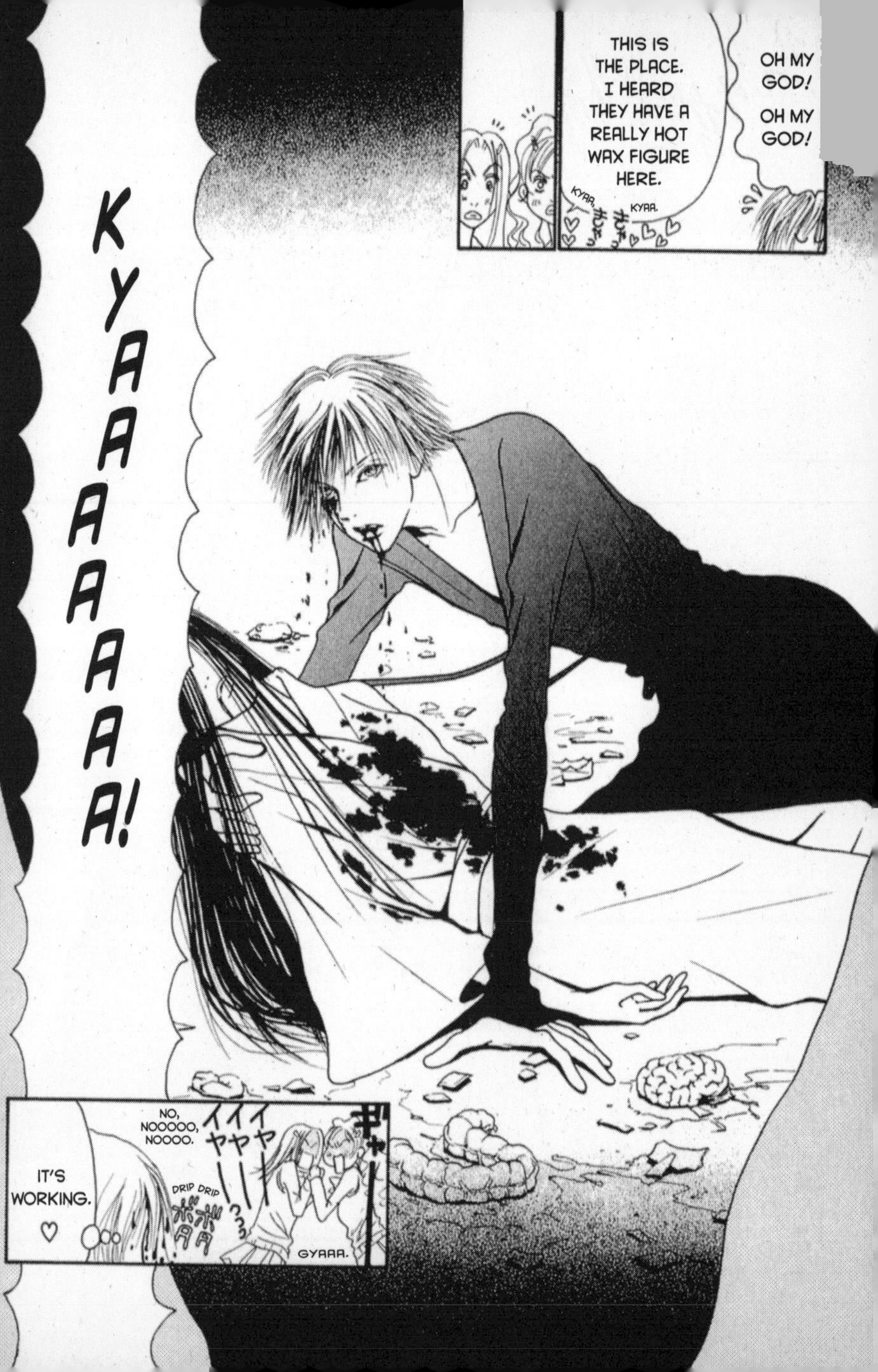

OH MY GOD!
OH MY GOD!
THIS IS THE PLACE. I HEARD THEY HAVE A REALLY HOT WAX FIGURE HERE.
KYAA.
KYAA.
KYAAAAAAAAA!
GYAAA.
NO, NOOOOO, NOOOO.
DRIP DRIP
IT'S WORKING. ♡

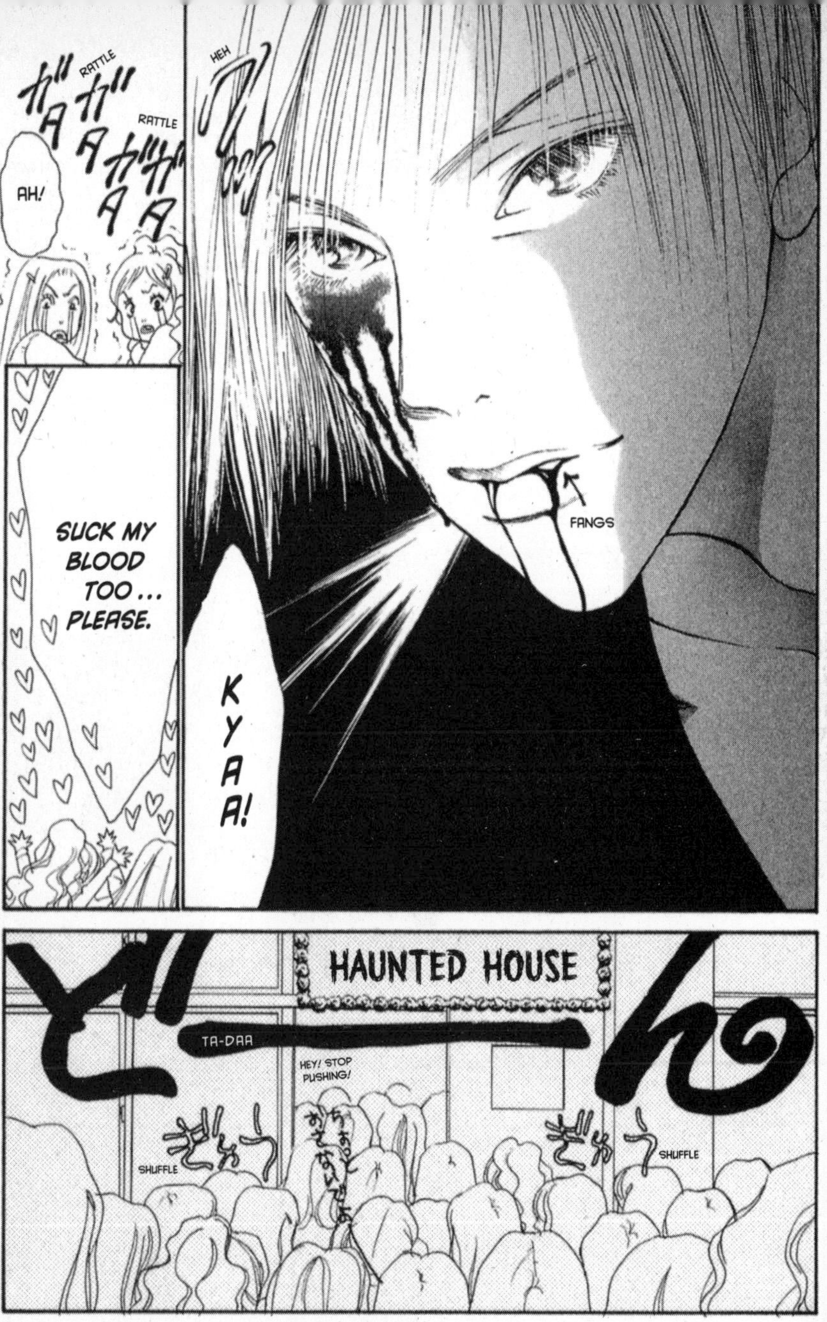
HEH
FANGS
KYAA!
RATTLE
RATTLE
AH!
SUCK MY BLOOD TOO... PLEASE.
HAUNTED HOUSE
TA-DAA
HEY! STOP PUSHING!
SHUFFLE
SHUFFLE

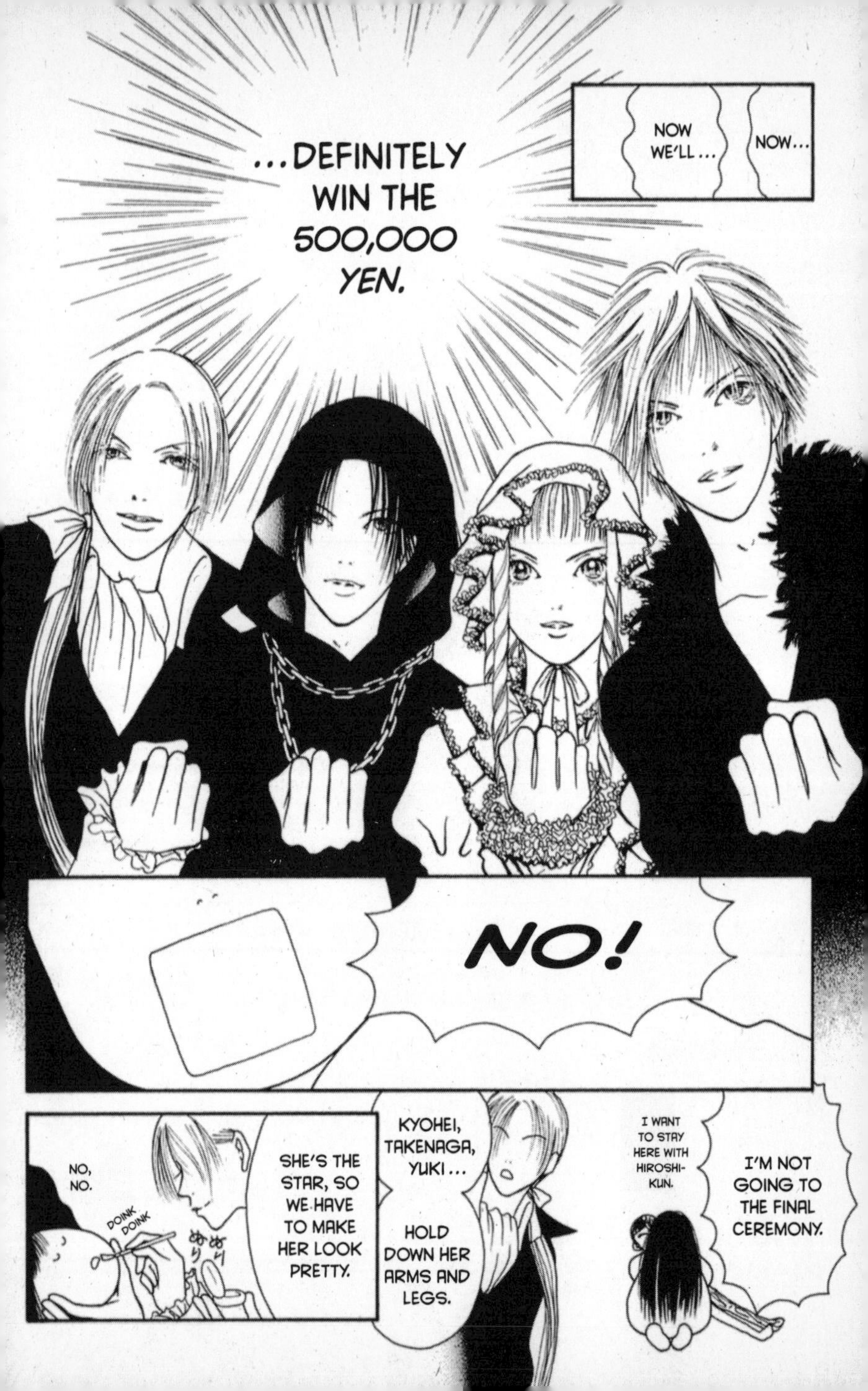
NOW...
NOW WE'LL...
...DEFINITELY WIN THE 500,000 YEN.
NO!
I'M NOT GOING TO THE FINAL CEREMONY.
I WANT TO STAY HERE WITH HIROSHI-KUN.
KYOHEI, TAKENAGA, YUKI...
HOLD DOWN HER ARMS AND LEGS.
SHE'S THE STAR, SO WE HAVE TO MAKE HER LOOK PRETTY.
NO, NO.
DOINK DOINK

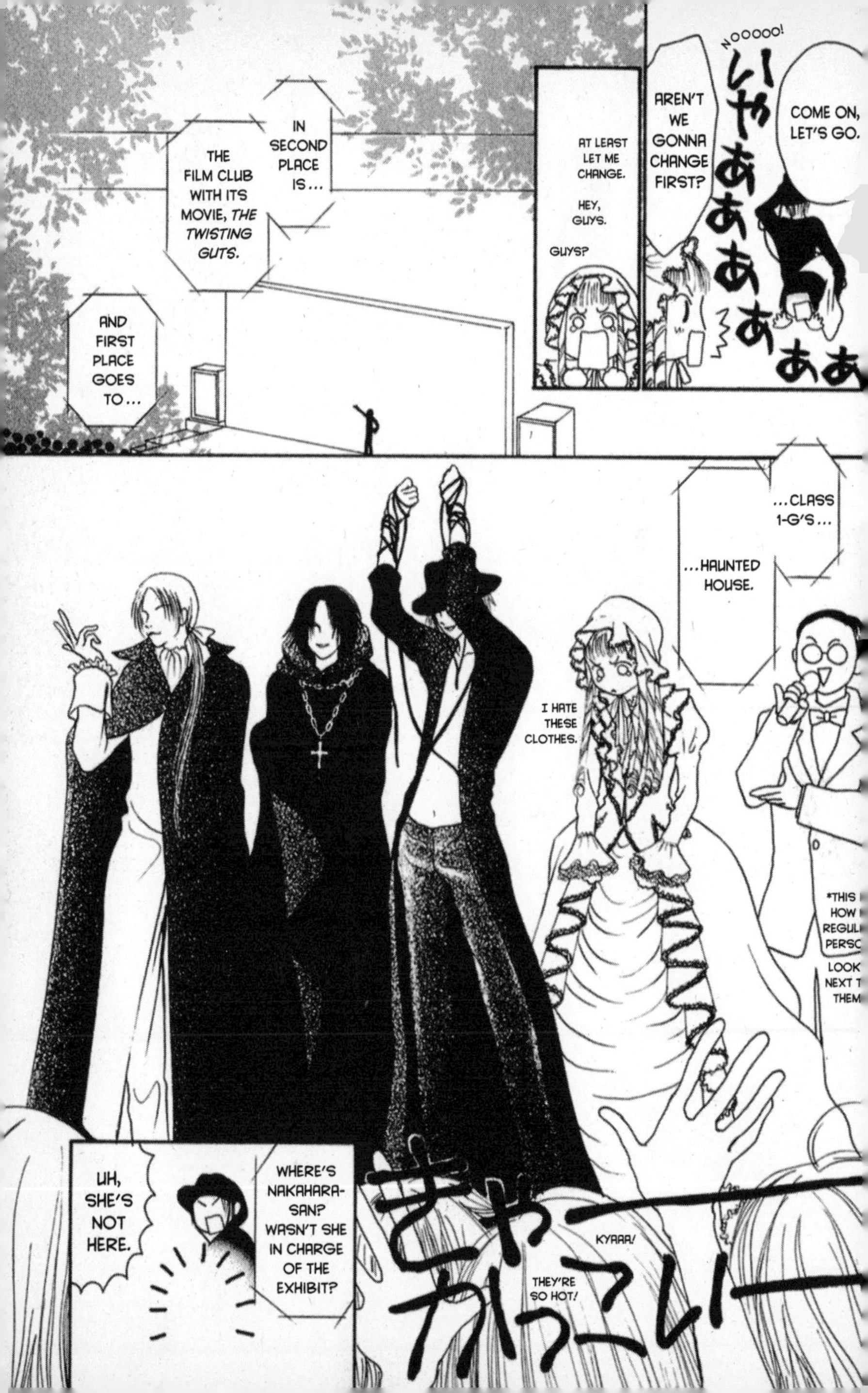
NOOOOO!
COME ON, LET'S GO.
AREN'T WE GONNA CHANGE FIRST?
AT LEAST LET ME CHANGE.
HEY, GUYS.
GUYS?
IN SECOND PLACE IS…
THE FILM CLUB WITH ITS MOVIE, *THE TWISTING GUTS.*
AND FIRST PLACE GOES TO…
…CLASS 1-G'S…
…HAUNTED HOUSE.
I HATE THESE CLOTHES.
KYAAA!
THEY'RE SO HOT!
WHERE'S NAKAHARA-SAN? WASN'T SHE IN CHARGE OF THE EXHIBIT?
UH, SHE'S NOT HERE.

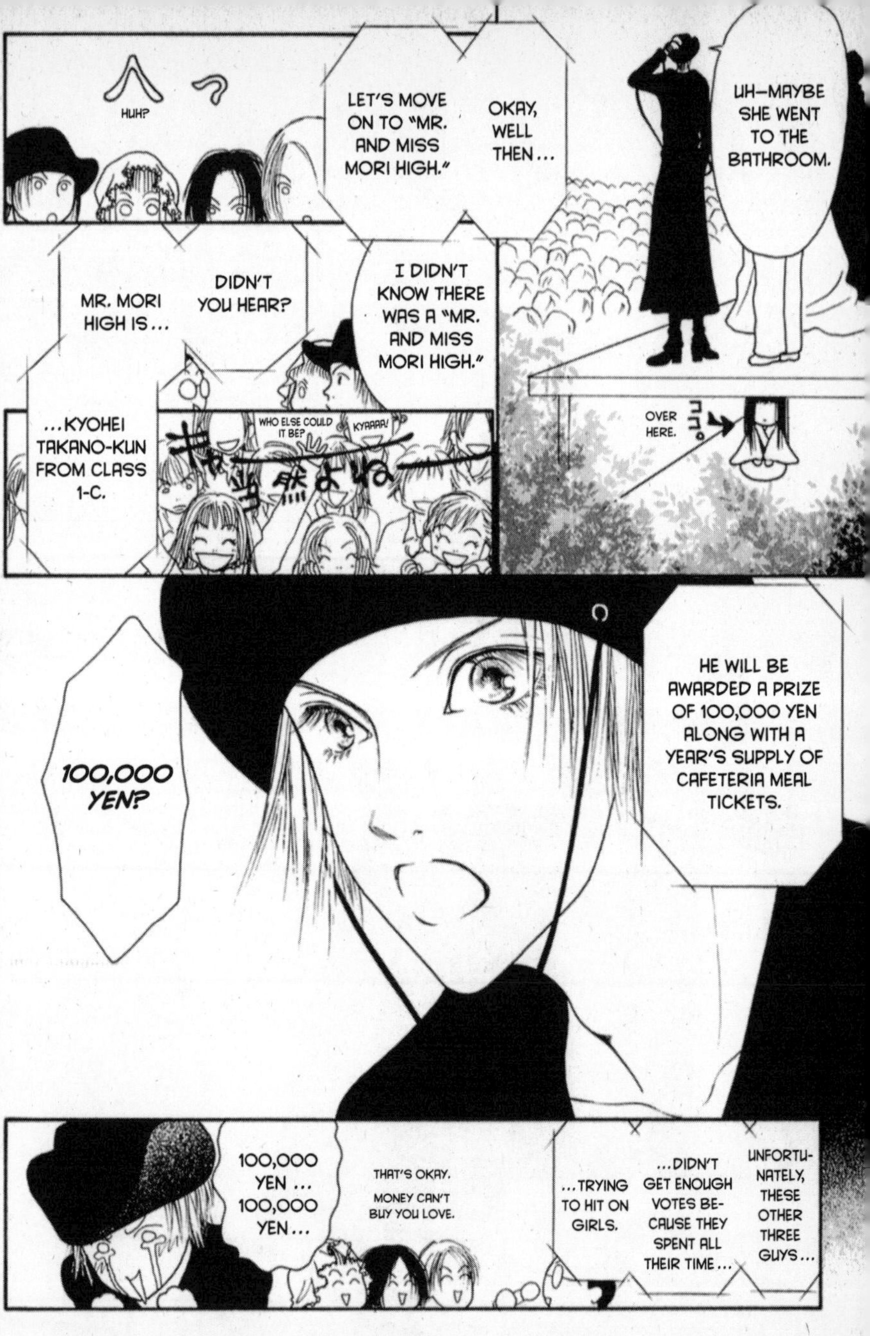
UH—MAYBE SHE WENT TO THE BATHROOM.
ココ
OVER HERE.
OKAY, WELL THEN…
LET'S MOVE ON TO "MR. AND MISS MORI HIGH."
へっ
HUH?
I DIDN'T KNOW THERE WAS A "MR. AND MISS MORI HIGH."
DIDN'T YOU HEAR?
MR. MORI HIGH IS…
…KYOHEI TAKANO-KUN FROM CLASS 1-C.
KYAAAA!
WHO ELSE COULD IT BE?
HE WILL BE AWARDED A PRIZE OF 100,000 YEN ALONG WITH A YEAR'S SUPPLY OF CAFETERIA MEAL TICKETS.
100,000 YEN?
UNFORTUNATELY, THESE OTHER THREE GUYS…
…DIDN'T GET ENOUGH VOTES BECAUSE THEY SPENT ALL THEIR TIME…
…TRYING TO HIT ON GIRLS.
THAT'S OKAY.
MONEY CAN'T BUY YOU LOVE.
100,000 YEN … 100,000 YEN…

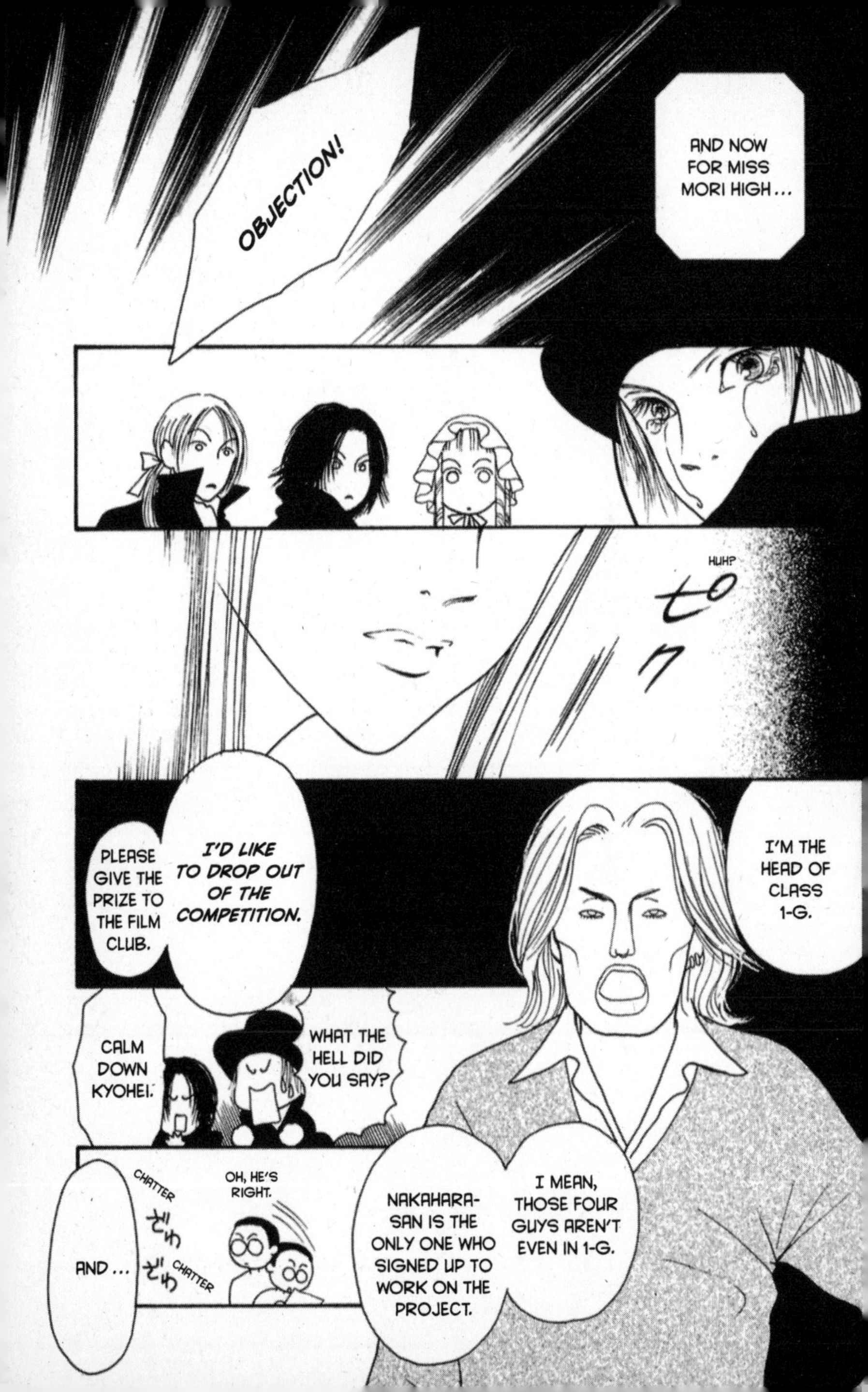
AND NOW FOR MISS MORI HIGH...
OBJECTION!
HUH?
ピク
I'M THE HEAD OF CLASS 1-G.
I'D LIKE TO DROP OUT OF THE COMPETITION.
PLEASE GIVE THE PRIZE TO THE FILM CLUB.
WHAT THE HELL DID YOU SAY?
CALM DOWN KYOHEI.
I MEAN, THOSE FOUR GUYS AREN'T EVEN IN 1-G.
NAKAHARA-SAN IS THE ONLY ONE WHO SIGNED UP TO WORK ON THE PROJECT.
OH, HE'S RIGHT.
CHATTER
ざわ
ざわ
CHATTER
AND...

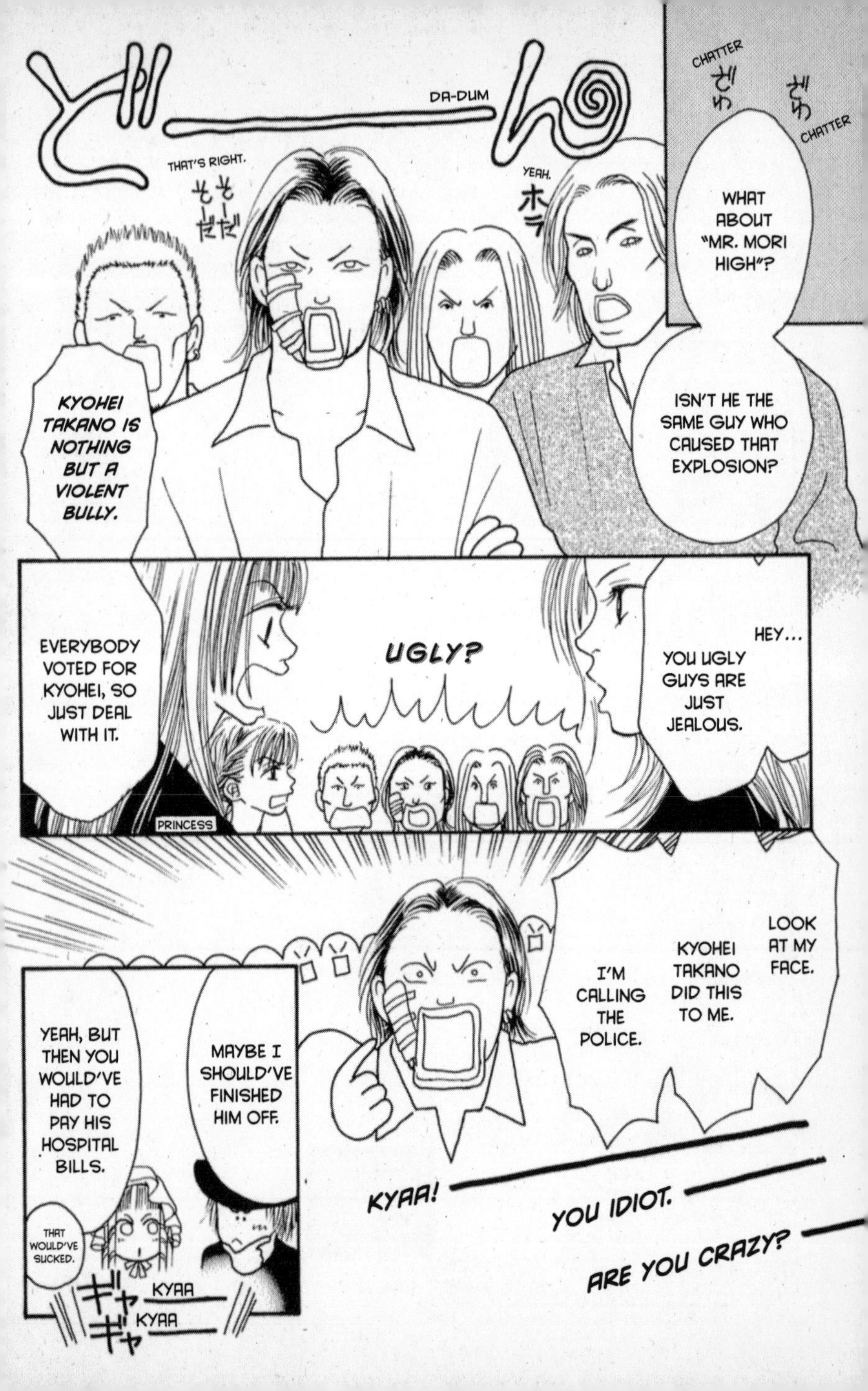
CHATTER
CHATTER
WHAT ABOUT "MR. MORI HIGH"?
ISN'T HE THE SAME GUY WHO CAUSED THAT EXPLOSION?
YEAH.
DA-DUM
THAT'S RIGHT.
KYOHEI TAKANO IS NOTHING BUT A VIOLENT BULLY.
HEY...
YOU UGLY GUYS ARE JUST JEALOUS.
UGLY?
EVERYBODY VOTED FOR KYOHEI, SO JUST DEAL WITH IT.
PRINCESS
LOOK AT MY FACE.
KYOHEI TAKANO DID THIS TO ME.
I'M CALLING THE POLICE.
KYAA!
YOU IDIOT.
ARE YOU CRAZY?
MAYBE I SHOULD'VE FINISHED HIM OFF.
YEAH, BUT THEN YOU WOULD'VE HAD TO PAY HIS HOSPITAL BILLS.
THAT WOULD'VE SUCKED.
KYAA
KYAA

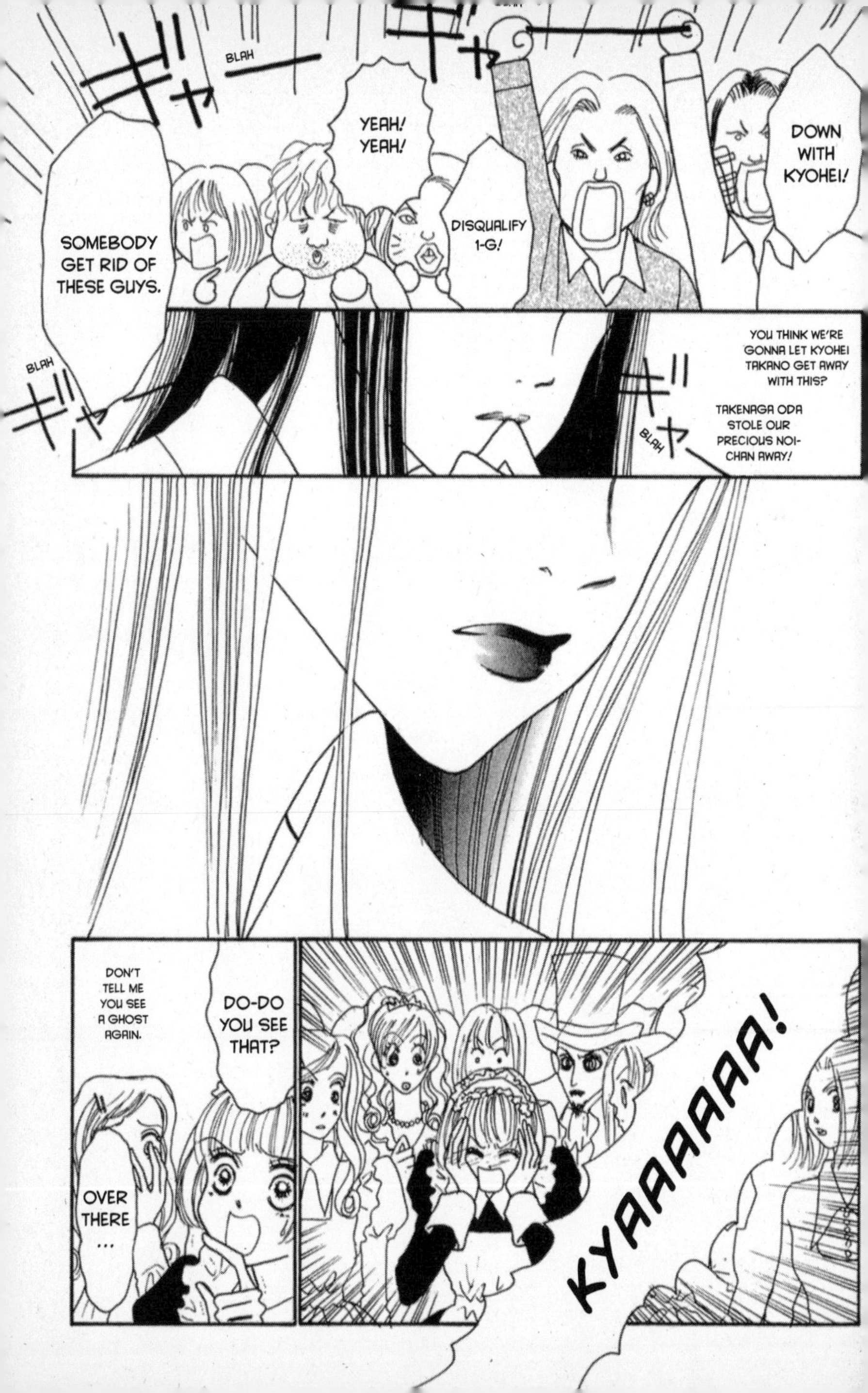
DOWN WITH KYOHEI!
DISQUALIFY 1-G!
YEAH! YEAH!
BLAH
SOMEBODY GET RID OF THESE GUYS.
YOU THINK WE'RE GONNA LET KYOHEI TAKANO GET AWAY WITH THIS?
TAKENAGA ODA STOLE OUR PRECIOUS NOI-CHAN AWAY!
BLAH
BLAH
KYAAAAAA!
DO-DO YOU SEE THAT?
DON'T TELL ME YOU SEE A GHOST AGAIN.
OVER THERE ...

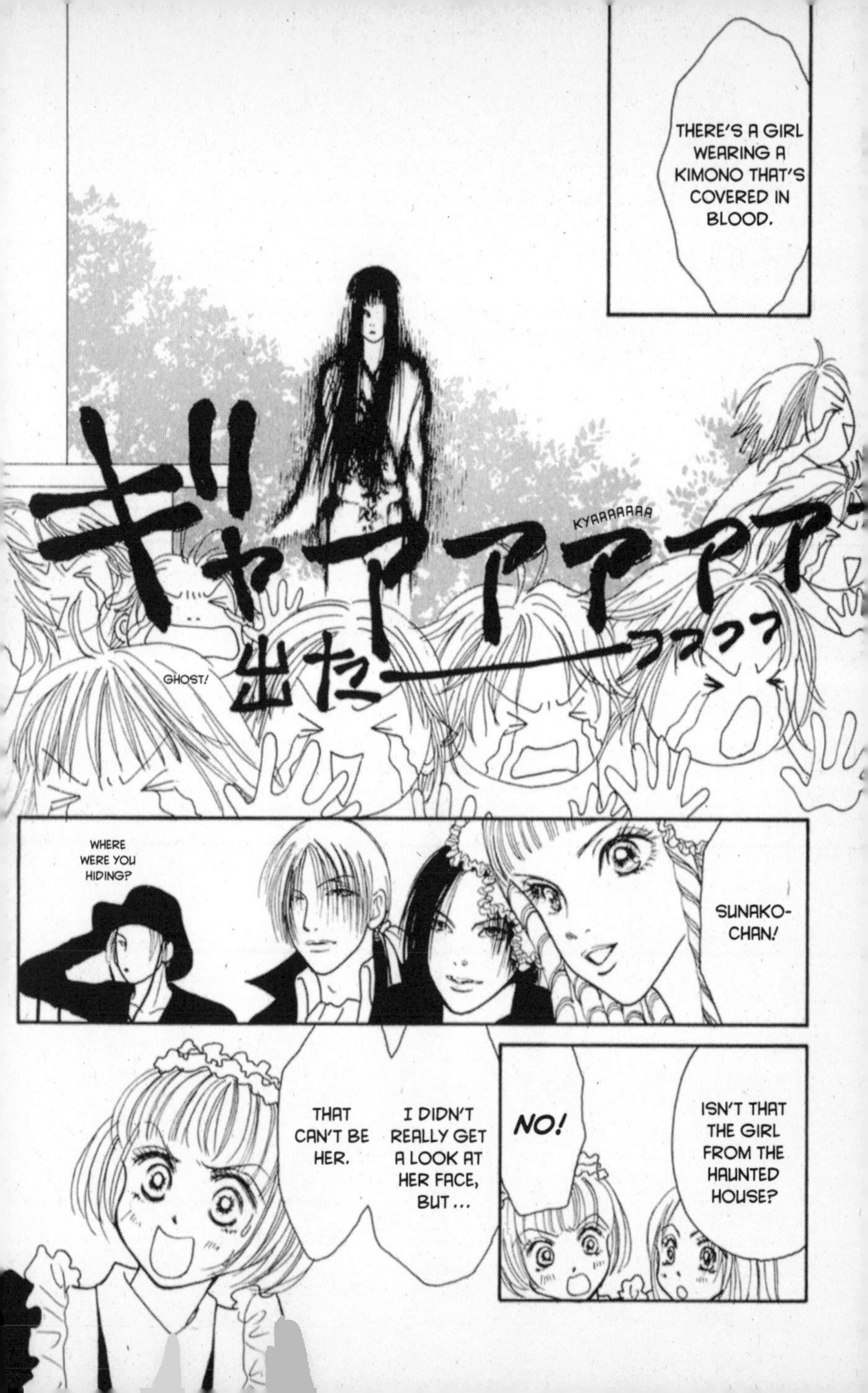
THERE'S A GIRL WEARING A KIMONO THAT'S COVERED IN BLOOD.
ギャアアアア
KYAAAAAAA
出たーっっっ
GHOST!
SUNAKO-CHAN!
WHERE WERE YOU HIDING?
ISN'T THAT THE GIRL FROM THE HAUNTED HOUSE?
NO!
I DIDN'T REALLY GET A LOOK AT HER FACE, BUT...
THAT CAN'T BE HER.

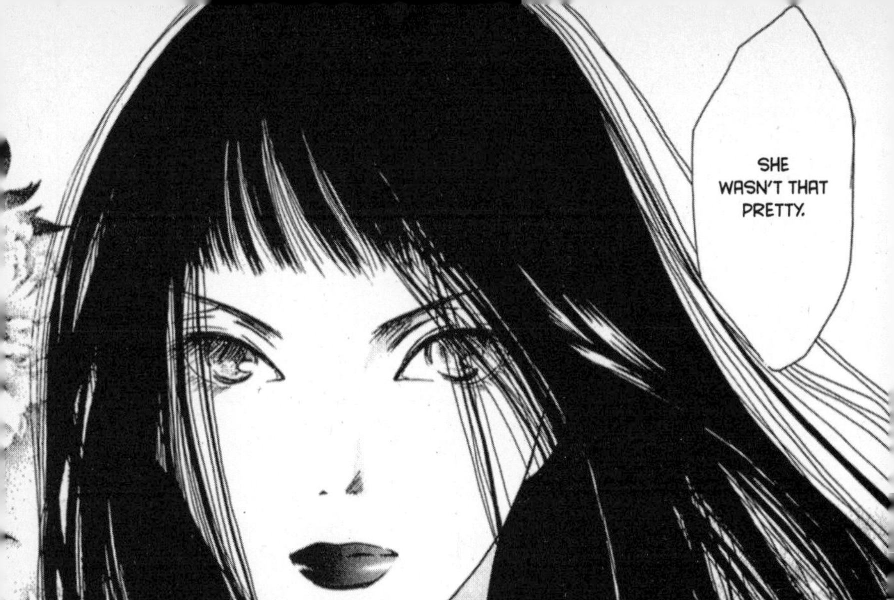
SHE WASN'T THAT PRETTY.
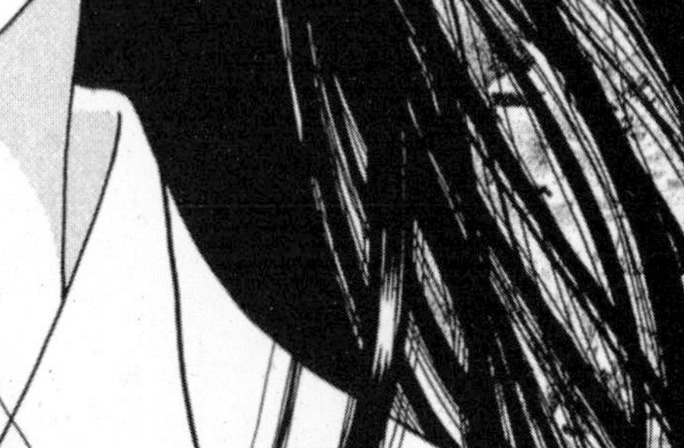
HYUU
KYAA! IT MOVED.
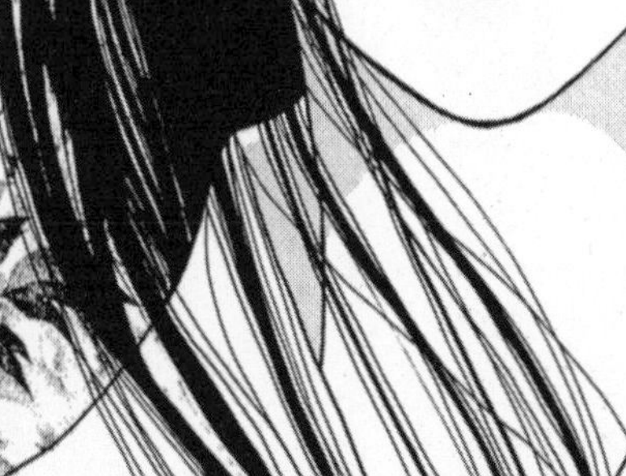
HYUU
HYUU
HYUU
HYUU

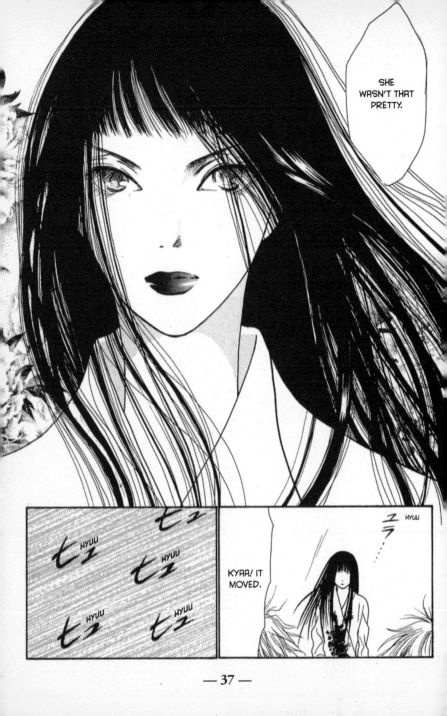

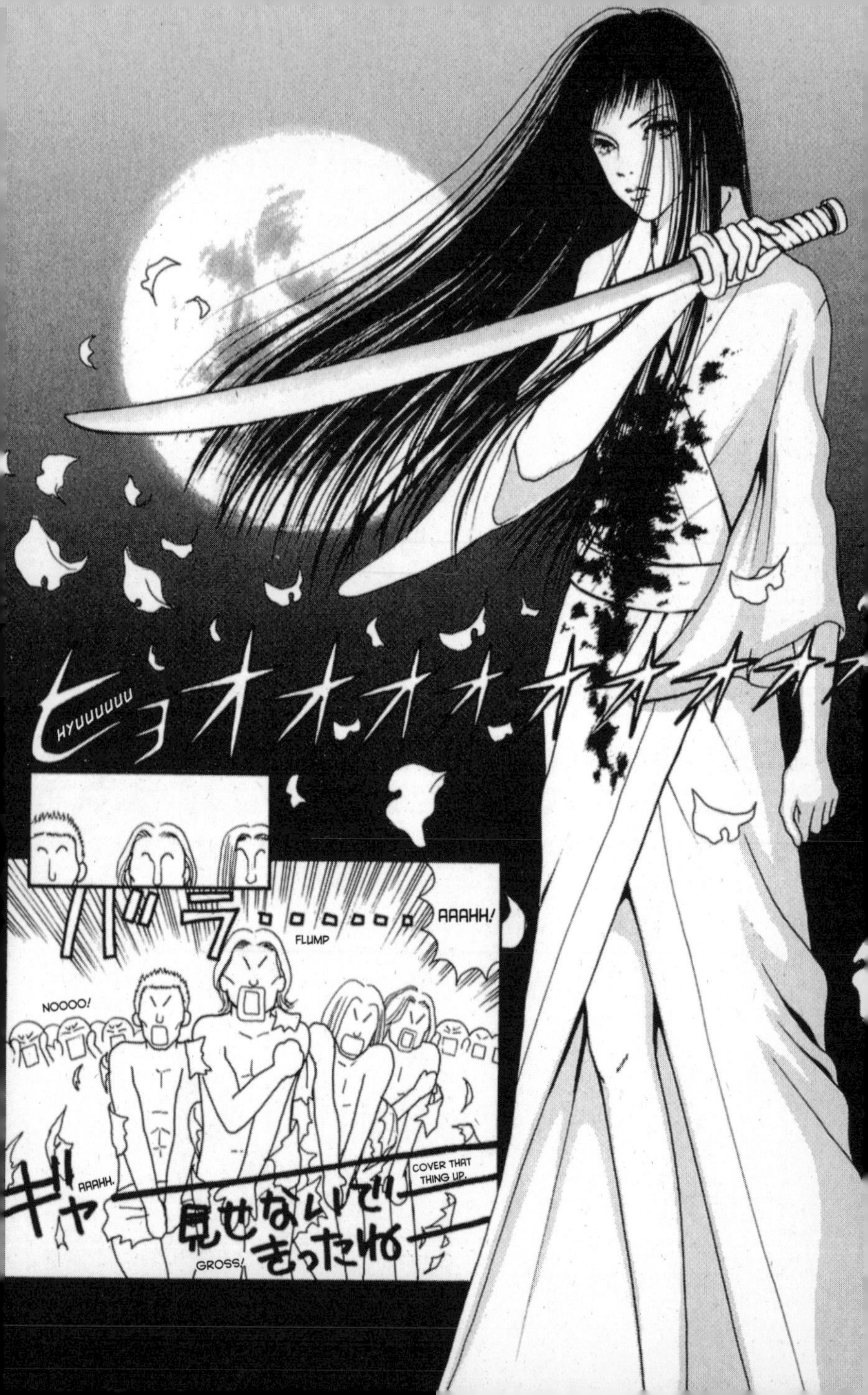

HYUUUUUU
AAAHH!
FLUMP
NOOOO!
COVER THAT THING UP.
AAAHH.
GROSS!

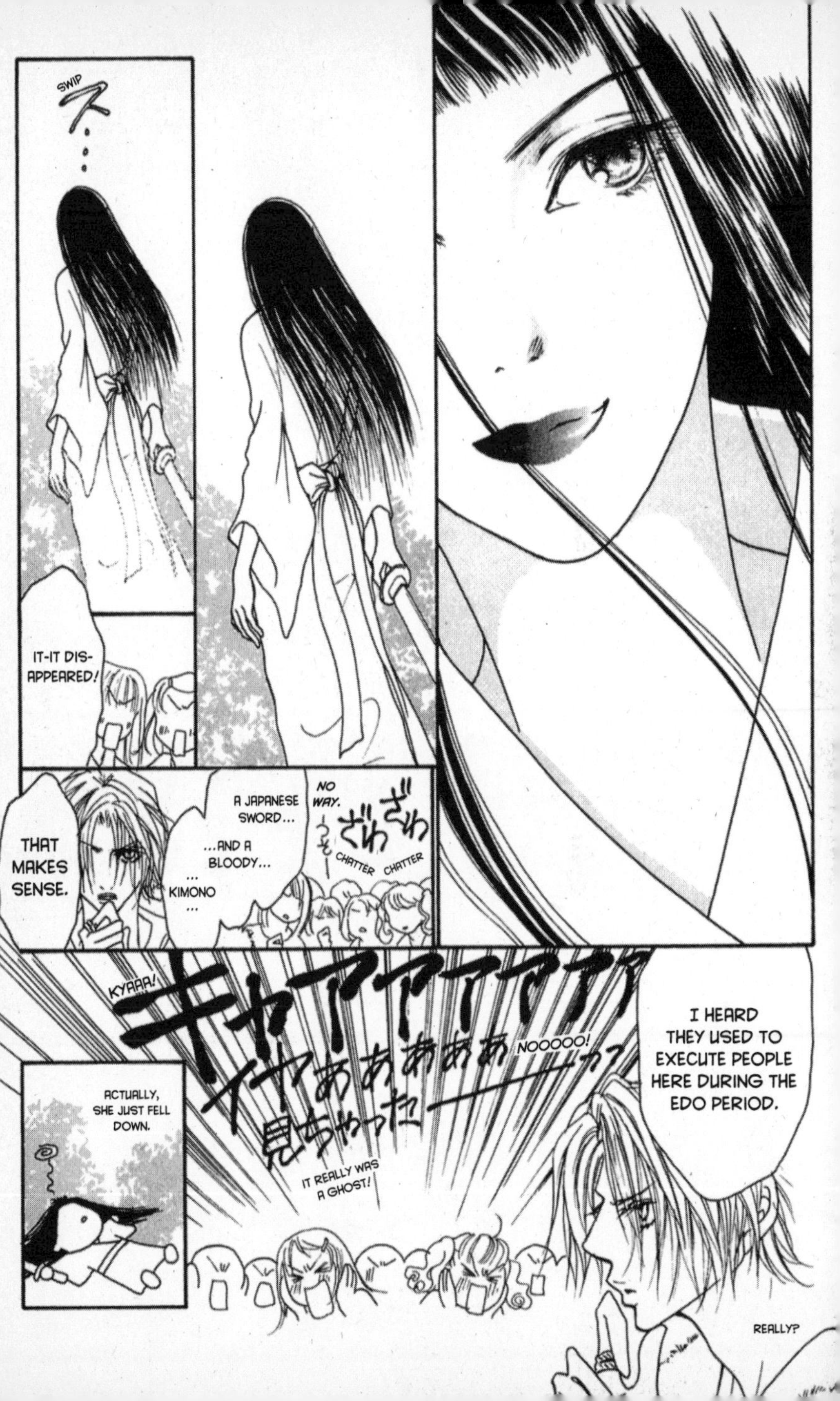
SWIP
ス…
IT-IT DIS-APPEARED!
NO WAY.
ざわざわ
CHATTER CHATTER
A JAPANESE SWORD…
…AND A BLOODY…
…KIMONO…
THAT MAKES SENSE.
I HEARD THEY USED TO EXECUTE PEOPLE HERE DURING THE EDO PERIOD.
キャアアアア
KYAAA!
イヤあああああ
NOOOOO!
見ちゃった
IT REALLY WAS A GHOST!
REALLY?
ACTUALLY, SHE JUST FELL DOWN.

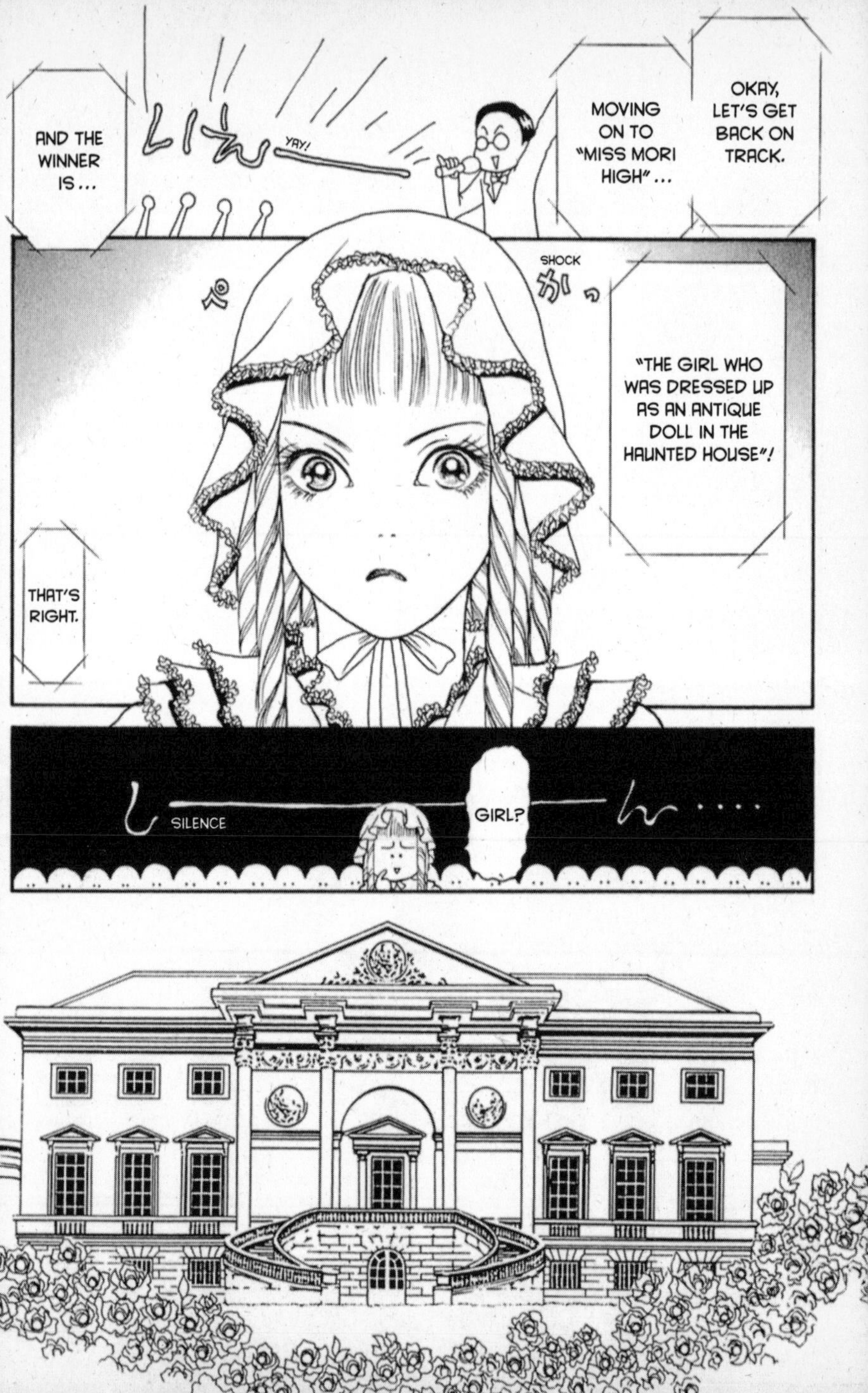
OKAY, LET'S GET BACK ON TRACK.
MOVING ON TO "MISS MORI HIGH"...
YAY!
AND THE WINNER IS...
SHOCK
"THE GIRL WHO WAS DRESSED UP AS AN ANTIQUE DOLL IN THE HAUNTED HOUSE"!
THAT'S RIGHT.
GIRL?
SILENCE

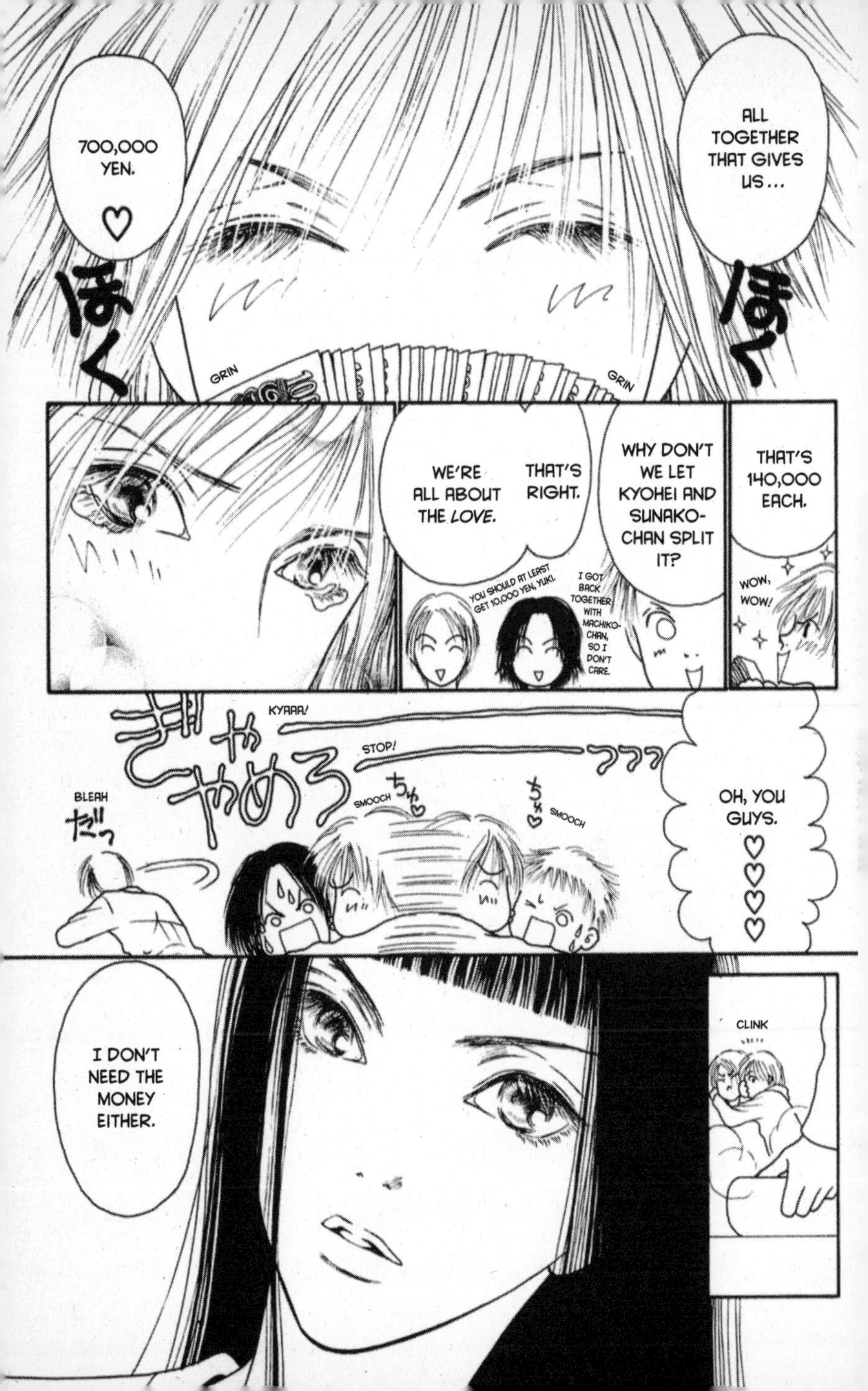

ALL TOGETHER THAT GIVES US...
ほく
700,000 YEN. ♡
ほく
GRIN
GRIN
THAT'S 140,000 EACH.
WOW, WOW!
WHY DON'T WE LET KYOHEI AND SUNAKO-CHAN SPLIT IT?
I GOT BACK TOGETHER WITH MACHIKO-CHAN, SO I DON'T CARE.
THAT'S RIGHT.
WE'RE ALL ABOUT THE *LOVE.*
YOU SHOULD AT LEAST GET 10,000 YEN, YUKI.
OH, YOU GUYS. ♡♡♡♡
KYAAA!
STOP!
SMOOCH
SMOOCH
BLEAH
CLINK
I DON'T NEED THE MONEY EITHER.

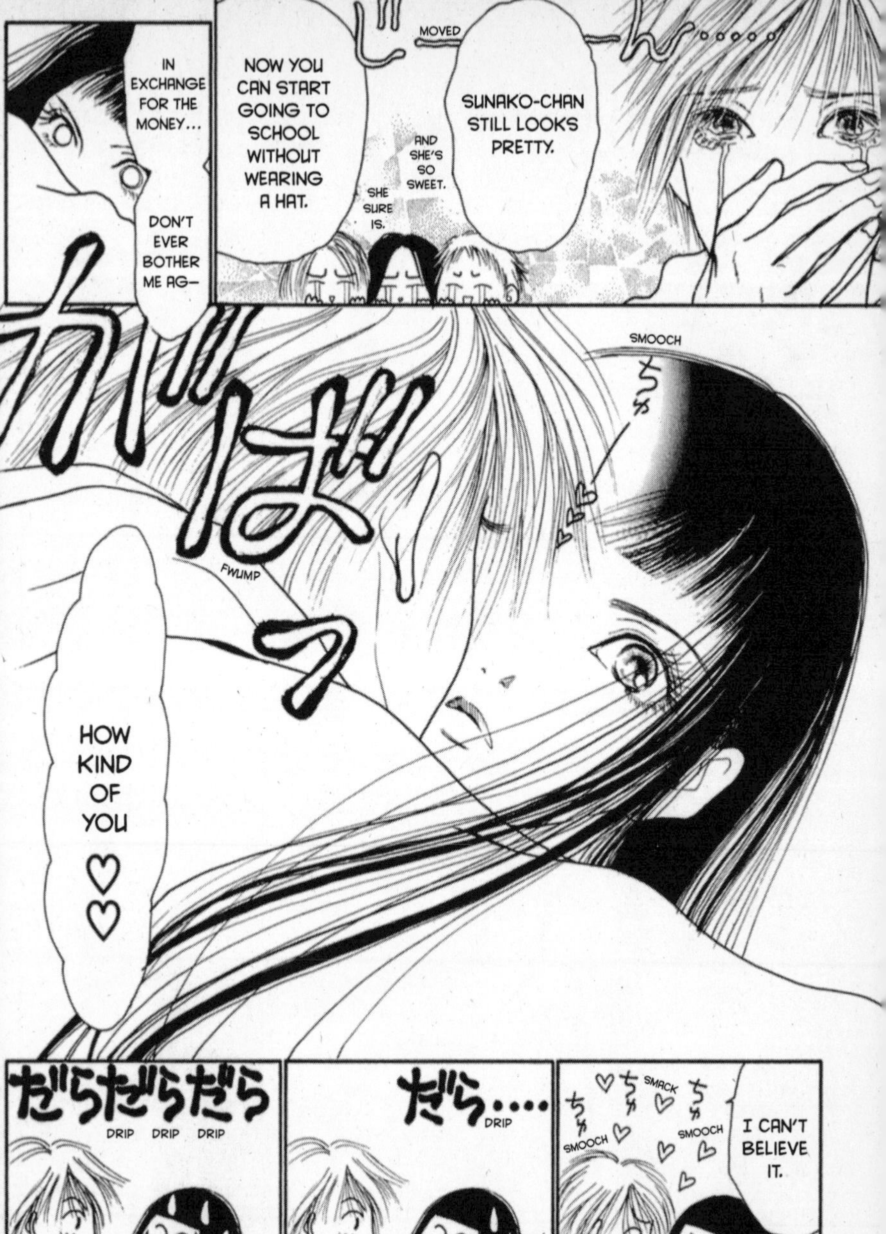
じーん……
MOVED
SUNAKO-CHAN STILL LOOKS PRETTY.
AND SHE'S SO SWEET.
SHE SURE IS.
NOW YOU CAN START GOING TO SCHOOL WITHOUT WEARING A HAT.
IN EXCHANGE FOR THE MONEY…
DON'T EVER BOTHER ME AG—
ちゅ
SMOOCH
がばっ
FWUMP
HOW KIND OF YOU ♡ ♡
I CAN'T BELIEVE IT.
ちゅ
SMOOCH
ちゅ
SMACK
ちゅ
SMOOCH
だら….
DRIP
だらだらだら
DRIP DRIP DRIP

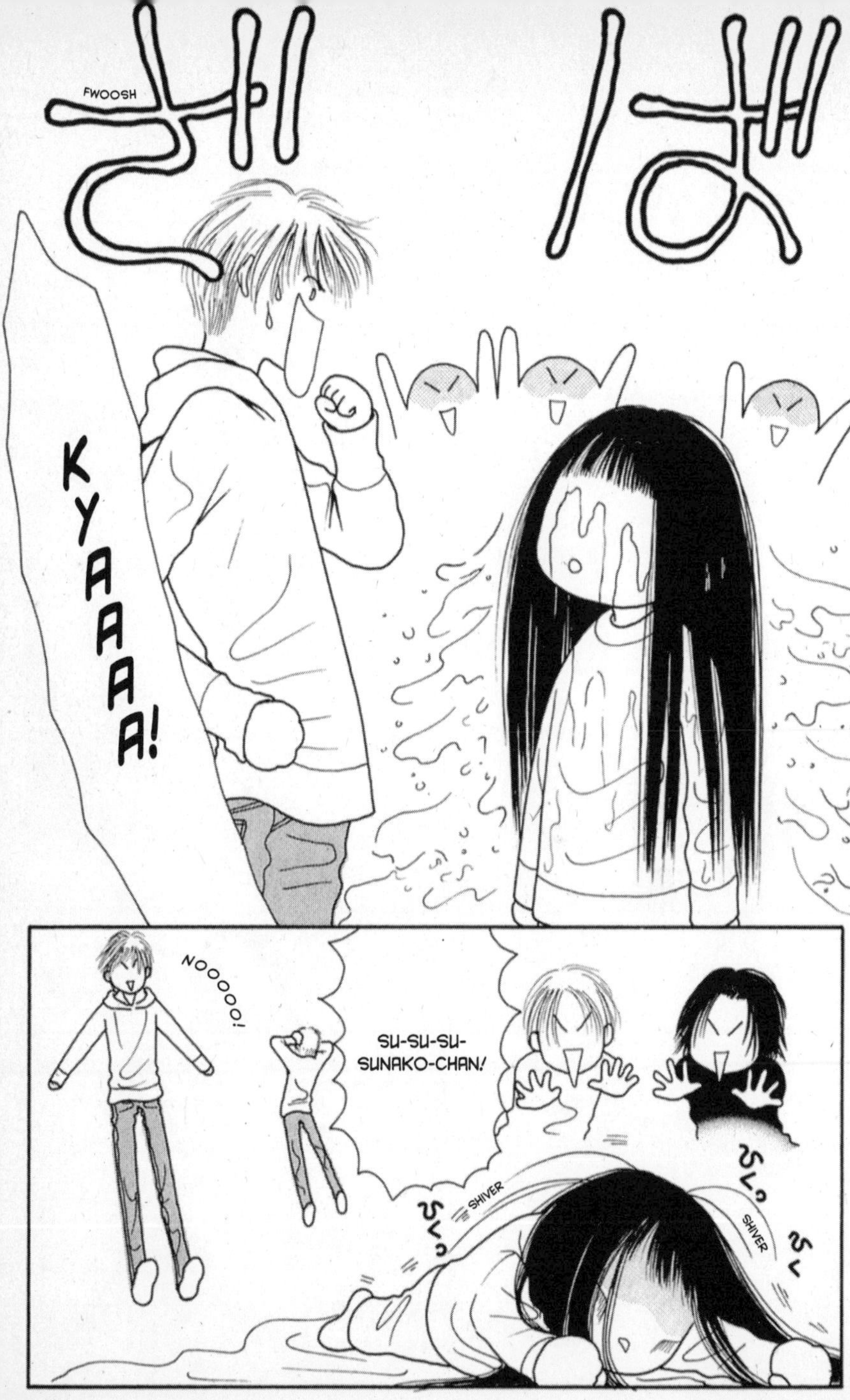

ざば
FWOOSH
KYAAAAA!
SHIVER
SHIVER
SU-SU-SU-SUNAKO-CHAN!
NOOOOOO!

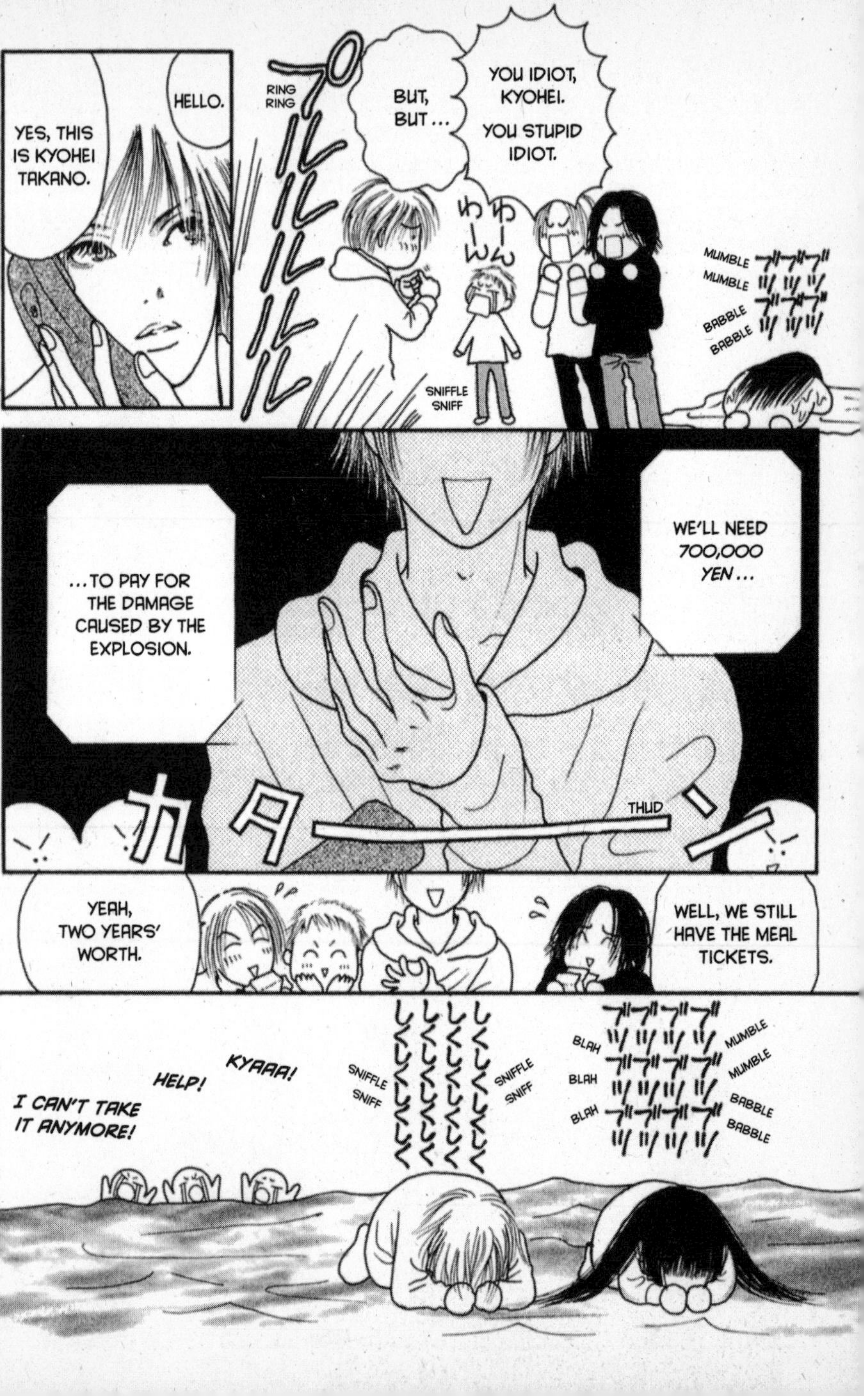
YOU IDIOT, KYOHEI.
YOU STUPID IDIOT.
BUT, BUT...
わーん
わーん
MUMBLE MUMBLE
BABBLE BABBLE
ブツブツ
ブツブツ
SNIFFLE SNIFF
RING RING
プルルルル
HELLO.
YES, THIS IS KYOHEI TAKANO.
WE'LL NEED 700,000 YEN...
...TO PAY FOR THE DAMAGE CAUSED BY THE EXPLOSION.
THUD
カタ
WELL, WE STILL HAVE THE MEAL TICKETS.
YEAH, TWO YEARS' WORTH.
MUMBLE MUMBLE
BABBLE BABBLE
BLAH BLAH BLAH
ブツブツブツブツ
SNIFFLE SNIFF
SNIFFLE SNIFF
しくしくしくしく
KYAAA!
HELP!
I CAN'T TAKE IT ANYMORE!

Chapter 7
Merry Scary Christmas!

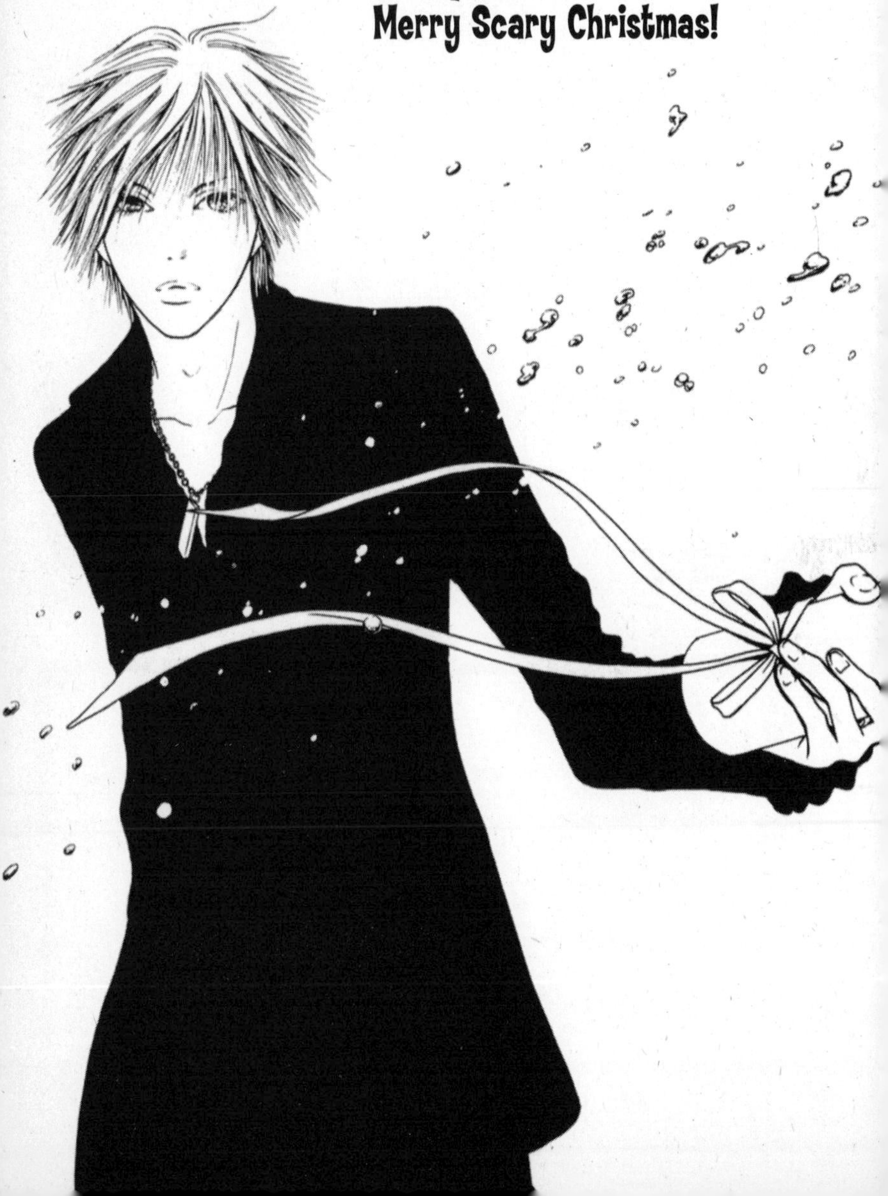

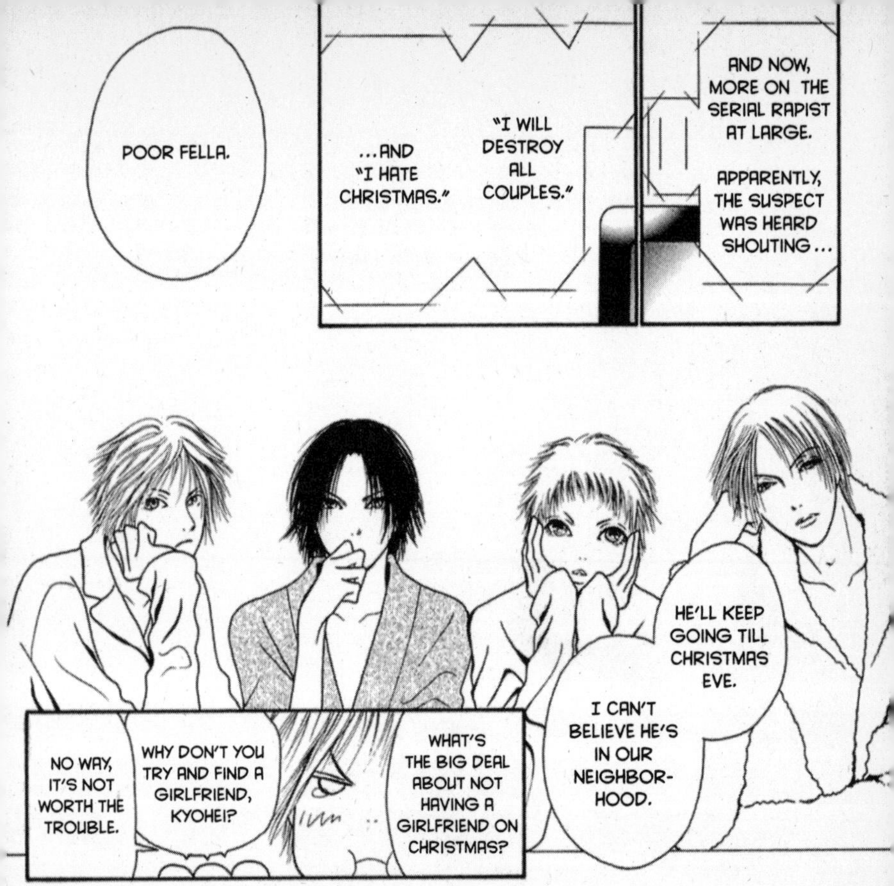
AND NOW, MORE ON THE SERIAL RAPIST AT LARGE.
APPARENTLY, THE SUSPECT WAS HEARD SHOUTING...
"I WILL DESTROY ALL COUPLES."
...AND "I HATE CHRISTMAS."
POOR FELLA.
HE'LL KEEP GOING TILL CHRISTMAS EVE.
I CAN'T BELIEVE HE'S IN OUR NEIGHBOR-HOOD.
WHAT'S THE BIG DEAL ABOUT NOT HAVING A GIRLFRIEND ON CHRISTMAS?
WHY DON'T YOU TRY AND FIND A GIRLFRIEND, KYOHEI?
NO WAY, IT'S NOT WORTH THE TROUBLE.

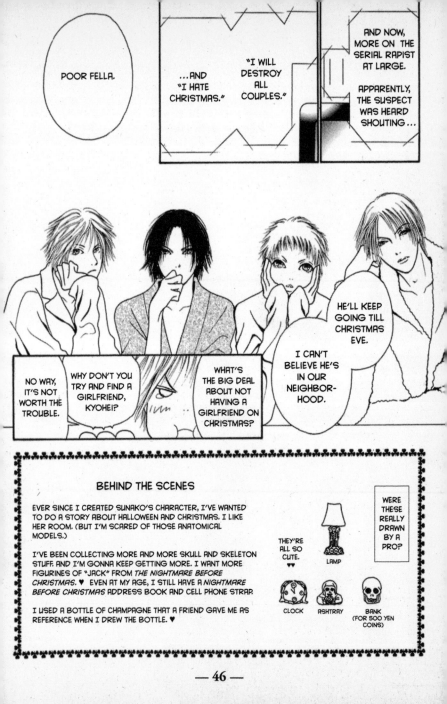

BEHIND THE SCENES

EVER SINCE I CREATED SUNAKO'S CHARACTER, I'VE WANTED TO DO A STORY ABOUT HALLOWEEN AND CHRISTMAS. I LIKE HER ROOM. (BUT I'M SCARED OF THOSE ANATOMICAL MODELS.)

I'VE BEEN COLLECTING MORE AND MORE SKULL AND SKELETON STUFF. AND I'M GONNA KEEP GETTING MORE. I WANT MORE FIGURINES OF "JACK" FROM *THE NIGHTMARE BEFORE CHRISTMAS*. ♥ EVEN AT MY AGE, I STILL HAVE A *NIGHTMARE BEFORE CHRISTMAS* ADDRESS BOOK AND CELL PHONE STRAP.

I USED A BOTTLE OF CHAMPAGNE THAT A FRIEND GAVE ME AS REFERENCE WHEN I DREW THE BOTTLE. ♥

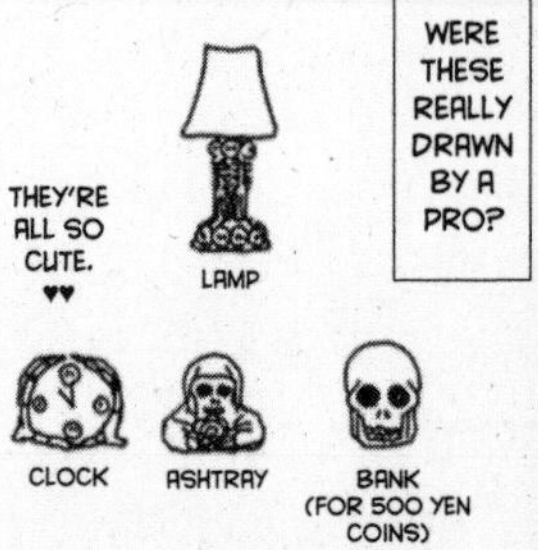
WERE THESE REALLY DRAWN BY A PRO?
THEY'RE ALL SO CUTE. ♥♥
LAMP
CLOCK
ASHTRAY
BANK (FOR 500 YEN COINS)

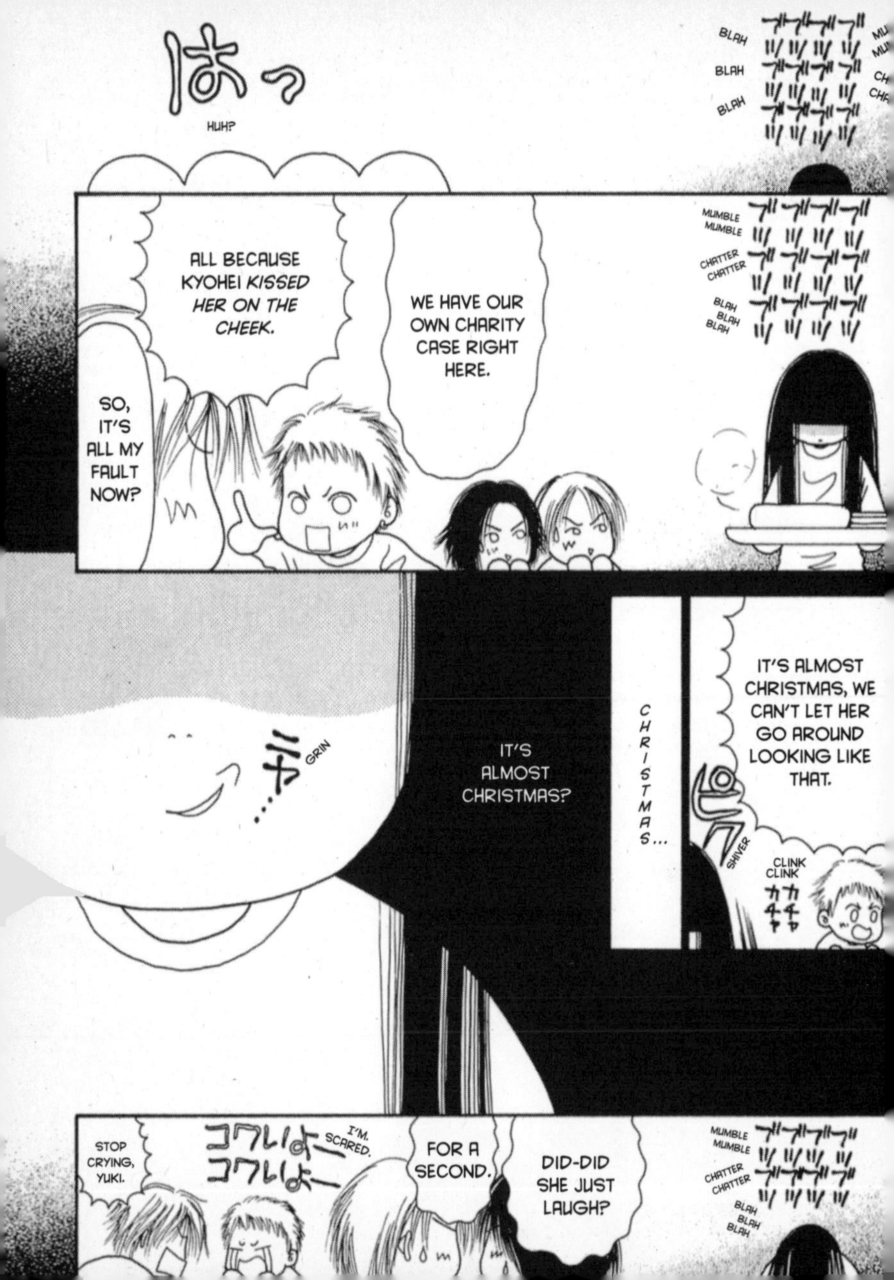
BLAH
BLAH
BLAH
はっ
HUH?
MUMBLE MUMBLE
CHATTER CHATTER
BLAH BLAH BLAH
WE HAVE OUR OWN CHARITY CASE RIGHT HERE.
ALL BECAUSE KYOHEI KISSED HER ON THE CHEEK.
SO, IT'S ALL MY FAULT NOW?
IT'S ALMOST CHRISTMAS, WE CAN'T LET HER GO AROUND LOOKING LIKE THAT.
SHIVER
CLINK CLINK
CHRISTMAS...
IT'S ALMOST CHRISTMAS?
GRIN
MUMBLE MUMBLE
CHATTER CHATTER
BLAH BLAH BLAH
DID-DID SHE JUST LAUGH?
FOR A SECOND.
I'M SCARED.
STOP CRYING, YUKI.

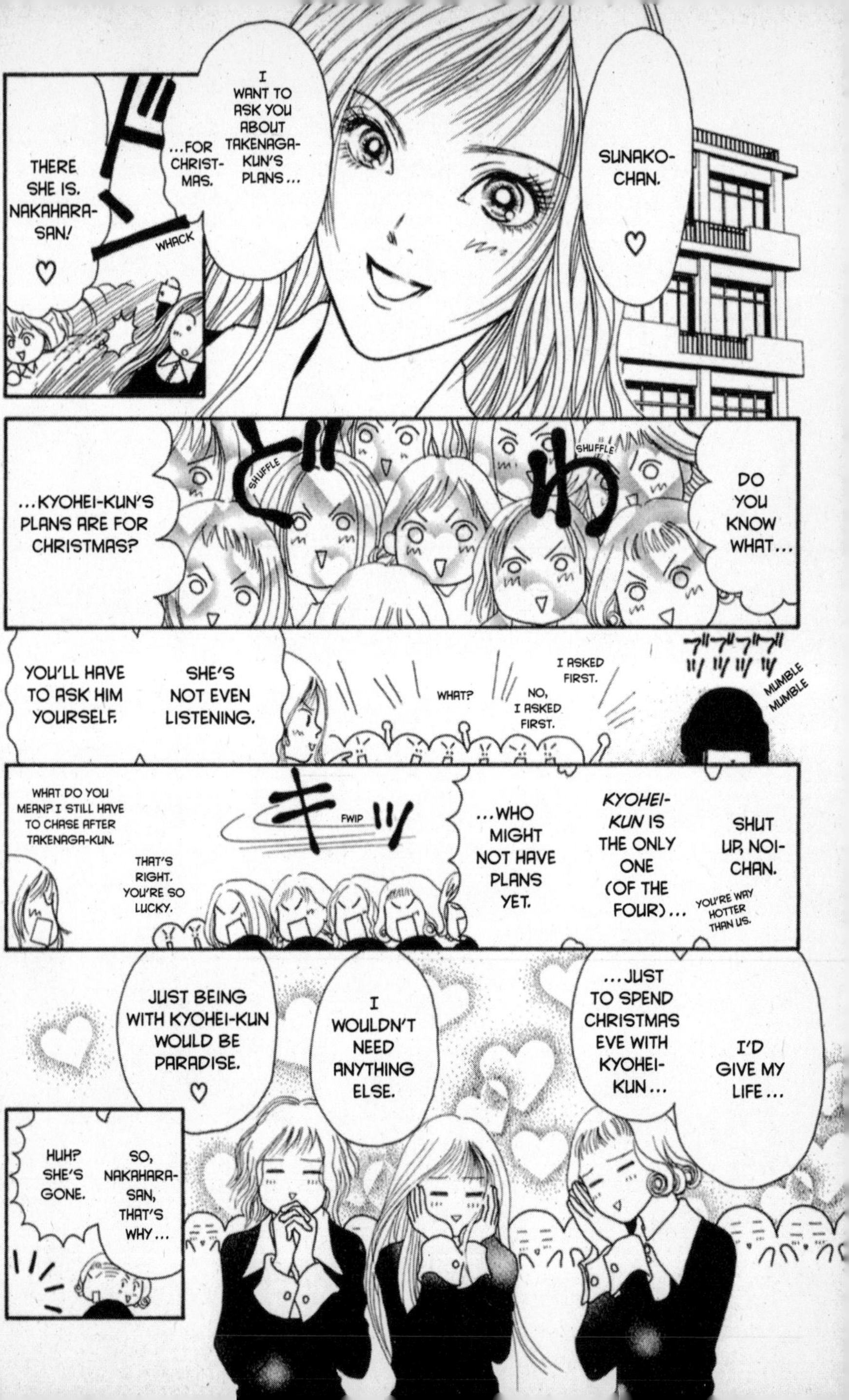
SUNAKO-CHAN. ♡
I WANT TO ASK YOU ABOUT TAKENAGA-KUN'S PLANS...
...FOR CHRIST-MAS.
WHACK
THERE SHE IS. NAKAHARA-SAN! ♡
DO YOU KNOW WHAT...
SHUFFLE
SHUFFLE
...KYOHEI-KUN'S PLANS ARE FOR CHRISTMAS?
MUMBLE MUMBLE
I ASKED FIRST.
NO, I ASKED FIRST.
WHAT?
SHE'S NOT EVEN LISTENING.
YOU'LL HAVE TO ASK HIM YOURSELF.
SHUT UP, NOI-CHAN.
YOU'RE WAY HOTTER THAN US.
KYOHEI-KUN IS THE ONLY ONE (OF THE FOUR)...
...WHO MIGHT NOT HAVE PLANS YET.
FWIP
WHAT DO YOU MEAN? I STILL HAVE TO CHASE AFTER TAKENAGA-KUN.
THAT'S RIGHT. YOU'RE SO LUCKY.
I'D GIVE MY LIFE...
...JUST TO SPEND CHRISTMAS EVE WITH KYOHEI-KUN...
I WOULDN'T NEED ANYTHING ELSE.
JUST BEING WITH KYOHEI-KUN WOULD BE PARADISE. ♡
SO, NAKAHARA-SAN, THAT'S WHY...
HUH? SHE'S GONE.

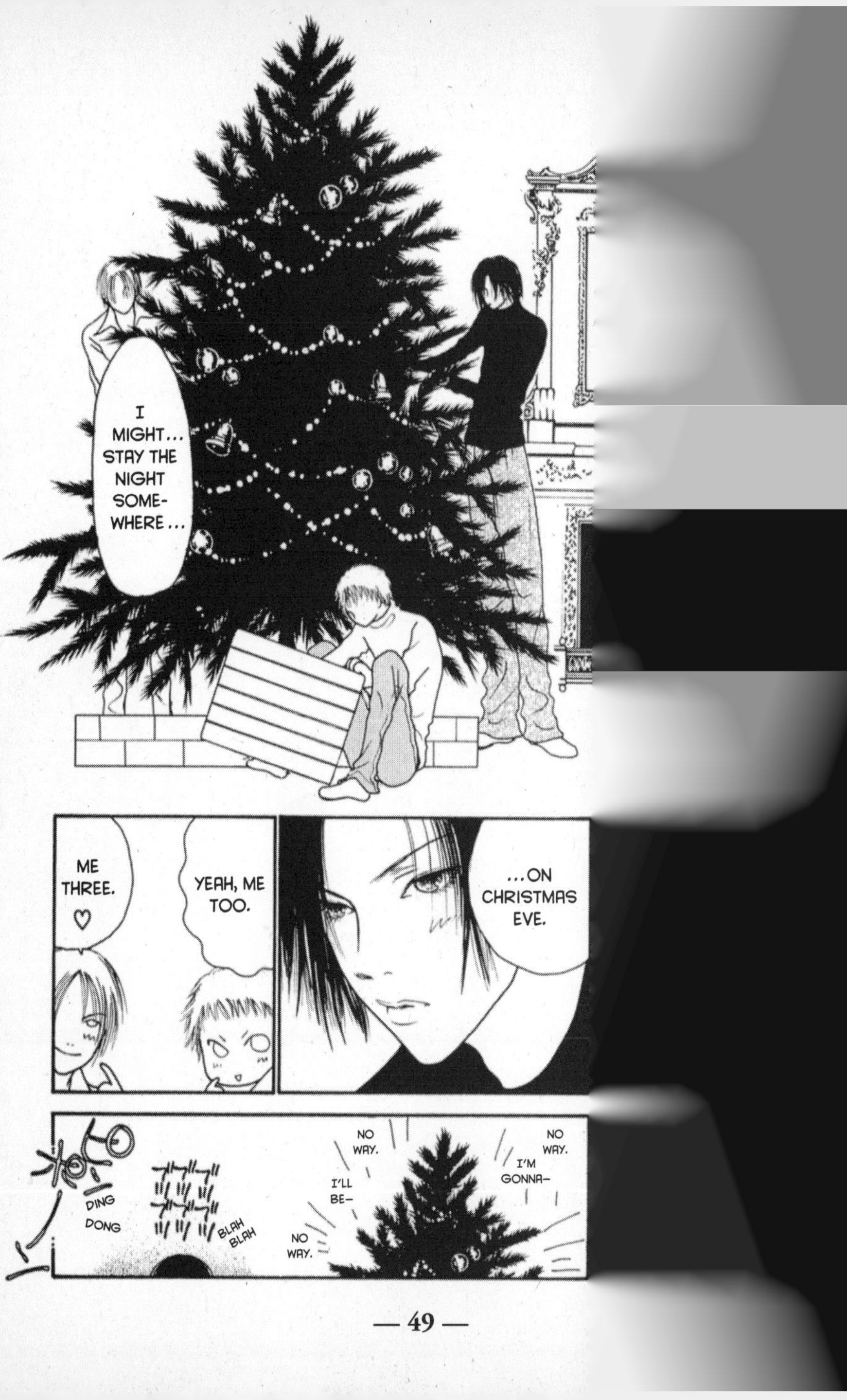
I MIGHT... STAY THE NIGHT SOMEWHERE...
...ON CHRISTMAS EVE.
YEAH, ME TOO.
ME THREE. ♡
NO WAY.
I'M GONNA–
NO WAY.
I'LL BE–
NO WAY.
BLAH BLAH
DING DONG

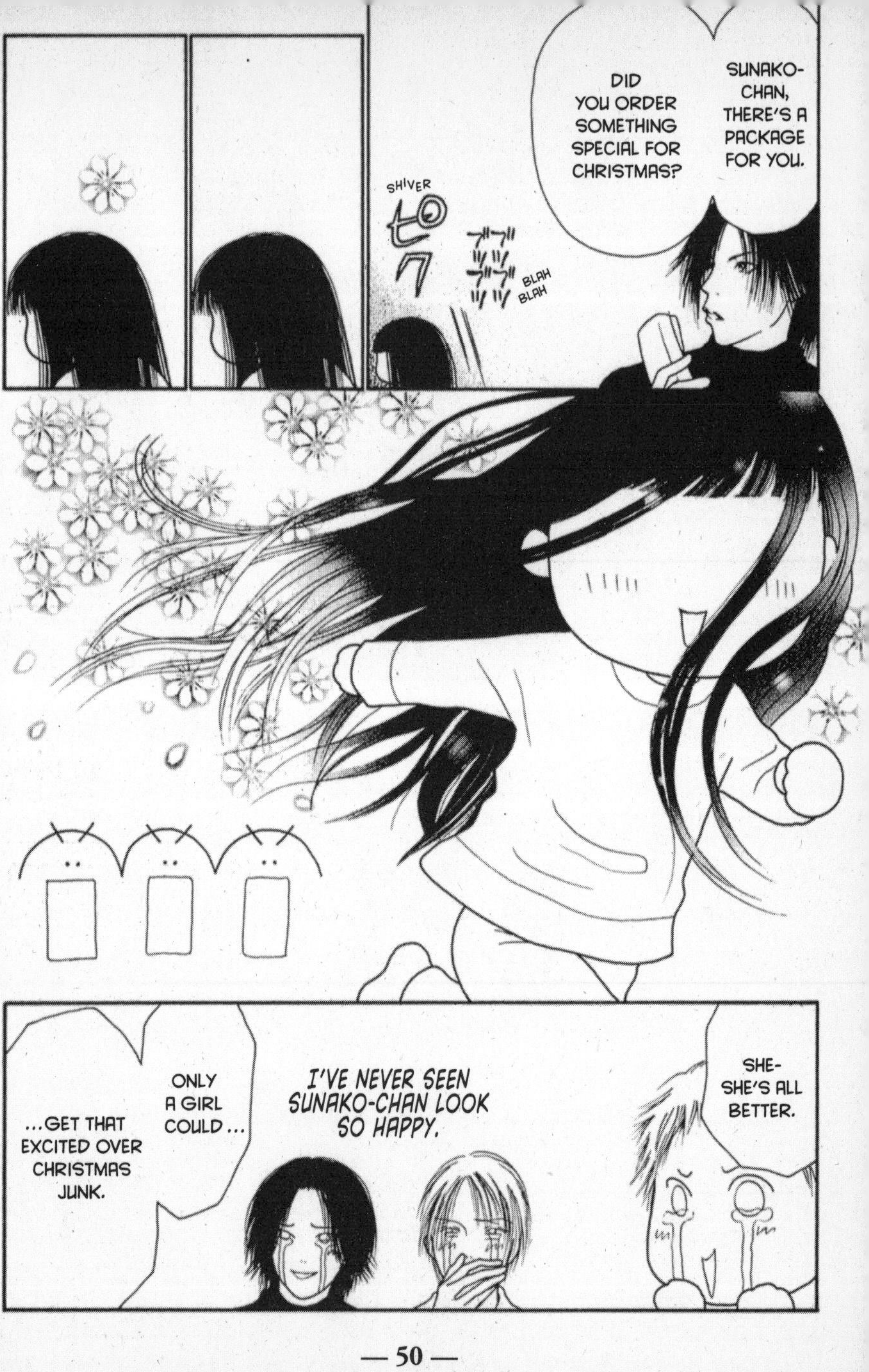
SUNAKO-CHAN, THERE'S A PACKAGE FOR YOU.
DID YOU ORDER SOMETHING SPECIAL FOR CHRISTMAS?
ブツブツ
BLAH BLAH
ピク
SHIVER
SHE-SHE'S ALL BETTER.
I'VE NEVER SEEN SUNAKO-CHAN LOOK SO HAPPY.
ONLY A GIRL COULD ...
...GET THAT EXCITED OVER CHRISTMAS JUNK.

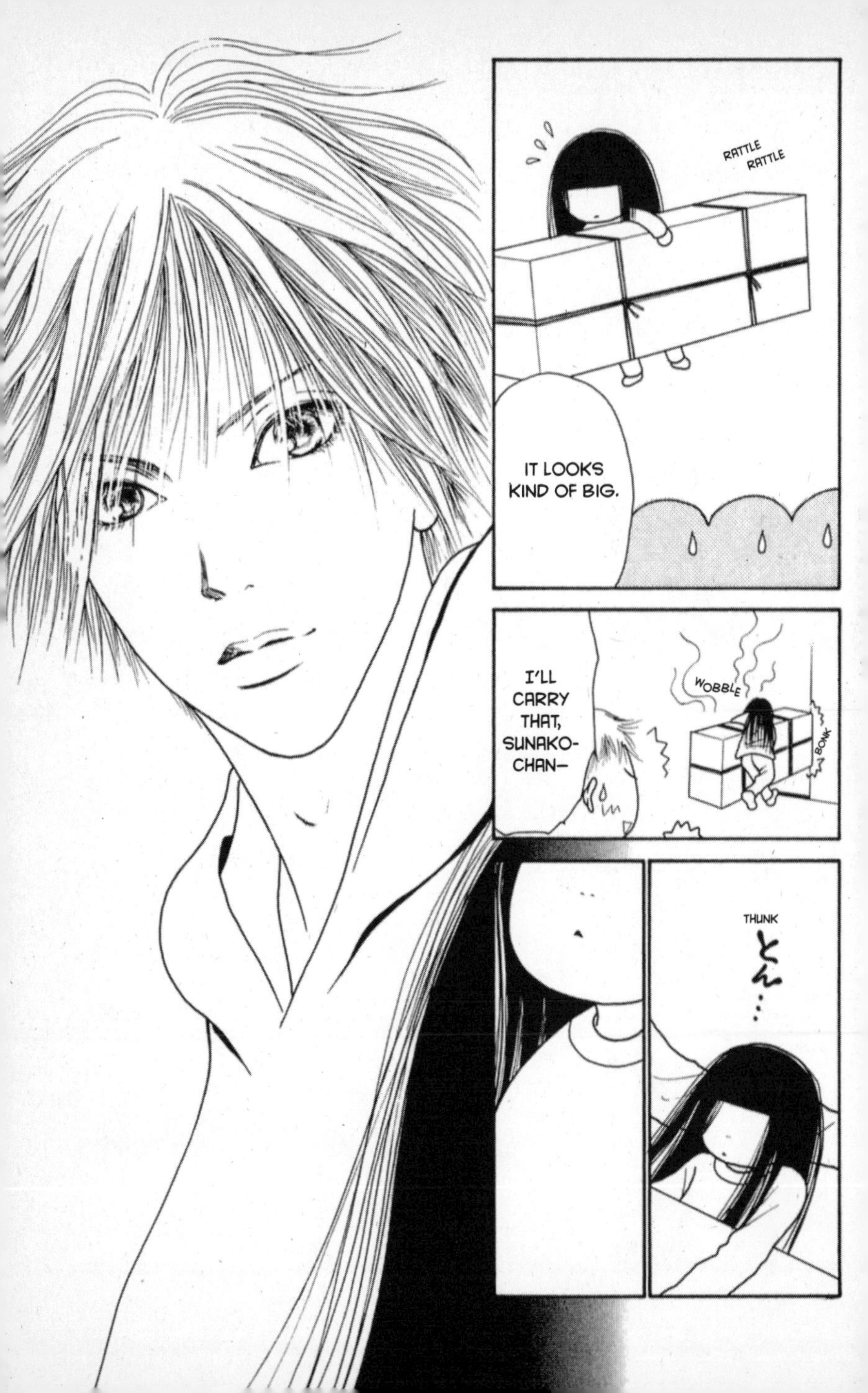
RATTLE RATTLE
IT LOOKS KIND OF BIG.
WOBBLE
BONK
I'LL CARRY THAT, SUNAKO-CHAN—
THUNK
とん…

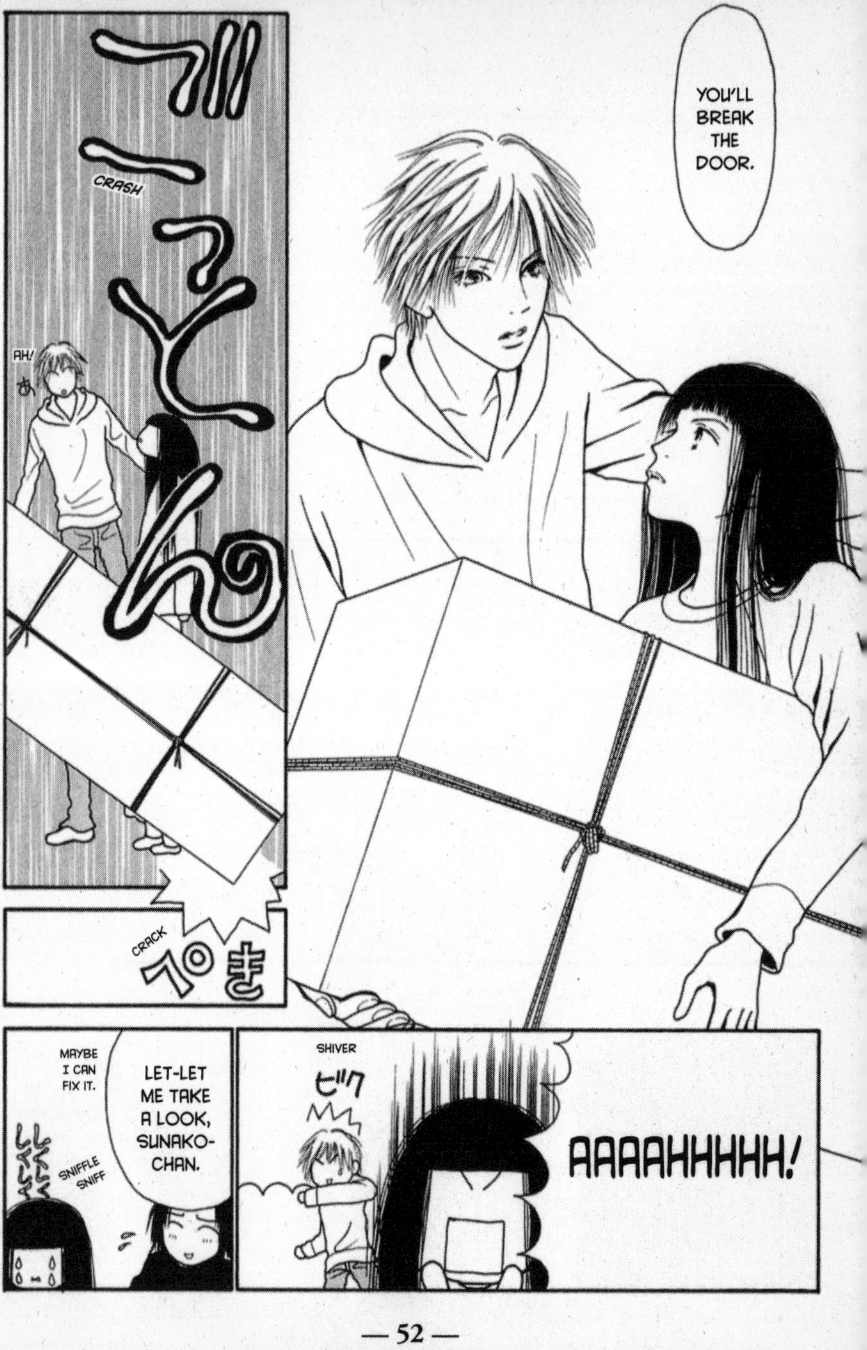
YOU'LL BREAK THE DOOR.
CRASH
AH!
CRACK
SHIVER
AAAAHHHHH!
LET-LET ME TAKE A LOOK, SUNAKO-CHAN.
MAYBE I CAN FIX IT.
SNIFFLE SNIFF

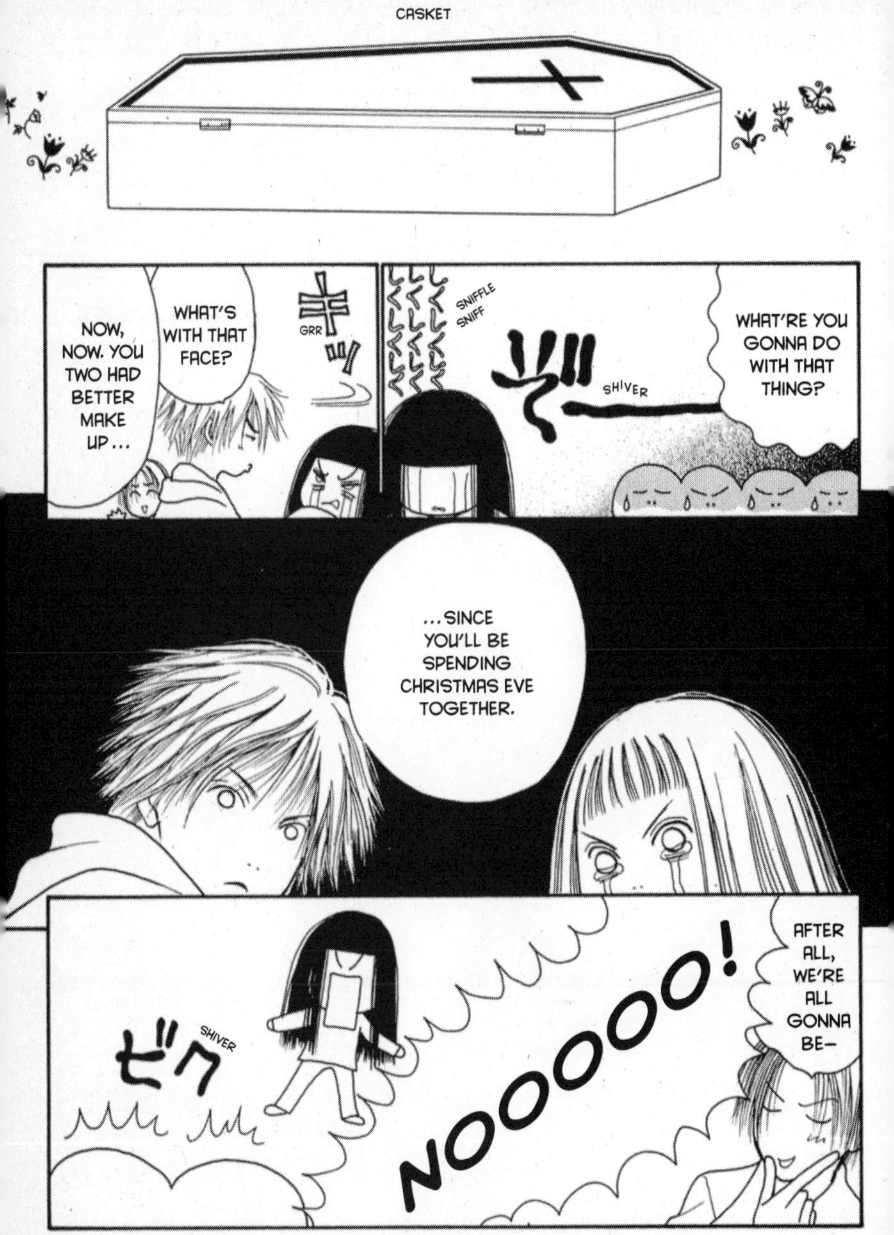
CASKET
WHAT'RE YOU GONNA DO WITH THAT THING?
SHIVER
SNIFFLE SNIFF
GRR
WHAT'S WITH THAT FACE?
NOW, NOW. YOU TWO HAD BETTER MAKE UP...
...SINCE YOU'LL BE SPENDING CHRISTMAS EVE TOGETHER.
AFTER ALL, WE'RE ALL GONNA BE—
NOOOOO!
SHIVER

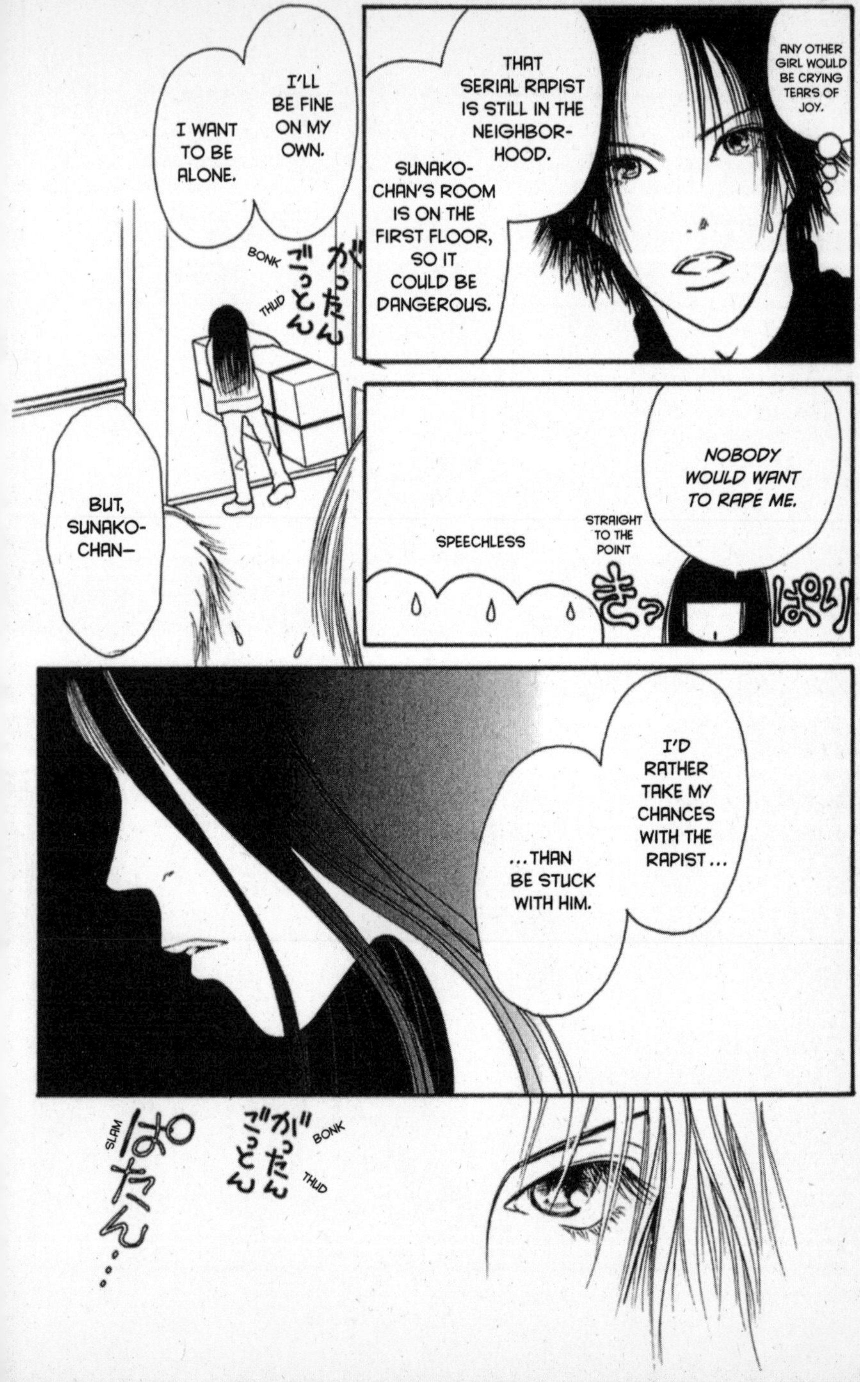
ANY OTHER GIRL WOULD BE CRYING TEARS OF JOY.
THAT SERIAL RAPIST IS STILL IN THE NEIGHBOR-HOOD.
SUNAKO-CHAN'S ROOM IS ON THE FIRST FLOOR, SO IT COULD BE DANGEROUS.
NOBODY WOULD WANT TO RAPE ME.
きっぱり
STRAIGHT TO THE POINT
SPEECHLESS
I'LL BE FINE ON MY OWN.
I WANT TO BE ALONE.
がったん
BONK
ごっとん
THUD
BUT, SUNAKO-CHAN—
I'D RATHER TAKE MY CHANCES WITH THE RAPIST...
...THAN BE STUCK WITH HIM.
がったん
BONK
ごっとん
THUD
ぱたん…
SLAM

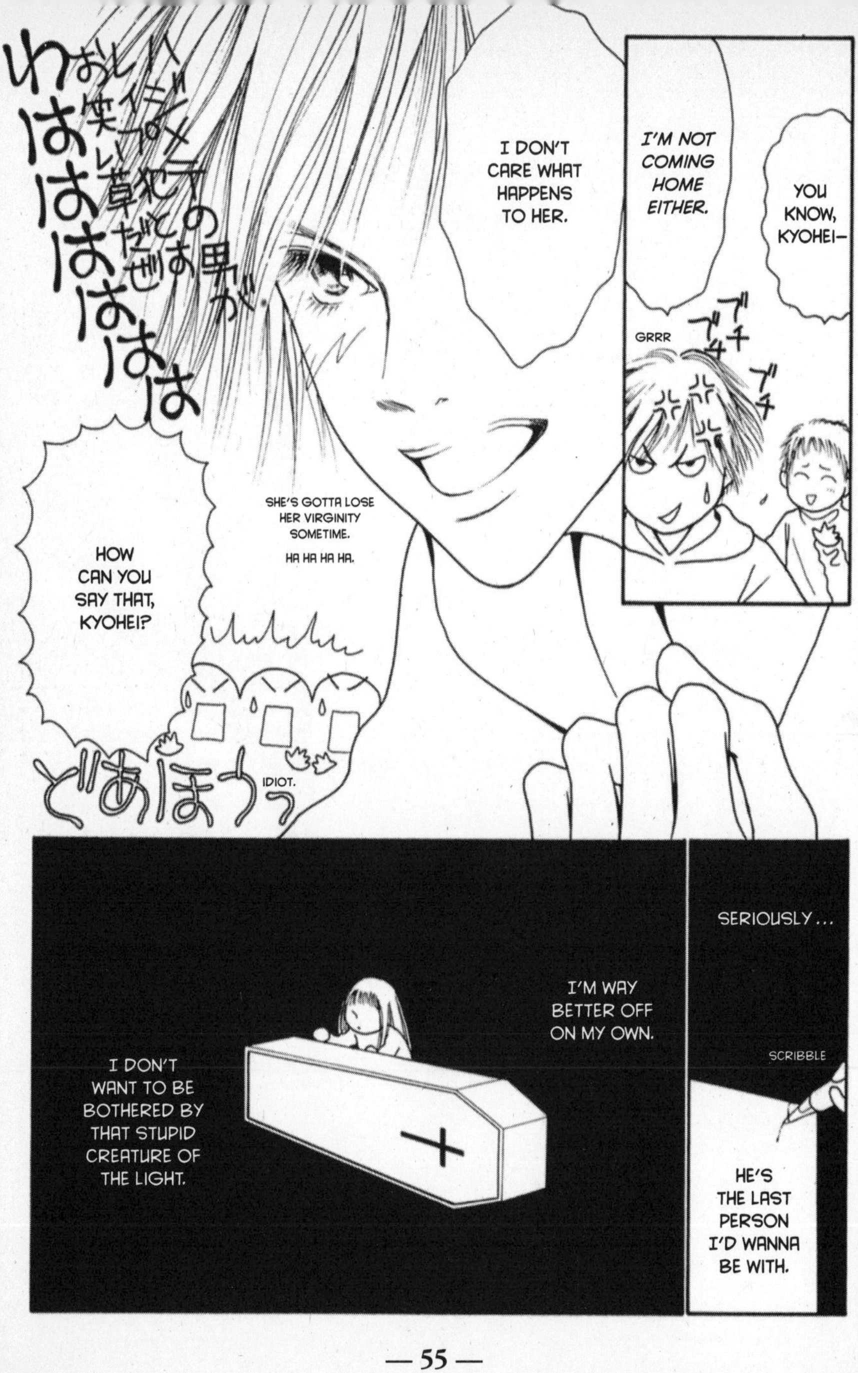

YOU KNOW, KYOHEI—
I'M NOT COMING HOME EITHER.
GRRR
I DON'T CARE WHAT HAPPENS TO HER.
SHE'S GOTTA LOSE HER VIRGINITY SOMETIME.
HA HA HA HA.
HOW CAN YOU SAY THAT, KYOHEI?
どあほぅっ
IDIOT.
SERIOUSLY...
SCRIBBLE
HE'S THE LAST PERSON I'D WANNA BE WITH.
I'M WAY BETTER OFF ON MY OWN.
I DON'T WANT TO BE BOTHERED BY THAT STUPID CREATURE OF THE LIGHT.

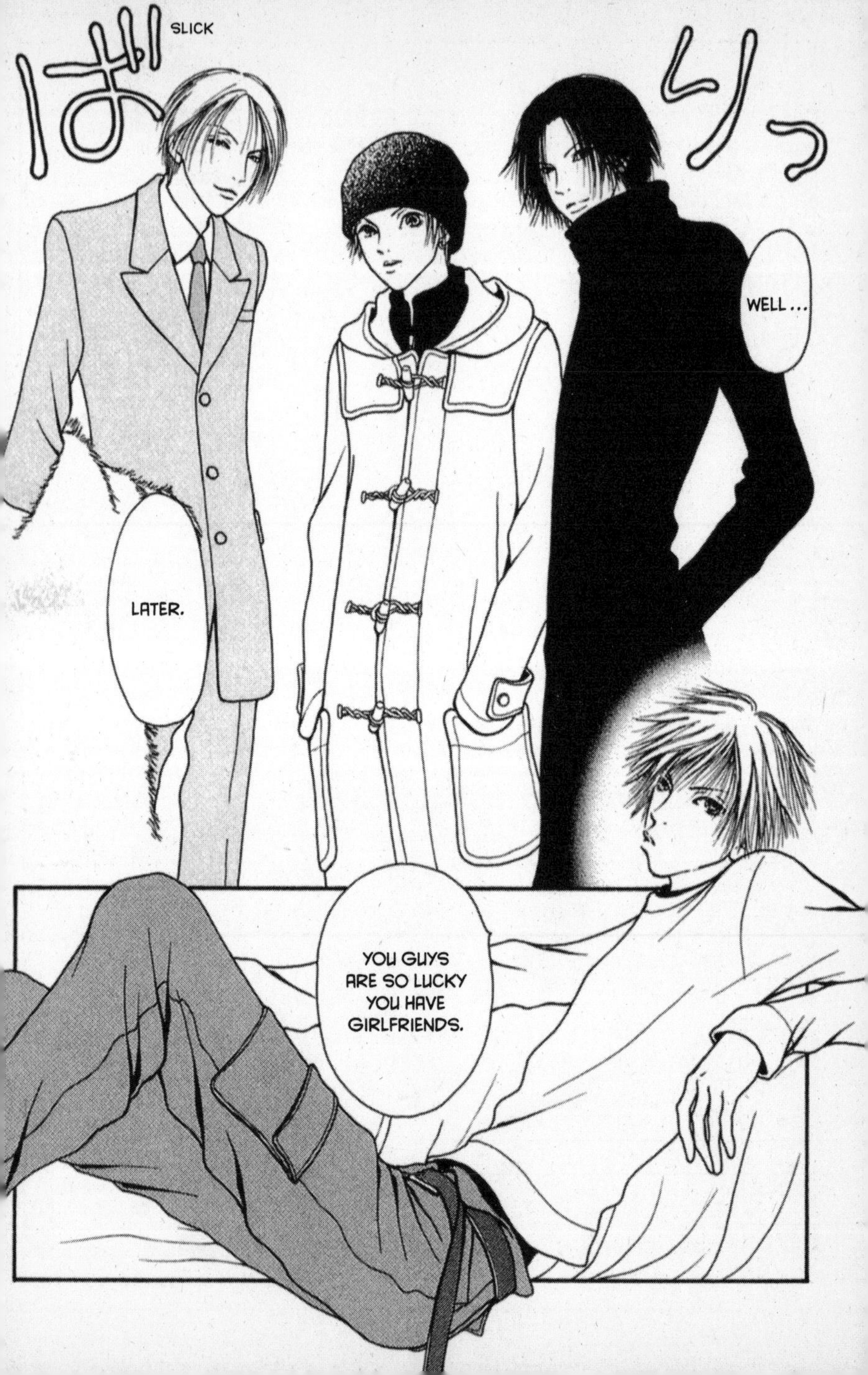
ばりっ
SLICK
WELL...
LATER.
YOU GUYS ARE SO LUCKY YOU HAVE GIRLFRIENDS.

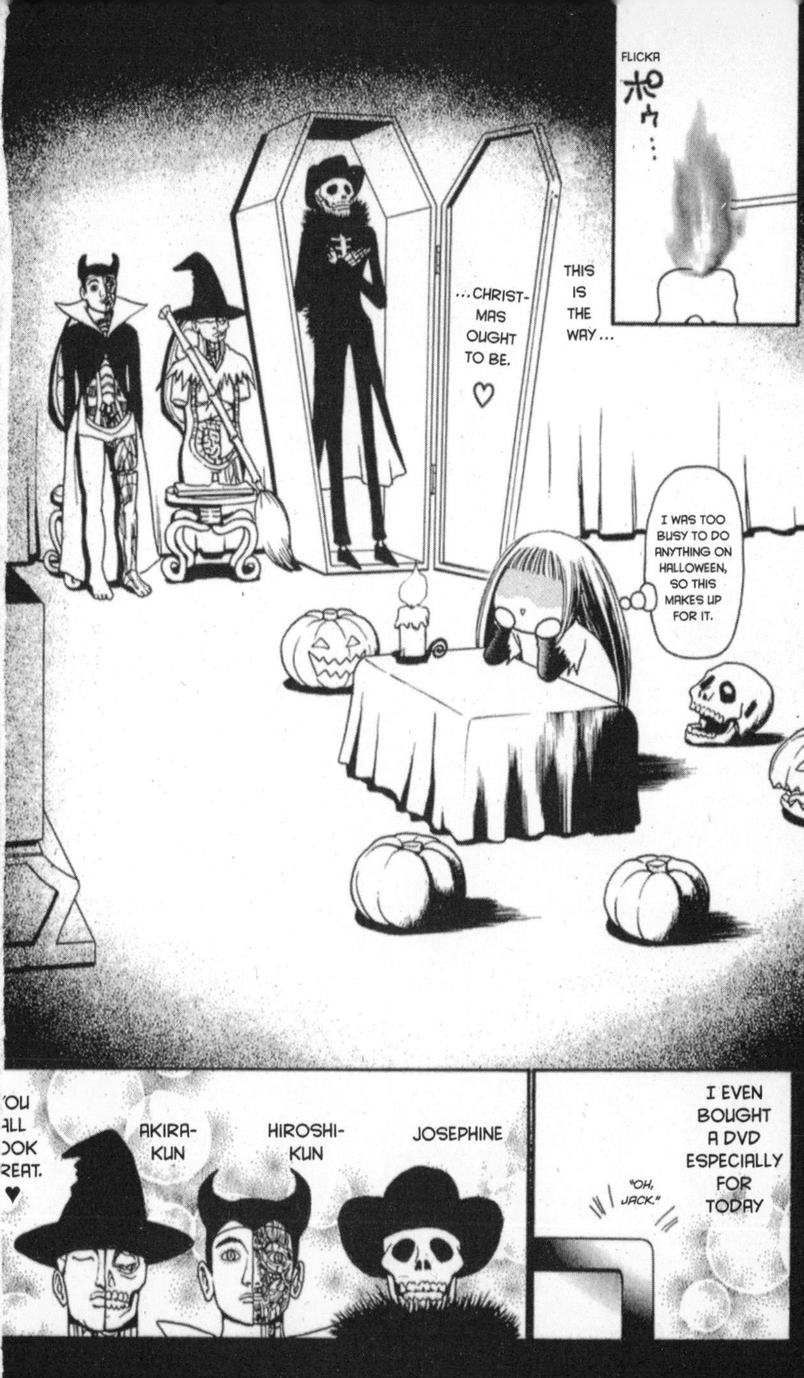
FLICKA
ポゥ…
THIS IS THE WAY…
…CHRISTMAS OUGHT TO BE. ♡
I WAS TOO BUSY TO DO ANYTHING ON HALLOWEEN, SO THIS MAKES UP FOR IT.
I EVEN BOUGHT A DVD ESPECIALLY FOR TODAY
"OH, JACK."
JOSEPHINE
HIROSHI-KUN
AKIRA-KUN
OU ALL OOK REAT. ♥

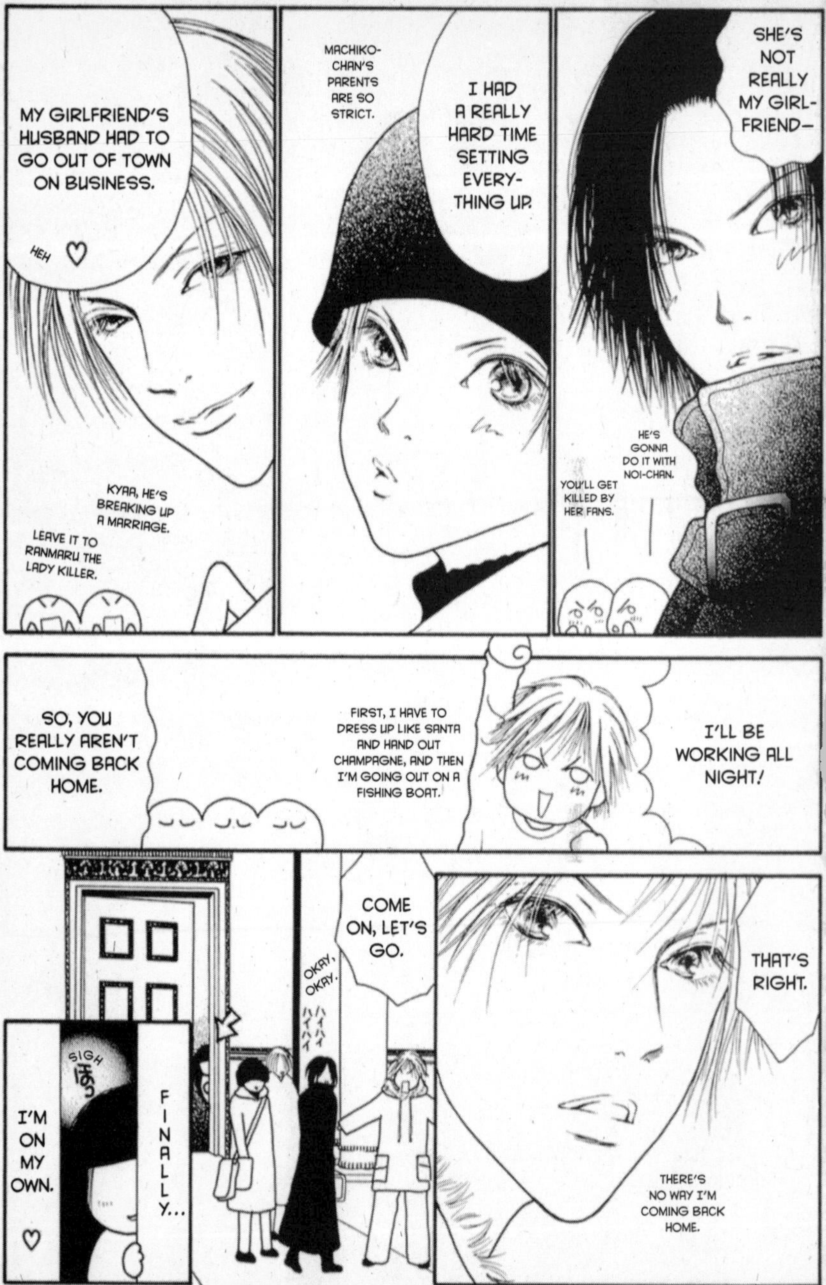
SHE'S NOT REALLY MY GIRL-FRIEND—
HE'S GONNA DO IT WITH NOI-CHAN.
YOU'LL GET KILLED BY HER FANS.
I HAD A REALLY HARD TIME SETTING EVERY-THING UP.
MACHIKO-CHAN'S PARENTS ARE SO STRICT.
MY GIRLFRIEND'S HUSBAND HAD TO GO OUT OF TOWN ON BUSINESS.
HEH ♡
KYAA, HE'S BREAKING UP A MARRIAGE.
LEAVE IT TO RANMARU THE LADY KILLER.
I'LL BE WORKING ALL NIGHT!
FIRST, I HAVE TO DRESS UP LIKE SANTA AND HAND OUT CHAMPAGNE, AND THEN I'M GOING OUT ON A FISHING BOAT.
SO, YOU REALLY AREN'T COMING BACK HOME.
THAT'S RIGHT.
THERE'S NO WAY I'M COMING BACK HOME.
COME ON, LET'S GO.
OKAY, OKAY.
FINALLY...
SIGH
I'M ON MY OWN.
♡

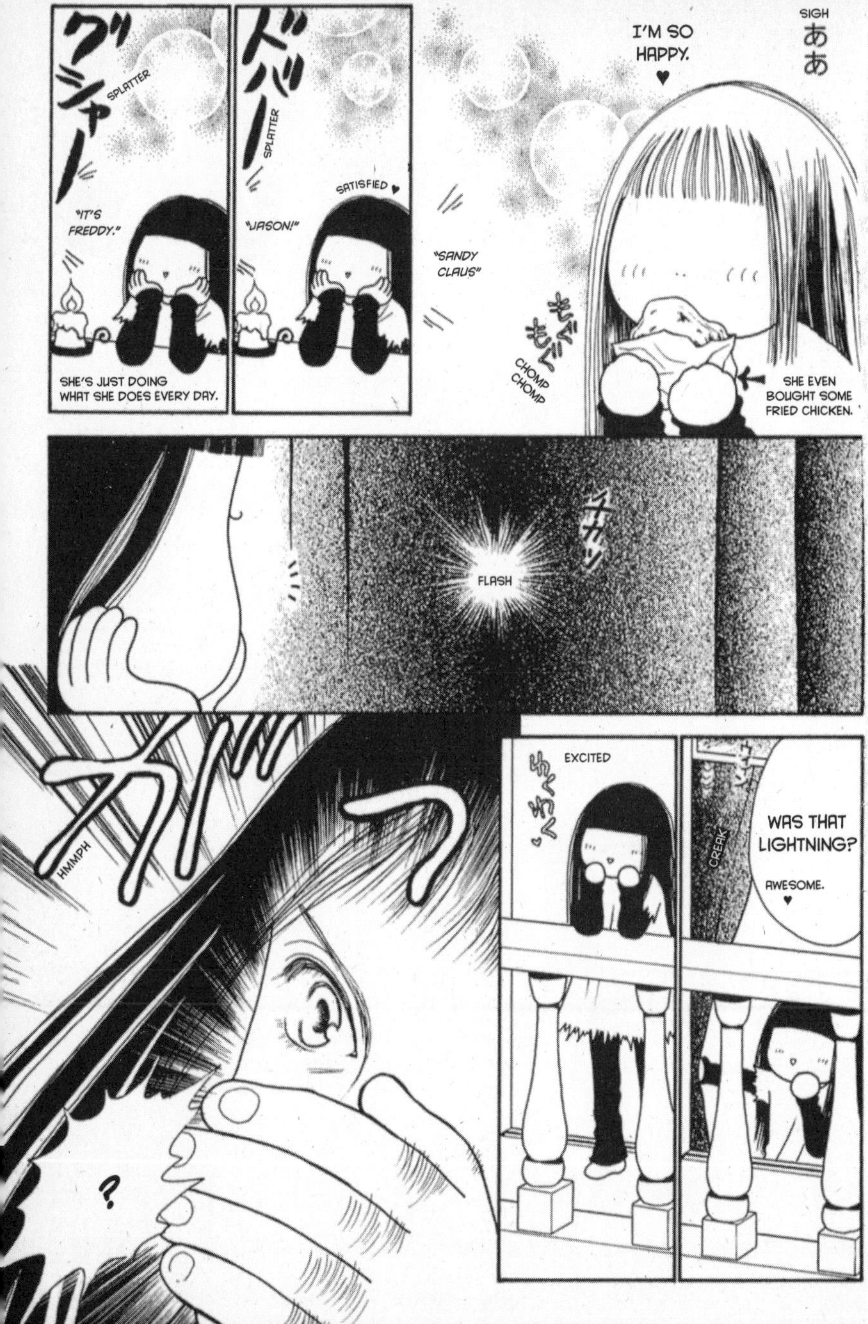
SIGH
ああ
I'M SO HAPPY. ♥
もぐもぐ
CHOMP CHOMP
SHE EVEN BOUGHT SOME FRIED CHICKEN.
"SANDY CLAUS"
SPLATTER
SATISFIED ♥
"JASON!"
SPLATTER
"IT'S FREDDY."
SHE'S JUST DOING WHAT SHE DOES EVERY DAY.
FLASH
WAS THAT LIGHTNING?
AWESOME. ♥
CREAK
EXCITED
HMMPH
?

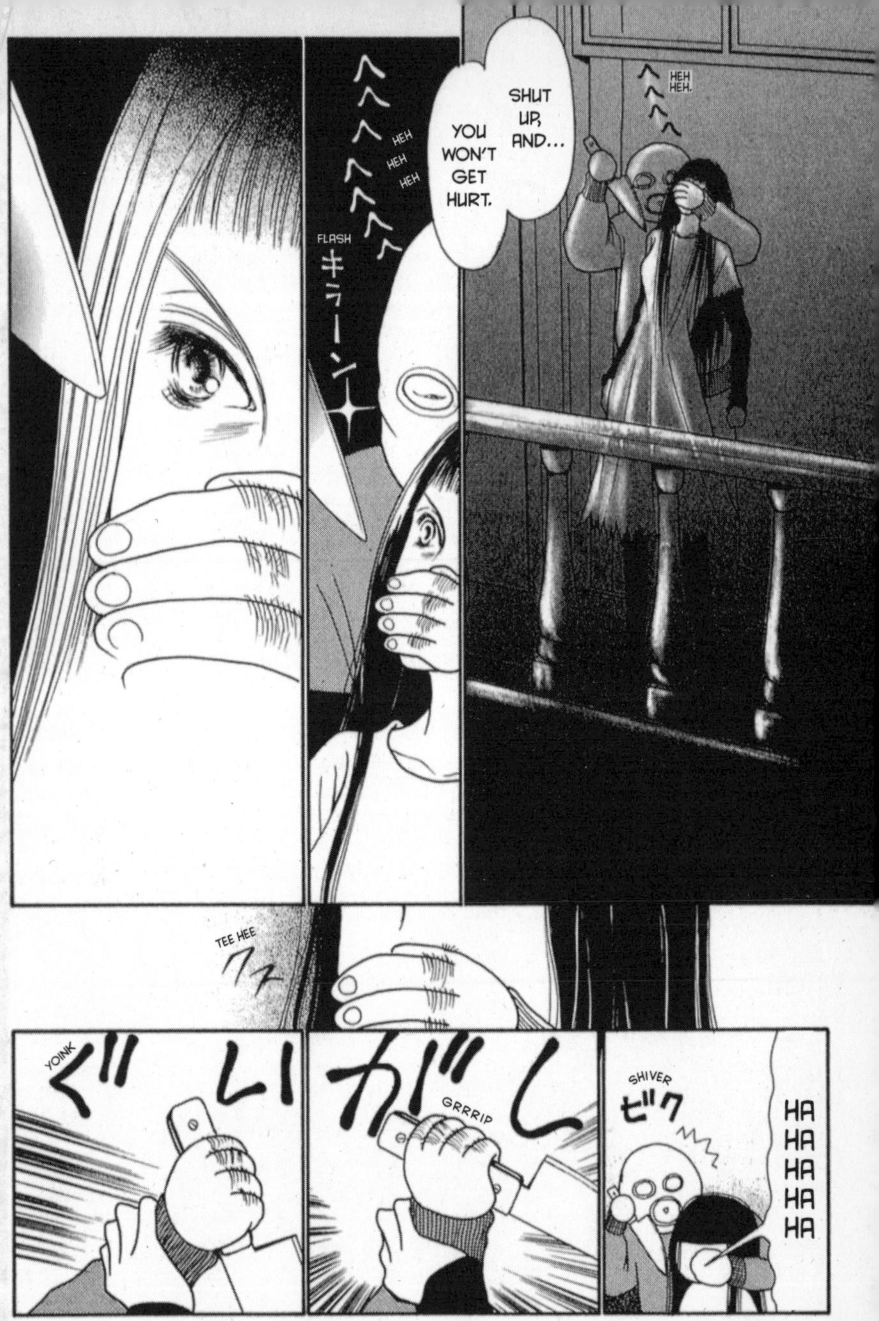

ヘヘヘヘ
HEH HEH.
SHUT UP, AND...
YOU WON'T GET HURT.
ヘヘヘヘヘヘヘ
HEH HEH HEH
FLASH
キラーン
TEE HEE
クク
HA HA HA HA HA HA
SHIVER
ビク
GRRRIP
がし
YOINK
ぐい

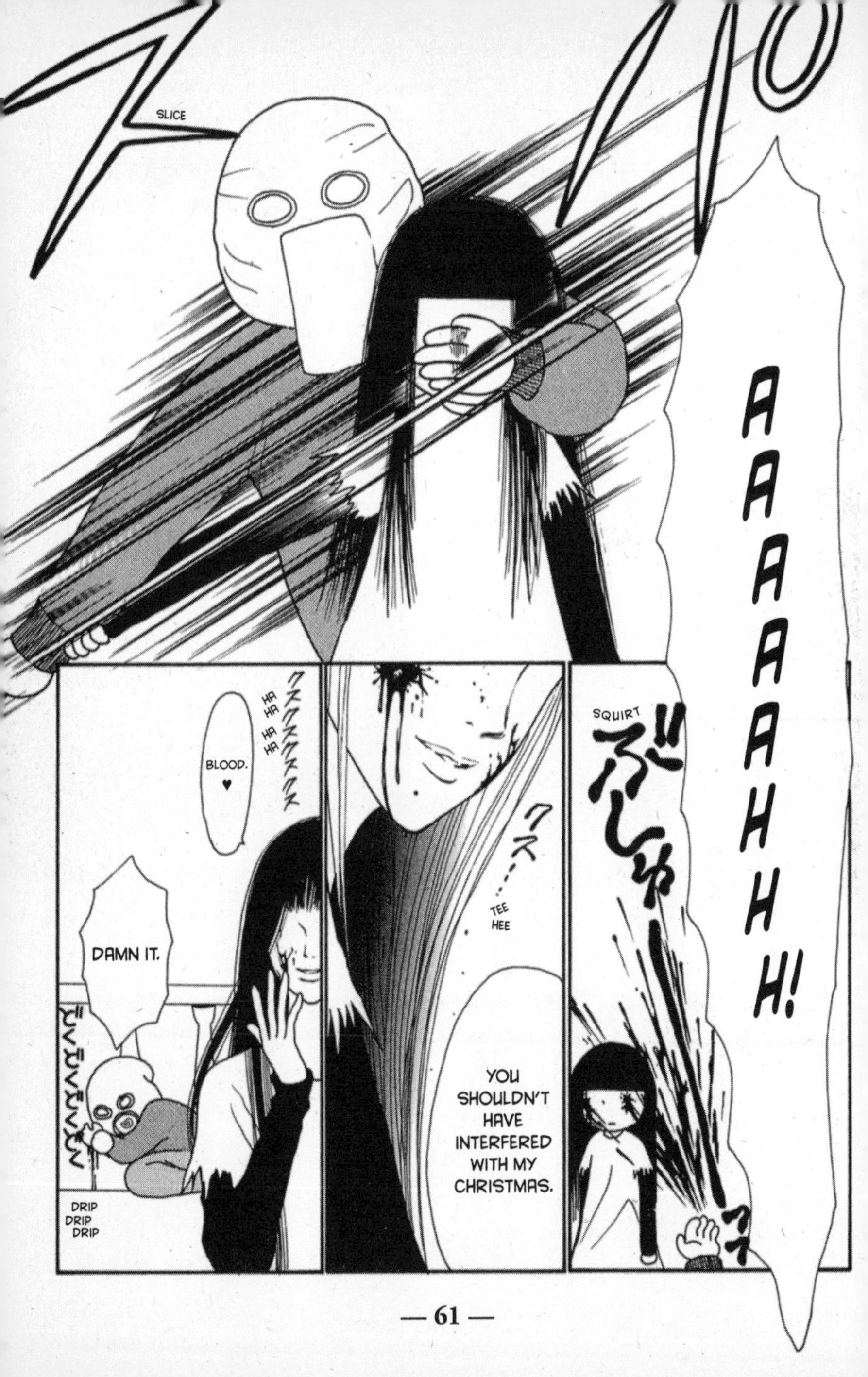
SLICE
AAAAAHHH!
SQUIRT
ぶしゅー
クス…
TEE HEE
YOU SHOULDN'T HAVE INTERFERED WITH MY CHRISTMAS.
HA HA HA HA
BLOOD. ♥
DAMN IT.
DRIP DRIP DRIP

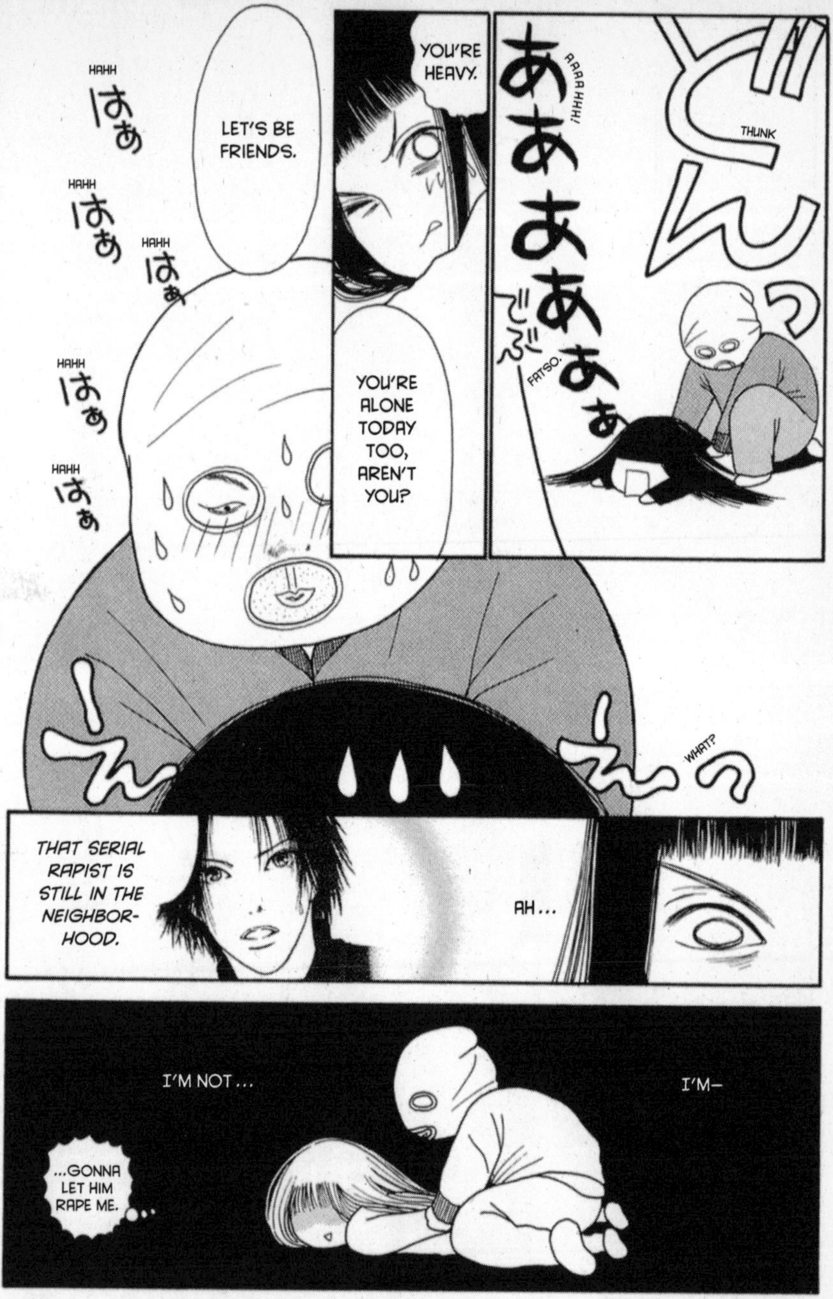
どんっ
THUNK
あああぁぁ
AAAAHHH!
でぶ
FATSO.
YOU'RE HEAVY.
YOU'RE ALONE TODAY TOO, AREN'T YOU?
LET'S BE FRIENDS.
はぁ
HAHH
はぁ
HAHH
はぁ
HAHH
はぁ
HAHH
はぁ
HAHH
んえっ
WHAT?
AH...
THAT SERIAL RAPIST IS STILL IN THE NEIGHBOR-HOOD.
I'M—
I'M NOT...
...GONNA LET HIM RAPE ME.

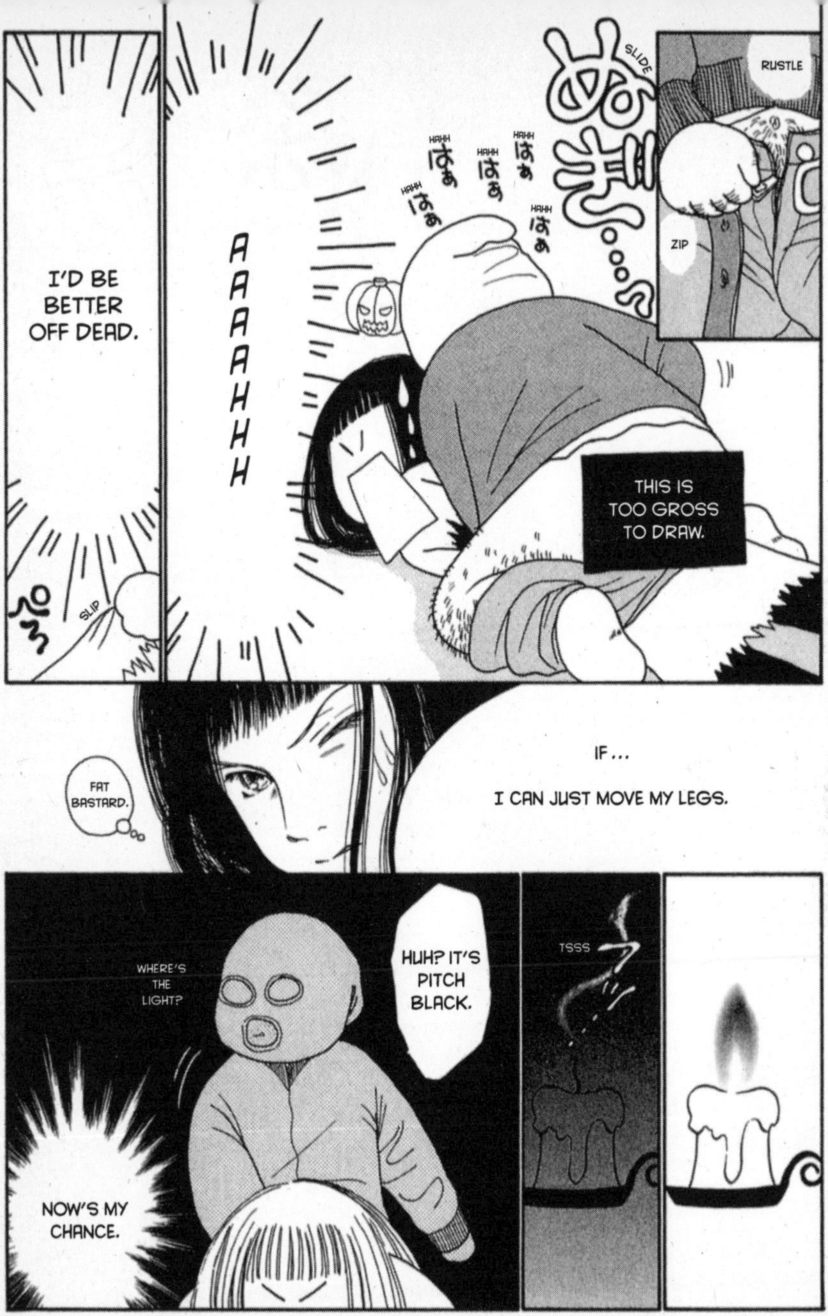
RUSTLE
ZIP
SLIDE
HAHH
はぁ
HAHH
はぁ
HAHH
はぁ
HAHH
はぁ
AAAAAHHHH
THIS IS TOO GROSS TO DRAW.
I'D BE BETTER OFF DEAD.
SLIP
IF...
I CAN JUST MOVE MY LEGS.
FAT BASTARD.
TSSS
HUH? IT'S PITCH BLACK.
WHERE'S THE LIGHT?
NOW'S MY CHANCE.

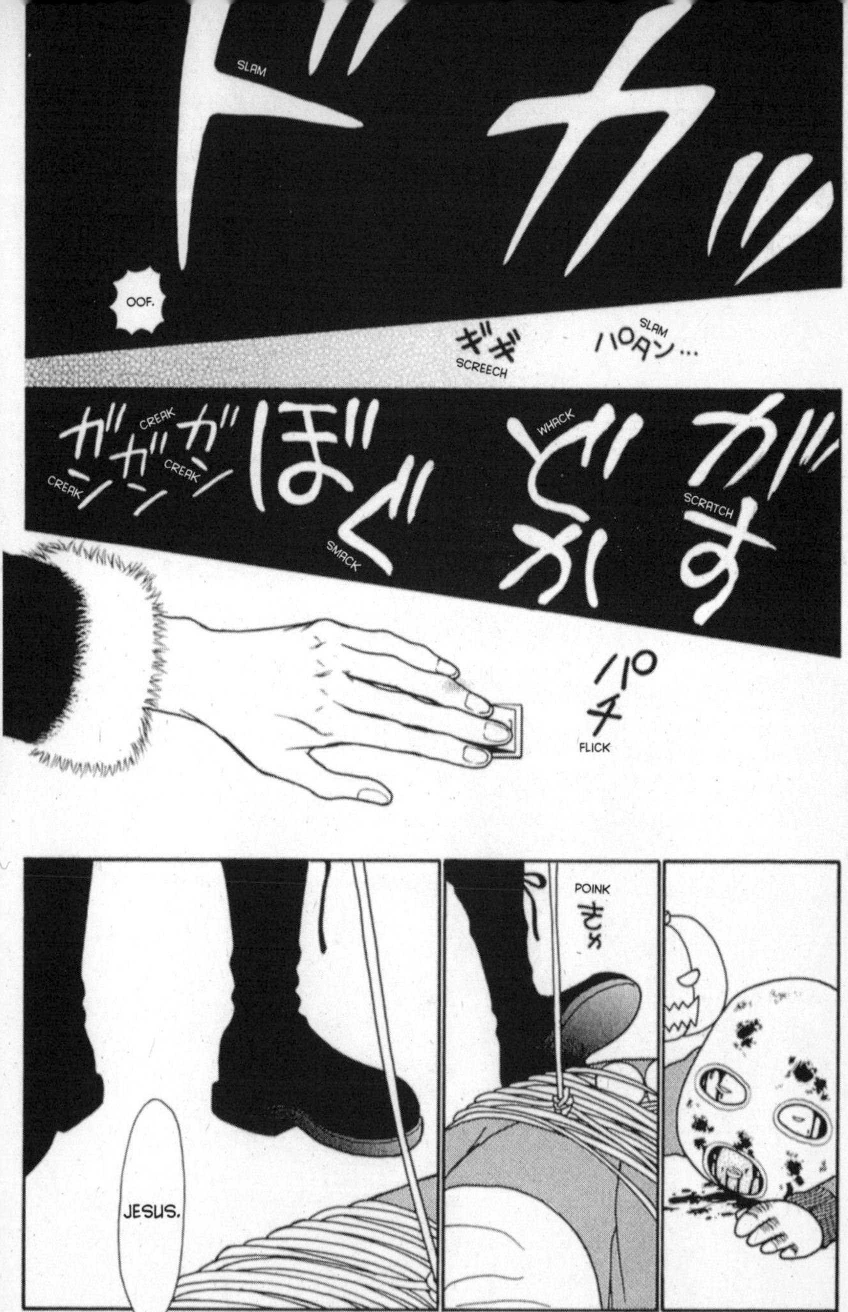
ドカッ
SLAM
OOF.
バタン…
SLAM
ギギ
SCREECH
がす
SCRATCH
どか
WHACK
ぼぐ
SMACK
ガンガンガン
CREAK
CREAK
CREAK
パチ
FLICK
POINK
JESUS.

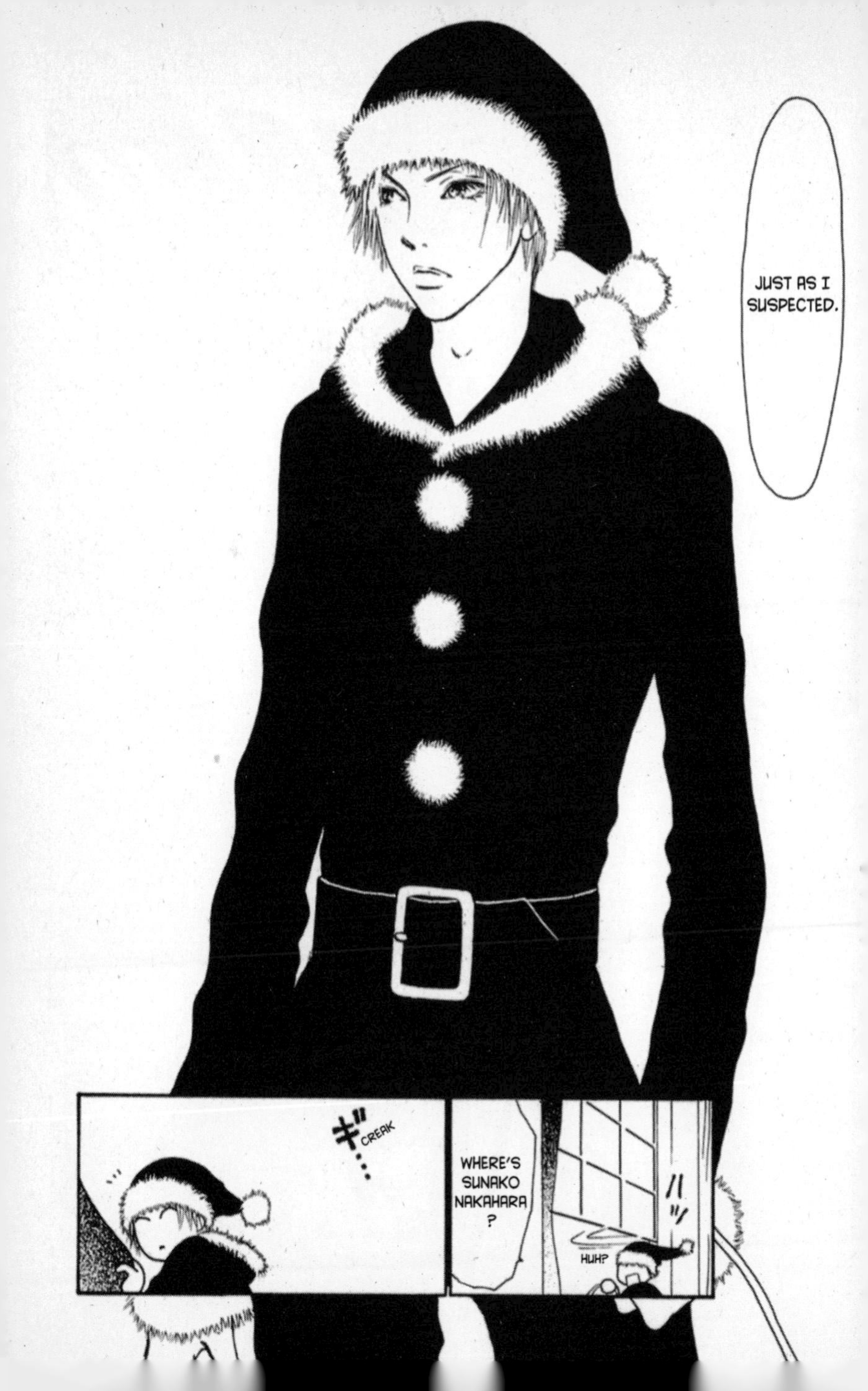
JUST AS I SUSPECTED.
ハッ
WHERE'S SUNAKO NAKAHARA?
HUH?
ギ
CREAK

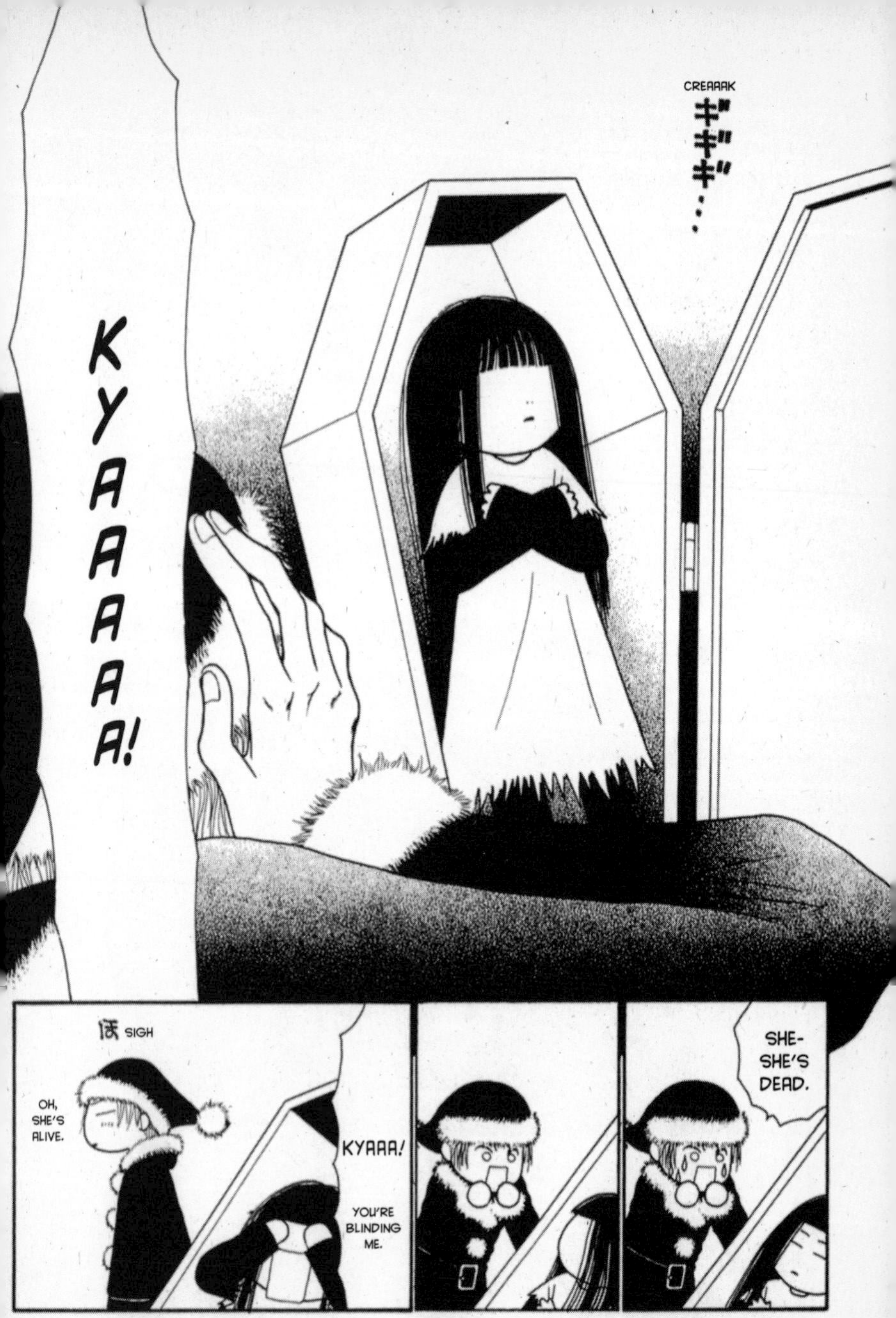
CREAAAK
ギギギ・・・
KYAAAAAAA!
SHE- SHE'S DEAD.
KYAAA!
YOU'RE BLINDING ME.
ほ SIGH
OH, SHE'S ALIVE.

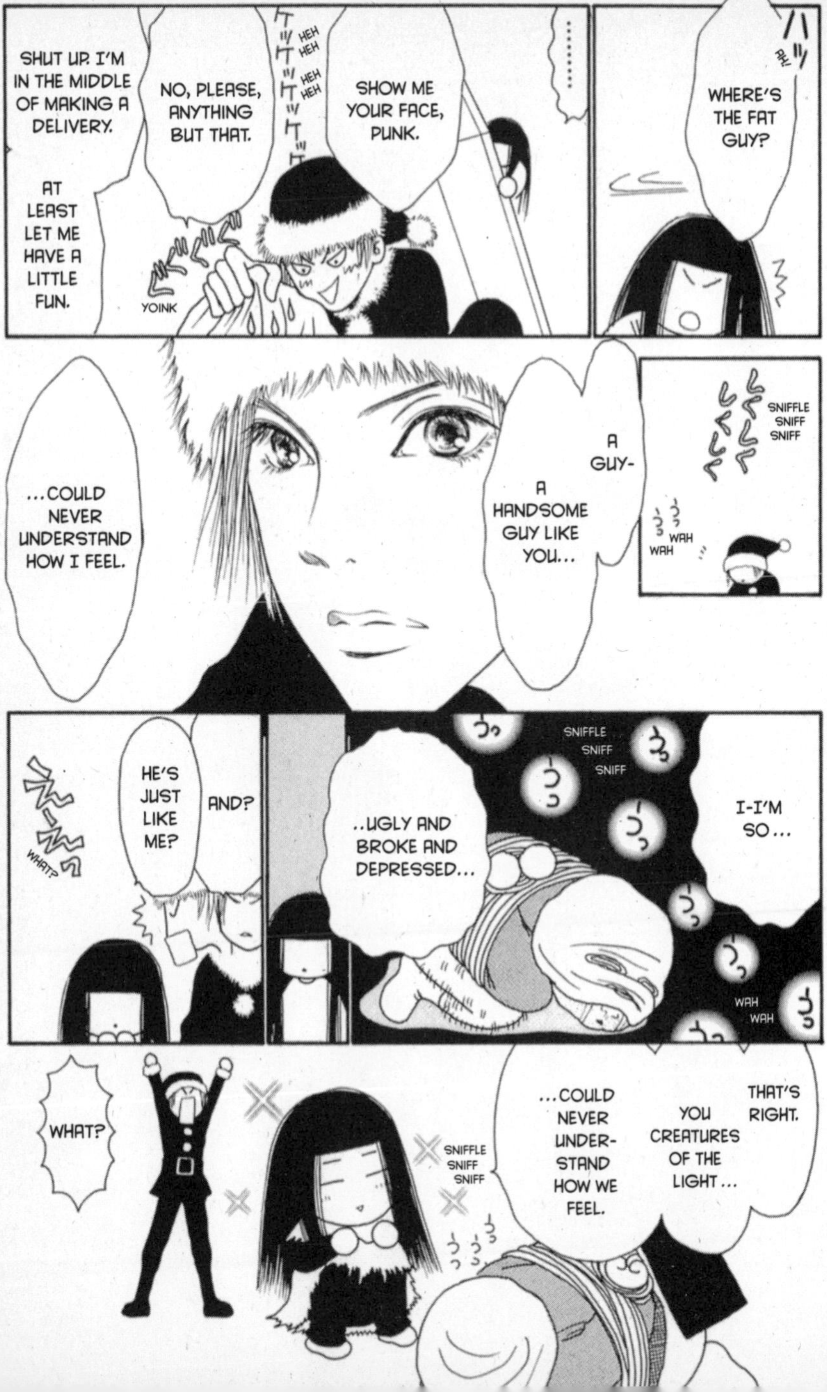
AH!
WHERE'S THE FAT GUY?
SHOW ME YOUR FACE, PUNK.
HEH HEH HEH HEH
NO, PLEASE, ANYTHING BUT THAT.
SHUT UP. I'M IN THE MIDDLE OF MAKING A DELIVERY.
AT LEAST LET ME HAVE A LITTLE FUN.
YOINK
SNIFFLE SNIFF SNIFF
WAH WAH
A GUY-
A HANDSOME GUY LIKE YOU...
...COULD NEVER UNDERSTAND HOW I FEEL.
I-I'M SO...
SNIFFLE SNIFF SNIFF
..UGLY AND BROKE AND DEPRESSED...
WAH WAH
AND?
HE'S JUST LIKE ME?
WHAT?
THAT'S RIGHT.
YOU CREATURES OF THE LIGHT...
...COULD NEVER UNDER-STAND HOW WE FEEL.
SNIFFLE SNIFF SNIFF
WHAT?

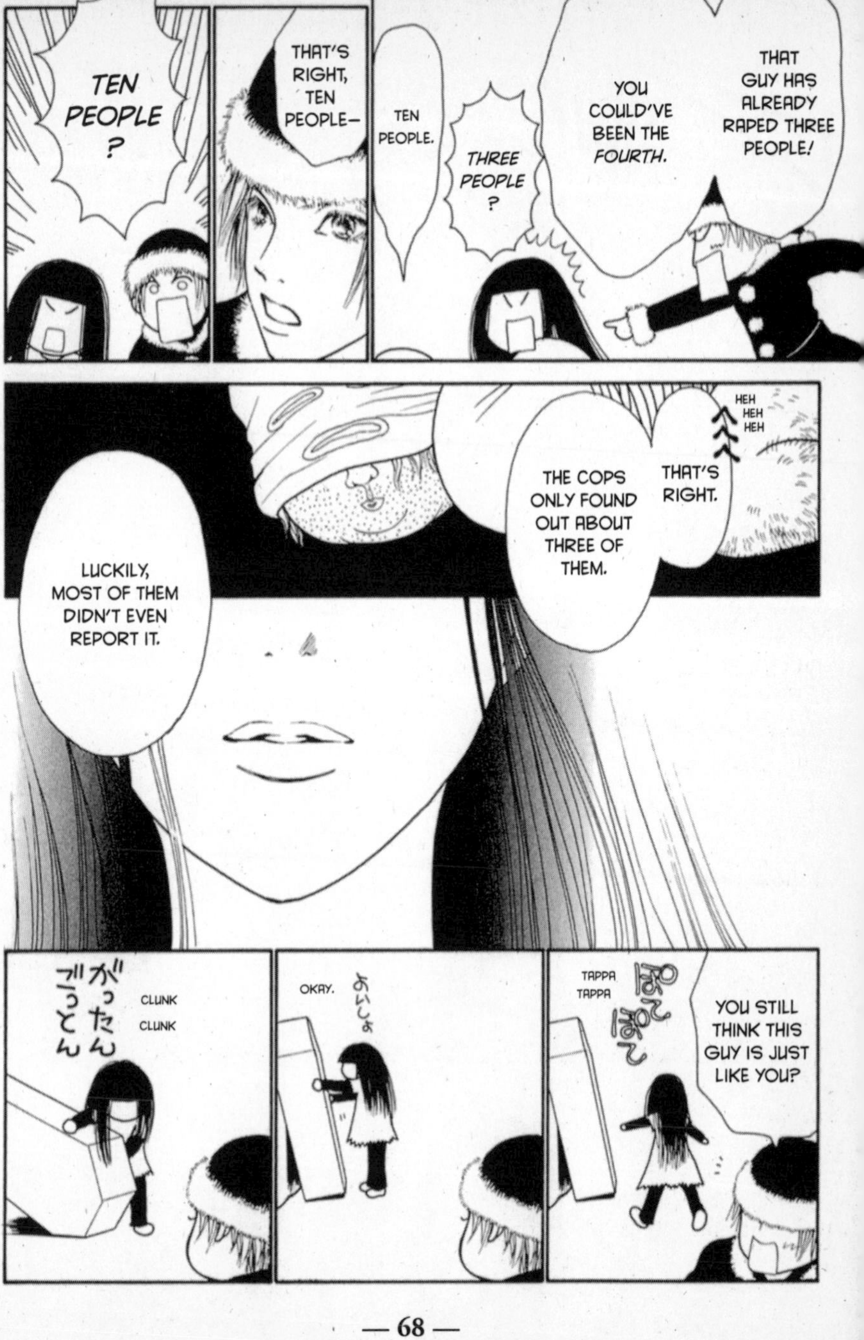
THAT GUY HAS ALREADY RAPED THREE PEOPLE!
YOU COULD'VE BEEN THE *FOURTH*.
THREE PEOPLE?
TEN PEOPLE.
THAT'S RIGHT, TEN PEOPLE—
TEN PEOPLE?
HEH HEH HEH
THAT'S RIGHT.
THE COPS ONLY FOUND OUT ABOUT THREE OF THEM.
LUCKILY, MOST OF THEM DIDN'T EVEN REPORT IT.
YOU STILL THINK THIS GUY IS JUST LIKE YOU?
ぽてぽて
TAPPA TAPPA
よいしょ
OKAY.
がったん ごっとん
CLUNK CLUNK

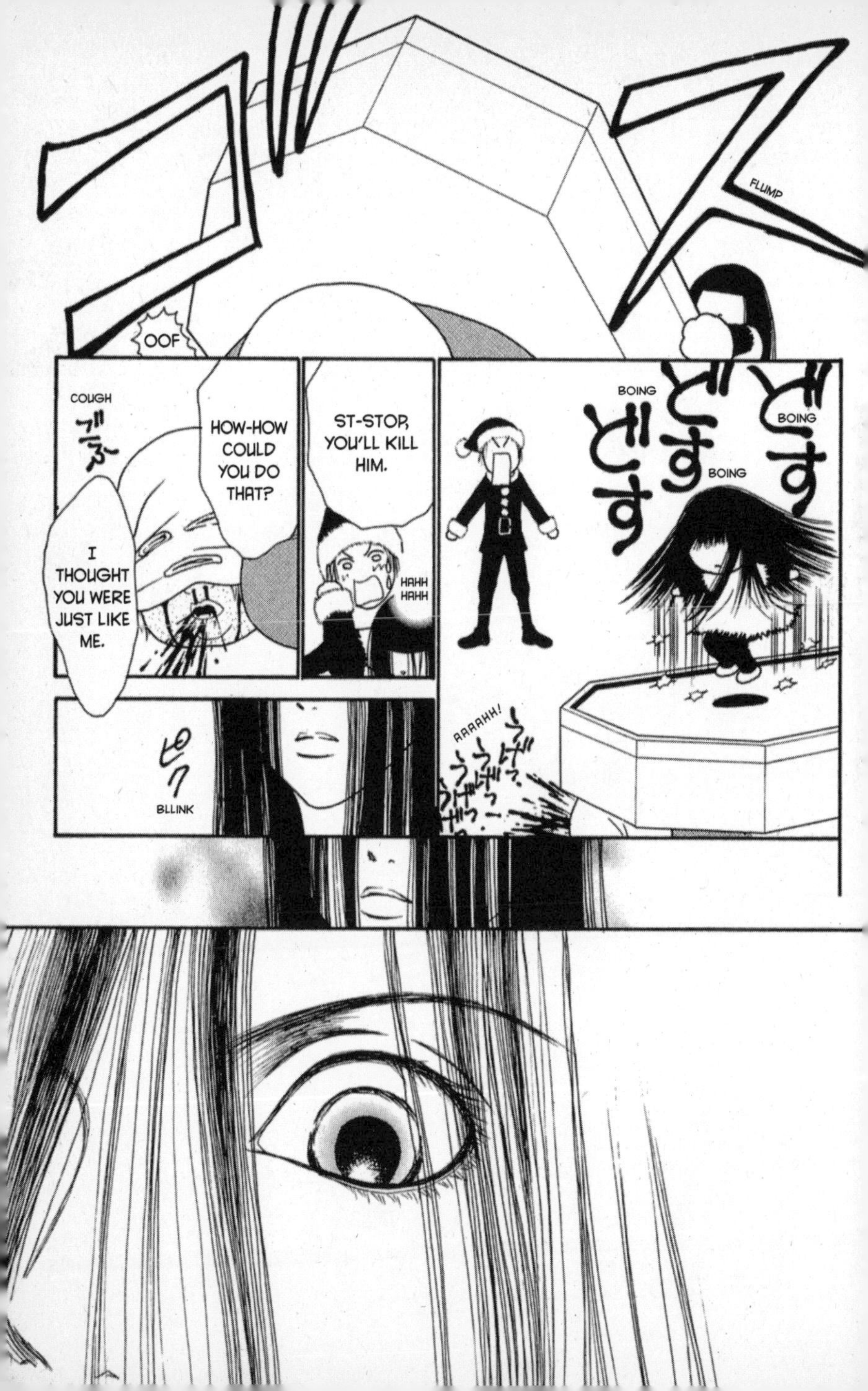
FLUMP
OOF
BOING
どす
どす
どす
BOING
BOING
AAAAHH!
ST-STOP, YOU'LL KILL HIM.
HAHH HAHH
HOW-HOW COULD YOU DO THAT?
COUGH
I THOUGHT YOU WERE JUST LIKE ME.
BLLINK

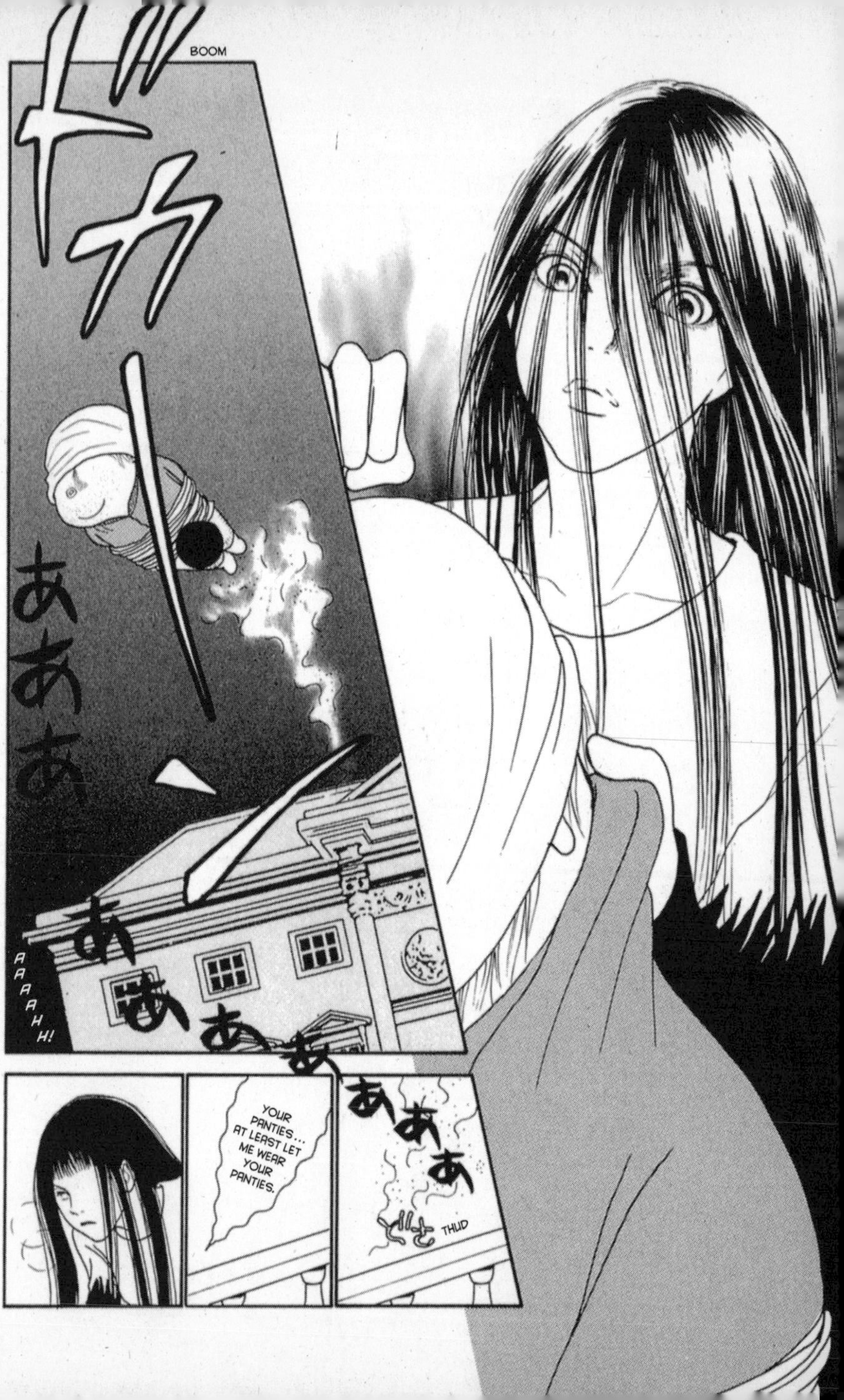
BOOM
AAAAAH!
THUD
YOUR PANTIES... AT LEAST LET ME WEAR YOUR PANTIES.

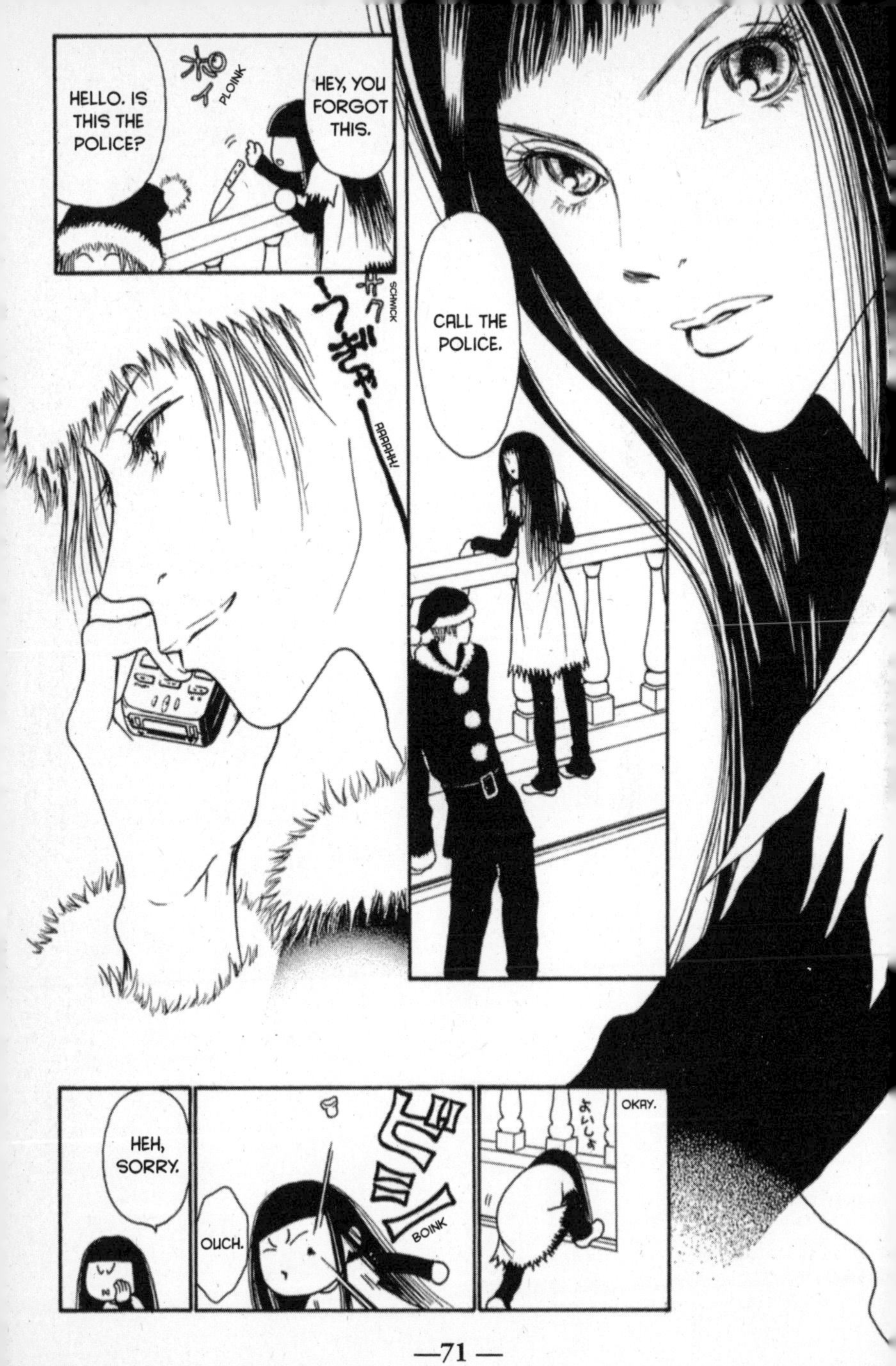
CALL THE POLICE.
HEY, YOU FORGOT THIS.
ポイ
PLOINK
HELLO. IS THIS THE POLICE?
ザク
SCHWICK
うぎゃ
AAAAHH!
OKAY.
よいしょ
BOINK
OUCH.
HEH, SORRY.

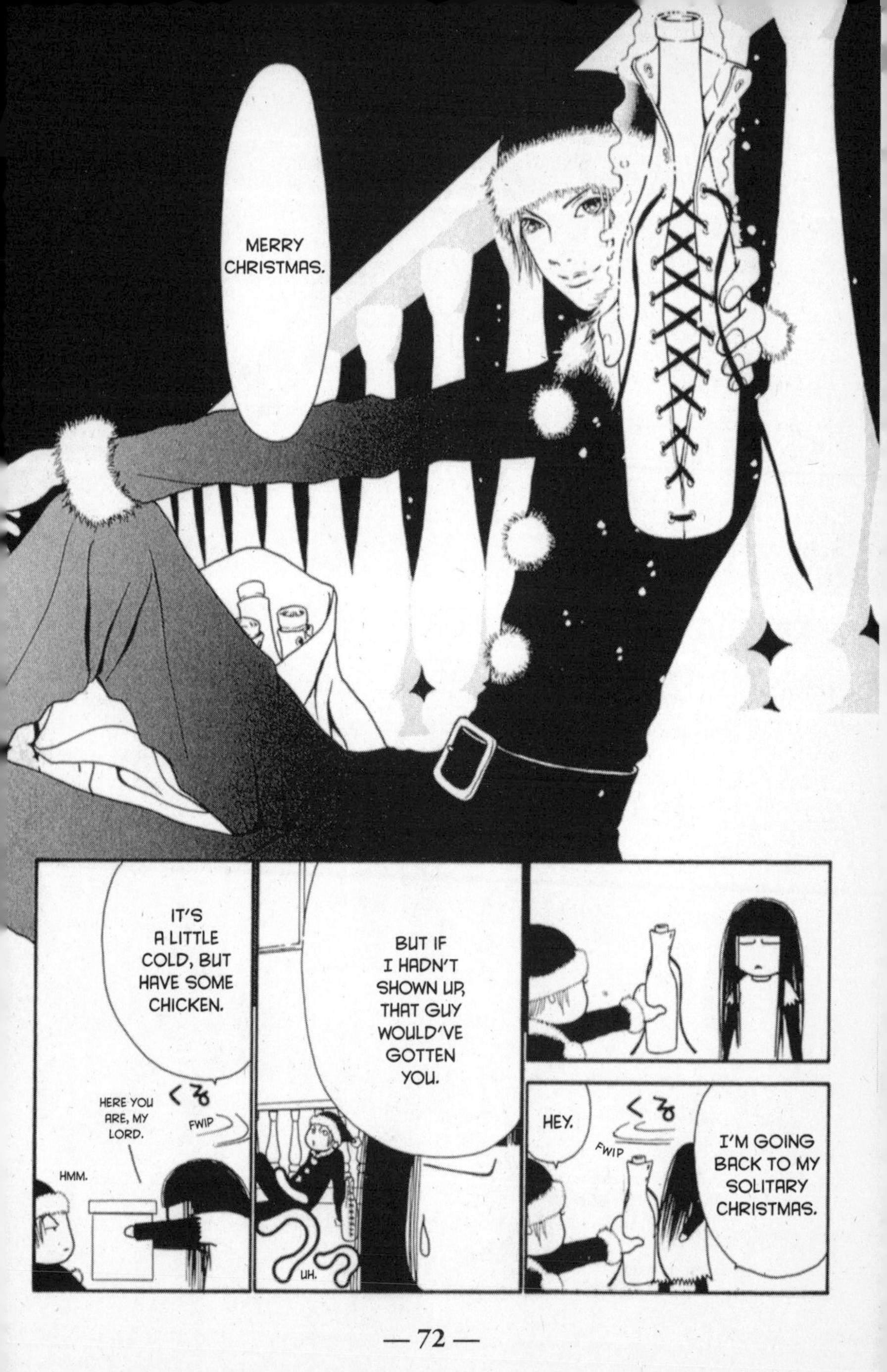
MERRY CHRISTMAS.
I'M GOING BACK TO MY SOLITARY CHRISTMAS.
くる
HEY.
FWIP
BUT IF I HADN'T SHOWN UP, THAT GUY WOULD'VE GOTTEN YOU.
UH.
IT'S A LITTLE COLD, BUT HAVE SOME CHICKEN.
くる
FWIP
HERE YOU ARE, MY LORD.
HMM.

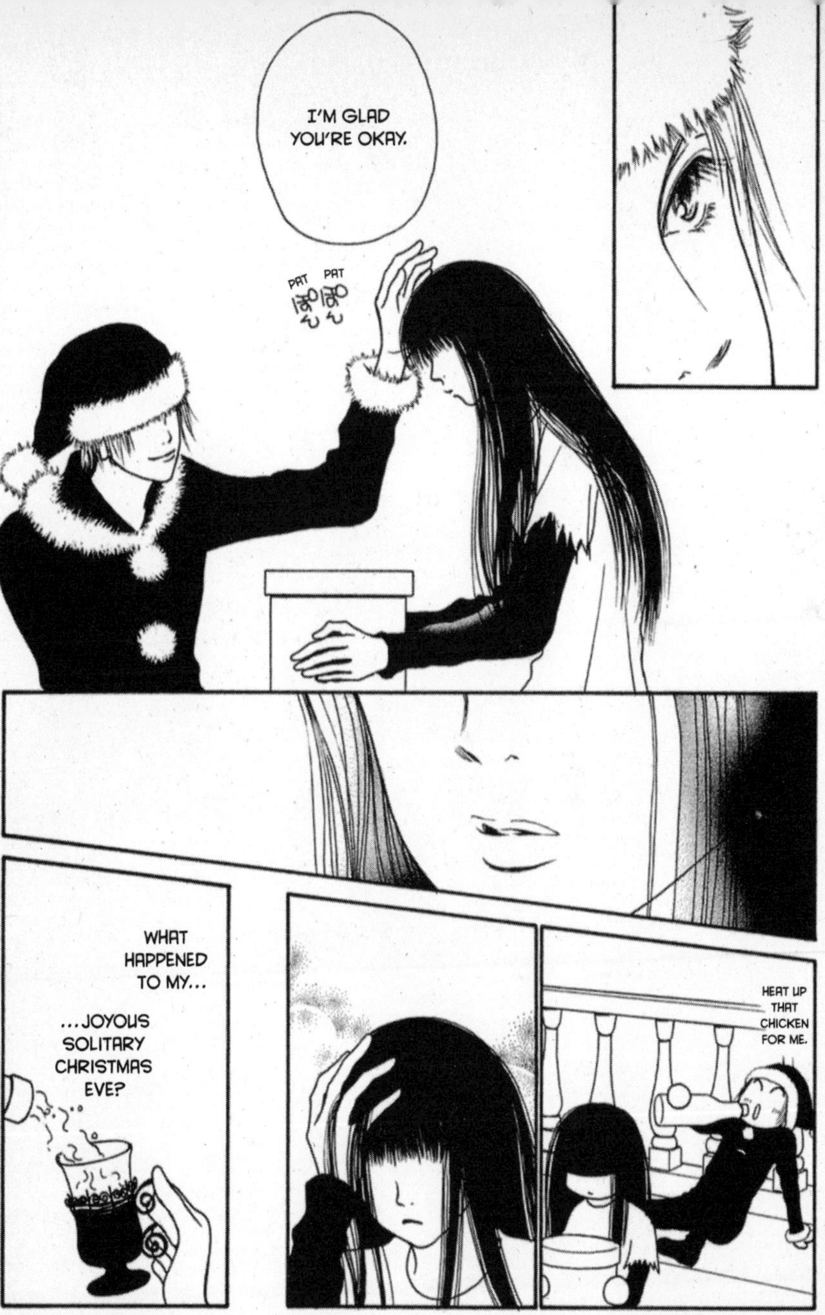
I'M GLAD YOU'RE OKAY.
PAT PAT
ぽんぽん
HEAT UP THAT CHICKEN FOR ME.
WHAT HAPPENED TO MY...
...JOYOUS SOLITARY CHRISTMAS EVE?

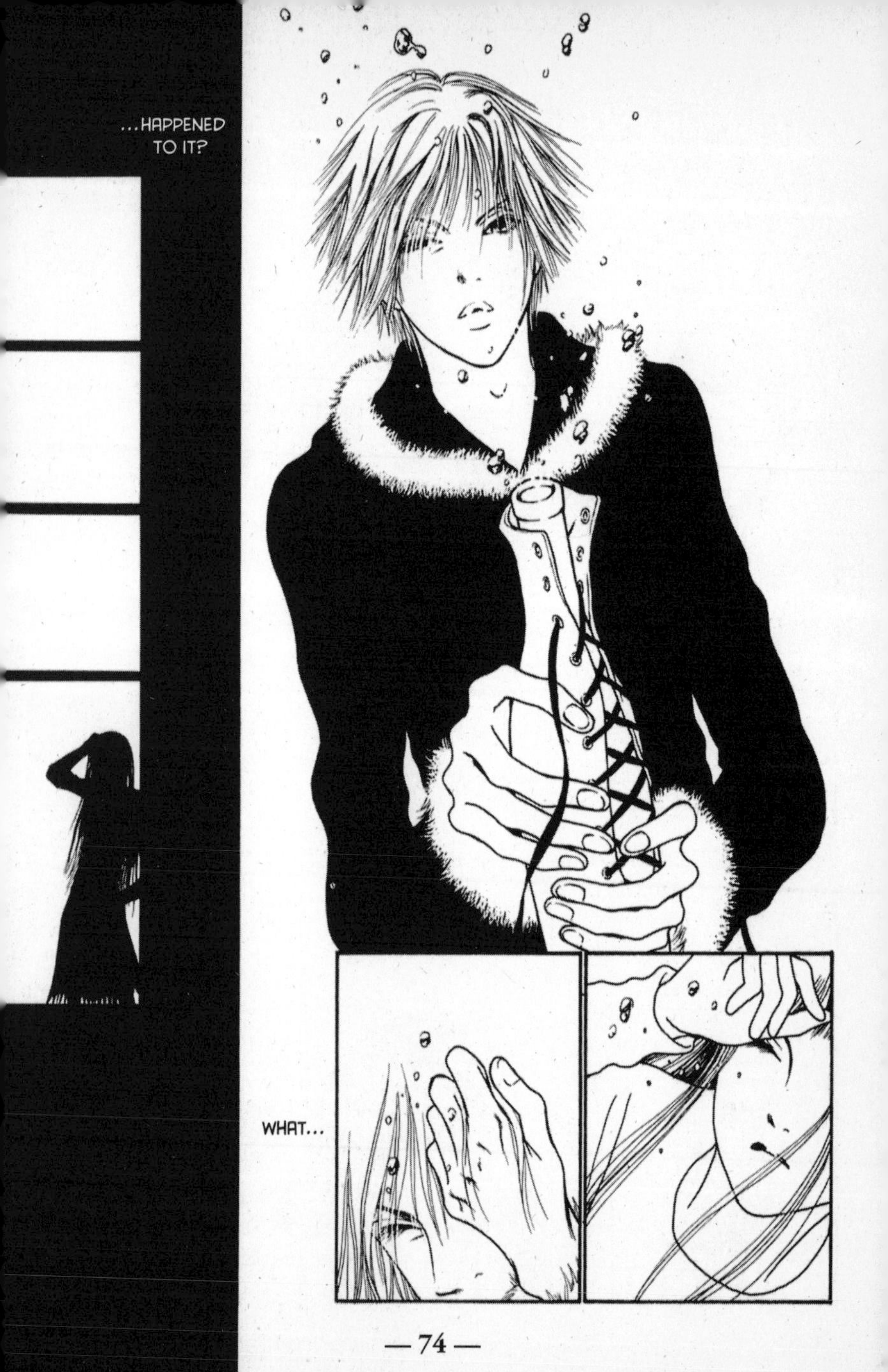
WHAT...
...HAPPENED TO IT?

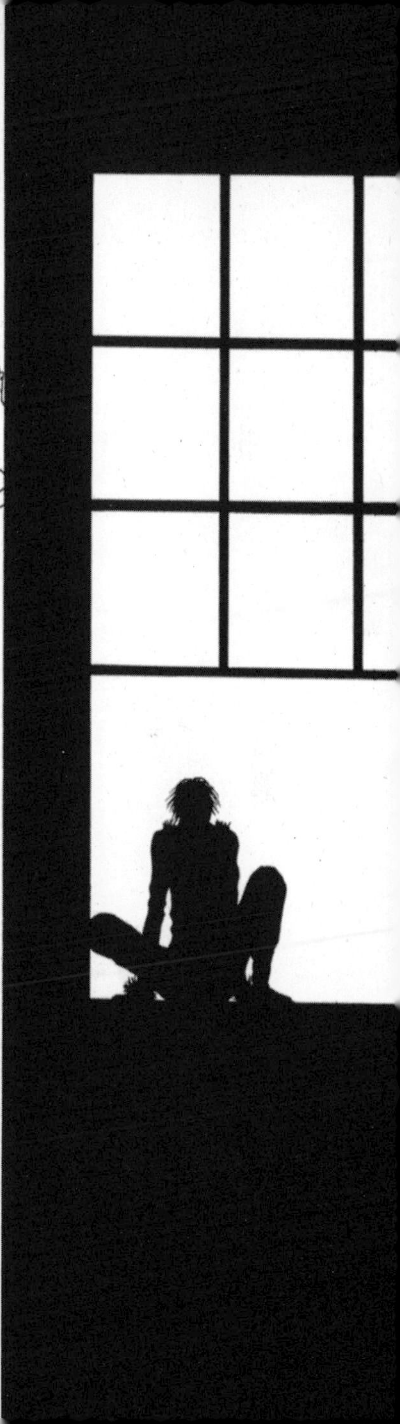

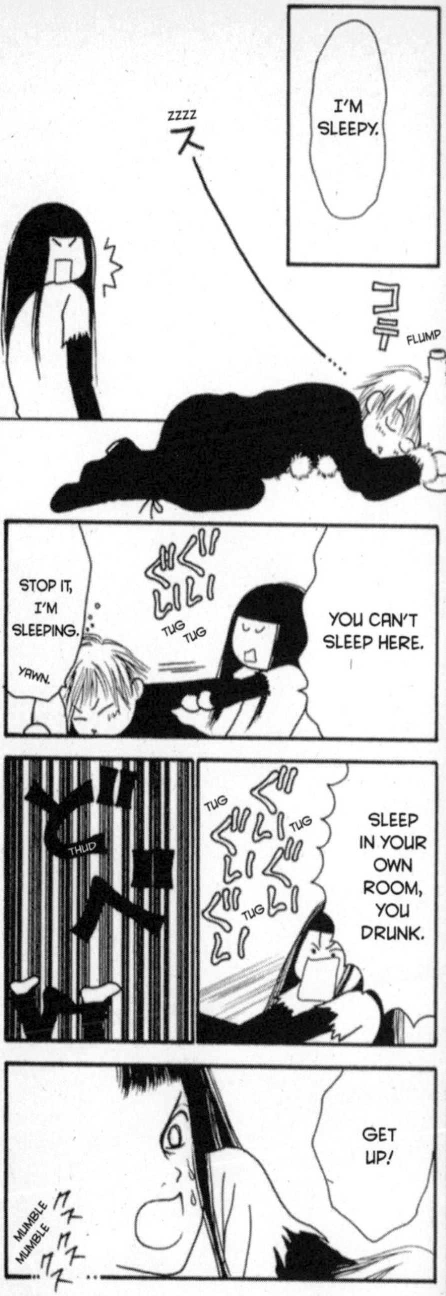

I'M SLEEPY.
ZZZZ
FLUMP
YOU CAN'T SLEEP HERE.
TUG TUG
STOP IT, I'M SLEEPING.
YAWN.
SLEEP IN YOUR OWN ROOM, YOU DRUNK.
TUG
TUG
TUG
THUD
GET UP!
MUMBLE MUMBLE

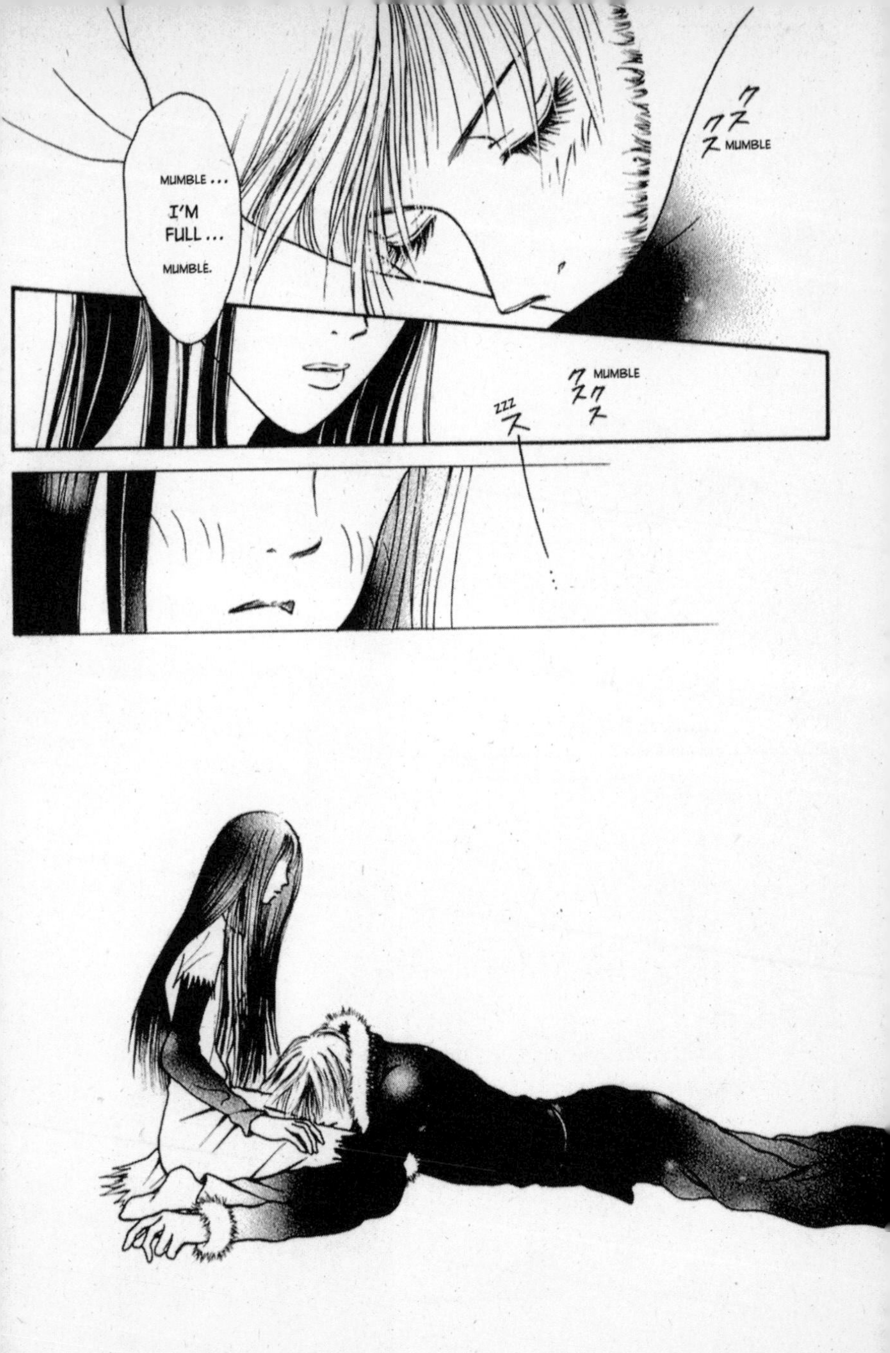
MUMBLE
MUMBLE... I'M FULL... MUMBLE.
MUMBLE
ZZZ

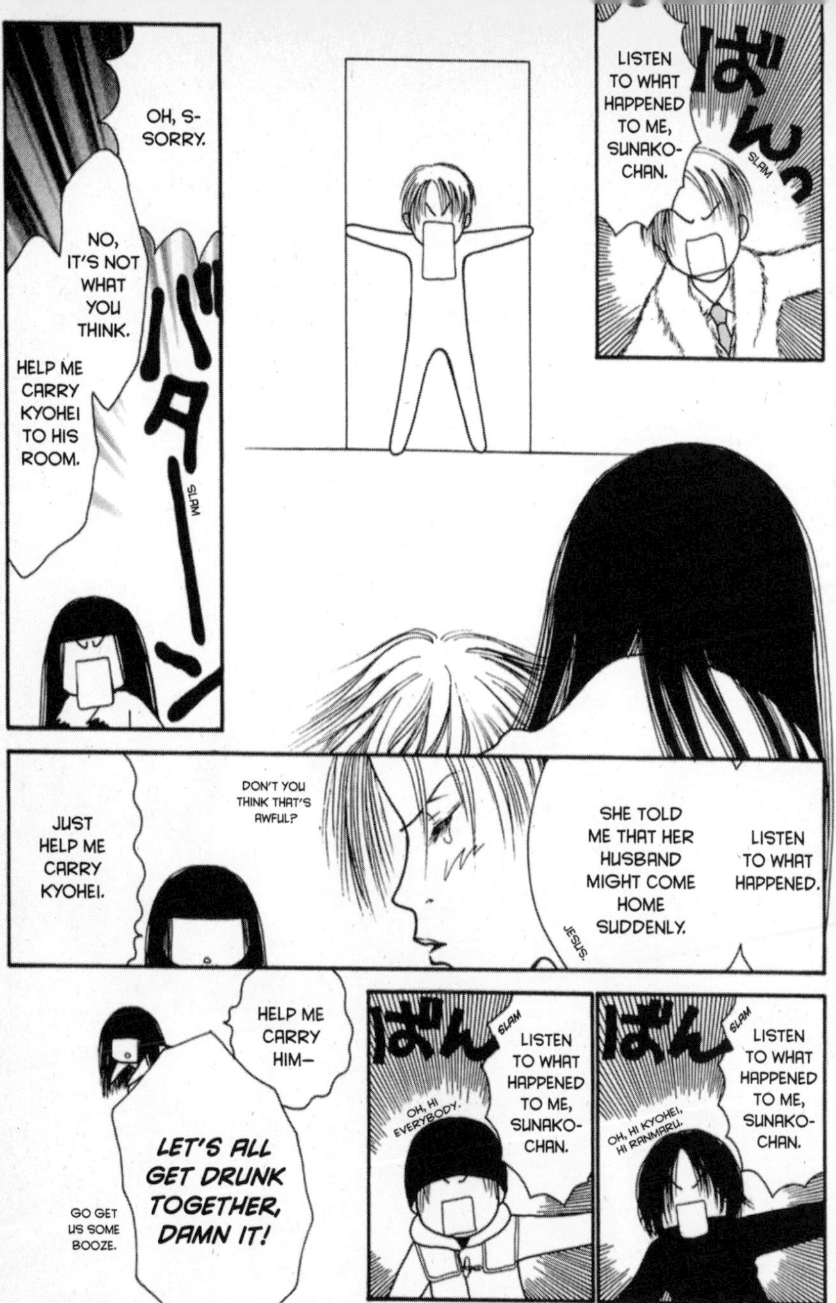
ばんっ
SLAM
LISTEN TO WHAT HAPPENED TO ME, SUNAKO-CHAN.
OH, S-SORRY.
NO, IT'S NOT WHAT YOU THINK.
HELP ME CARRY KYOHEI TO HIS ROOM.
バターン
SLAM
LISTEN TO WHAT HAPPENED.
SHE TOLD ME THAT HER HUSBAND MIGHT COME HOME SUDDENLY.
JESUS.
DON'T YOU THINK THAT'S AWFUL?
JUST HELP ME CARRY KYOHEI.
ばん
SLAM
LISTEN TO WHAT HAPPENED TO ME, SUNAKO-CHAN.
OH, HI KYOHEI, HI RANMARU.
ばん
SLAM
LISTEN TO WHAT HAPPENED TO ME, SUNAKO-CHAN.
OH, HI EVERYBODY.
HELP ME CARRY HIM—
LET'S ALL GET DRUNK TOGETHER, DAMN IT!
GO GET US SOME BOOZE.

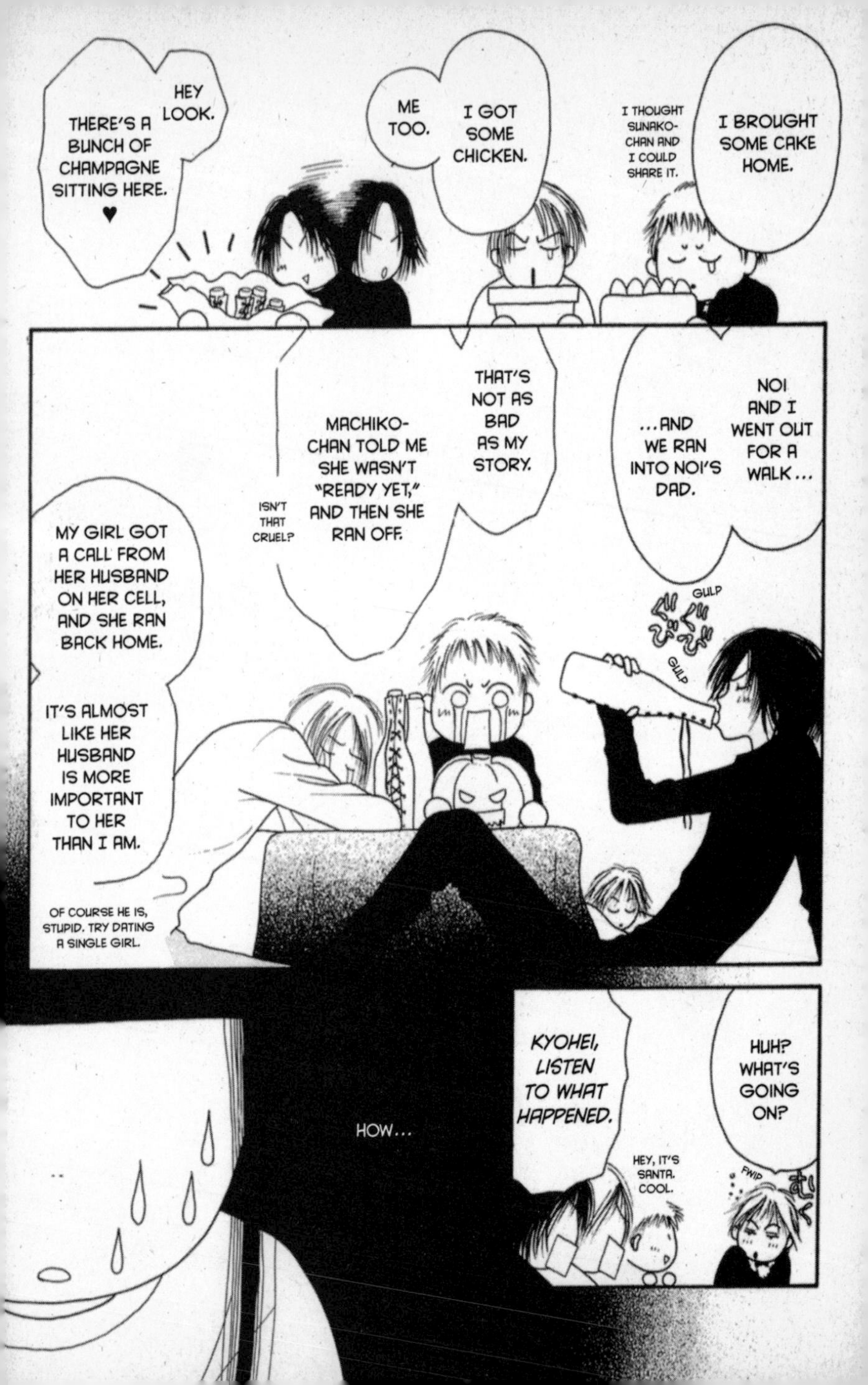
I BROUGHT SOME CAKE HOME.
I THOUGHT SUNAKO-CHAN AND I COULD SHARE IT.
I GOT SOME CHICKEN.
ME TOO.
HEY LOOK.
THERE'S A BUNCH OF CHAMPAGNE SITTING HERE. ♥
NOI AND I WENT OUT FOR A WALK...
...AND WE RAN INTO NOI'S DAD.
THAT'S NOT AS BAD AS MY STORY.
MACHIKO-CHAN TOLD ME SHE WASN'T "READY YET," AND THEN SHE RAN OFF.
ISN'T THAT CRUEL?
GULP
GULP
MY GIRL GOT A CALL FROM HER HUSBAND ON HER CELL, AND SHE RAN BACK HOME.
IT'S ALMOST LIKE HER HUSBAND IS MORE IMPORTANT TO HER THAN I AM.
OF COURSE HE IS, STUPID. TRY DATING A SINGLE GIRL.
HUH? WHAT'S GOING ON?
FWIP
KYOHEI, LISTEN TO WHAT HAPPENED.
HEY, IT'S SANTA. COOL.
HOW...
..

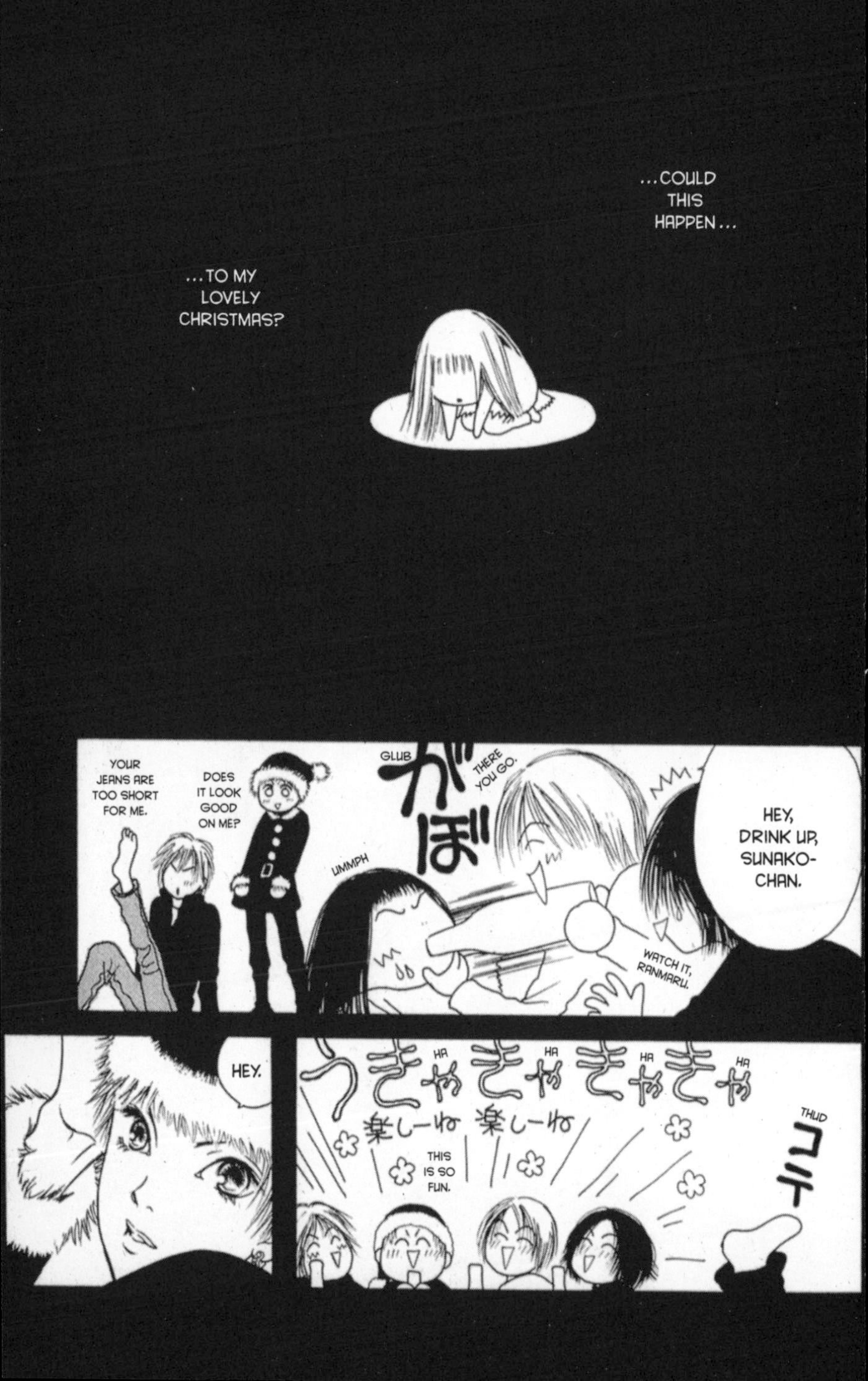
...COULD THIS HAPPEN...
...TO MY LOVELY CHRISTMAS?
HEY, DRINK UP, SUNAKO-CHAN.
WATCH IT, RANMARU.
THERE YOU GO.
がぼ
GLUB
UMMPH
DOES IT LOOK GOOD ON ME?
YOUR JEANS ARE TOO SHORT FOR ME.
コテ
THUD
うきゃきゃきゃきゃ
HA HA HA HA
楽しーね 楽しーね
THIS IS SO FUN.
HEY.

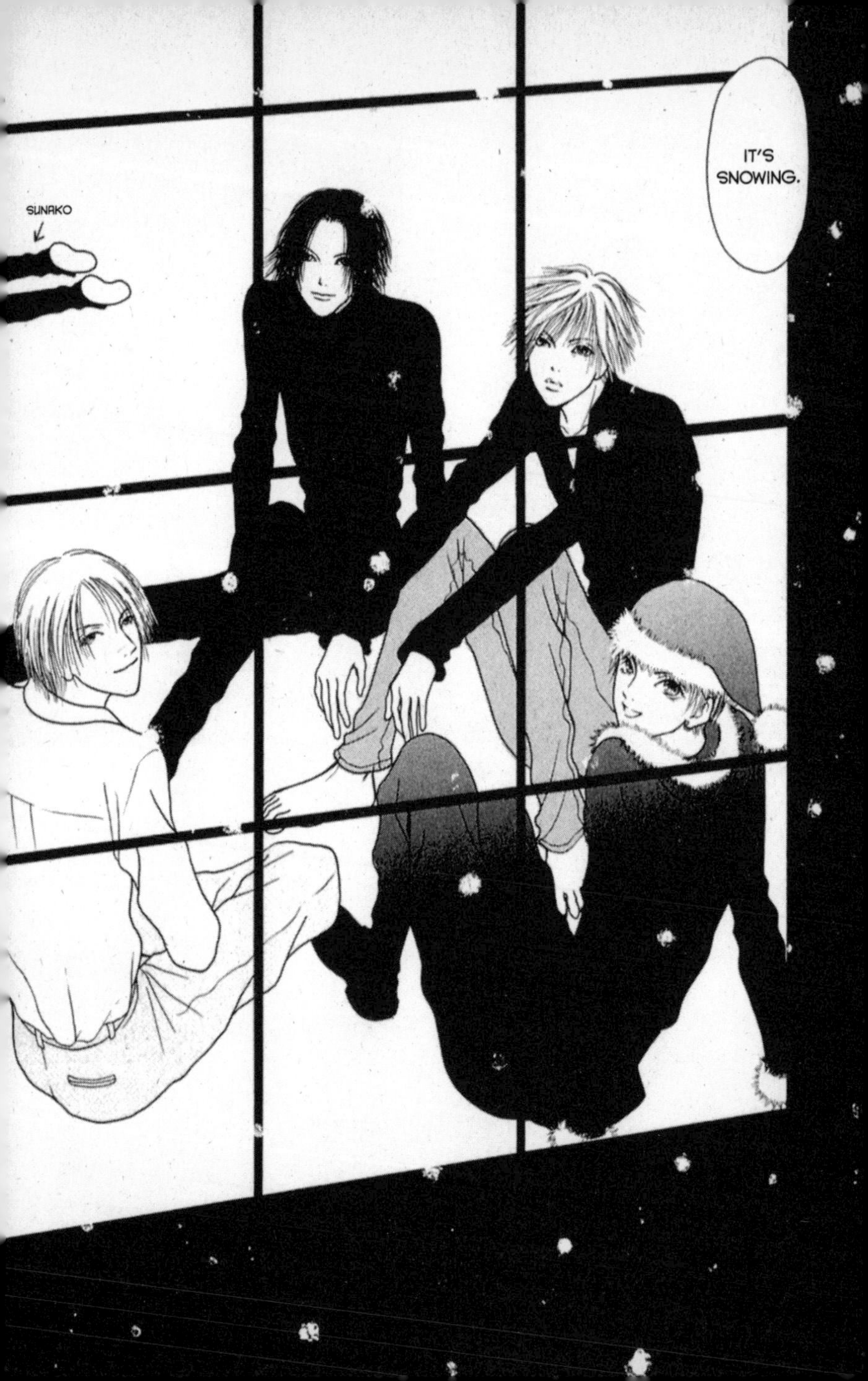
IT'S SNOWING.
SUNAKO

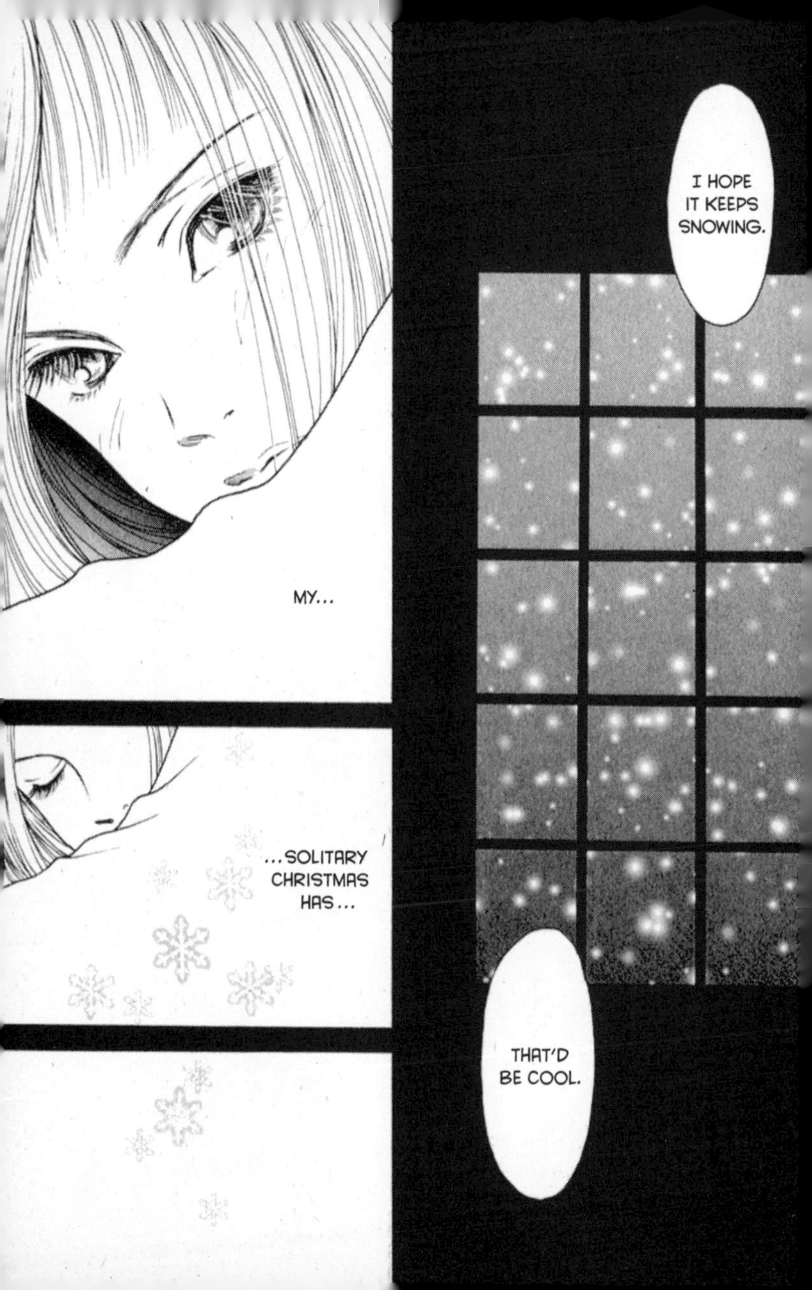
I HOPE IT KEEPS SNOWING.
THAT'D BE COOL.
MY...
...SOLITARY CHRISTMAS HAS...

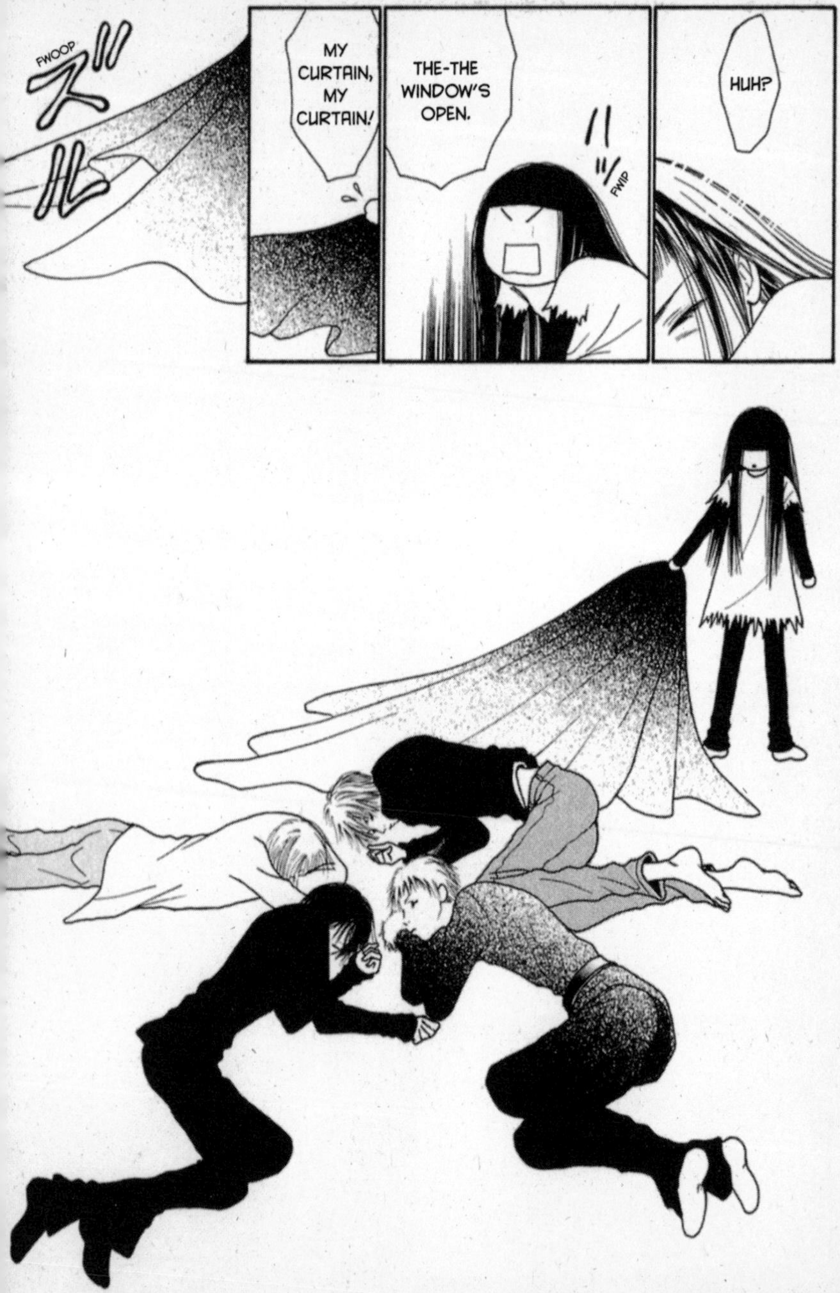
HUH?
THE-THE WINDOW'S OPEN.
FWIP
MY CURTAIN, MY CURTAIN!
FWOOP
ズル

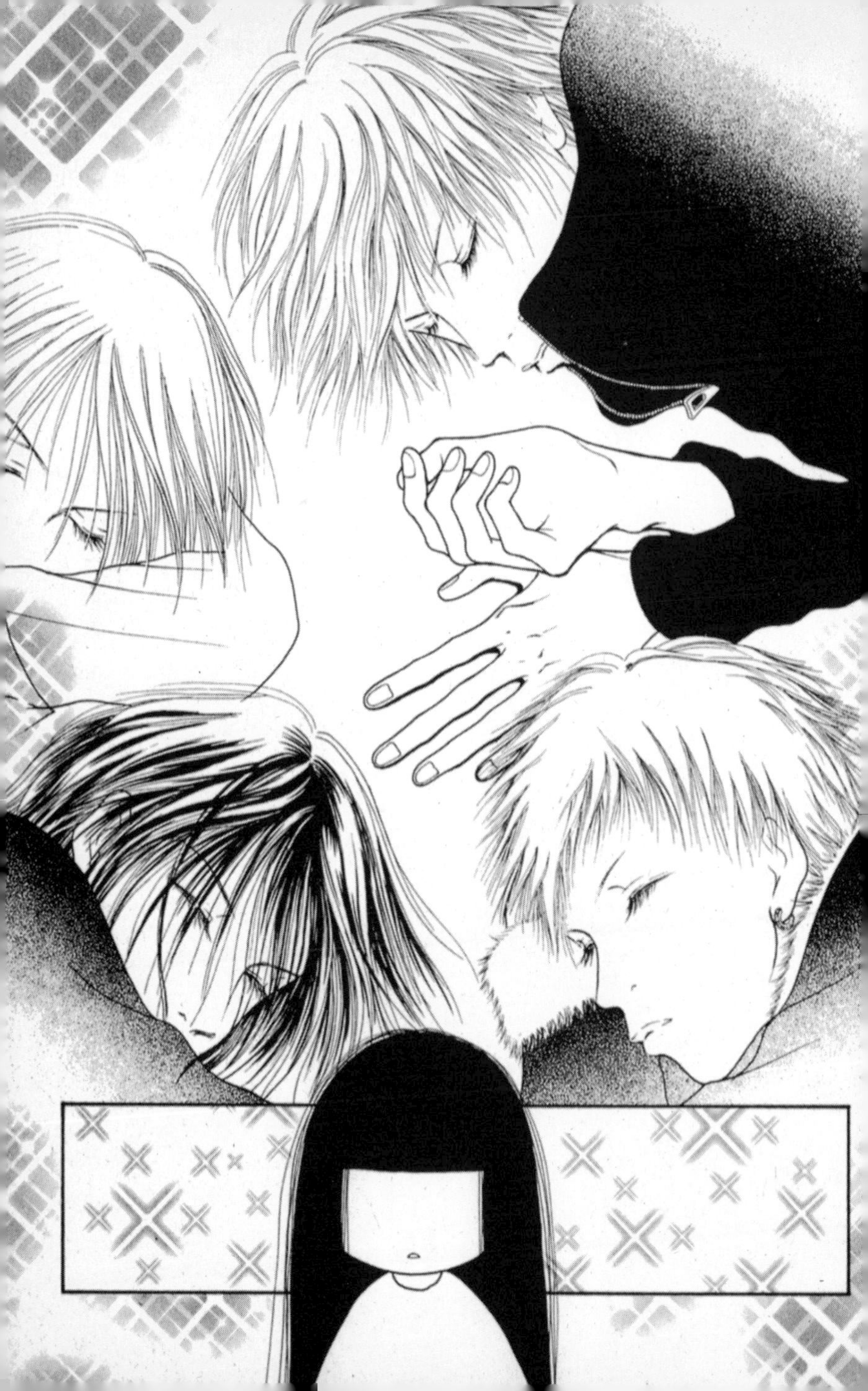

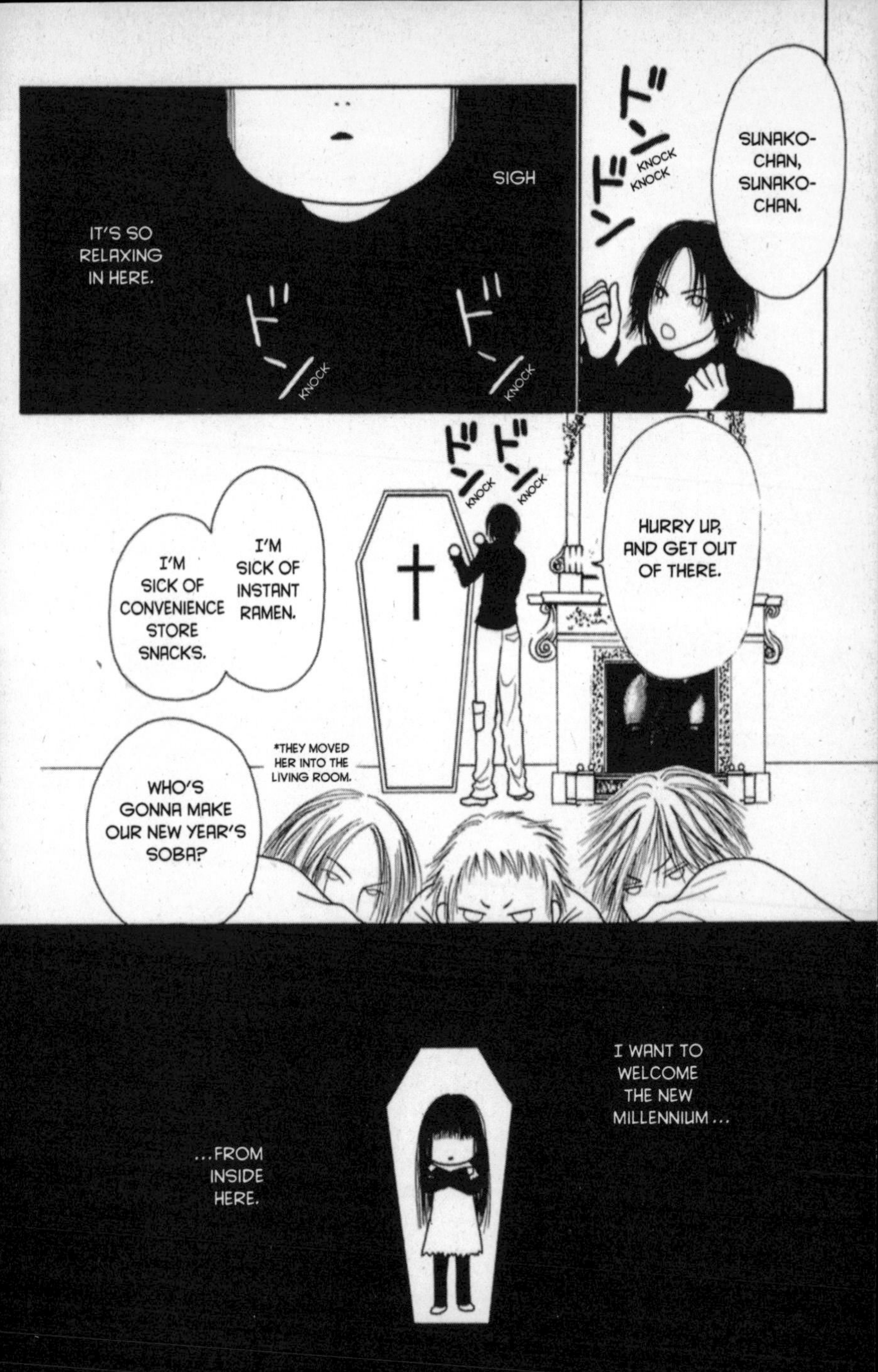
SUNAKO-CHAN, SUNAKO-CHAN.
ドンドン
KNOCK KNOCK
SIGH
IT'S SO RELAXING IN HERE.
ドン ドン
KNOCK KNOCK
ドンドン
KNOCK KNOCK
HURRY UP, AND GET OUT OF THERE.
I'M SICK OF INSTANT RAMEN.
I'M SICK OF CONVENIENCE STORE SNACKS.
*THEY MOVED HER INTO THE LIVING ROOM.
WHO'S GONNA MAKE OUR NEW YEAR'S SOBA?
I WANT TO WELCOME THE NEW MILLENNIUM...
...FROM INSIDE HERE.

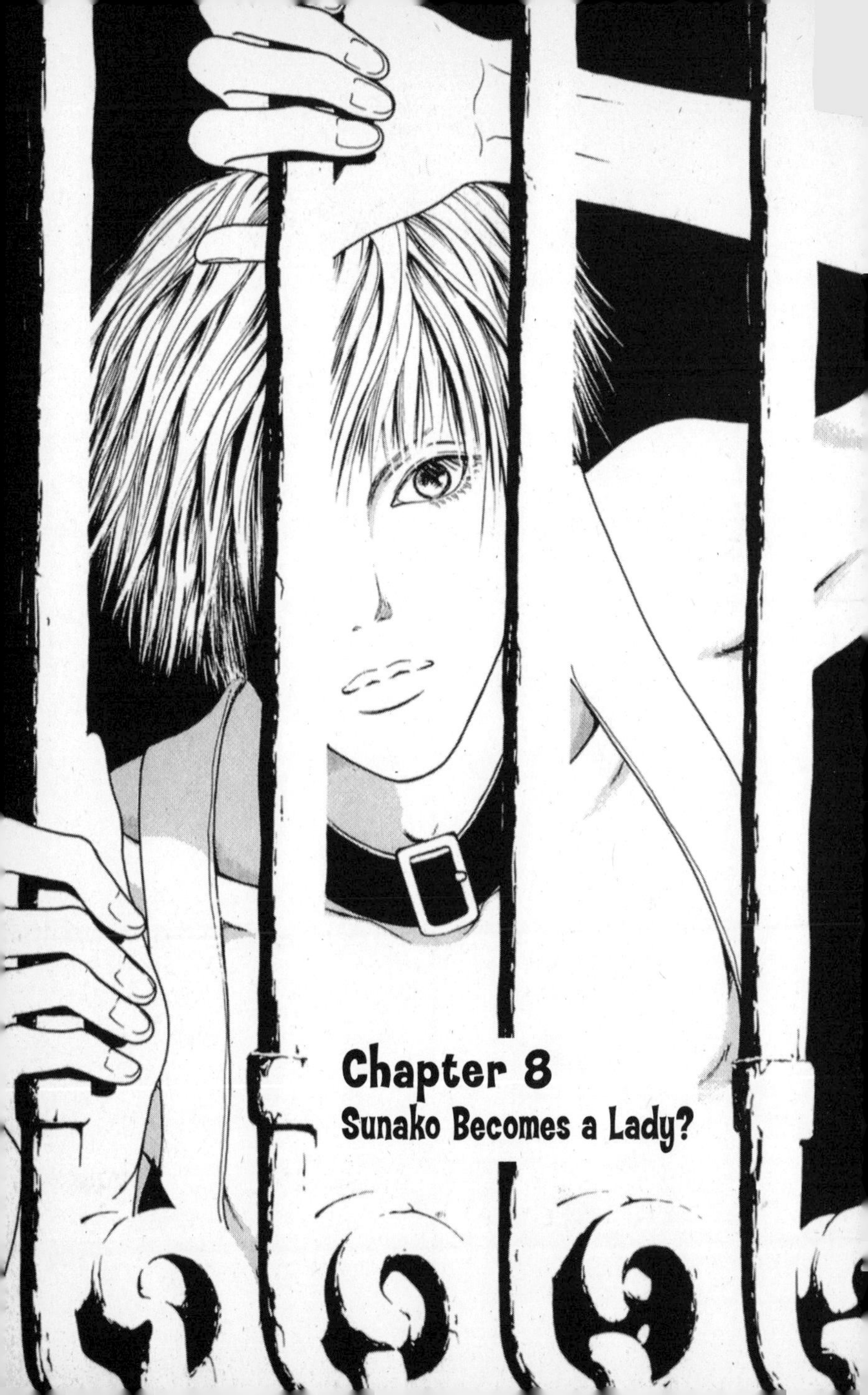
Chapter 8
Sunako Becomes a Lady?

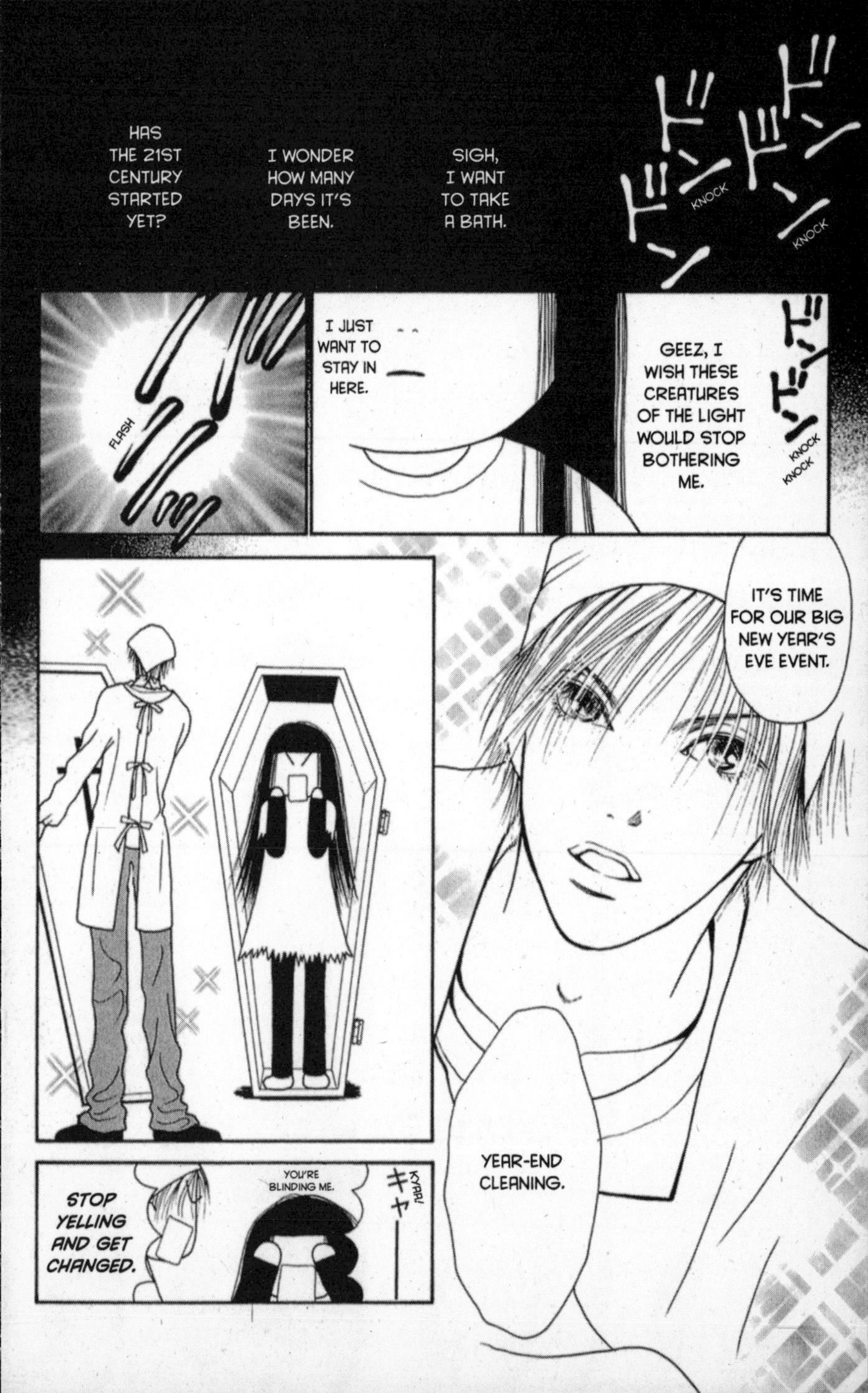
KNOCK
KNOCK
SIGH, I WANT TO TAKE A BATH.
I WONDER HOW MANY DAYS IT'S BEEN.
HAS THE 21ST CENTURY STARTED YET?
KNOCK KNOCK
GEEZ, I WISH THESE CREATURES OF THE LIGHT WOULD STOP BOTHERING ME.
I JUST WANT TO STAY IN HERE.
FLASH
IT'S TIME FOR OUR BIG NEW YEAR'S EVE EVENT.
YEAR-END CLEANING.
KYA!
YOU'RE BLINDING ME.
STOP YELLING AND GET CHANGED.

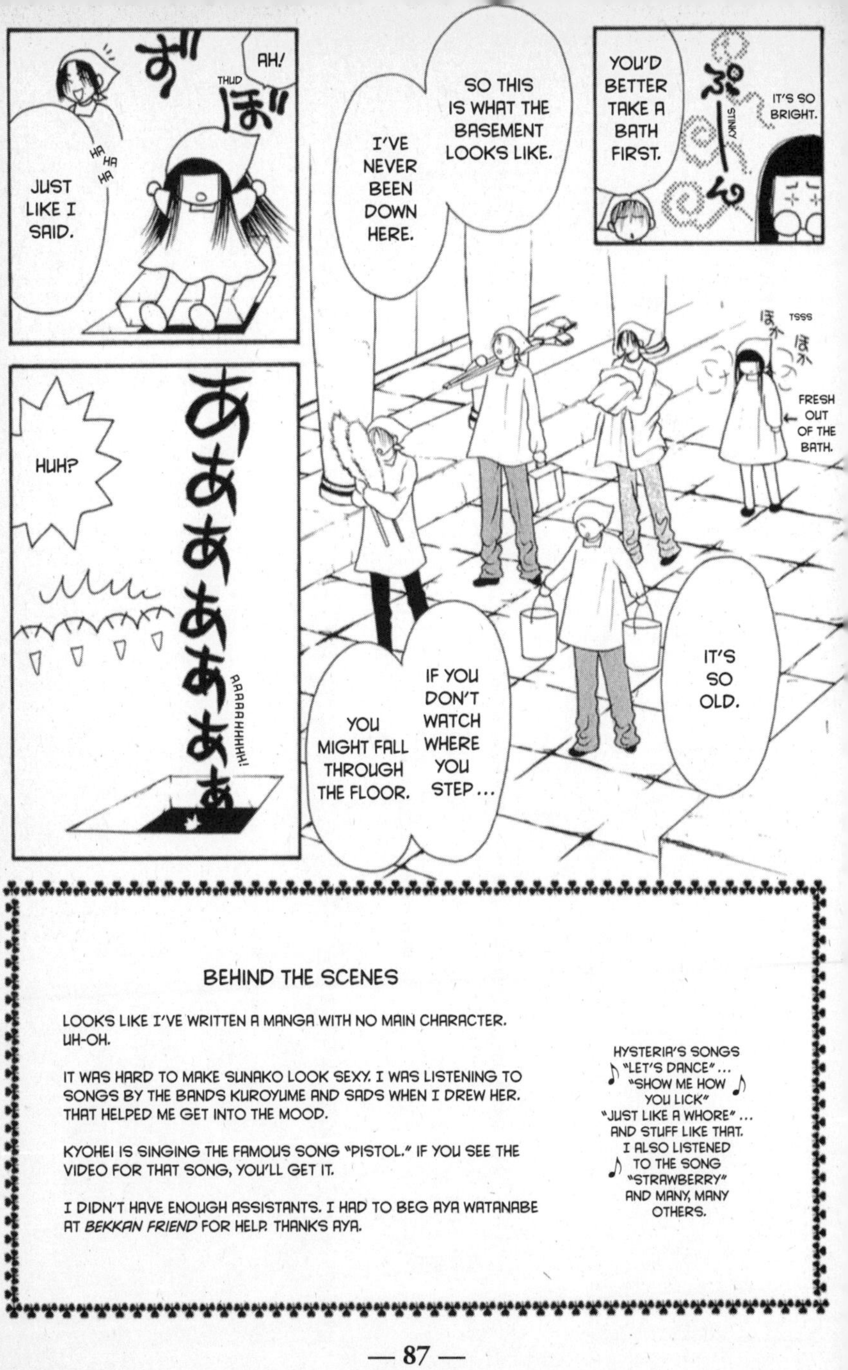
YOU'D BETTER TAKE A BATH FIRST.
STINKY
IT'S SO BRIGHT.
SO THIS IS WHAT THE BASEMENT LOOKS LIKE.
I'VE NEVER BEEN DOWN HERE.
TSSS
FRESH OUT OF THE BATH.
IT'S SO OLD.
IF YOU DON'T WATCH WHERE YOU STEP…
YOU MIGHT FALL THROUGH THE FLOOR.
AH!
THUD
HA HA HA
JUST LIKE I SAID.
HUH?
AAAAAHHHHH!

BEHIND THE SCENES

LOOKS LIKE I'VE WRITTEN A MANGA WITH NO MAIN CHARACTER. UH-OH.

IT WAS HARD TO MAKE SUNAKO LOOK SEXY. I WAS LISTENING TO SONGS BY THE BANDS KUROYUME AND SADS WHEN I DREW HER. THAT HELPED ME GET INTO THE MOOD.

KYOHEI IS SINGING THE FAMOUS SONG "PISTOL." IF YOU SEE THE VIDEO FOR THAT SONG, YOU'LL GET IT.

I DIDN'T HAVE ENOUGH ASSISTANTS. I HAD TO BEG AYA WATANABE AT *BEKKAN FRIEND* FOR HELP. THANKS AYA.

HYSTERIA'S SONGS ♪ "LET'S DANCE"… "SHOW ME HOW YOU LICK" ♪ "JUST LIKE A WHORE"… AND STUFF LIKE THAT. I ALSO LISTENED ♪ TO THE SONG "STRAWBERRY" AND MANY, MANY OTHERS.

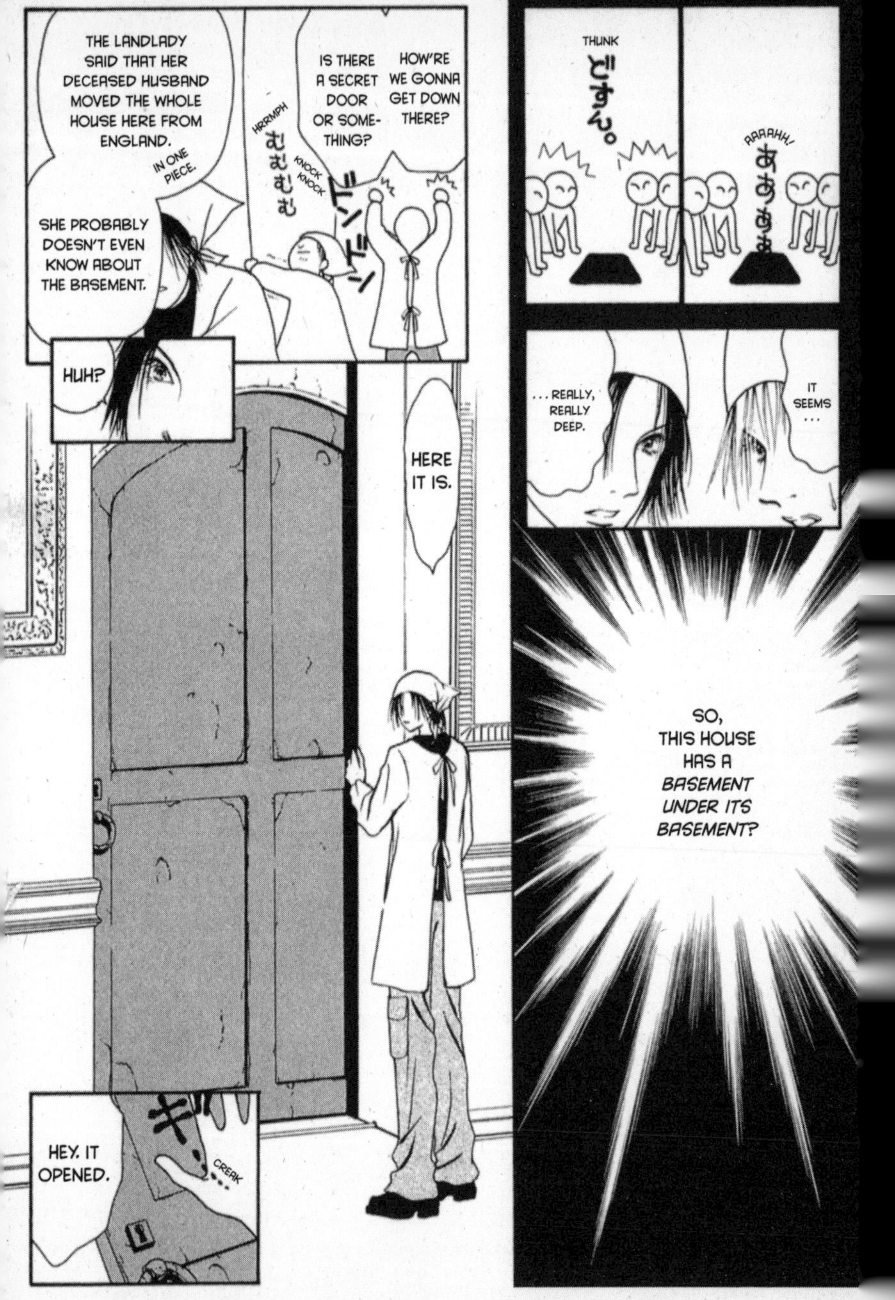

HOW'RE WE GONNA GET DOWN THERE?
IS THERE A SECRET DOOR OR SOME-THING?
HRRMPH
KNOCK KNOCK
THE LANDLADY SAID THAT HER DECEASED HUSBAND MOVED THE WHOLE HOUSE HERE FROM ENGLAND.
IN ONE PIECE.
SHE PROBABLY DOESN'T EVEN KNOW ABOUT THE BASEMENT.
HUH?
HERE IT IS.
HEY. IT OPENED.
CREAK
THUNK
AAAAHH!
IT SEEMS . . .
. . . REALLY, REALLY DEEP.
SO, THIS HOUSE HAS A *BASEMENT UNDER ITS BASEMENT?*

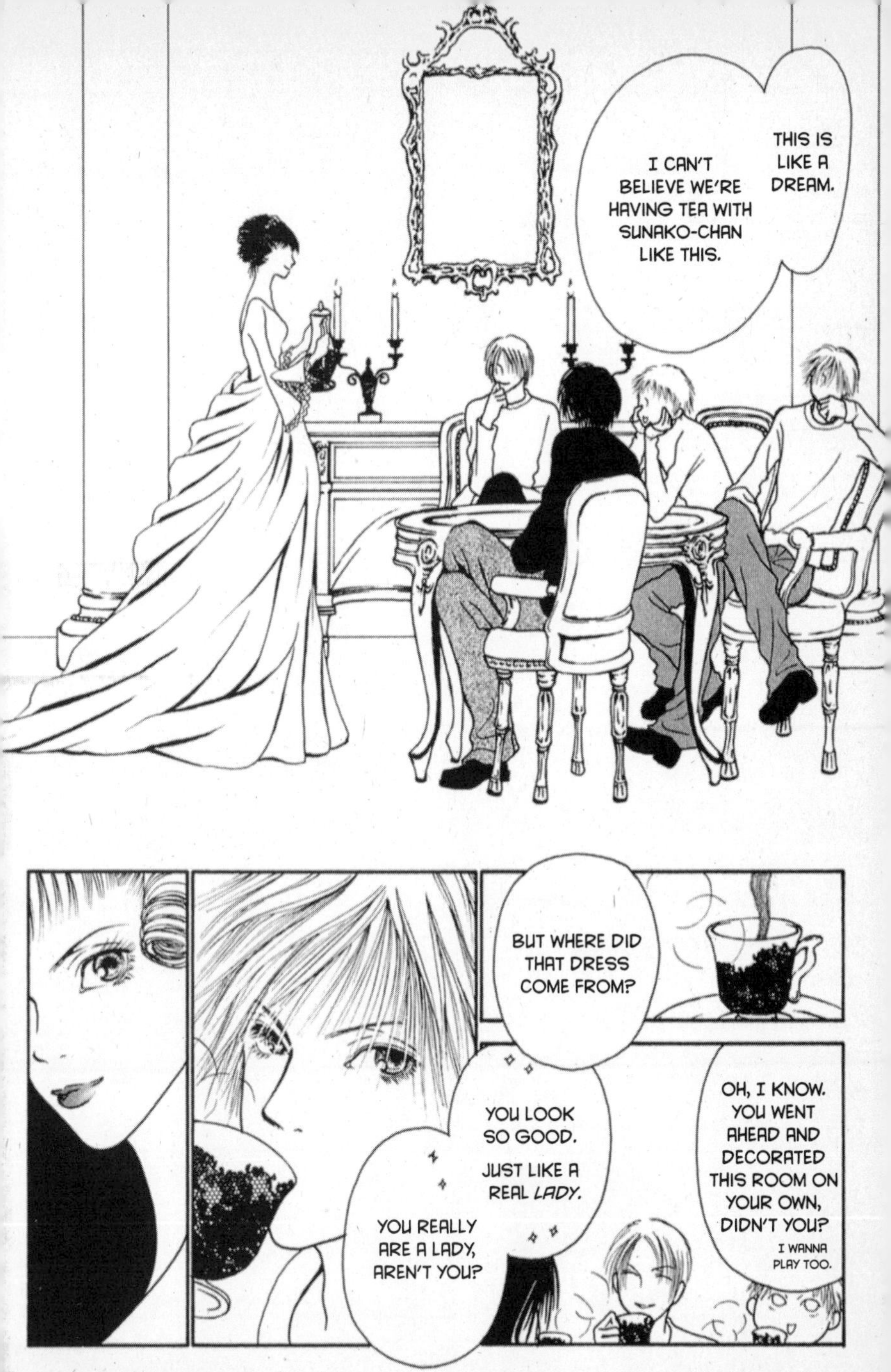
THIS IS LIKE A DREAM.
I CAN'T BELIEVE WE'RE HAVING TEA WITH SUNAKO-CHAN LIKE THIS.
BUT WHERE DID THAT DRESS COME FROM?
OH, I KNOW. YOU WENT AHEAD AND DECORATED THIS ROOM ON YOUR OWN, DIDN'T YOU?
I WANNA PLAY TOO.
YOU LOOK SO GOOD.
JUST LIKE A REAL *LADY*.
YOU REALLY ARE A LADY, AREN'T YOU?

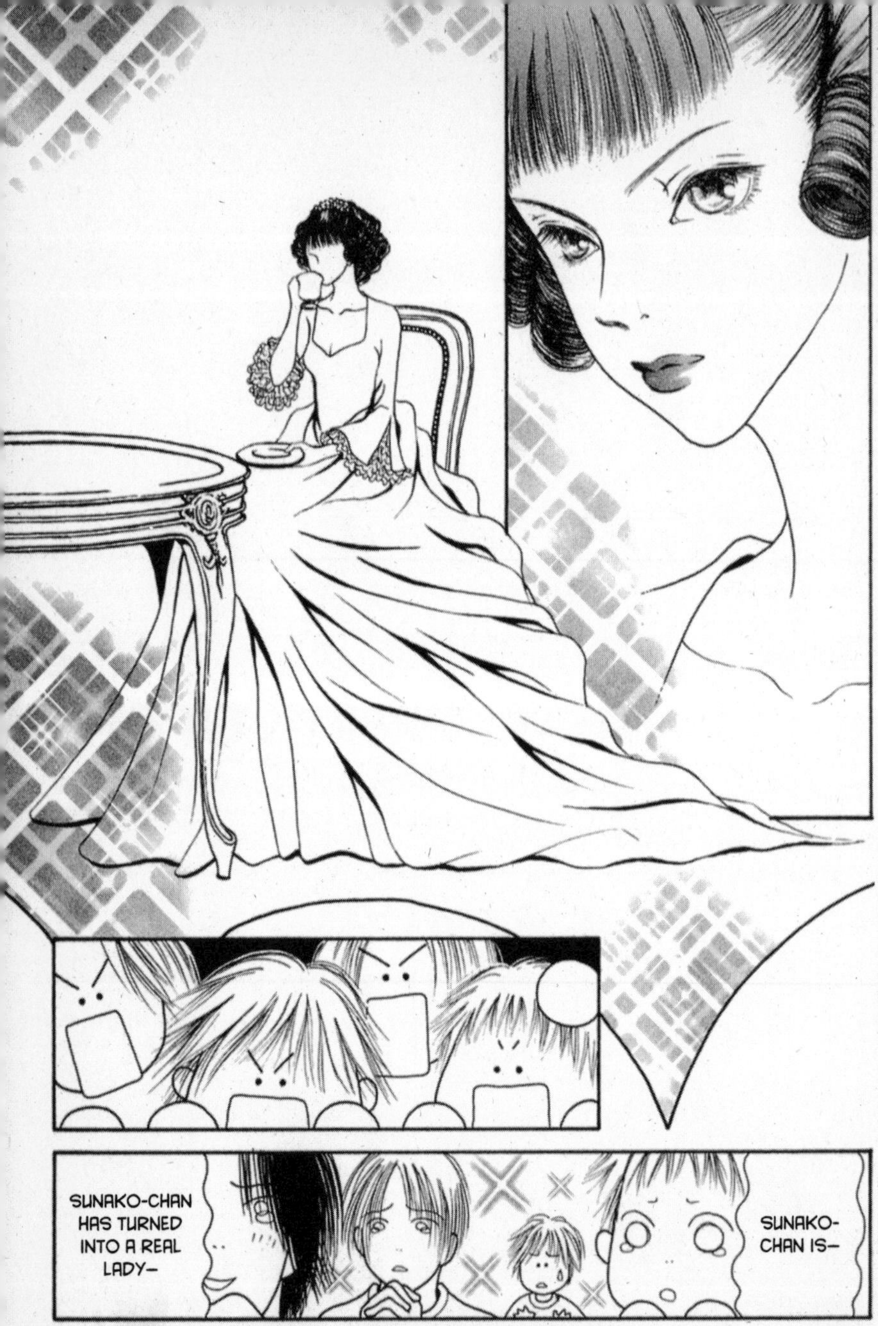
SUNAKO-CHAN IS—
SUNAKO-CHAN HAS TURNED INTO A REAL LADY—

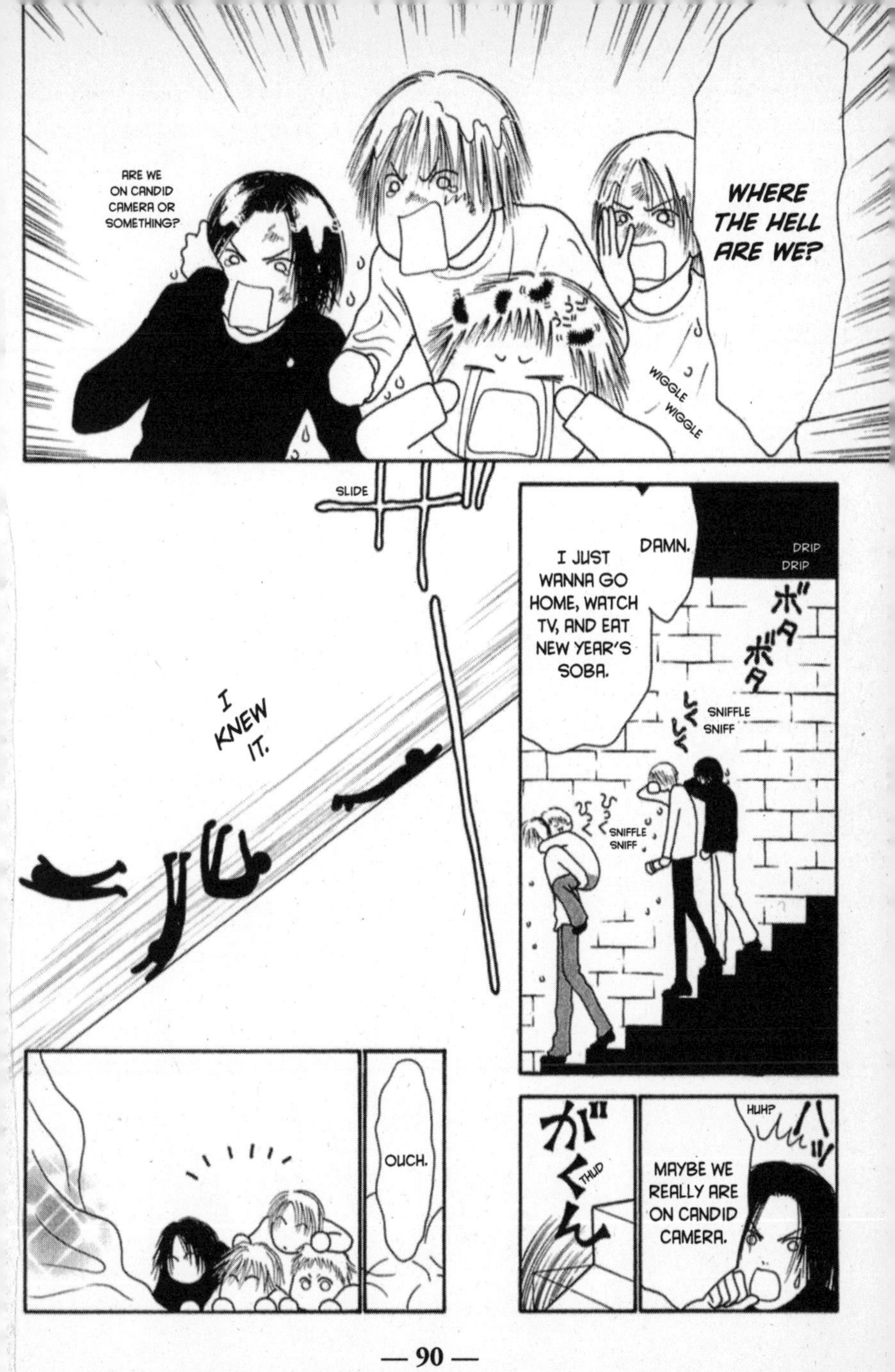
WHERE THE HELL ARE WE?
WIGGLE WIGGLE
ARE WE ON CANDID CAMERA OR SOMETHING?
DAMN.
I JUST WANNA GO HOME, WATCH TV, AND EAT NEW YEAR'S SOBA.
DRIP DRIP
ボタボタ
SNIFFLE SNIFF
SNIFFLE SNIFF
SLIDE
I KNEW IT.
HUH?
ハッ
MAYBE WE REALLY ARE ON CANDID CAMERA.
がくん
THUD
OUCH.

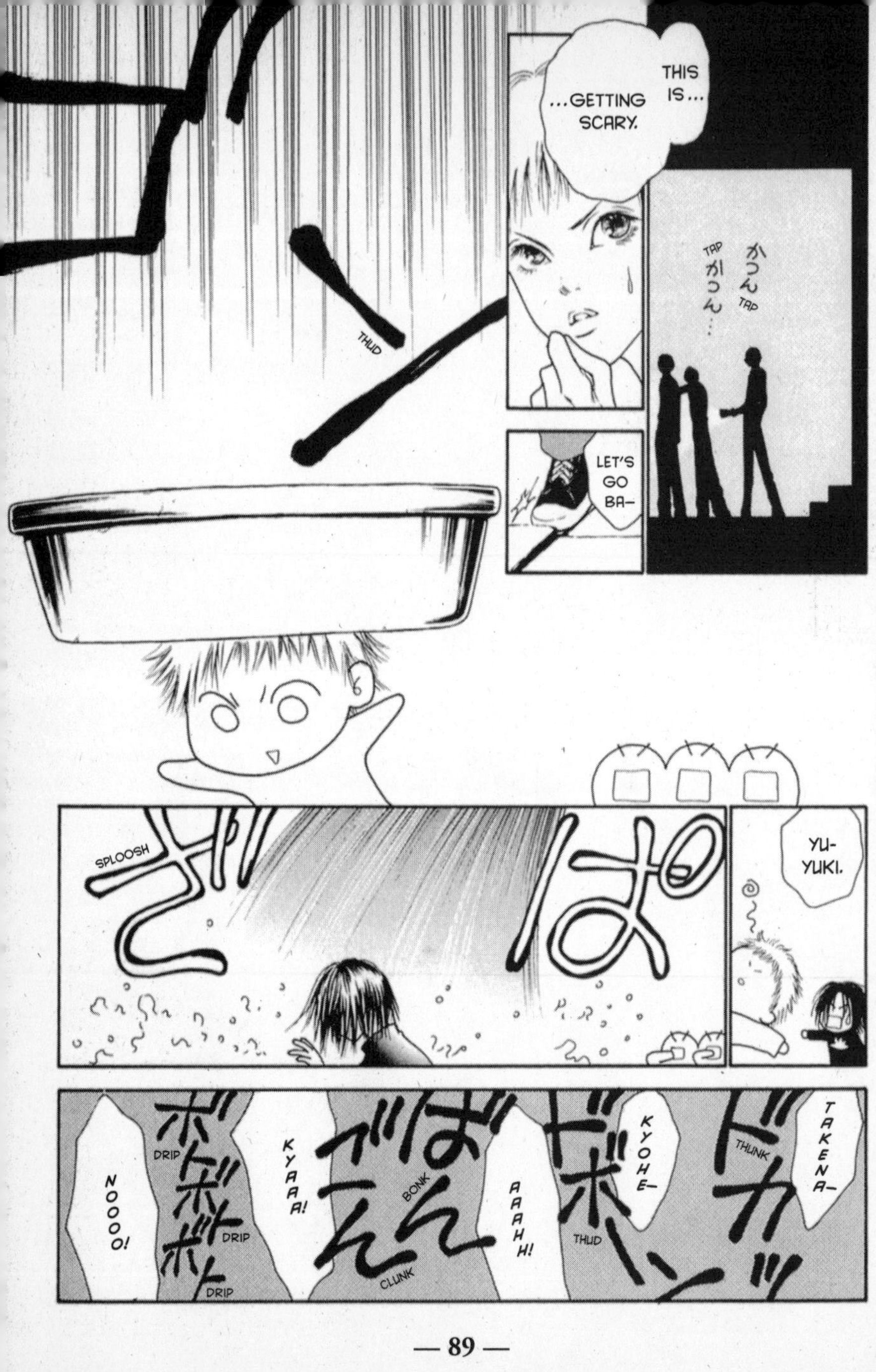

かつん かつん…
TAP TAP
THIS IS…
…GETTING SCARY.
LET'S GO BA—
THUD
YU-YUKI.
SPLOOSH
TAKENA—
THUNK
KYOHE—
THUD
AAAAH!
BONK
CLUNK
KYAAAA!
DRIP
DRIP
DRIP
NOOOO!

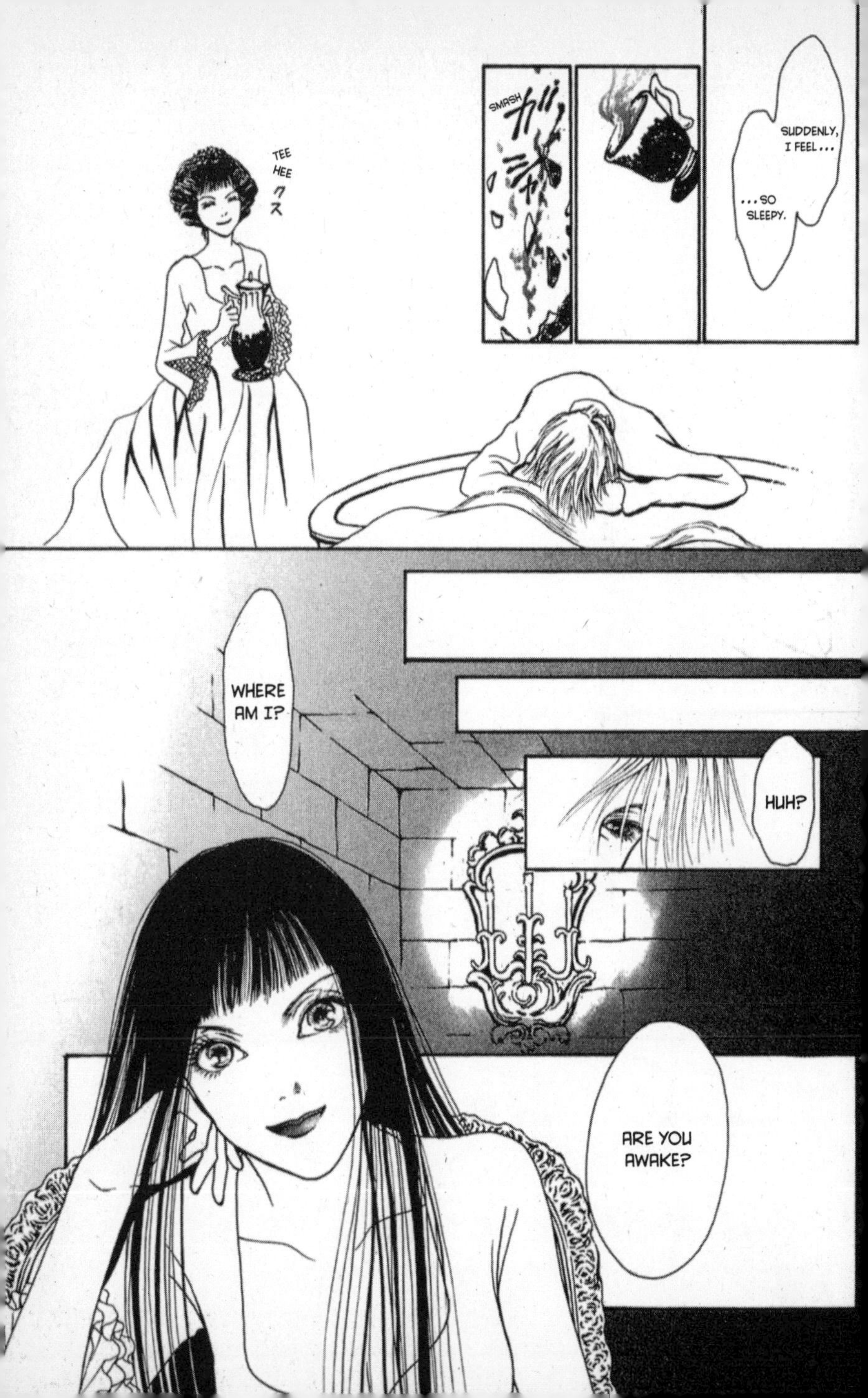

SUDDENLY, I FEEL...
...SO SLEEPY.
SMASH
TEE HEE
クス
WHERE AM I?
HUH?
ARE YOU AWAKE?

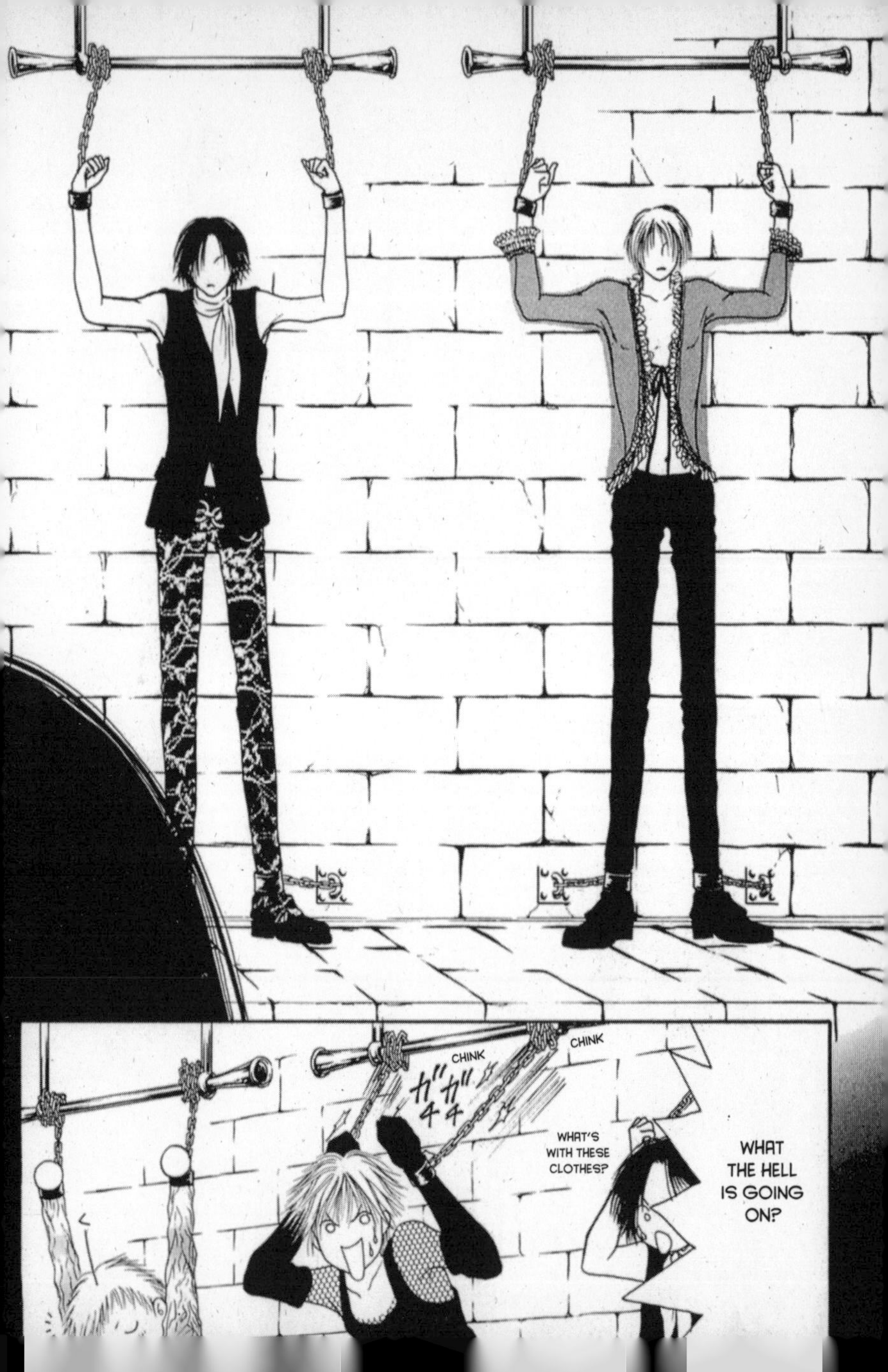
WHAT THE HELL IS GOING ON?
WHAT'S WITH THESE CLOTHES?
CHINK
ガチガチ
CHINK

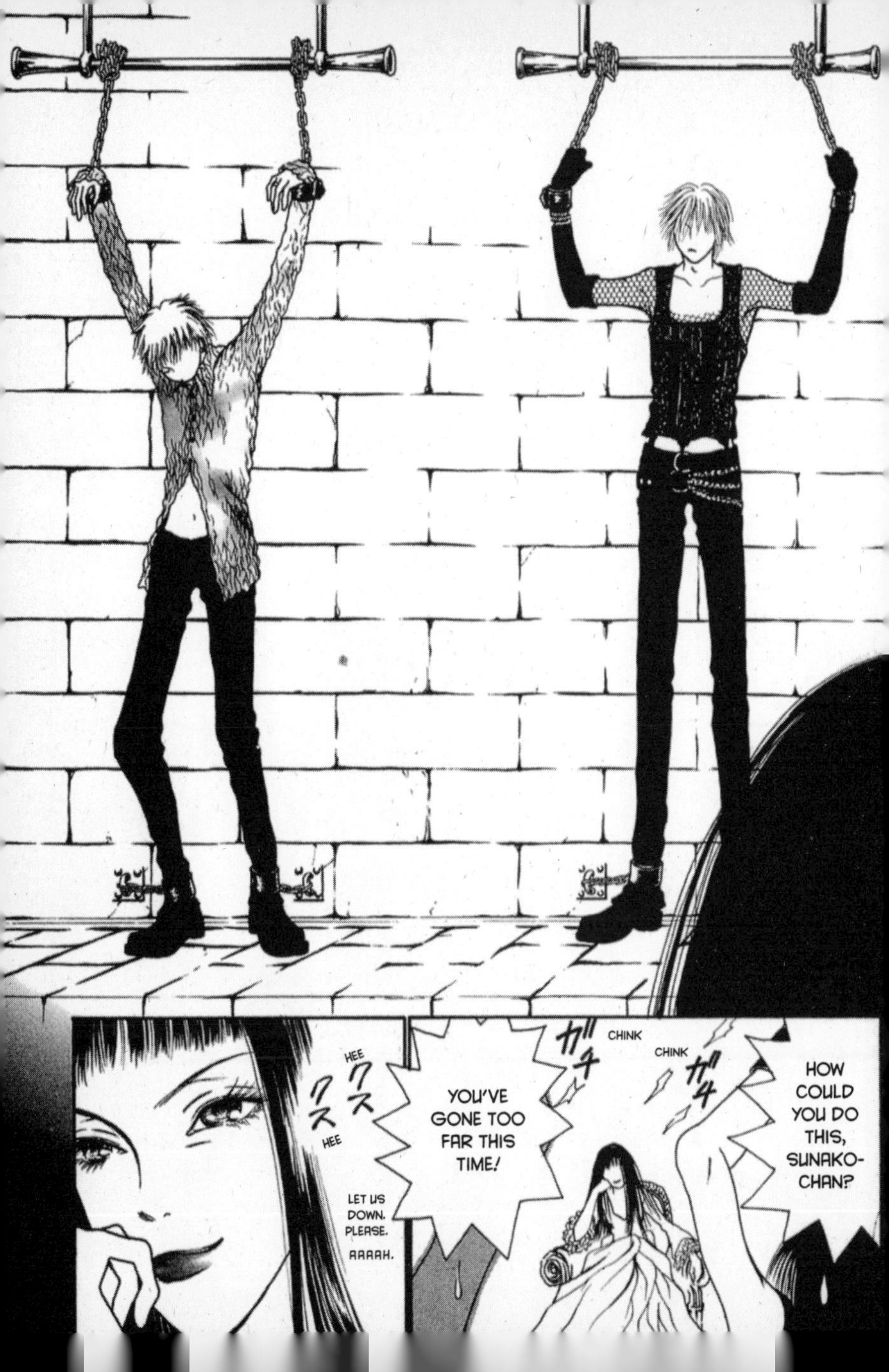
HOW COULD YOU DO THIS, SUNAKO-CHAN?
CHINK
ガチ
CHINK
ガチ
YOU'VE GONE TOO FAR THIS TIME!
HEE
クスクス
HEE
LET US DOWN. PLEASE.
AAAAH.

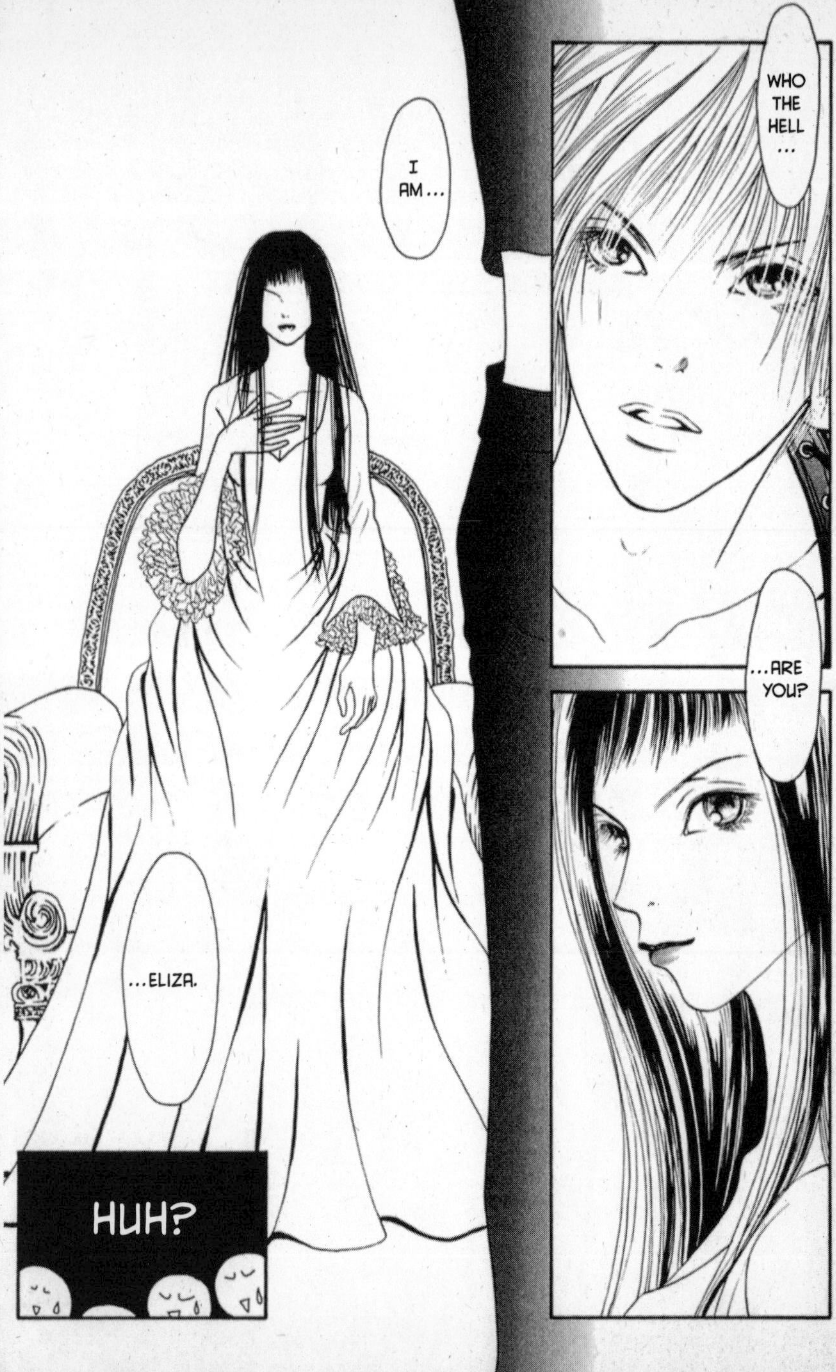
WHO THE HELL...
...ARE YOU?
I AM...
...ELIZA.
HUH?

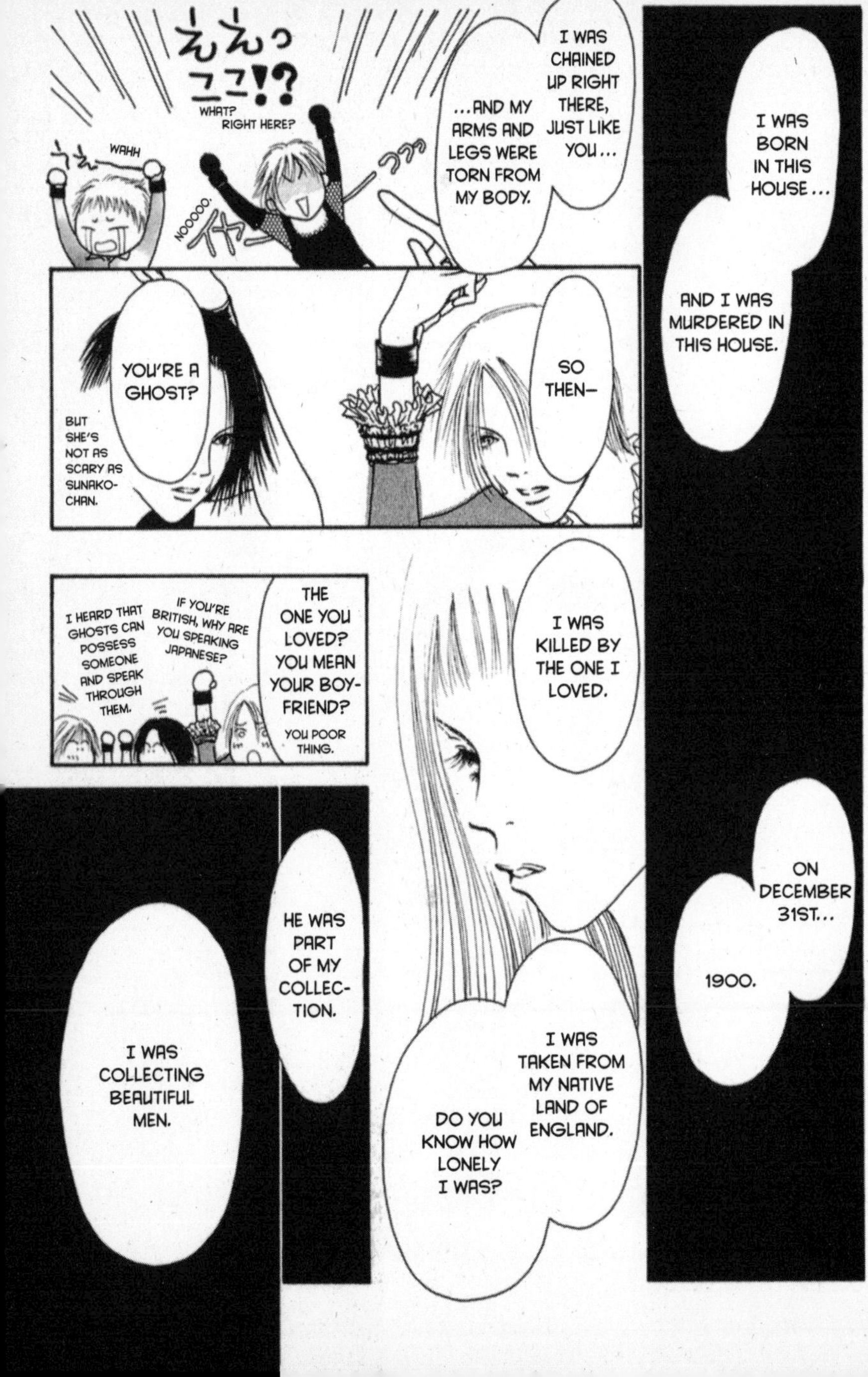
I WAS BORN IN THIS HOUSE…
AND I WAS MURDERED IN THIS HOUSE.
ON DECEMBER 31ST…
1900.
I WAS CHAINED UP RIGHT THERE, JUST LIKE YOU…
…AND MY ARMS AND LEGS WERE TORN FROM MY BODY.
ええっ ここ!?
WHAT? RIGHT HERE?
イヤー
NOOOOO.
WAHH
SO THEN—
YOU'RE A GHOST?
BUT SHE'S NOT AS SCARY AS SUNAKO-CHAN.
I WAS KILLED BY THE ONE I LOVED.
THE ONE YOU LOVED? YOU MEAN YOUR BOY-FRIEND?
YOU POOR THING.
IF YOU'RE BRITISH, WHY ARE YOU SPEAKING JAPANESE?
I HEARD THAT GHOSTS CAN POSSESS SOMEONE AND SPEAK THROUGH THEM.
I WAS TAKEN FROM MY NATIVE LAND OF ENGLAND.
DO YOU KNOW HOW LONELY I WAS?
HE WAS PART OF MY COLLEC-TION.
I WAS COLLECTING BEAUTIFUL MEN.

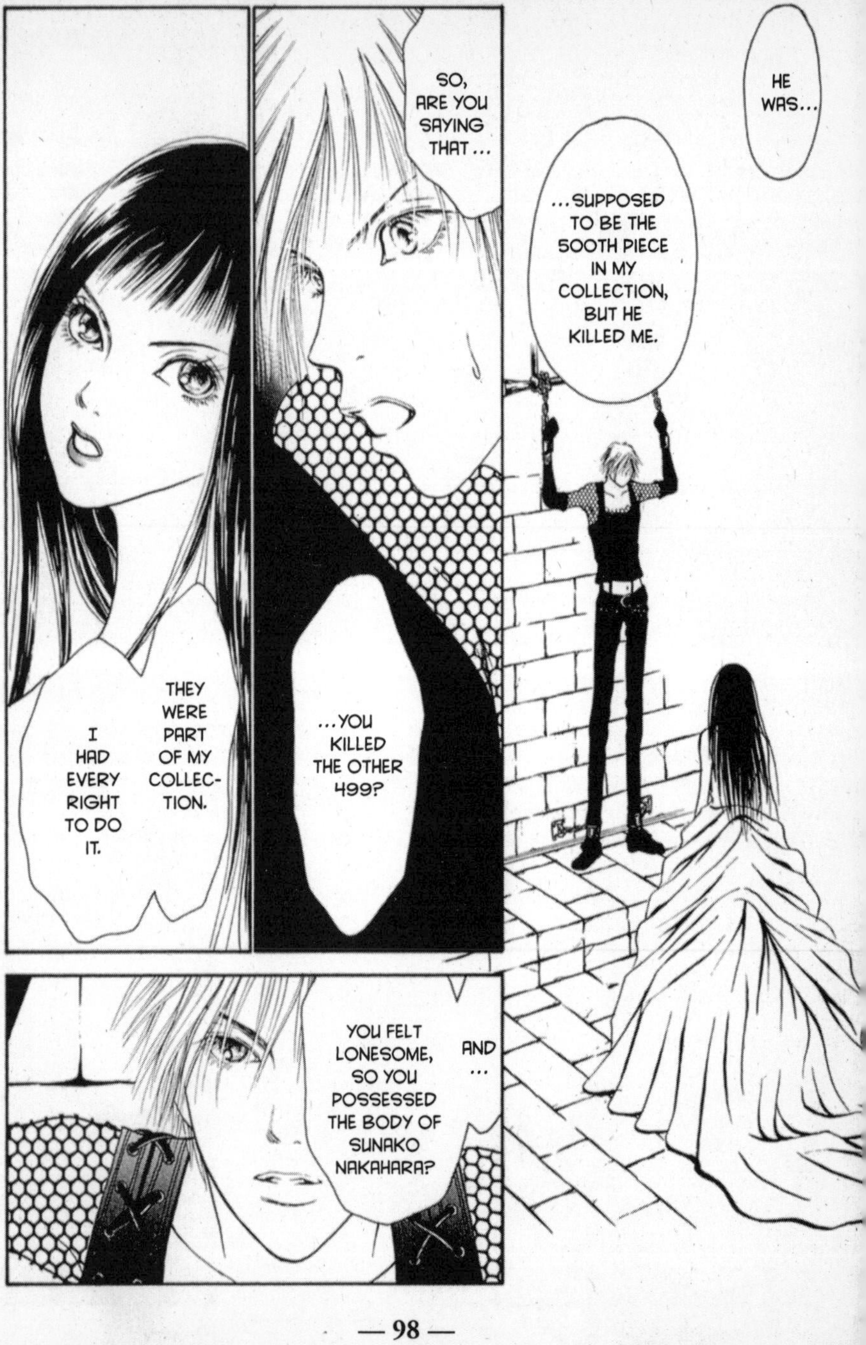
HE WAS...
...SUPPOSED TO BE THE 500TH PIECE IN MY COLLECTION, BUT HE KILLED ME.
SO, ARE YOU SAYING THAT...
...YOU KILLED THE OTHER 499?
THEY WERE PART OF MY COLLECTION.
I HAD EVERY RIGHT TO DO IT.
AND...
YOU FELT LONESOME, SO YOU POSSESSED THE BODY OF SUNAKO NAKAHARA?

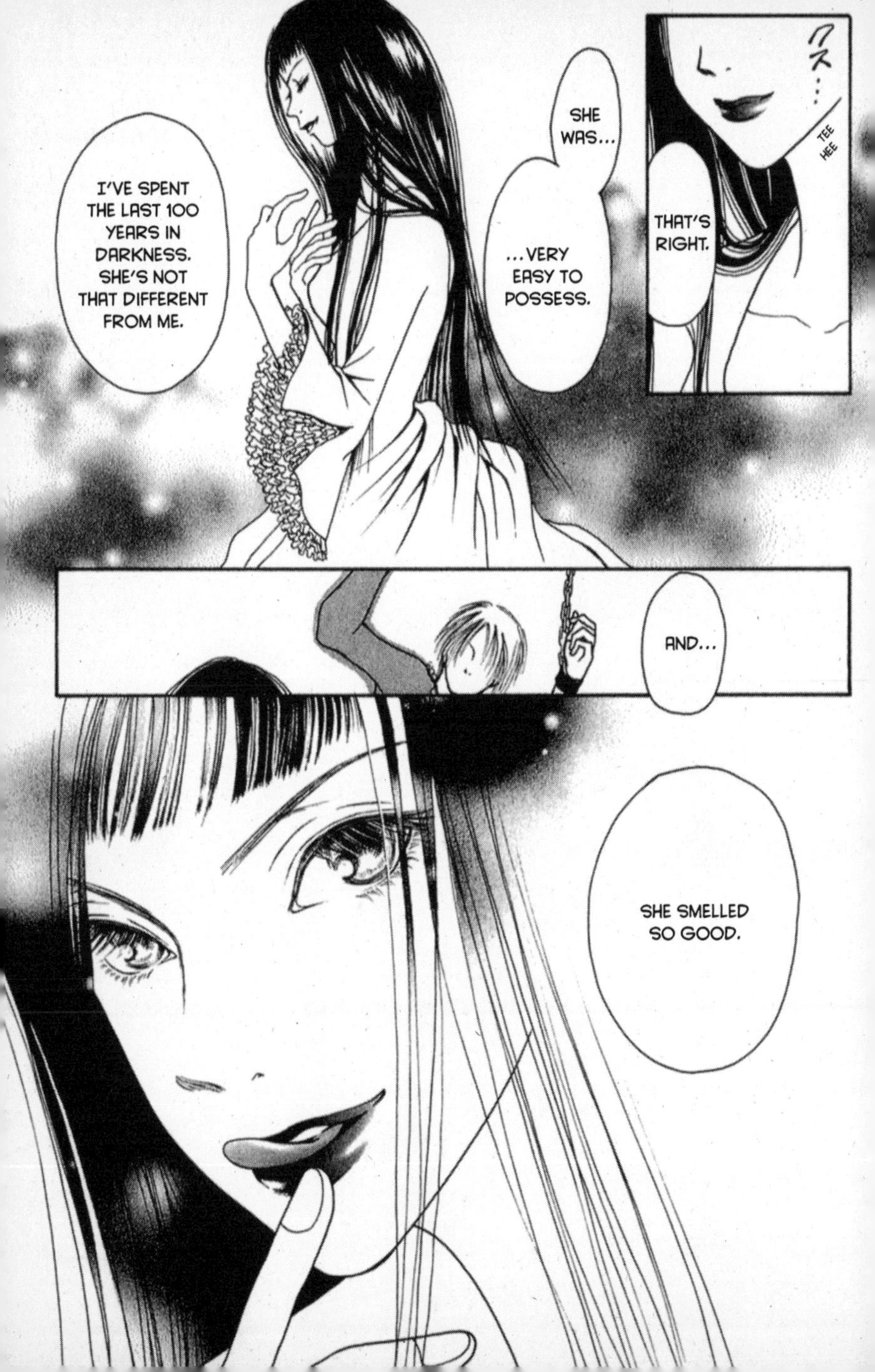

クス…
TEE HEE
THAT'S RIGHT.
SHE WAS...
...VERY EASY TO POSSESS.
I'VE SPENT THE LAST 100 YEARS IN DARKNESS. SHE'S NOT THAT DIFFERENT FROM ME.
AND...
SHE SMELLED SO GOOD.

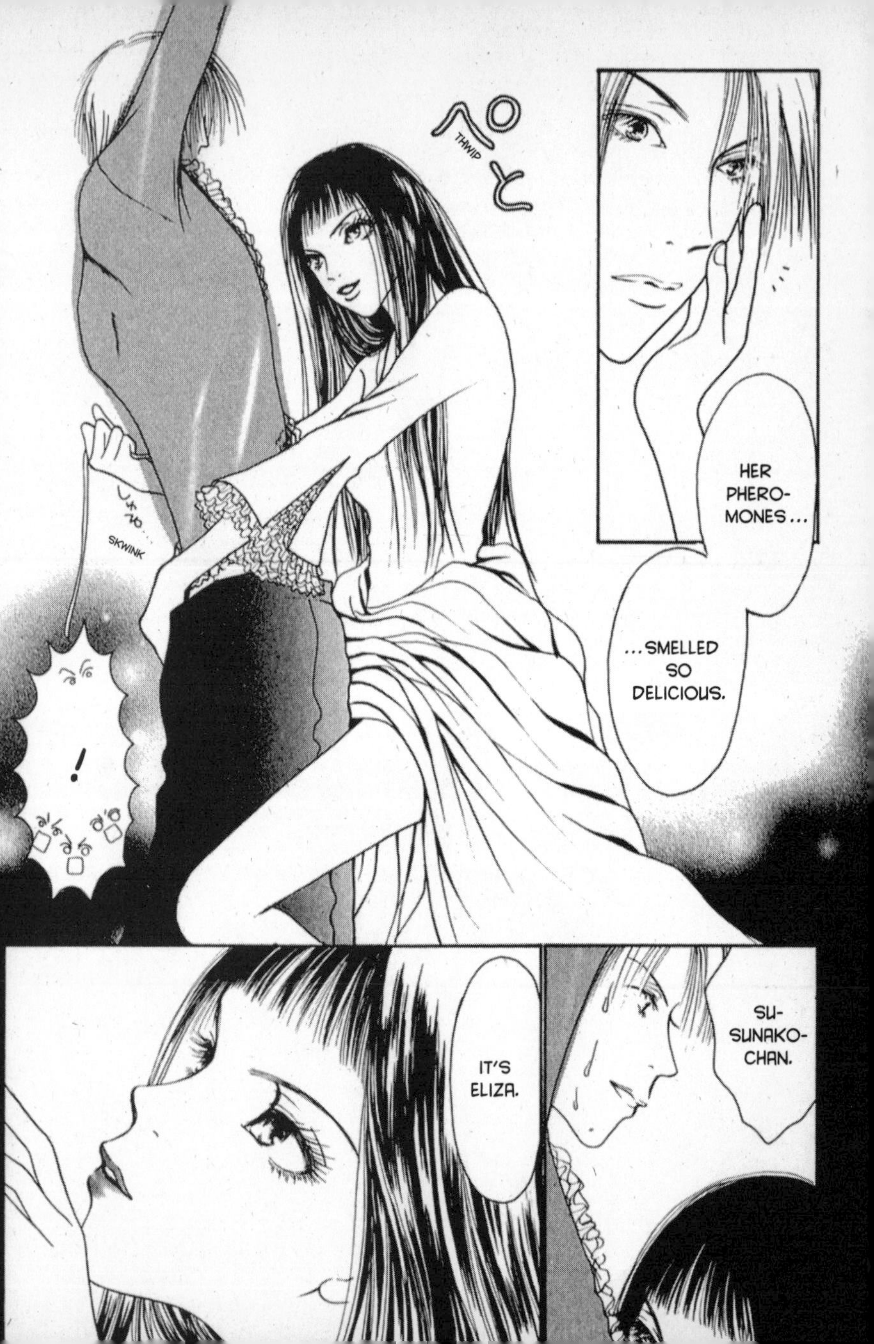
HER PHEROMONES...
...SMELLED SO DELICIOUS.
ぺと
THWIP
しゅる…
SKWINK
!
SU-SUNAKO-CHAN.
IT'S ELIZA.

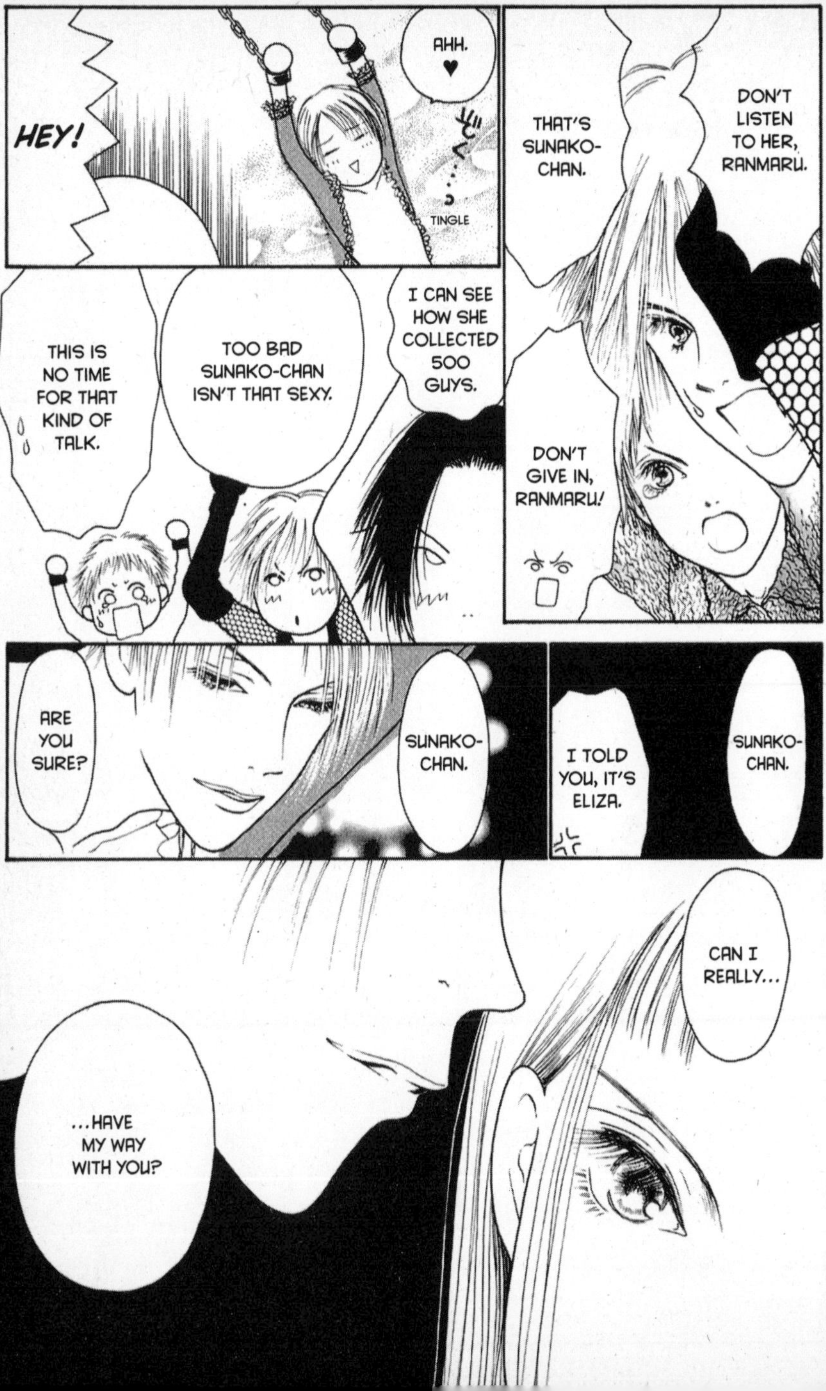
DON'T LISTEN TO HER, RANMARU.
THAT'S SUNAKO-CHAN.
DON'T GIVE IN, RANMARU!
AHH. ♥
TINGLE
HEY!
I CAN SEE HOW SHE COLLECTED 500 GUYS.
TOO BAD SUNAKO-CHAN ISN'T THAT SEXY.
THIS IS NO TIME FOR THAT KIND OF TALK.
SUNAKO-CHAN.
I TOLD YOU, IT'S ELIZA.
SUNAKO-CHAN.
ARE YOU SURE?
CAN I REALLY...
...HAVE MY WAY WITH YOU?

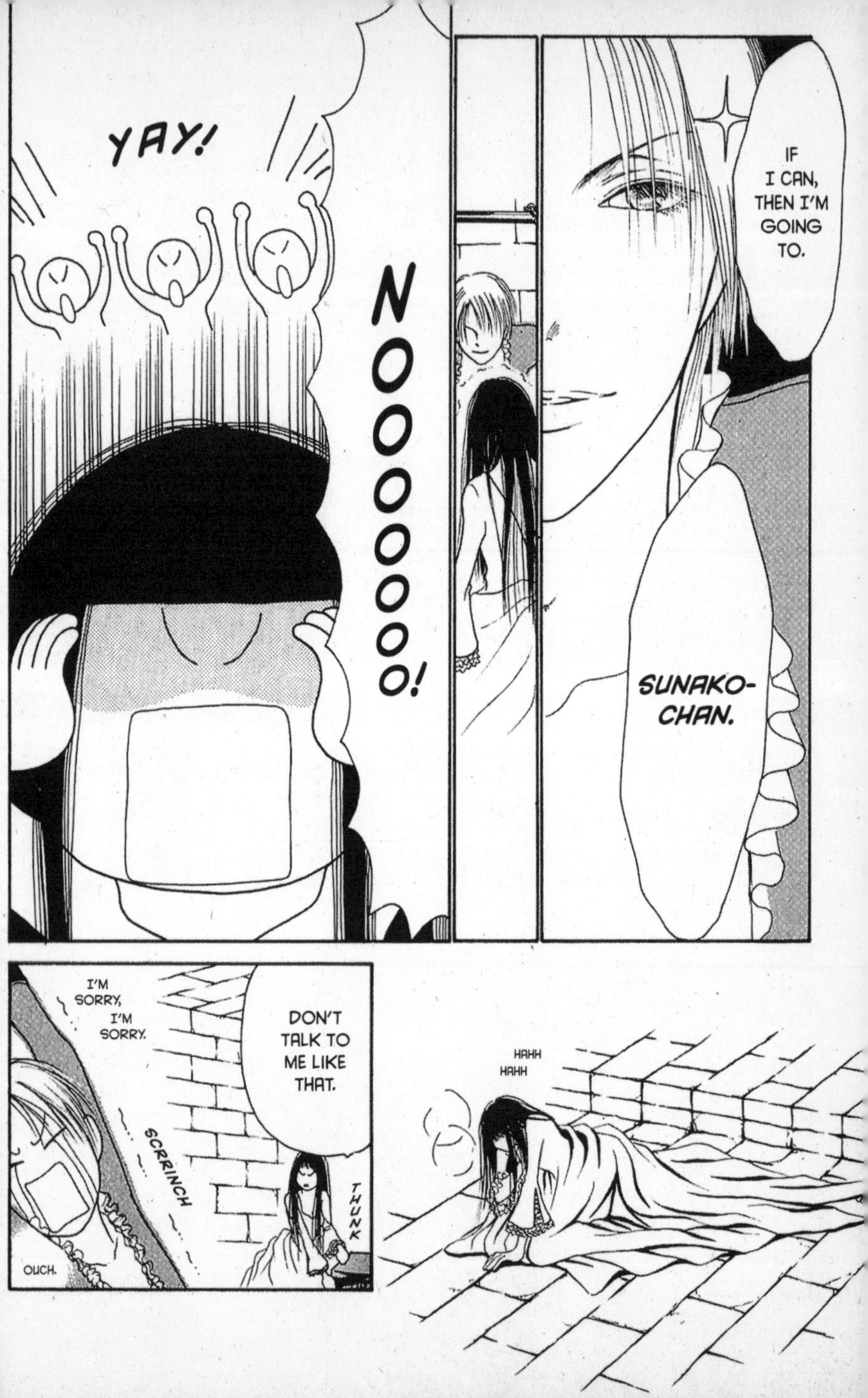
IF I CAN, THEN I'M GOING TO.
SUNAKO-CHAN.
YAY!
NOOOOOOO!
HAHH HAHH
DON'T TALK TO ME LIKE THAT.
I'M SORRY, I'M SORRY.
THUNK
SCRRINCH
OUCH.

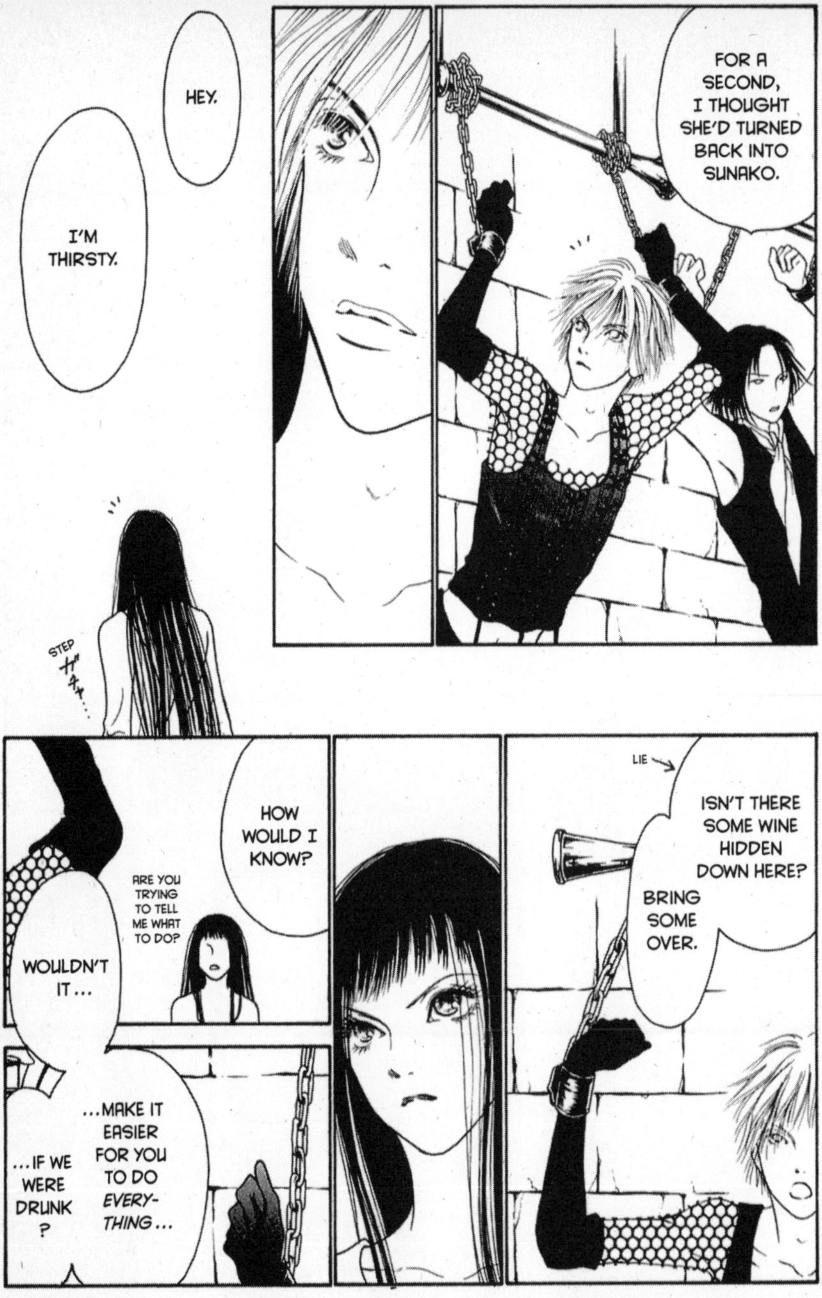
FOR A SECOND, I THOUGHT SHE'D TURNED BACK INTO SUNAKO.
HEY.
I'M THIRSTY.
STEP
LIE
ISN'T THERE SOME WINE HIDDEN DOWN HERE?
BRING SOME OVER.
HOW WOULD I KNOW?
ARE YOU TRYING TO TELL ME WHAT TO DO?
WOULDN'T IT...
...MAKE IT EASIER FOR YOU TO DO *EVERYTHING*...
...IF WE WERE DRUNK?

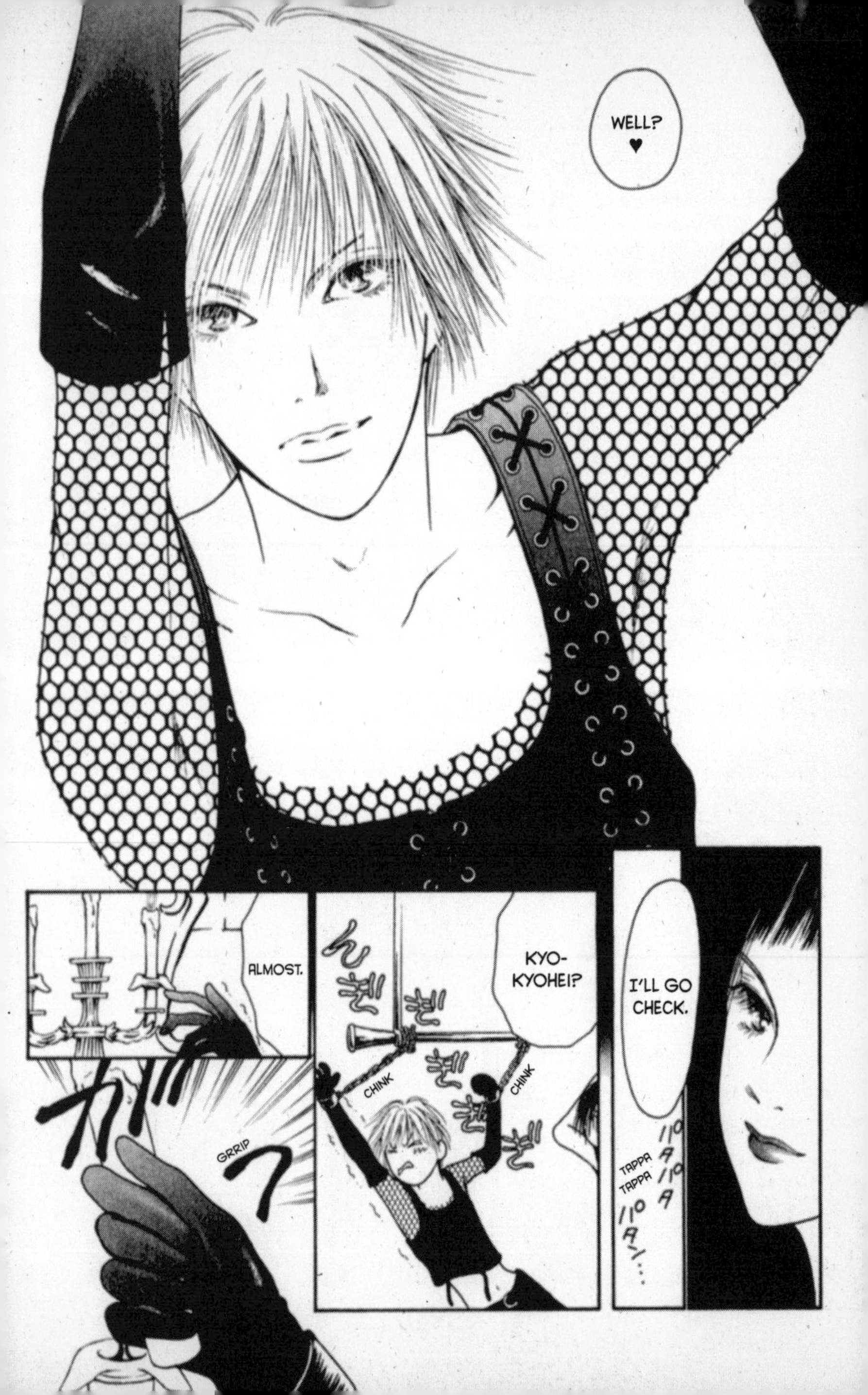
WELL? ♥
I'LL GO CHECK.
TAPPA TAPPA
KYO-KYOHEI!?
CHINK
CHINK
ALMOST.
GRRIP

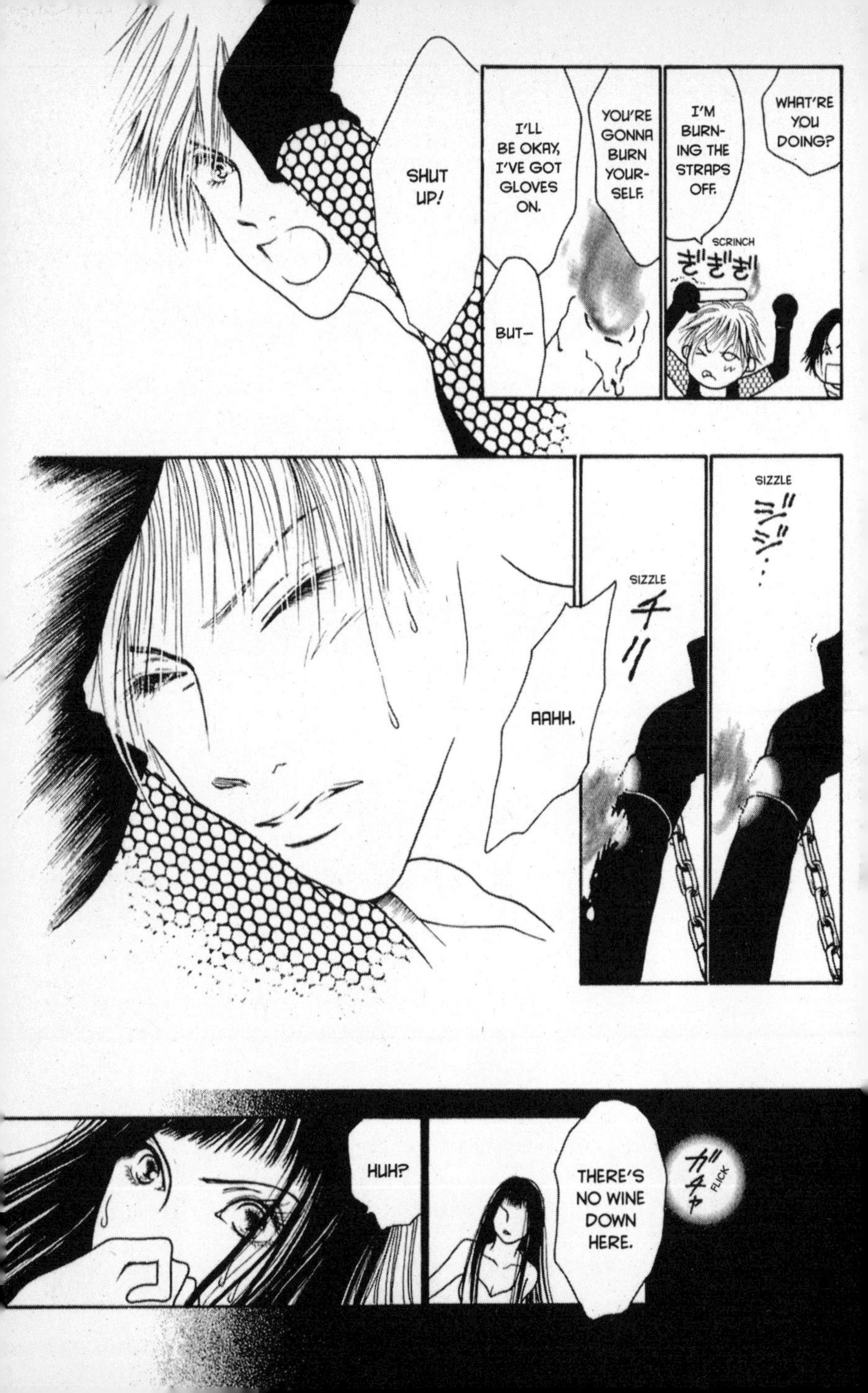
WHAT'RE YOU DOING?
I'M BURNING THE STRAPS OFF.
SCRINCH
ぎぎぎ
YOU'RE GONNA BURN YOURSELF.
I'LL BE OKAY, I'VE GOT GLOVES ON.
BUT—
SHUT UP!
SIZZLE
ジジジ…
SIZZLE
チリ
AAHH.
ガチャ
FLICK
THERE'S NO WINE DOWN HERE.
HUH?

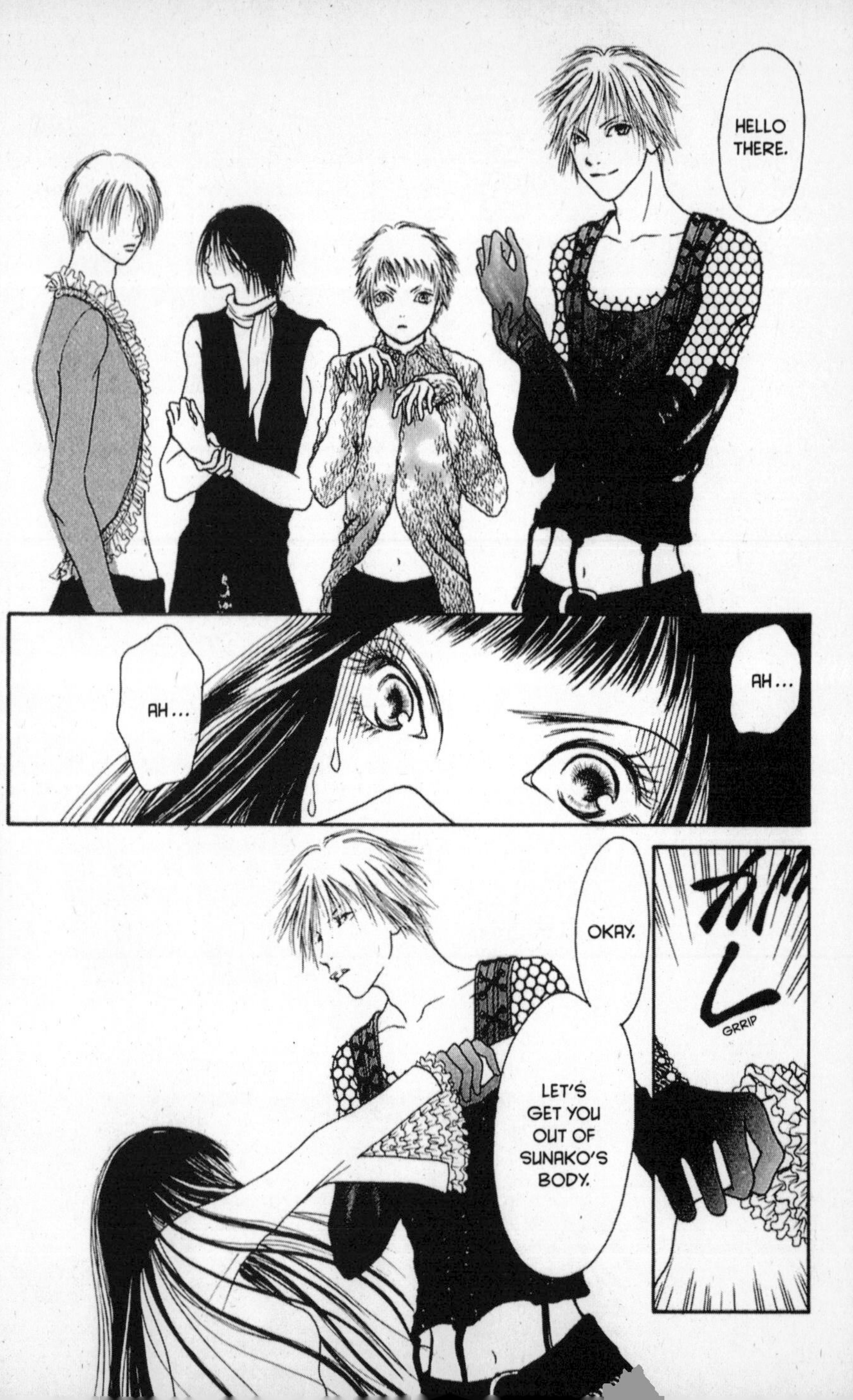
HELLO THERE.
AH...
AH...
GRRIP
OKAY.
LET'S GET YOU OUT OF SUNAKO'S BODY.

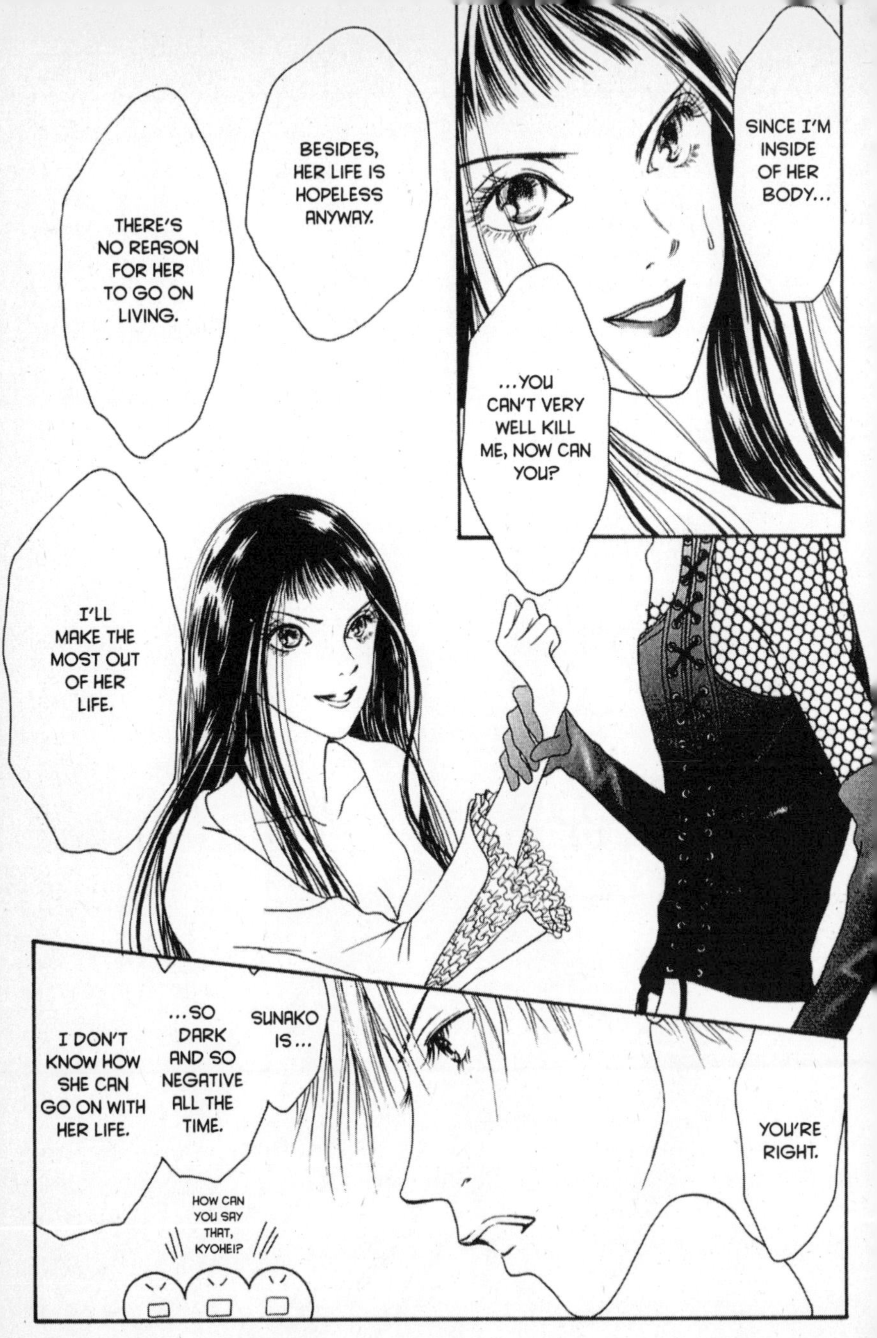
SINCE I'M INSIDE OF HER BODY...
...YOU CAN'T VERY WELL KILL ME, NOW CAN YOU?
BESIDES, HER LIFE IS HOPELESS ANYWAY.
THERE'S NO REASON FOR HER TO GO ON LIVING.
I'LL MAKE THE MOST OUT OF HER LIFE.
YOU'RE RIGHT.
SUNAKO IS...
...SO DARK AND SO NEGATIVE ALL THE TIME.
I DON'T KNOW HOW SHE CAN GO ON WITH HER LIFE.
HOW CAN YOU SAY THAT, KYOHEI!?

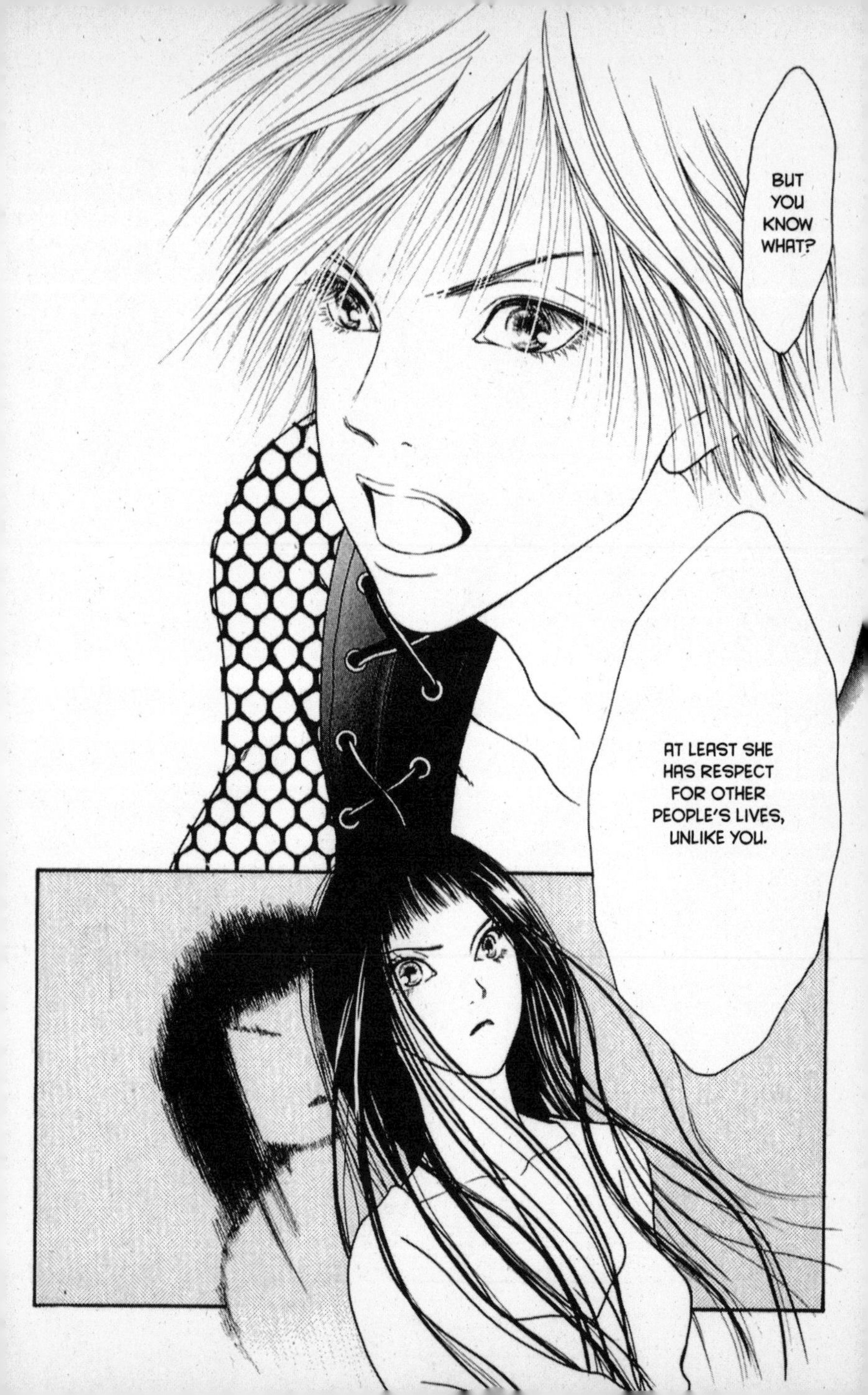
BUT YOU KNOW WHAT?
AT LEAST SHE HAS RESPECT FOR OTHER PEOPLE'S LIVES, UNLIKE YOU.

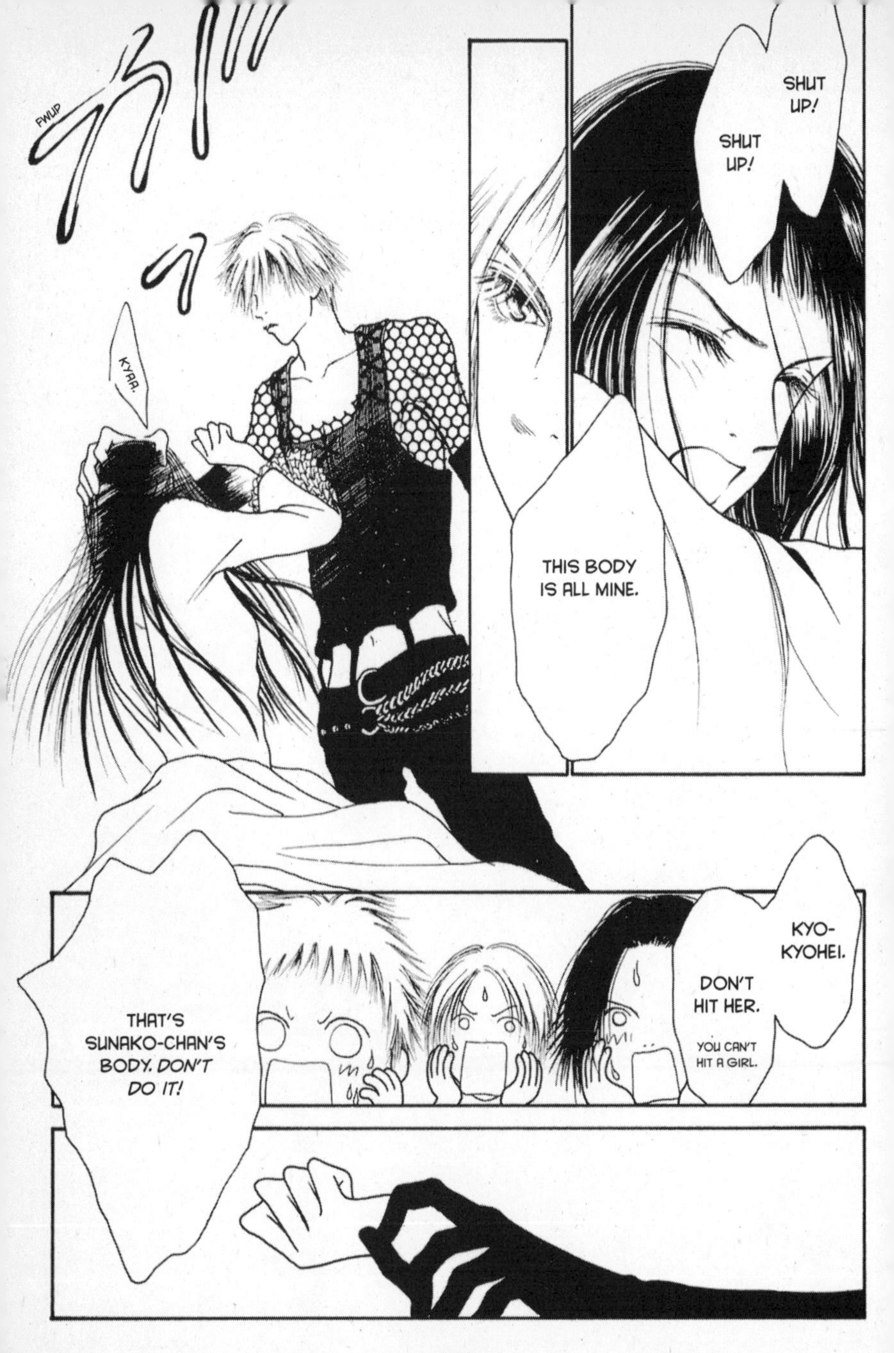
SHUT UP!
SHUT UP!
THIS BODY IS ALL MINE.
FWUP
KYAA.
KYO-KYOHEI.
DON'T HIT HER.
YOU CAN'T HIT A GIRL.
THAT'S SUNAKO-CHAN'S BODY. *DON'T DO IT!*

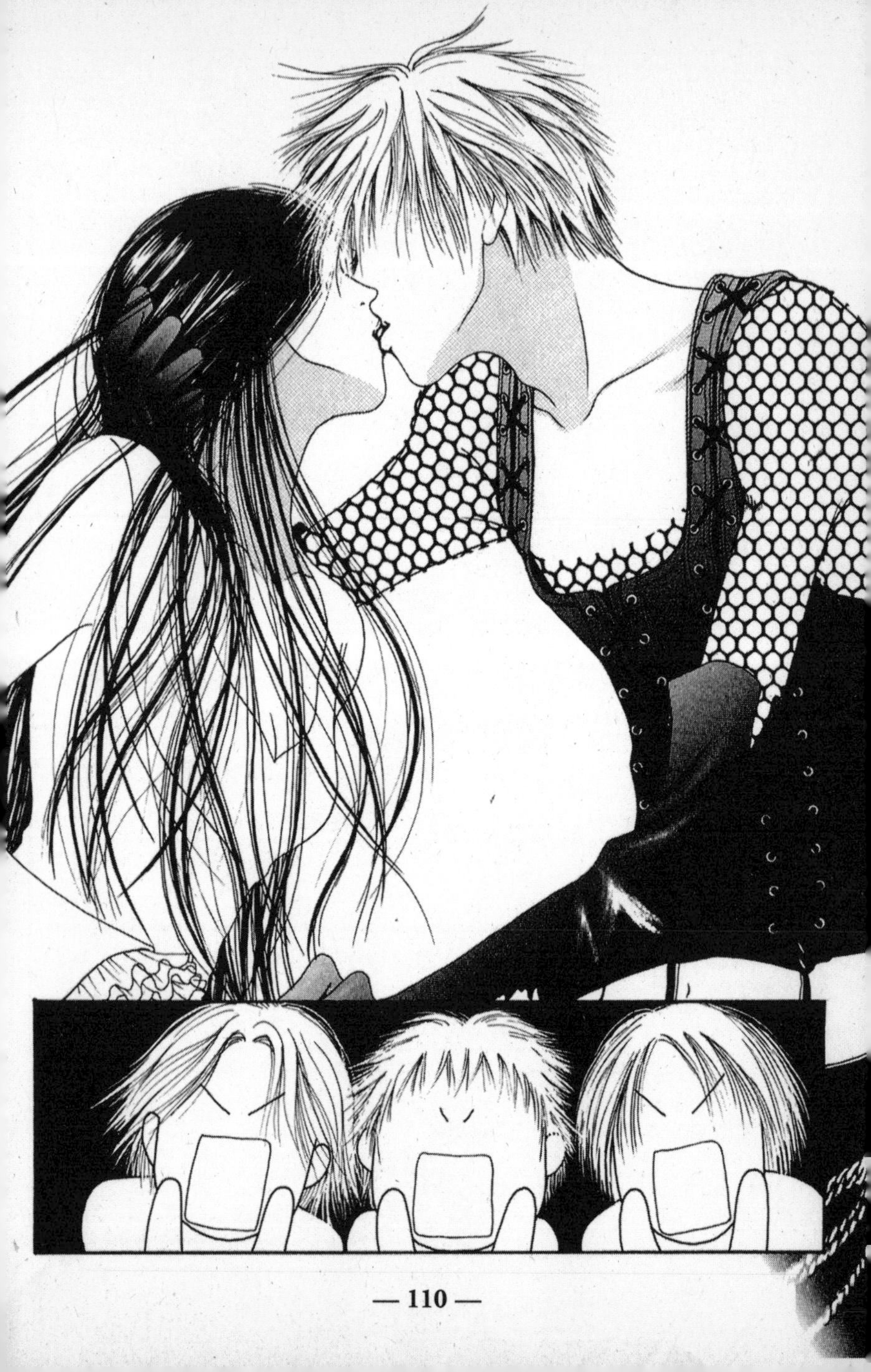

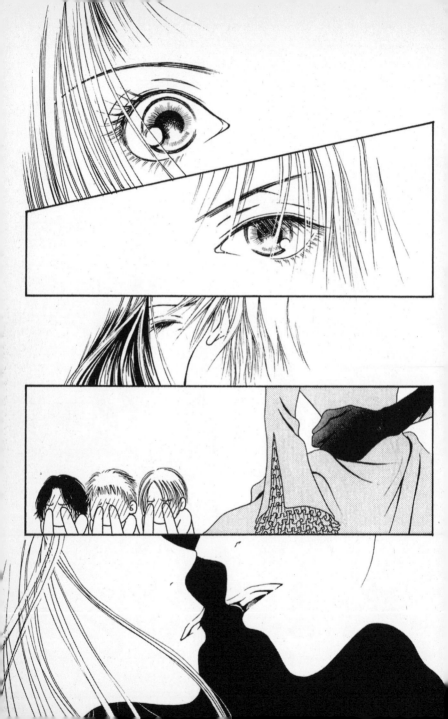

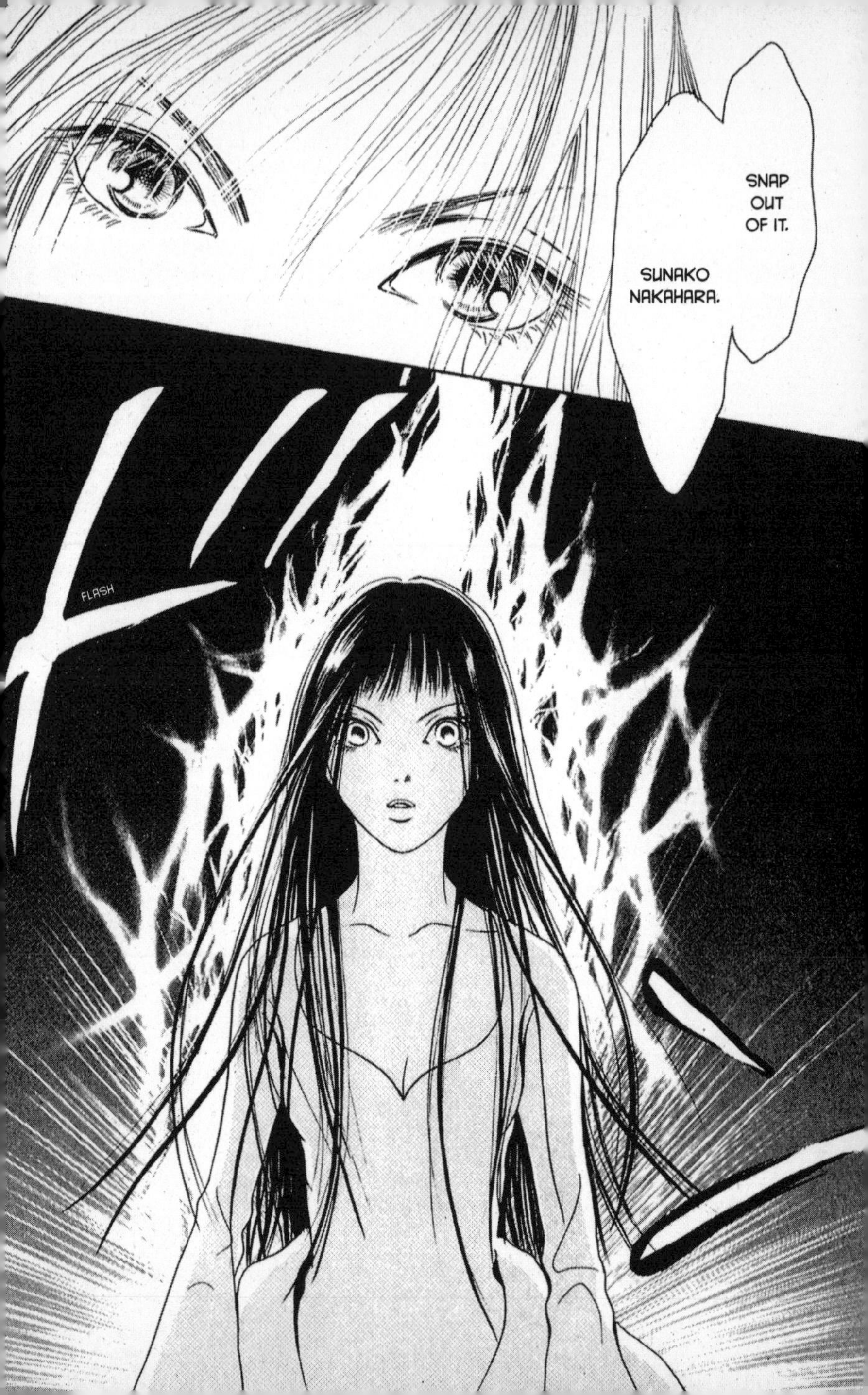
SNAP OUT OF IT.
SUNAKO NAKAHARA.
FLASH

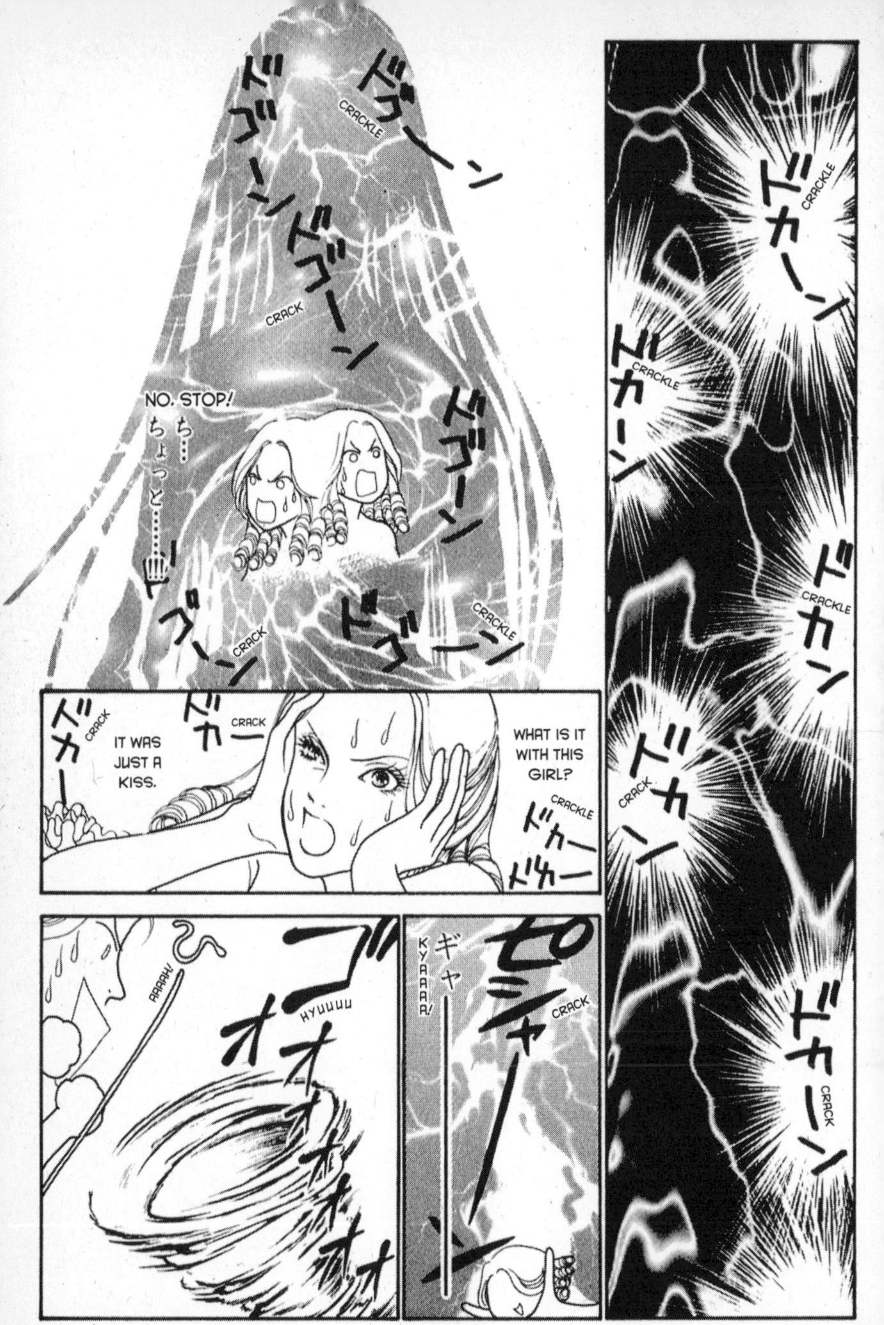
ドカーン
CRACKLE
ドカーン
CRACKLE
ドカン
CRACKLE
ドカーン
CRACK
ドカーン
CRACK
ドゴーン
CRACKLE
ドゴーン
ドゴーン
CRACK
ドゴーン
NO. STOP!
ち…ちょっと……
ドゴーン
CRACKLE
ドブーン
CRACK
WHAT IS IT WITH THIS GIRL?
CRACKLE
ドカー
ドカー
IT WAS JUST A KISS.
ドカー
CRACK
ドカー
CRACK
ピシャーン
CRACK
ギャ
KYAAAA!
ゴオオオオオ
HYUUUU
AAAAH!
ひ

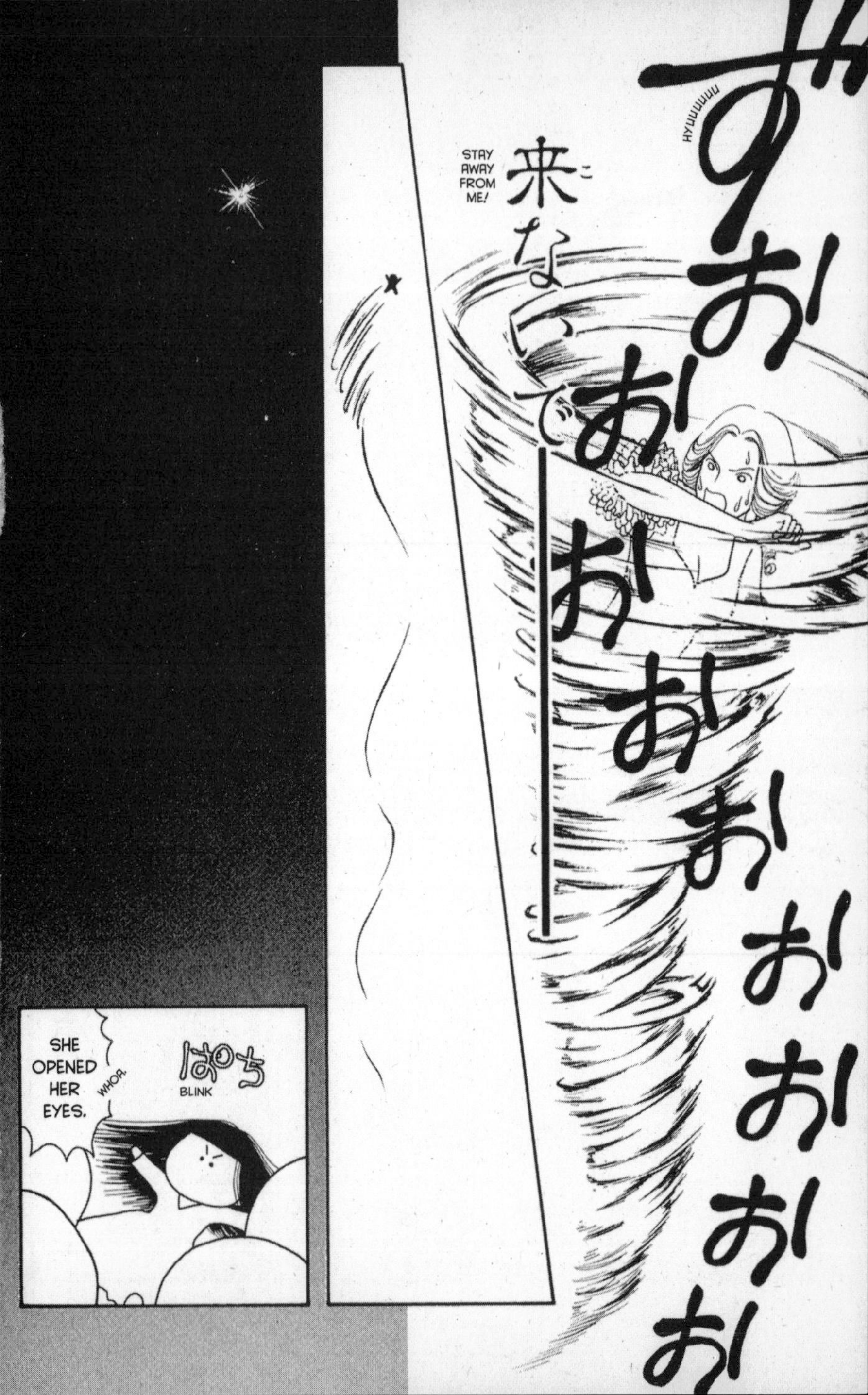
おおおおおおおおお
HYUUUUNNN
来ないで——
STAY AWAY FROM ME!
SHE OPENED HER EYES.
WHOA.
ぱちっ
BLINK

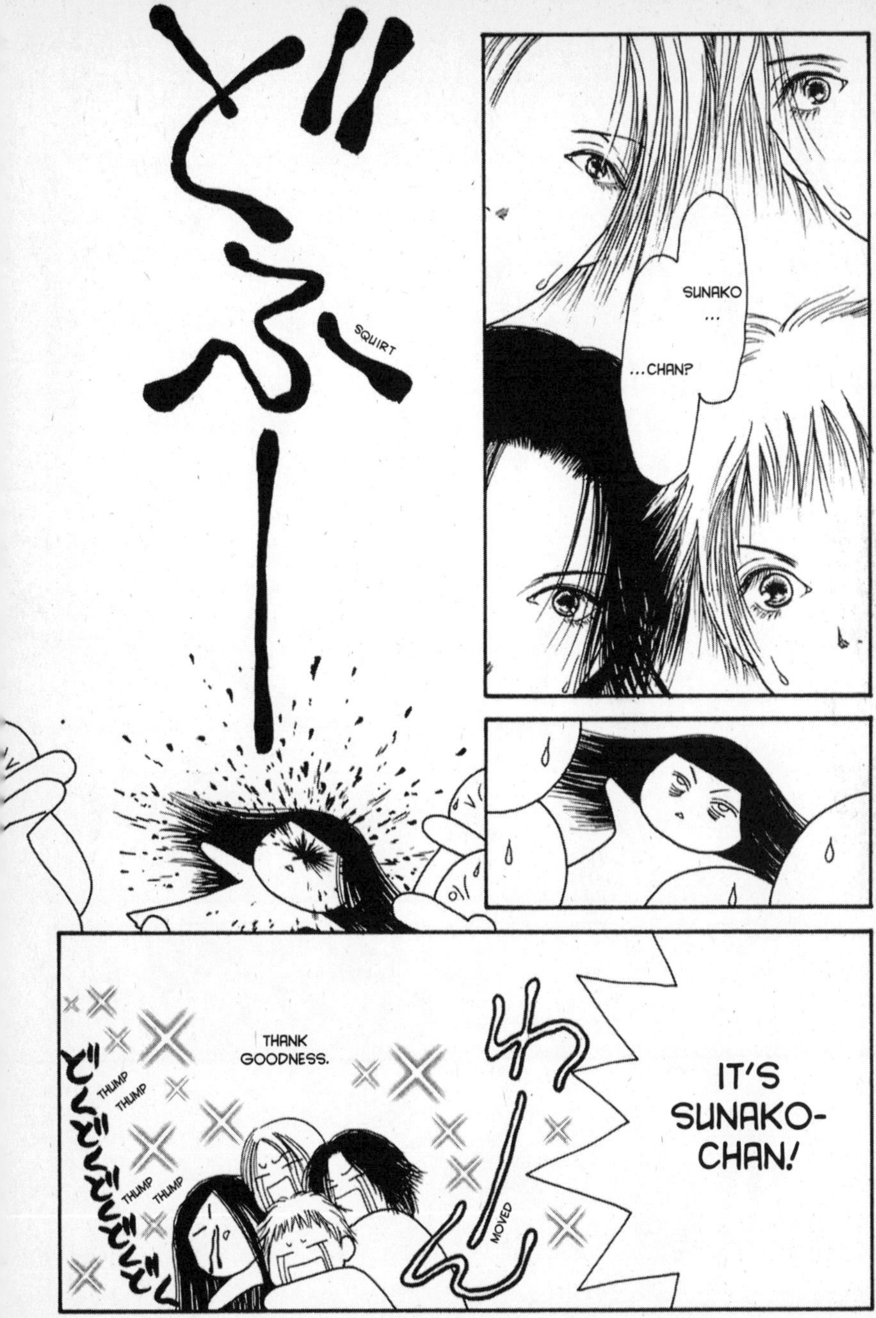
SUNAKO ... ...CHAN?
SQUIRT
IT'S SUNAKO-CHAN!
MOVED
THANK GOODNESS.
THUMP THUMP
THUMP THUMP

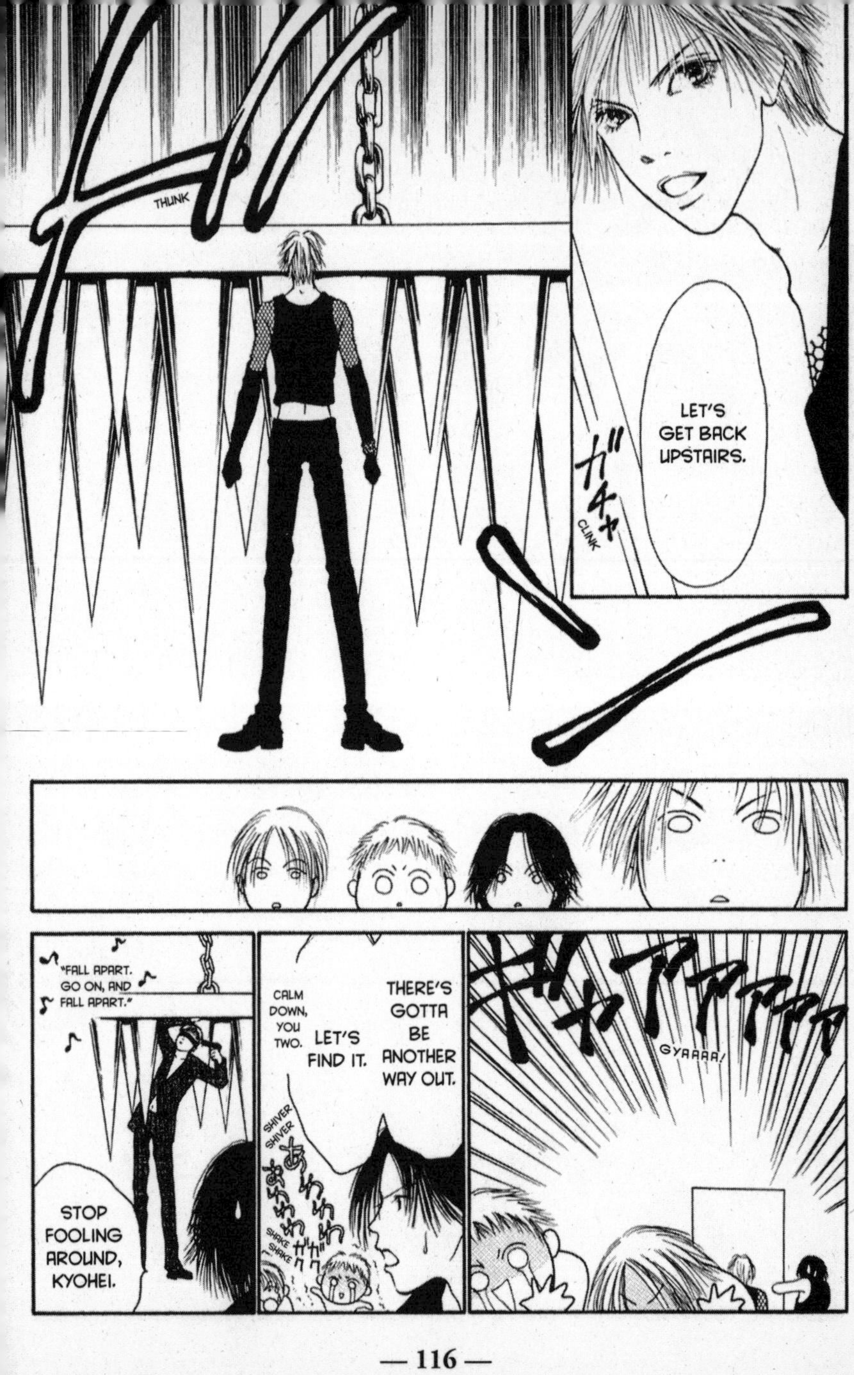
LET'S GET BACK UPSTAIRS.
ガチャ
CLINK
THUNK
GYAAAA!
THERE'S GOTTA BE ANOTHER WAY OUT.
LET'S FIND IT.
CALM DOWN, YOU TWO.
SHIVER SHIVER
SHAKE SHAKE
"FALL APART. GO ON, AND FALL APART."
STOP FOOLING AROUND, KYOHEI.

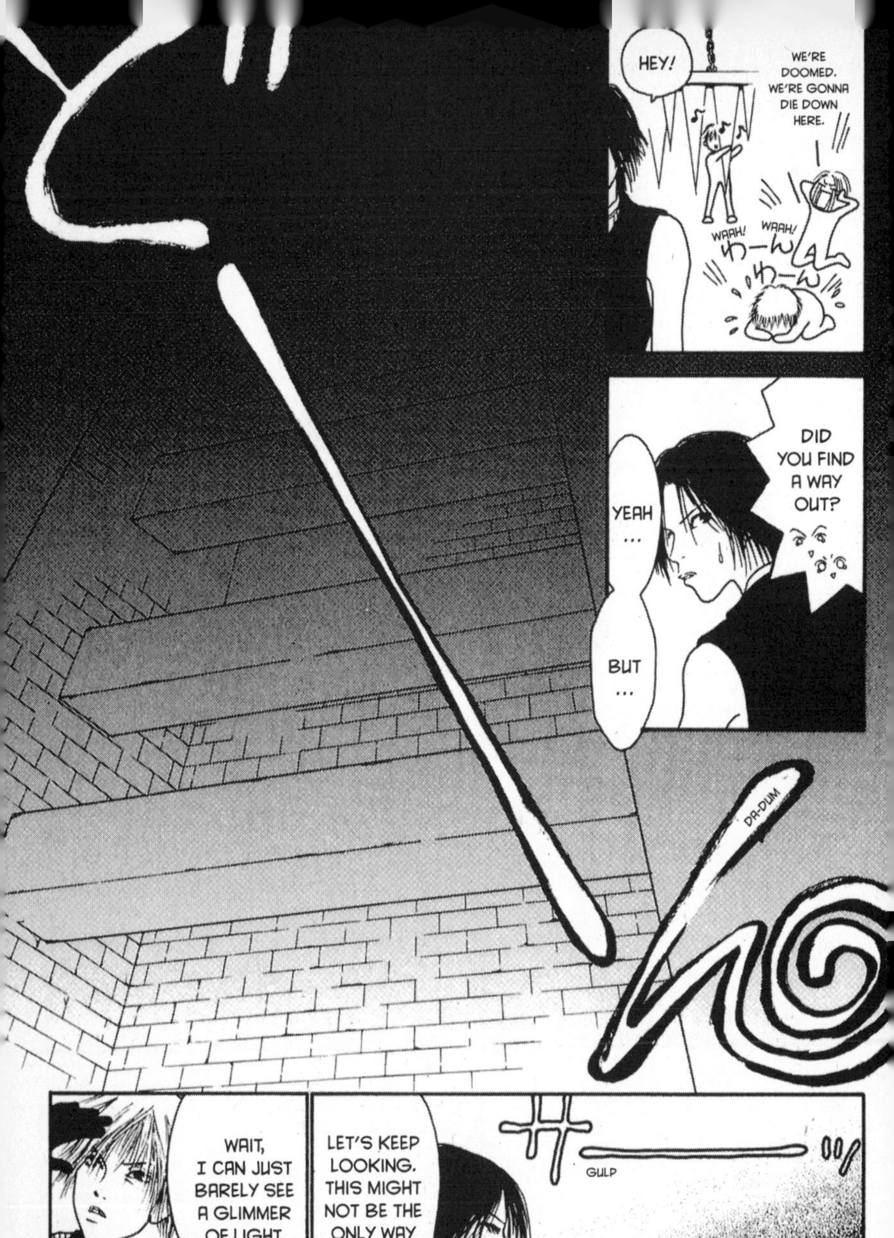
WE'RE DOOMED. WE'RE GONNA DIE DOWN HERE.
HEY!
WAAH! WAAH!
わーん
わーん
DID YOU FIND A WAY OUT?
YEAH ...
BUT ...
DA-DUM
LET'S KEEP LOOKING. THIS MIGHT NOT BE THE ONLY WAY OUT.
GULP
WAIT, I CAN JUST BARELY SEE A GLIMMER OF LIGHT.

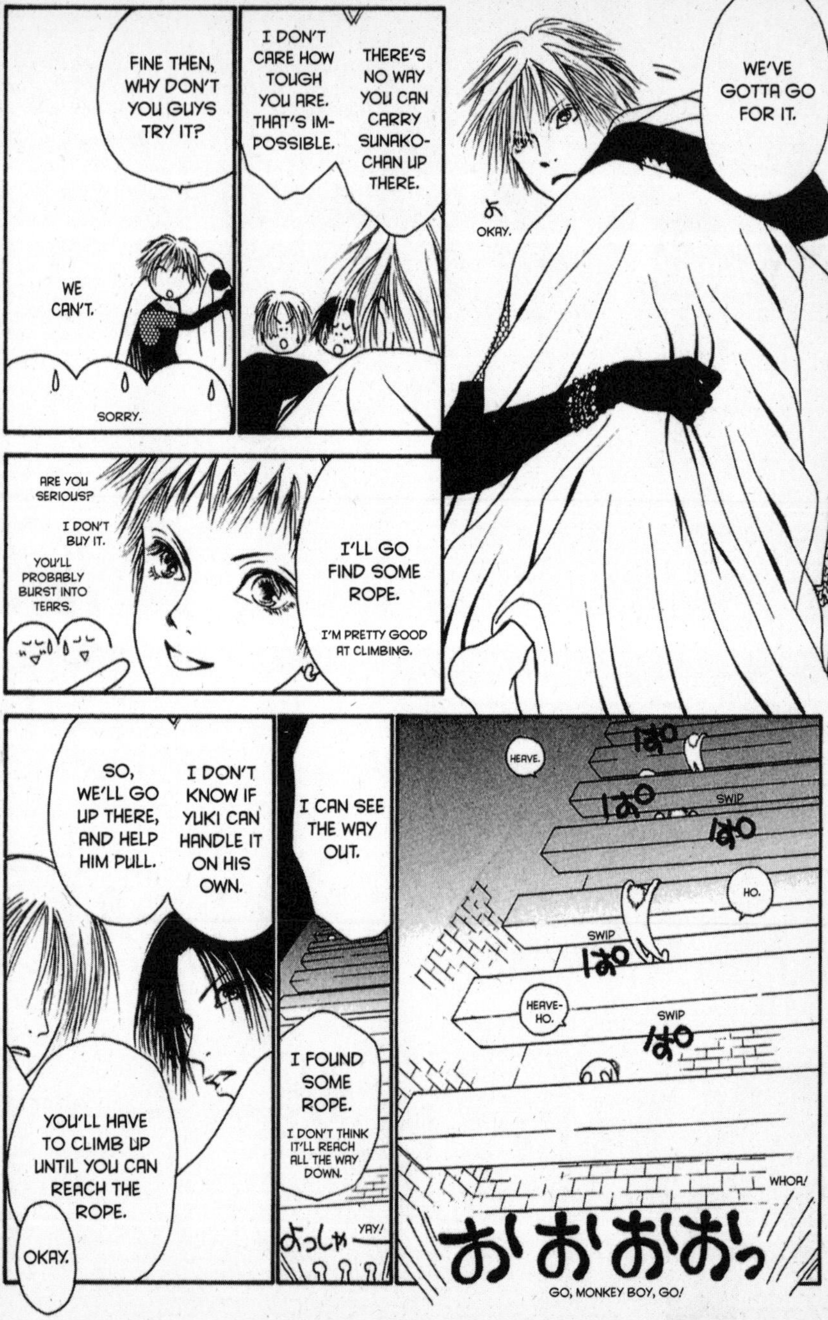
WE'VE GOTTA GO FOR IT.
OKAY.
THERE'S NO WAY YOU CAN CARRY SUNAKO-CHAN UP THERE.
I DON'T CARE HOW TOUGH YOU ARE. THAT'S IM-POSSIBLE.
FINE THEN, WHY DON'T YOU GUYS TRY IT?
WE CAN'T.
SORRY.
I'LL GO FIND SOME ROPE.
I'M PRETTY GOOD AT CLIMBING.
ARE YOU SERIOUS?
I DON'T BUY IT.
YOU'LL PROBABLY BURST INTO TEARS.
HEAVE.
SWIP
HO.
SWIP
HEAVE-HO.
SWIP
WHOA!
GO, MONKEY BOY, GO!
I CAN SEE THE WAY OUT.
I FOUND SOME ROPE.
I DON'T THINK IT'LL REACH ALL THE WAY DOWN.
YAY!
I DON'T KNOW IF YUKI CAN HANDLE IT ON HIS OWN.
SO, WE'LL GO UP THERE, AND HELP HIM PULL.
YOU'LL HAVE TO CLIMB UP UNTIL YOU CAN REACH THE ROPE.
OKAY.

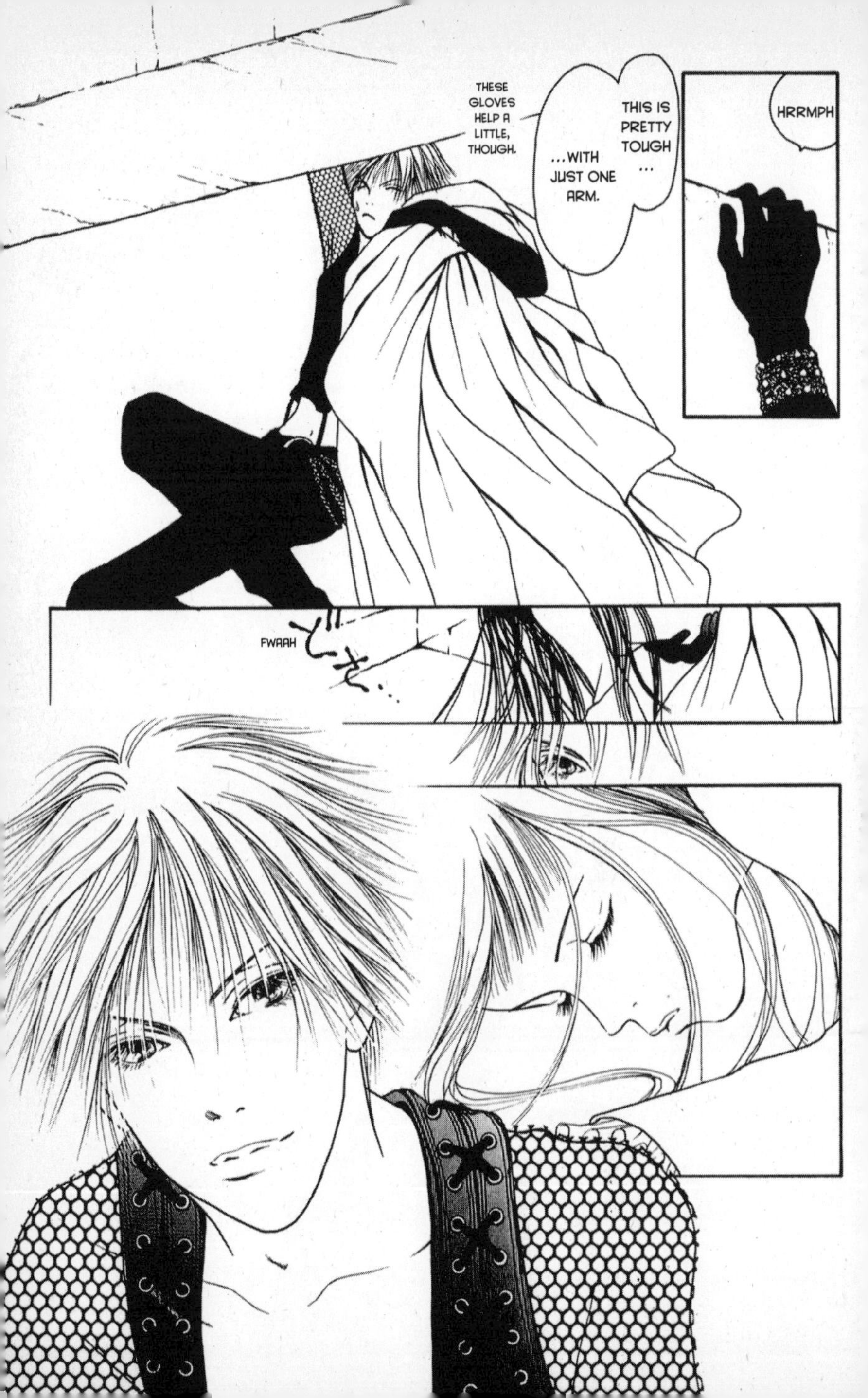
HRRMPH
THIS IS PRETTY TOUGH ...
...WITH JUST ONE ARM.
THESE GLOVES HELP A LITTLE, THOUGH.
FWAAH

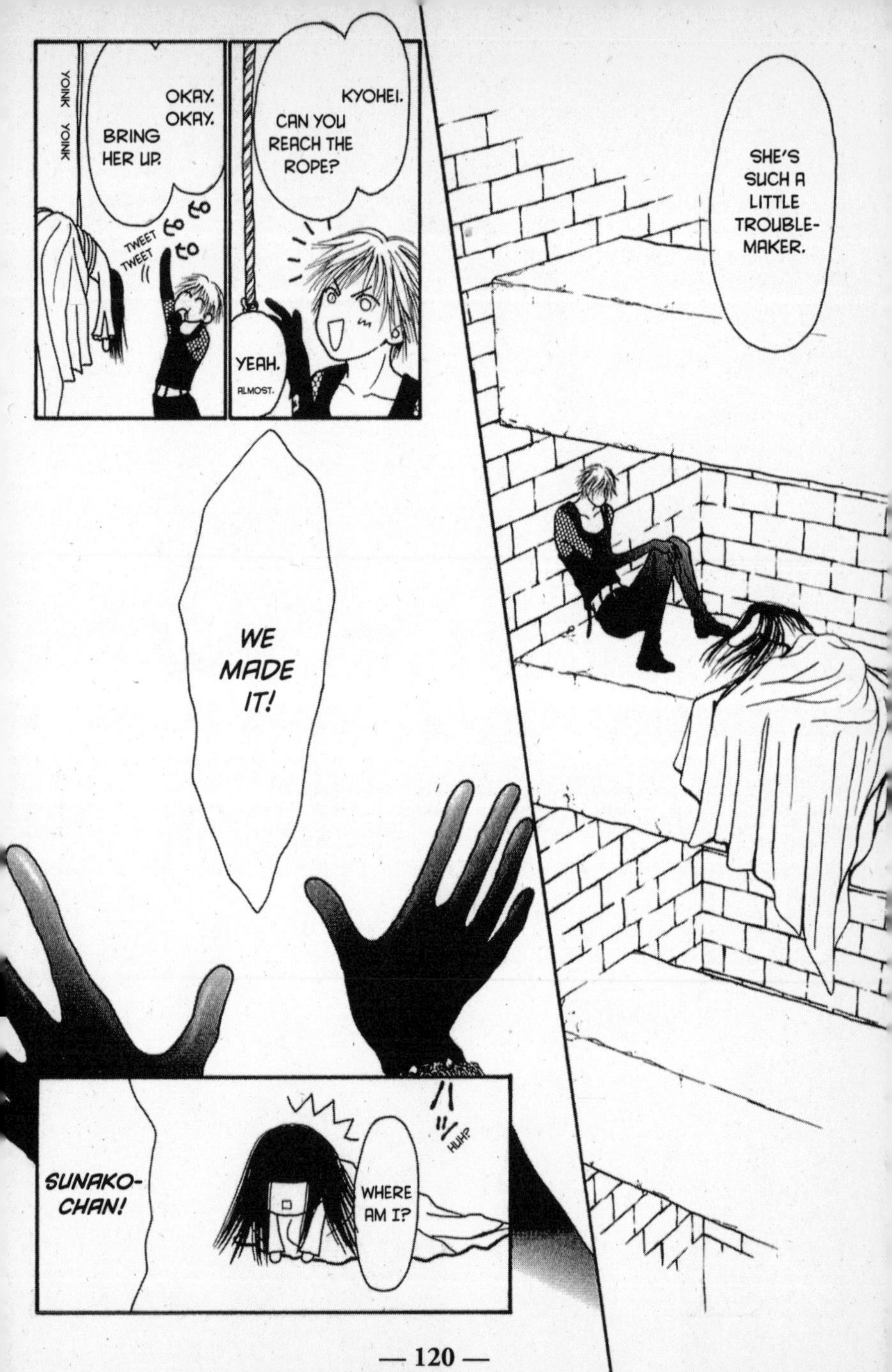
SHE'S SUCH A LITTLE TROUBLE-MAKER.
KYOHEI. CAN YOU REACH THE ROPE?
YEAH. ALMOST.
OKAY. OKAY. BRING HER UP.
TWEET TWEET
YOINK YOINK
WE MADE IT!
HUH?
WHERE AM I?
SUNAKO-CHAN!

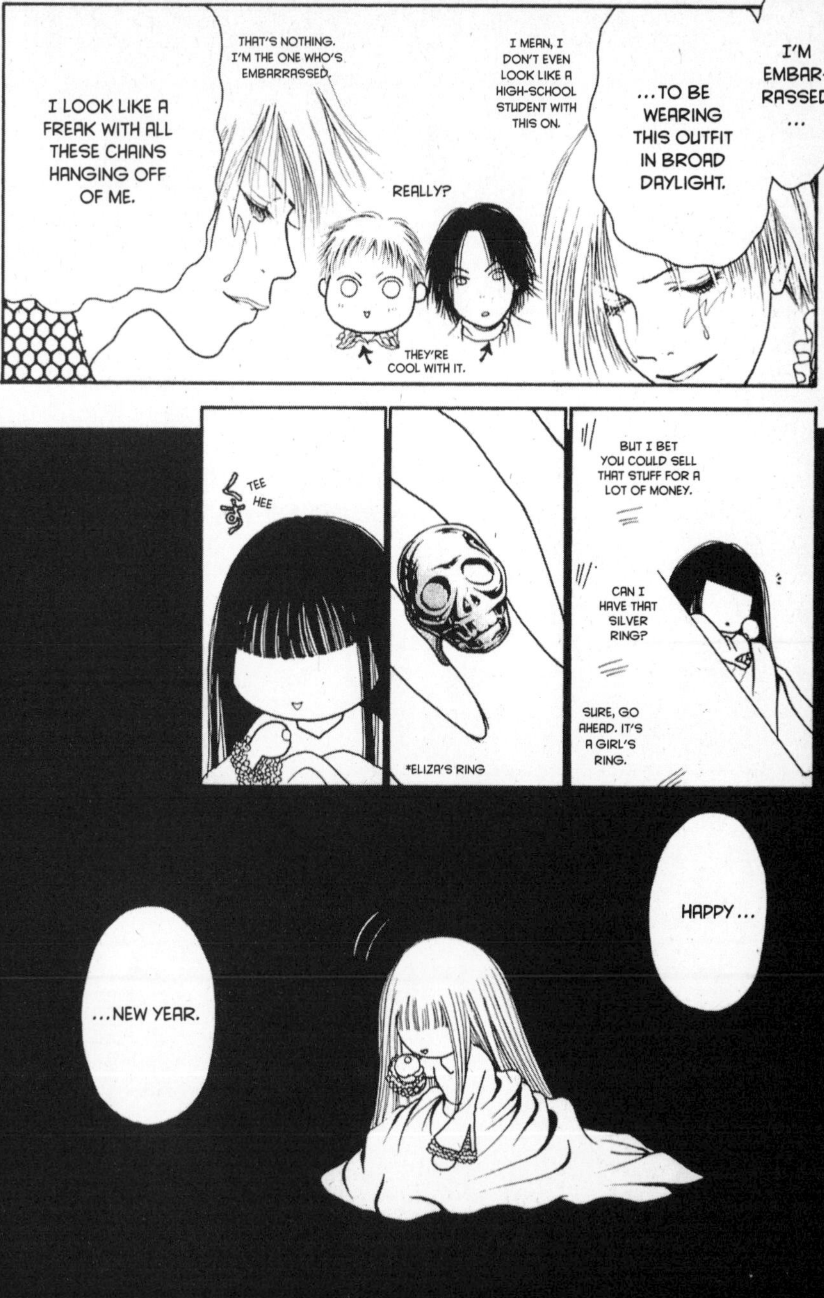
I'M EMBARRASSED...
...TO BE WEARING THIS OUTFIT IN BROAD DAYLIGHT.
I MEAN, I DON'T EVEN LOOK LIKE A HIGH-SCHOOL STUDENT WITH THIS ON.
THAT'S NOTHING. I'M THE ONE WHO'S EMBARRASSED.
I LOOK LIKE A FREAK WITH ALL THESE CHAINS HANGING OFF OF ME.
REALLY?
THEY'RE COOL WITH IT.
BUT I BET YOU COULD SELL THAT STUFF FOR A LOT OF MONEY.
CAN I HAVE THAT SILVER RING?
SURE, GO AHEAD. IT'S A GIRL'S RING.
*ELIZA'S RING
TEE HEE
HAPPY...
...NEW YEAR.

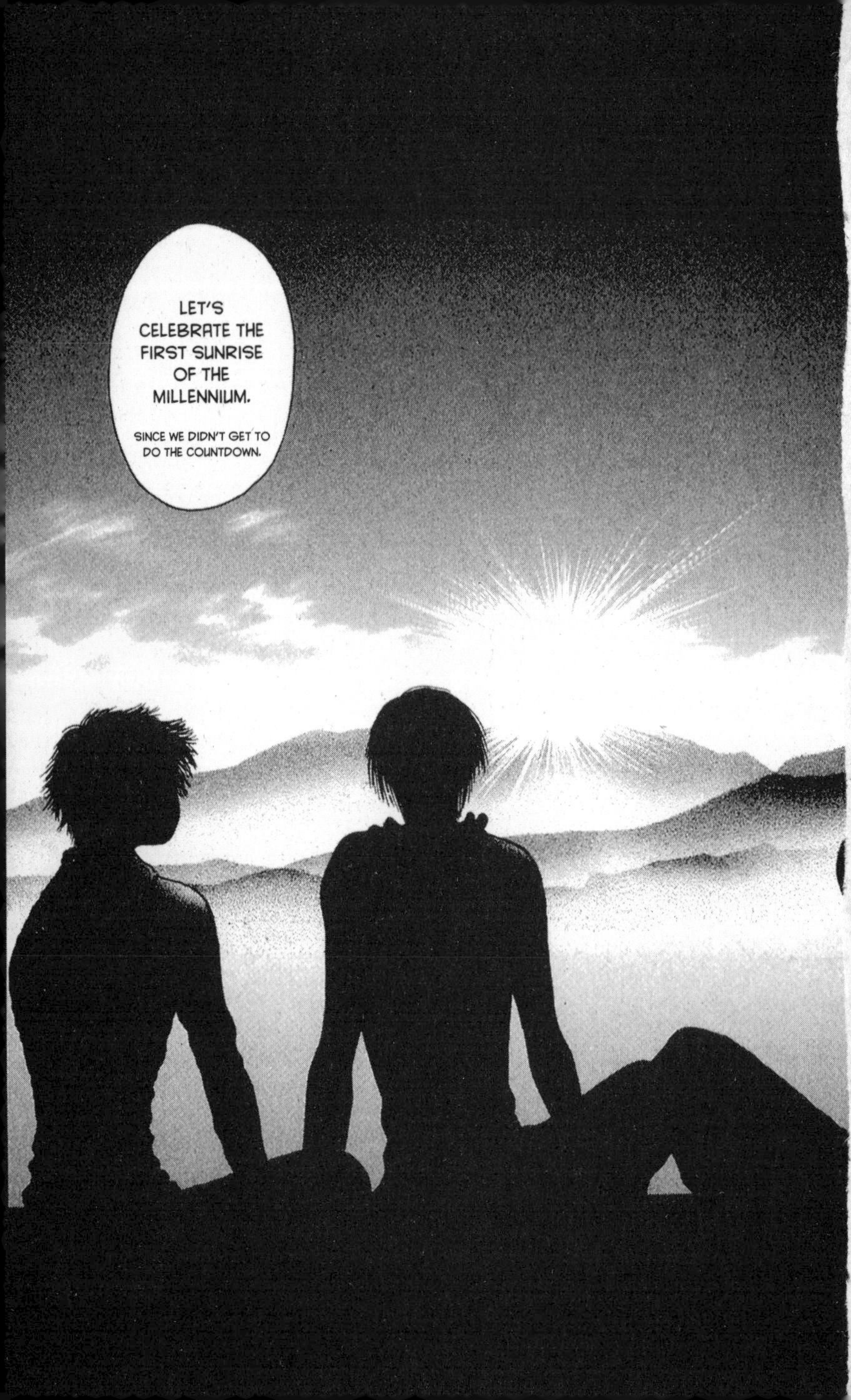
LET'S CELEBRATE THE FIRST SUNRISE OF THE MILLENNIUM.
SINCE WE DIDN'T GET TO DO THE COUNTDOWN.

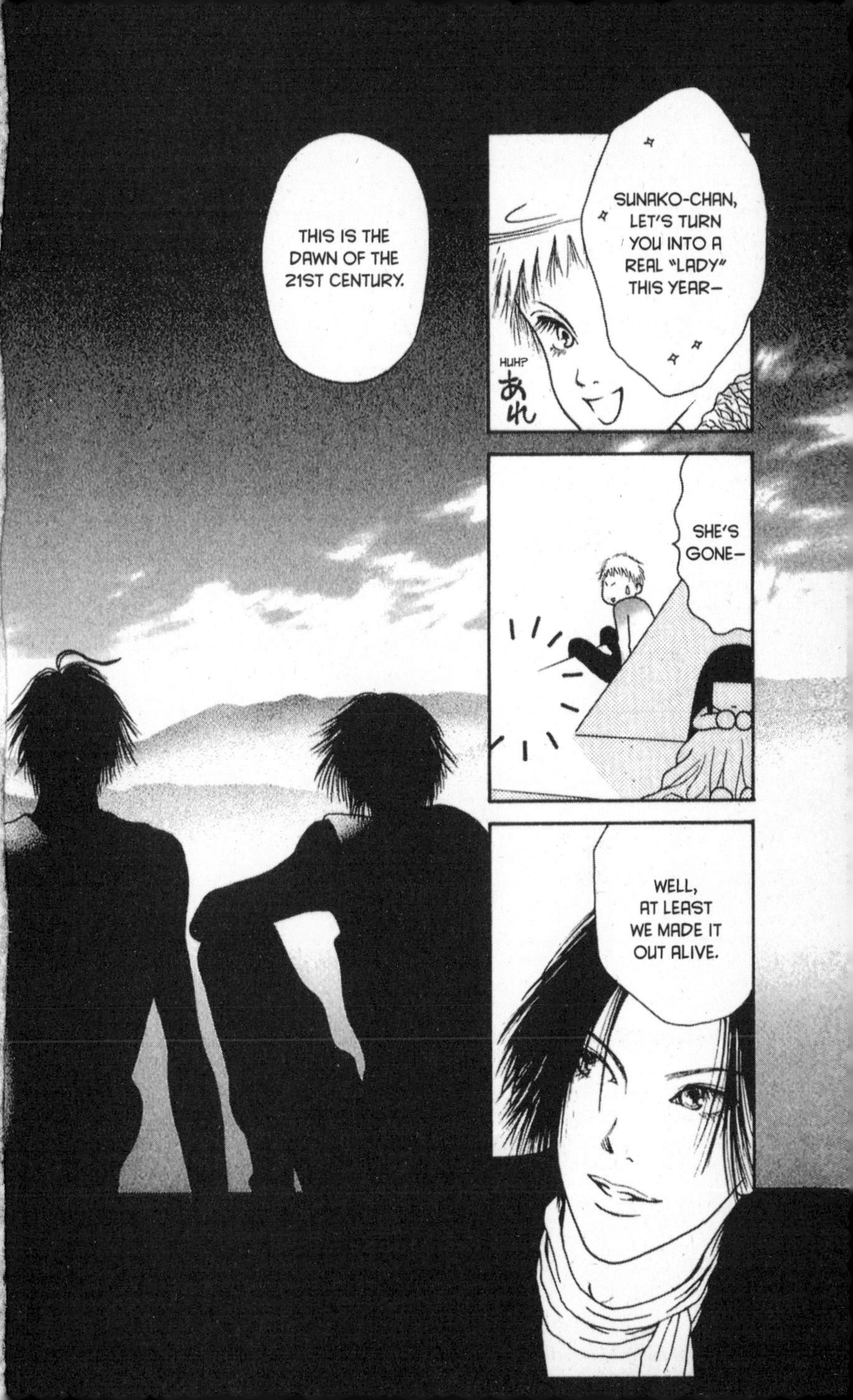
SUNAKO-CHAN, LET'S TURN YOU INTO A REAL "LADY" THIS YEAR—
HUH?
あれ
SHE'S GONE—
WELL, AT LEAST WE MADE IT OUT ALIVE.
THIS IS THE DAWN OF THE 21ST CENTURY.

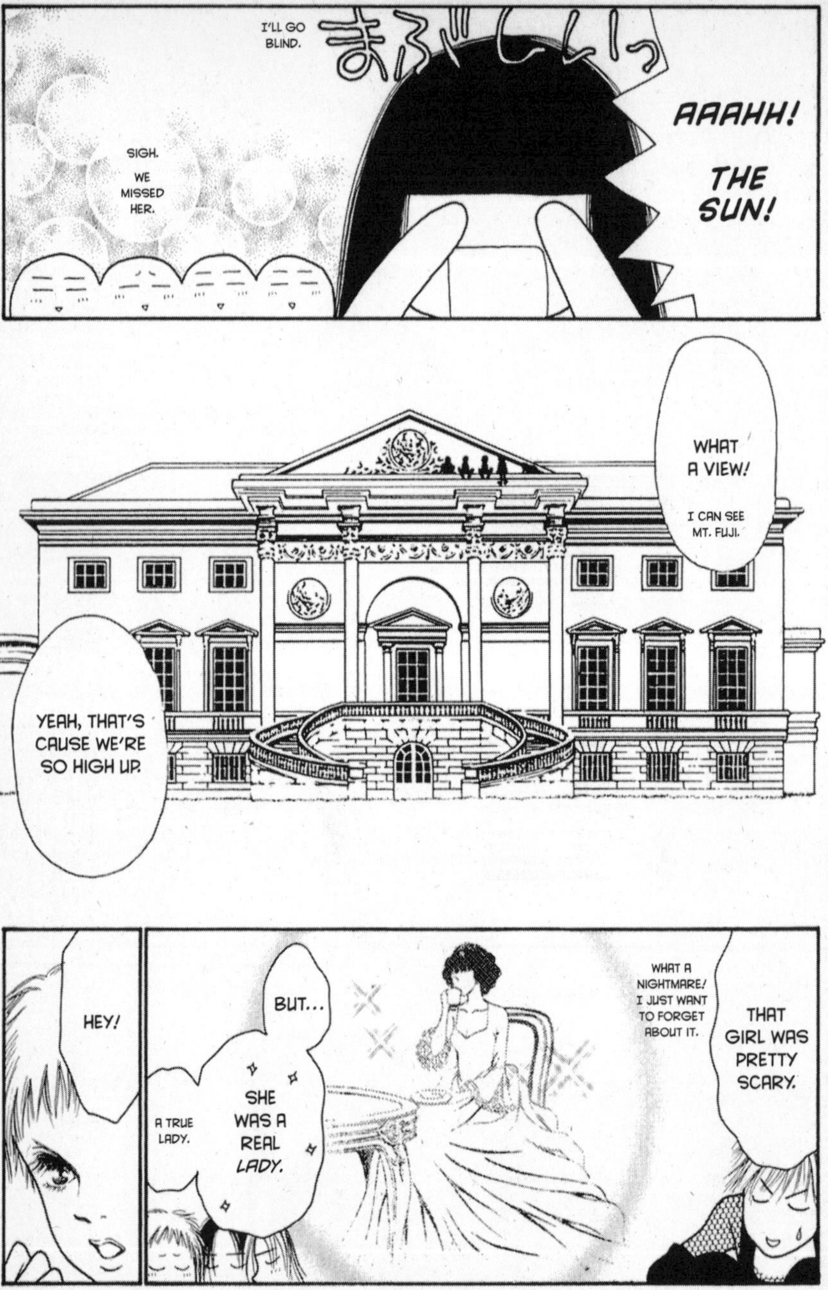
AAAHH!
THE SUN!
I'LL GO BLIND.
SIGH.
WE MISSED HER.
WHAT A VIEW!
I CAN SEE MT. FUJI.
YEAH, THAT'S CAUSE WE'RE SO HIGH UP.
THAT GIRL WAS PRETTY SCARY.
WHAT A NIGHTMARE! I JUST WANT TO FORGET ABOUT IT.
BUT...
SHE WAS A REAL *LADY.*
A TRUE LADY.
HEY!

Chapter 9
Blood-Splatteringly Steamy Love at the Hot Springs
PART 1

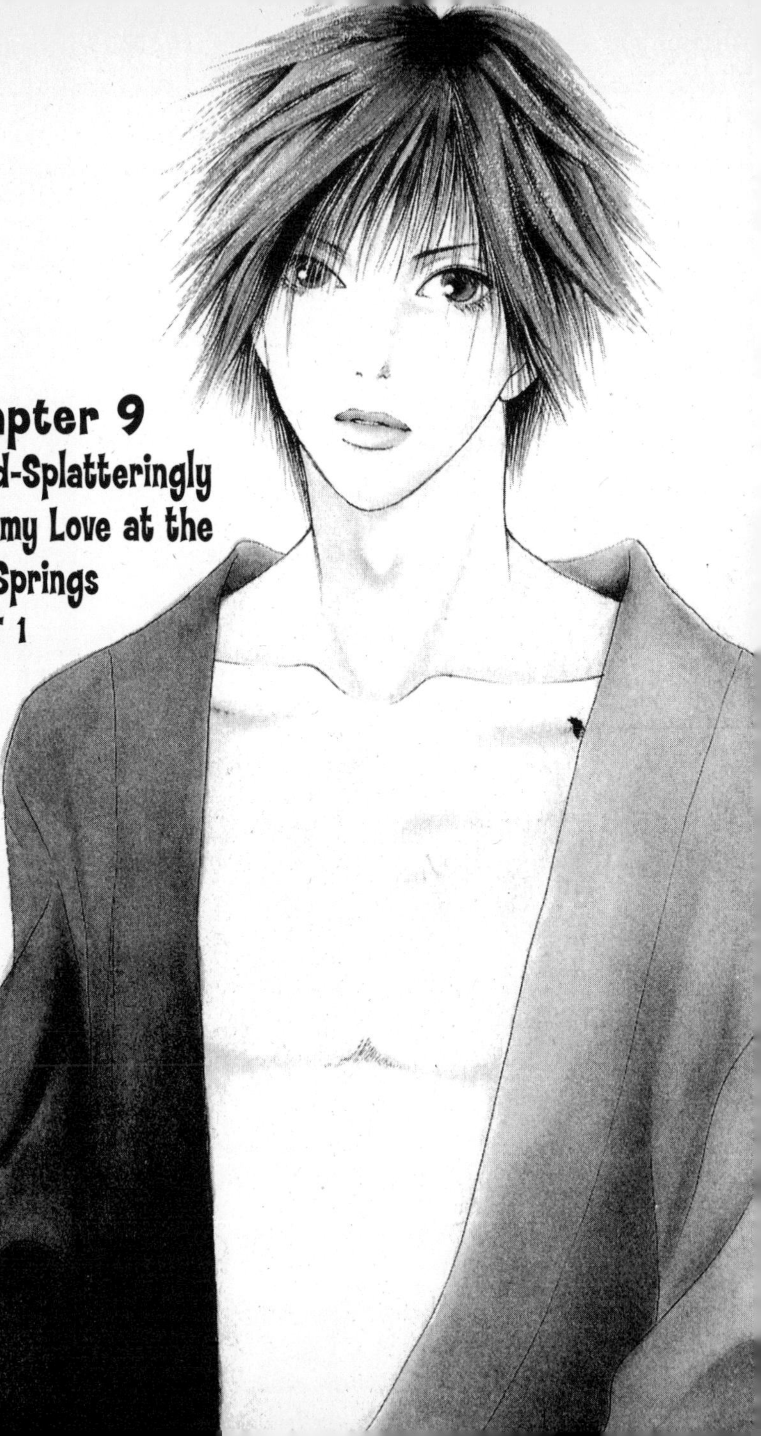

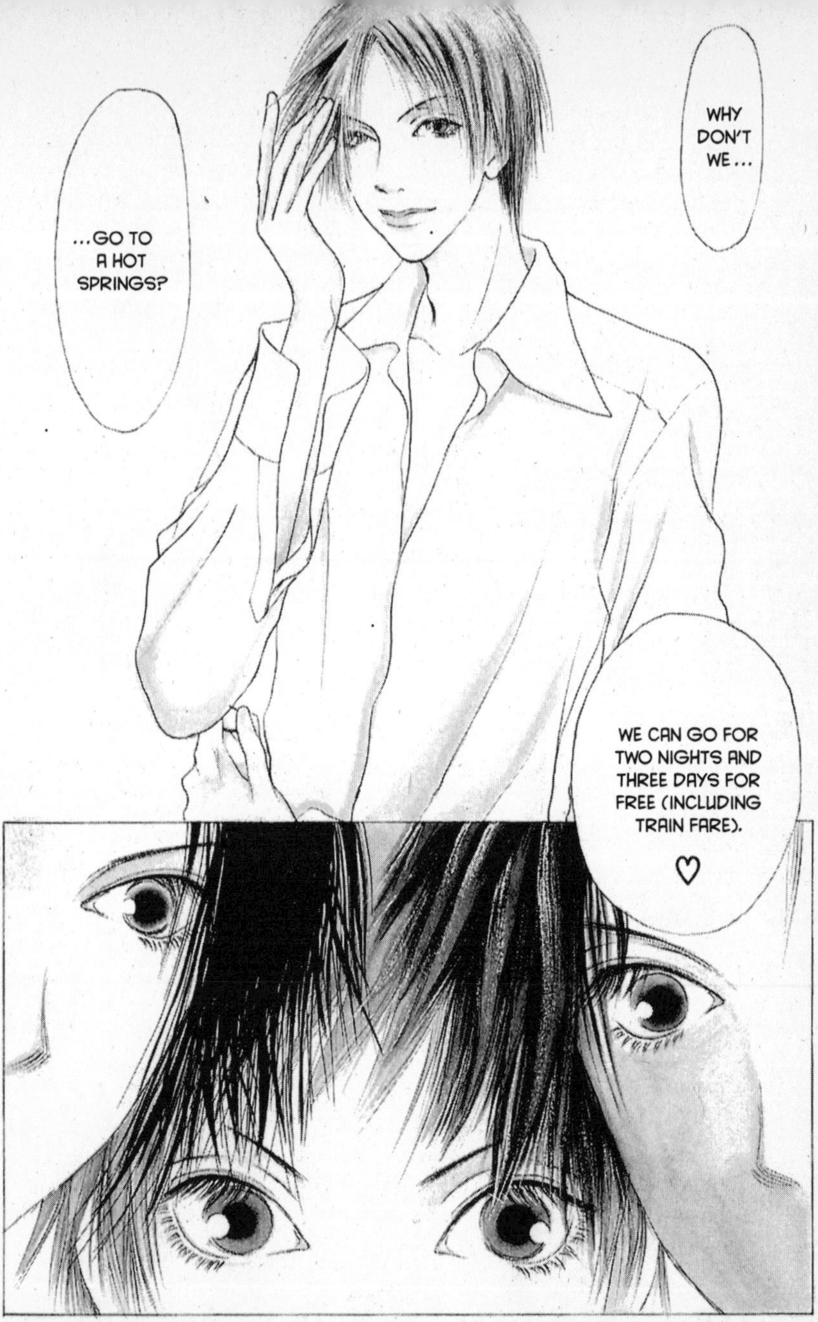
WHY DON'T WE...
...GO TO A HOT SPRINGS?
WE CAN GO FOR TWO NIGHTS AND THREE DAYS FOR FREE (INCLUDING TRAIN FARE). ♡

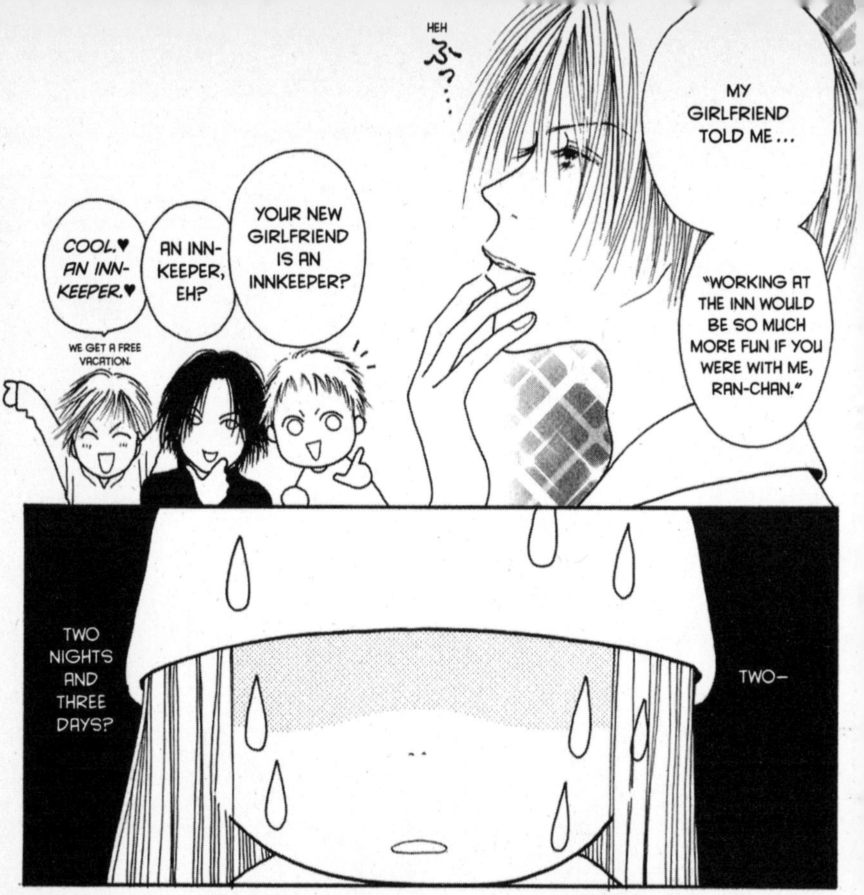
MY GIRLFRIEND TOLD ME...
HEH
ふ
"WORKING AT THE INN WOULD BE SO MUCH MORE FUN IF YOU WERE WITH ME, RAN-CHAN."
YOUR NEW GIRLFRIEND IS AN INNKEEPER?
AN INN-KEEPER, EH?
COOL.♥ AN INN-KEEPER.♥
WE GET A FREE VACATION.
TWO—
TWO NIGHTS AND THREE DAYS?

BEHIND THE SCENES

WHILE I WAS WRITING THIS STORY, I WANTED TO GO TO A HOT SPRINGS SO BADLY. (I ENDED UP NOT BEING ABLE TO GO, BUT ...) I STILL REALLY WANNA GO. YEAH. HOT SPRINGS ROCK!

YEAH. I WENT TO A HOT SPRINGS IN THE SUMMER, AND THE INNKEEPER WAS A REAL BITCH. (WE FOUGHT.)

I WAS ACTUALLY GONNA MAKE THIS STORY ABOUT AN UGLY INNKEEPER VS. A BEAUTIFUL MAID. I ENDED UP NOT USING THAT ELEMENT IN THE STORY, SO I MADE HER BEAUTIFUL INSTEAD. IF SHE WERE AN UGLY INNKEEPER, I WOULD'VE NAMED HER "YUKO." THAT'S RIGHT, I'M TALKING ABOUT YOU, YUKO! I'M NEVER GOING BACK THERE. THE MAID WAS REALLY NICE, AND SO WAS THE GIRL AT THE FRONT DESK.

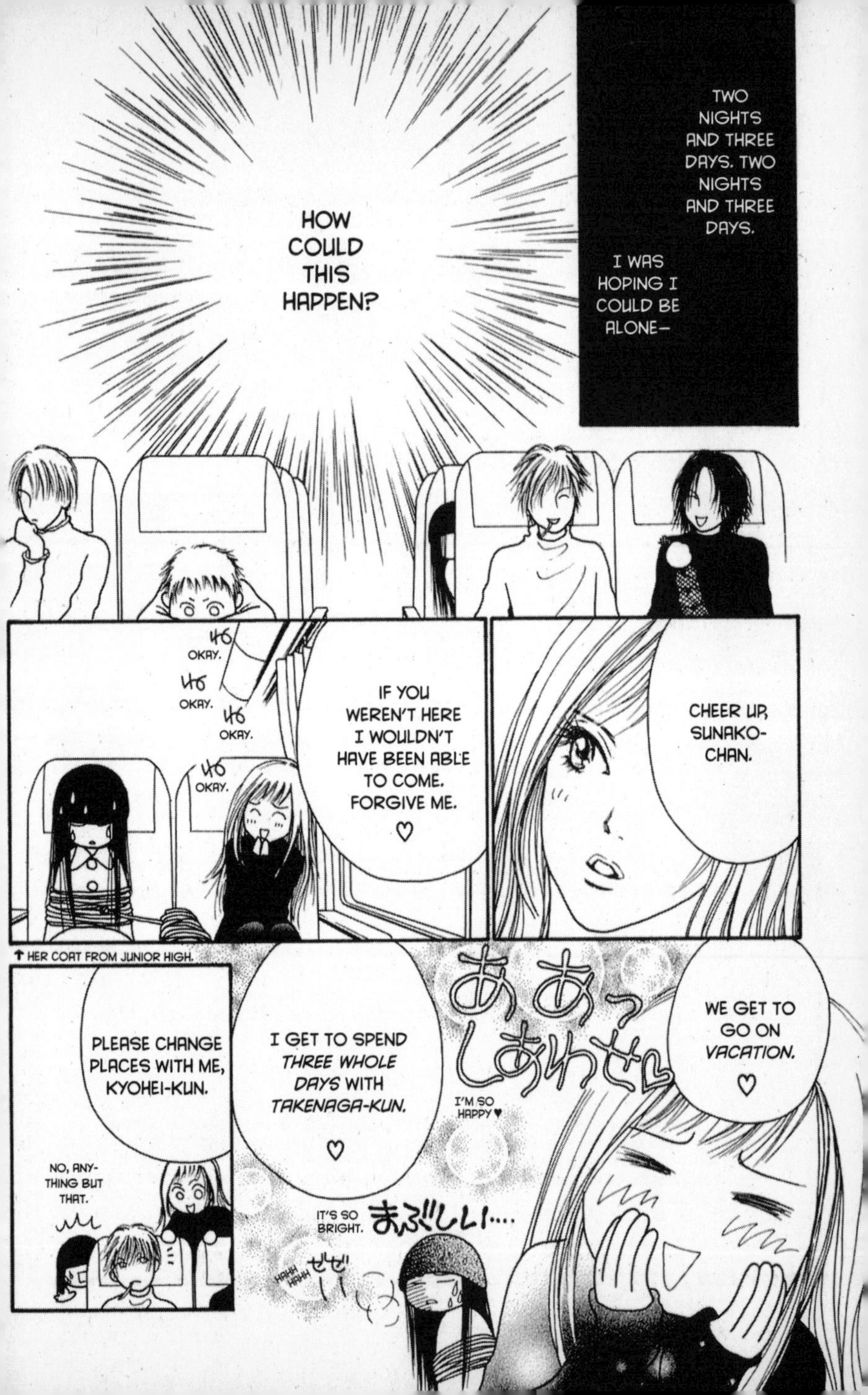
TWO NIGHTS AND THREE DAYS. TWO NIGHTS AND THREE DAYS.
I WAS HOPING I COULD BE ALONE—
HOW COULD THIS HAPPEN?
CHEER UP, SUNAKO-CHAN.
IF YOU WEREN'T HERE I WOULDN'T HAVE BEEN ABLE TO COME. FORGIVE ME. ♡
OKAY.
OKAY.
OKAY.
OKAY.
↑ HER COAT FROM JUNIOR HIGH.
WE GET TO GO ON *VACATION.* ♡
ああっしあわせ♡
I'M SO HAPPY♥
I GET TO SPEND *THREE WHOLE DAYS* WITH *TAKENAGA-KUN.* ♡
まぶしい…
IT'S SO BRIGHT.
ぜぜ
HAHH HAHH
PLEASE CHANGE PLACES WITH ME, KYOHEI-KUN.
NO, ANY-THING BUT THAT.

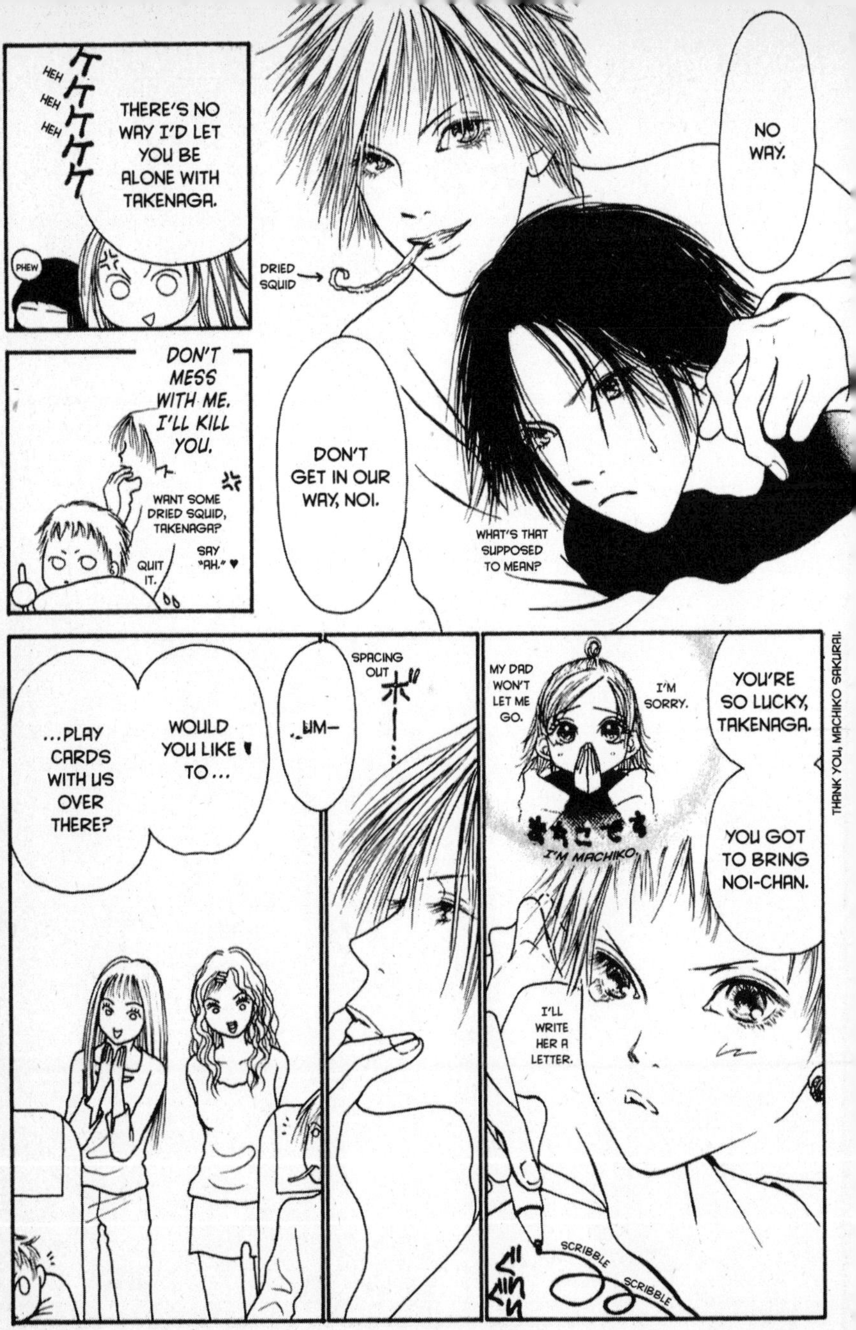
NO WAY.
DRIED SQUID
DON'T GET IN OUR WAY, NOI.
WHAT'S THAT SUPPOSED TO MEAN?
HEH HEH HEH
THERE'S NO WAY I'D LET YOU BE ALONE WITH TAKENAGA.
PHEW
DON'T MESS WITH ME. I'LL KILL YOU.
WANT SOME DRIED SQUID, TAKENAGA?
SAY "AH." ♥
QUIT IT.
YOU'RE SO LUCKY, TAKENAGA.
YOU GOT TO BRING NOI-CHAN.
I'M SORRY.
MY DAD WON'T LET ME GO.
I'M MACHIKO.
I'LL WRITE HER A LETTER.
SCRIBBLE
SCRIBBLE
SPACING OUT
UM—
WOULD YOU LIKE TO...
...PLAY CARDS WITH US OVER THERE?

THANK YOU, MACHIKO SAKURAI.

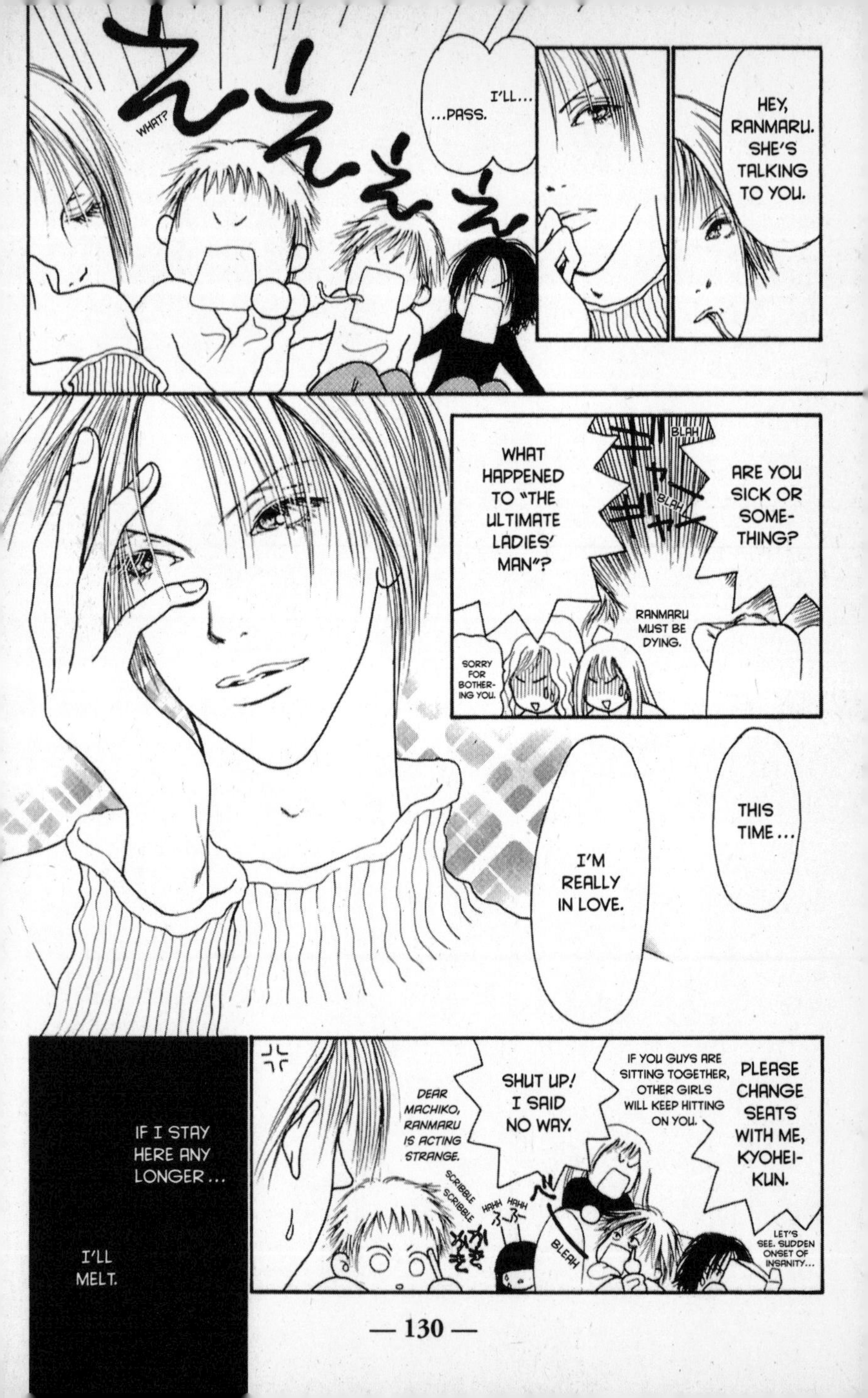
HEY, RANMARU. SHE'S TALKING TO YOU.
I'LL... ...PASS.
WHAT?
ARE YOU SICK OR SOME-THING?
BLAH BLAH
WHAT HAPPENED TO "THE ULTIMATE LADIES' MAN"?
RANMARU MUST BE DYING.
SORRY FOR BOTHER-ING YOU.
THIS TIME...
I'M REALLY IN LOVE.
PLEASE CHANGE SEATS WITH ME, KYOHEI-KUN.
IF YOU GUYS ARE SITTING TOGETHER, OTHER GIRLS WILL KEEP HITTING ON YOU.
LET'S SEE. SUDDEN ONSET OF INSANITY...
SHUT UP! I SAID NO WAY.
BLEAH
HAHH HAHH
DEAR MACHIKO, RANMARU IS ACTING STRANGE.
SCRIBBLE SCRIBBLE
IF I STAY HERE ANY LONGER...
I'LL MELT.

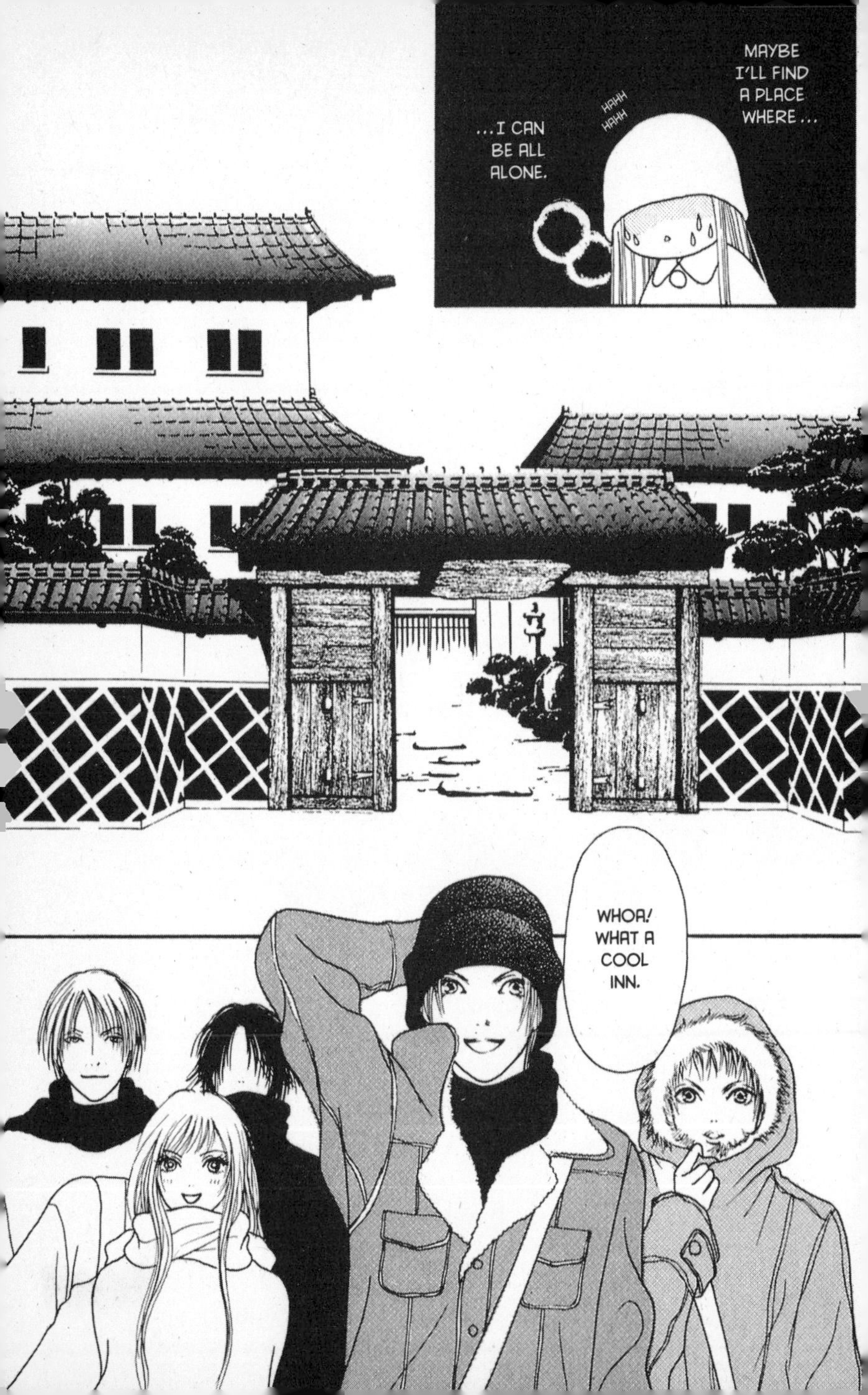
MAYBE I'LL FIND A PLACE WHERE...
HAHH HAHH
...I CAN BE ALL ALONE.
WHOA! WHAT A COOL INN.

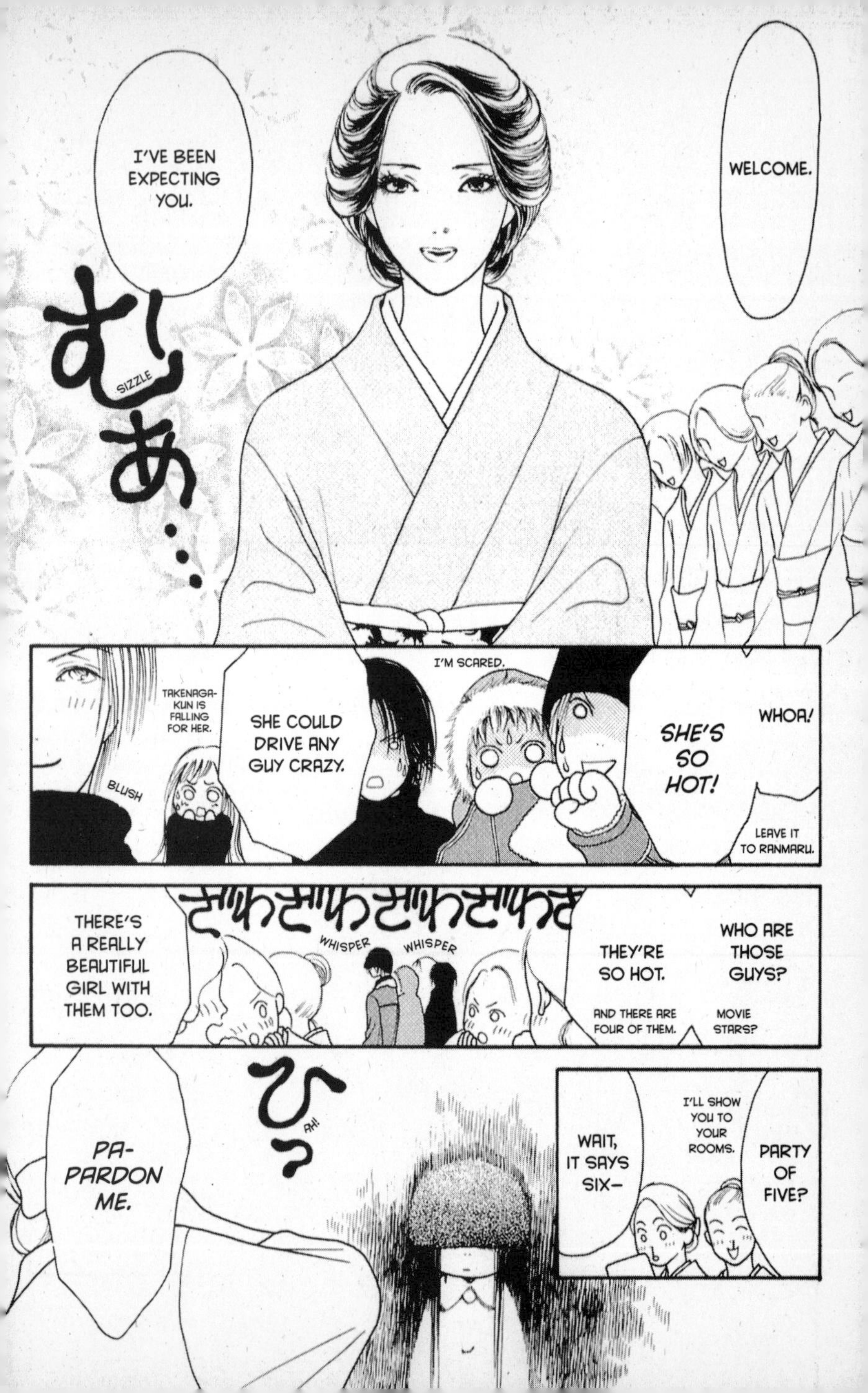
WELCOME.
I'VE BEEN EXPECTING YOU.
むあ…
SIZZLE
WHOA!
SHE'S SO HOT!
LEAVE IT TO RANMARU.
I'M SCARED.
SHE COULD DRIVE ANY GUY CRAZY.
TAKENAGA-KUN IS FALLING FOR HER.
BLUSH
WHO ARE THOSE GUYS?
MOVIE STARS?
THEY'RE SO HOT.
AND THERE ARE FOUR OF THEM.
ざわざわざわざわざ
WHISPER WHISPER
THERE'S A REALLY BEAUTIFUL GIRL WITH THEM TOO.
PARTY OF FIVE?
I'LL SHOW YOU TO YOUR ROOMS.
WAIT, IT SAYS SIX—
ひっ
AH!
PA-PARDON ME.

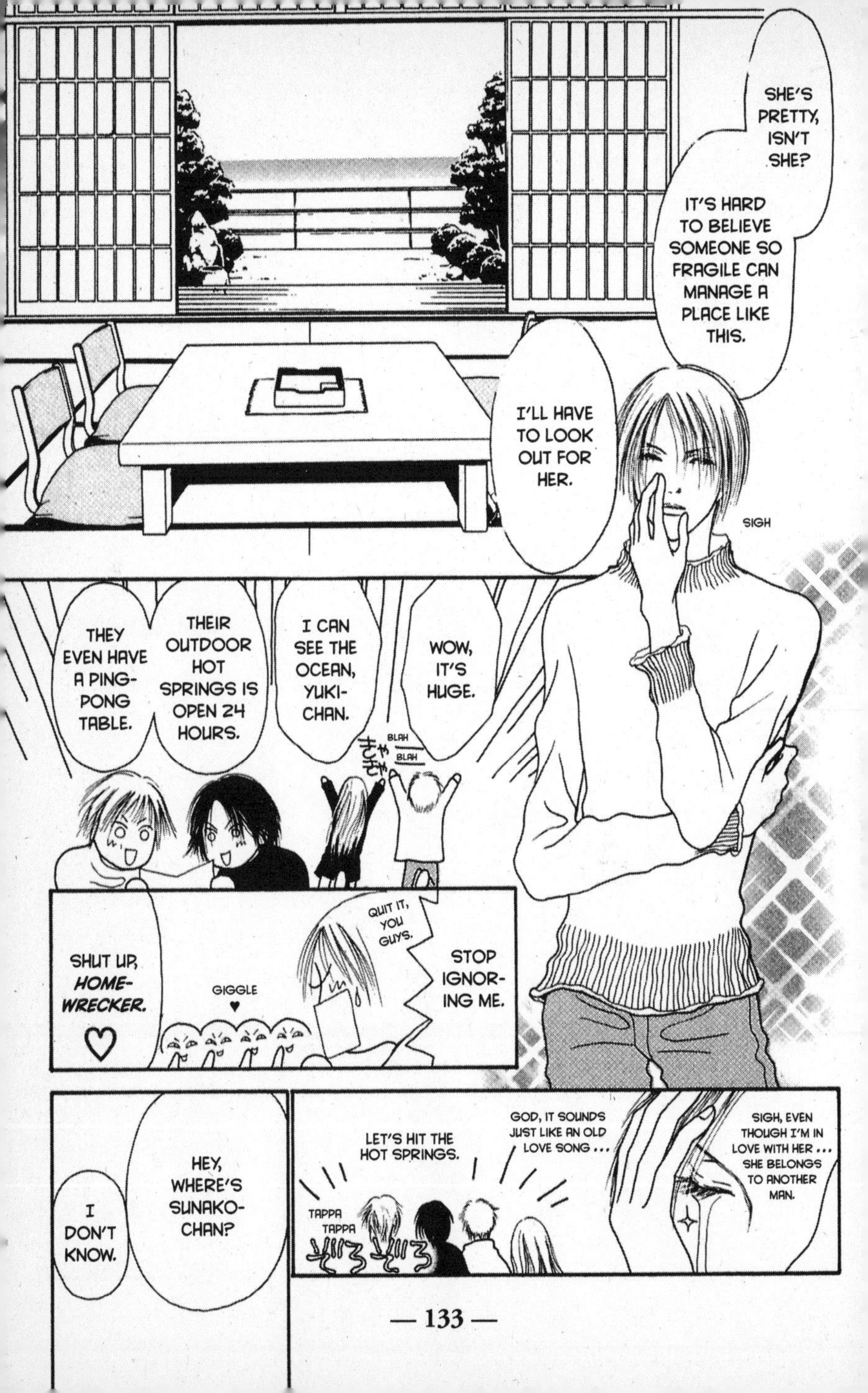
SHE'S PRETTY, ISN'T SHE?
IT'S HARD TO BELIEVE SOMEONE SO FRAGILE CAN MANAGE A PLACE LIKE THIS.
I'LL HAVE TO LOOK OUT FOR HER.
SIGH
WOW, IT'S HUGE.
I CAN SEE THE OCEAN, YUKI-CHAN.
BLAH BLAH
THEIR OUTDOOR HOT SPRINGS IS OPEN 24 HOURS.
THEY EVEN HAVE A PING-PONG TABLE.
STOP IGNORING ME.
QUIT IT, YOU GUYS.
GIGGLE ♥
SHUT UP, *HOME-WRECKER.* ♡
SIGH, EVEN THOUGH I'M IN LOVE WITH HER ... SHE BELONGS TO ANOTHER MAN.
GOD, IT SOUNDS JUST LIKE AN OLD LOVE SONG ...
LET'S HIT THE HOT SPRINGS.
TAPPA TAPPA
HEY, WHERE'S SUNAKO-CHAN?
I DON'T KNOW.

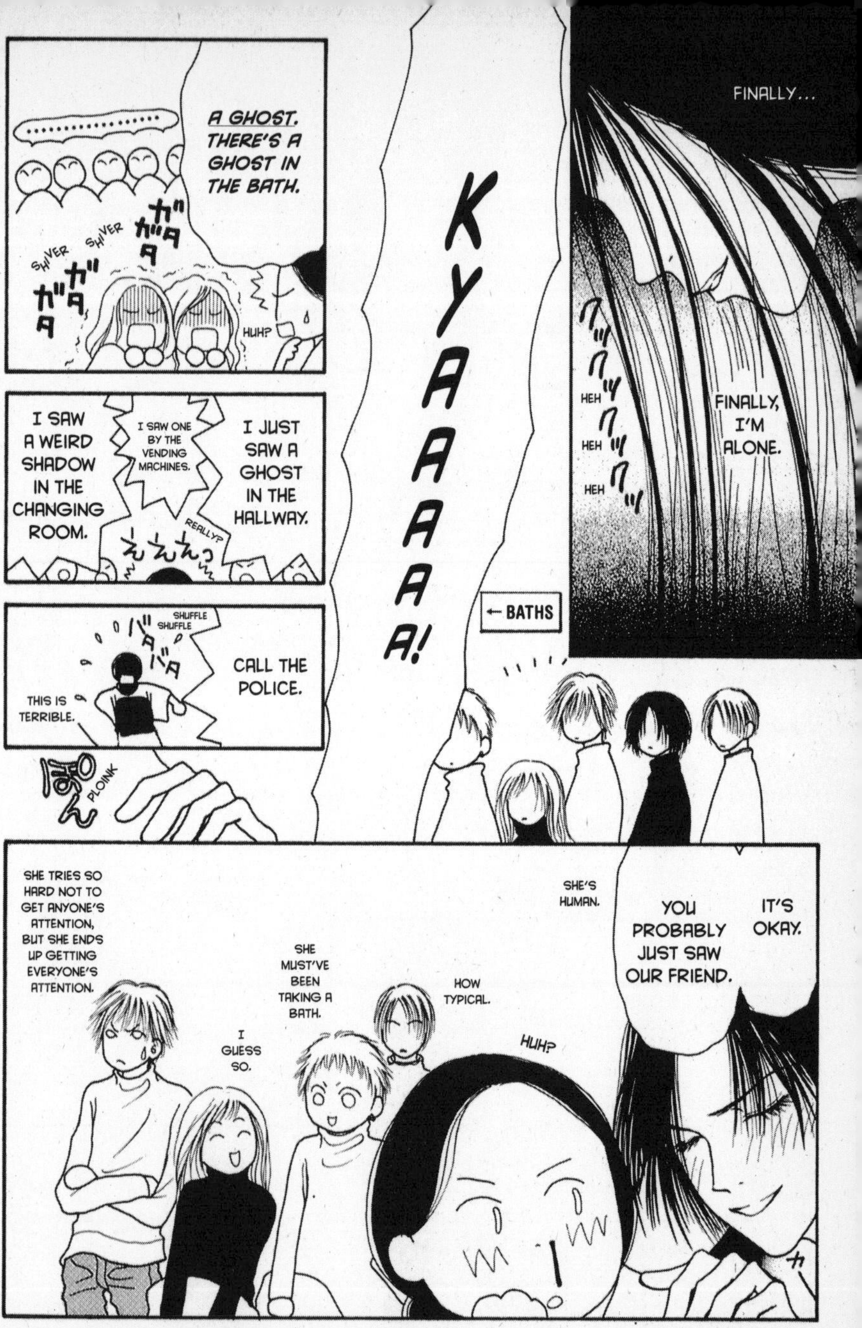
FINALLY...
HEH HEH HEH
FINALLY, I'M ALONE.
KYAAAAAAA!
← BATHS
A GHOST. THERE'S A GHOST IN THE BATH.
....
SHIVER SHIVER
HUH?
I JUST SAW A GHOST IN THE HALLWAY.
I SAW ONE BY THE VENDING MACHINES.
I SAW A WEIRD SHADOW IN THE CHANGING ROOM.
REALLY?
CALL THE POLICE.
SHUFFLE SHUFFLE
THIS IS TERRIBLE.
PLOINK
IT'S OKAY.
YOU PROBABLY JUST SAW OUR FRIEND.
SHE'S HUMAN.
HUH?
HOW TYPICAL.
SHE MUST'VE BEEN TAKING A BATH.
I GUESS SO.
SHE TRIES SO HARD NOT TO GET ANYONE'S ATTENTION, BUT SHE ENDS UP GETTING EVERYONE'S ATTENTION.

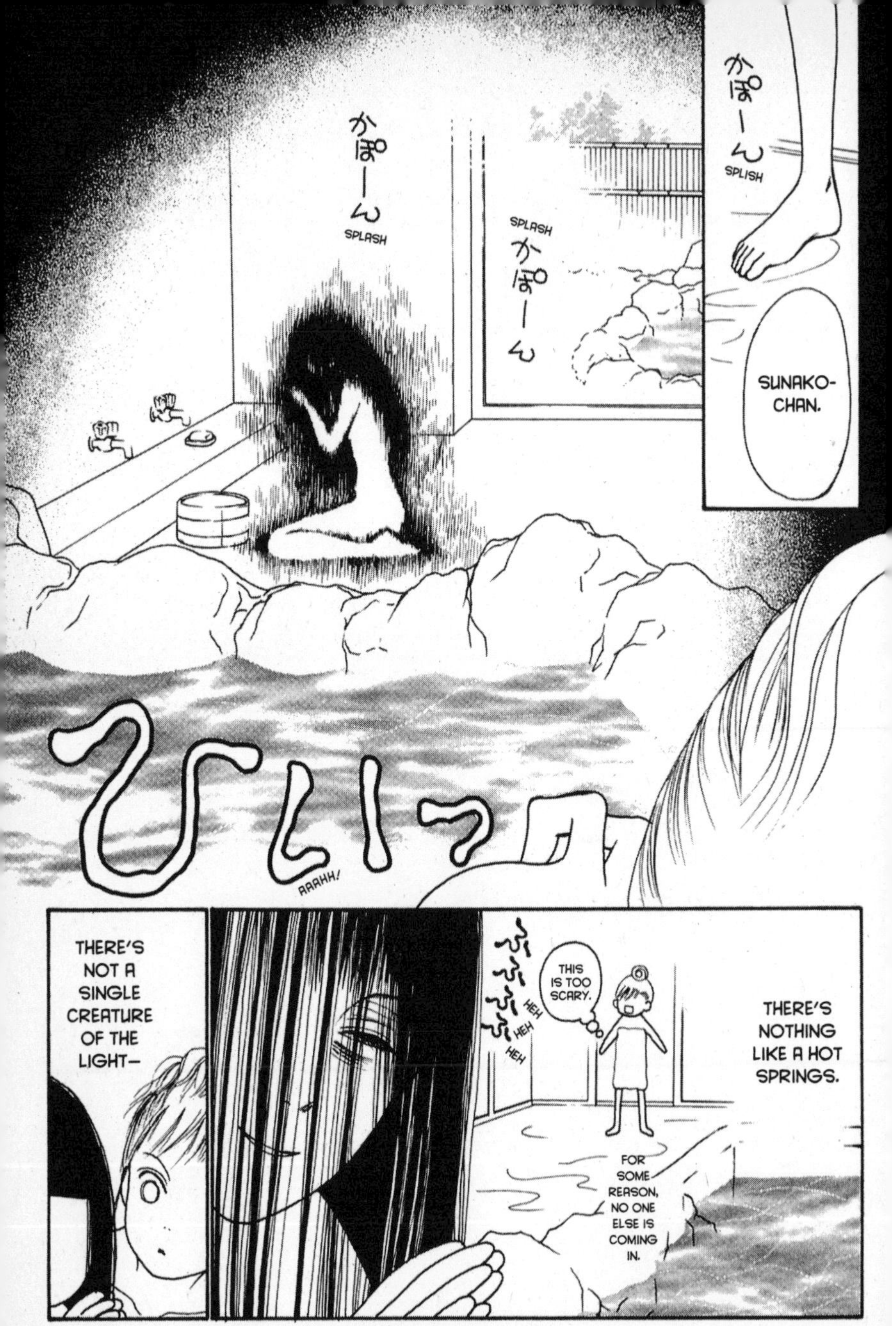
かぽーん
SPLISH
SUNAKO-CHAN.
SPLASH
かぽーん
かぽーん
SPLASH
ひいっ
AAAHH!
THERE'S NOTHING LIKE A HOT SPRINGS.
THIS IS TOO SCARY.
FOR SOME REASON, NO ONE ELSE IS COMING IN.
ふふふふ
HEH HEH HEH
THERE'S NOT A SINGLE CREATURE OF THE LIGHT—

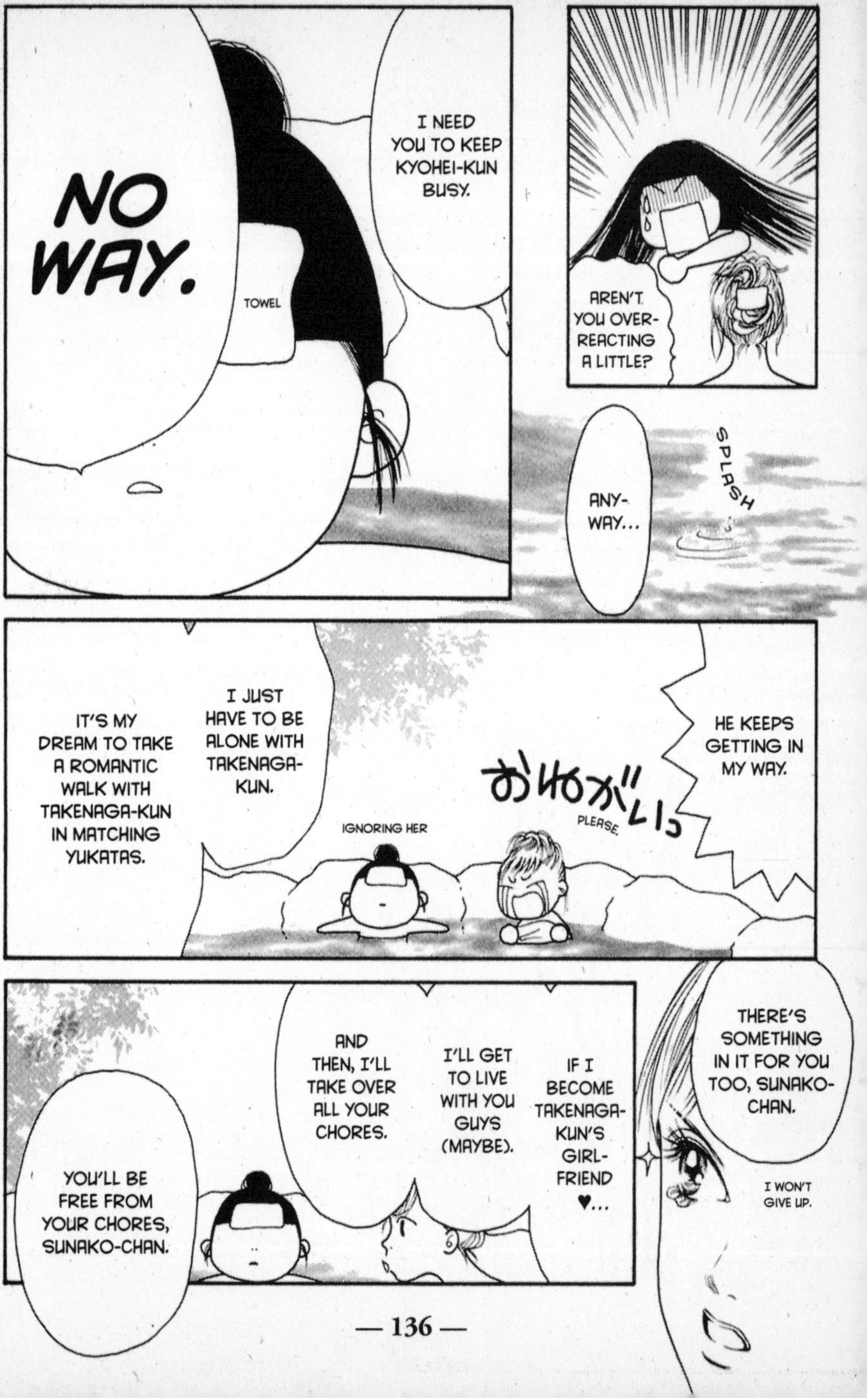
AREN'T YOU OVER-REACTING A LITTLE?
SPLASH
ANY-WAY...
I NEED YOU TO KEEP KYOHEI-KUN BUSY.
NO WAY.
TOWEL
HE KEEPS GETTING IN MY WAY.
おねがいっ
PLEASE.
I JUST HAVE TO BE ALONE WITH TAKENAGA-KUN.
IT'S MY DREAM TO TAKE A ROMANTIC WALK WITH TAKENAGA-KUN IN MATCHING YUKATAS.
IGNORING HER
THERE'S SOMETHING IN IT FOR YOU TOO, SUNAKO-CHAN.
I WON'T GIVE UP.
IF I BECOME TAKENAGA-KUN'S GIRL-FRIEND ♥...
I'LL GET TO LIVE WITH YOU GUYS (MAYBE).
AND THEN, I'LL TAKE OVER ALL YOUR CHORES.
YOU'LL BE FREE FROM YOUR CHORES, SUNAKO-CHAN.

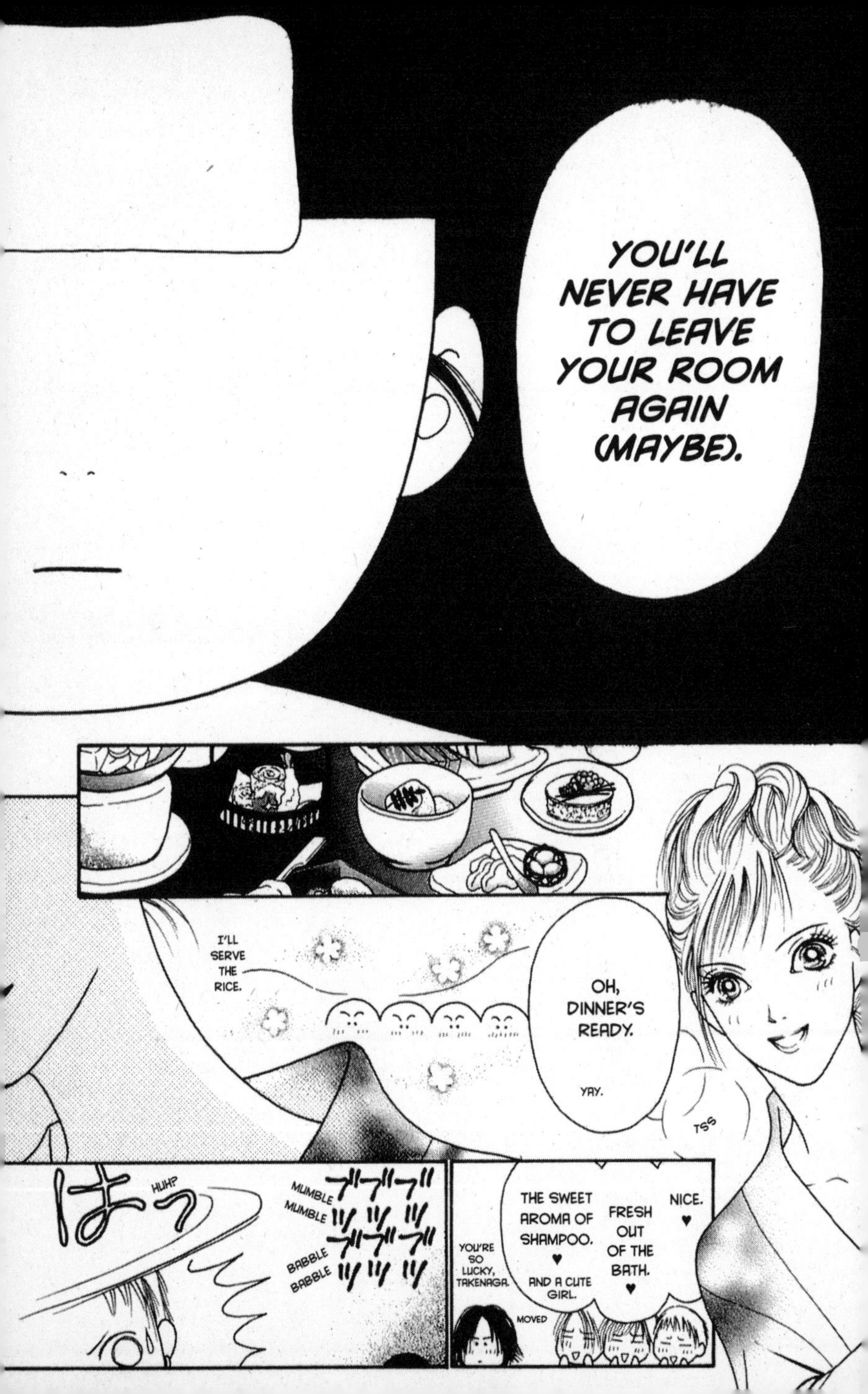
YOU'LL NEVER HAVE TO LEAVE YOUR ROOM AGAIN (MAYBE).
OH, DINNER'S READY.
TSS
YAY.
I'LL SERVE THE RICE.
NICE. ♥
FRESH OUT OF THE BATH. ♥
THE SWEET AROMA OF SHAMPOO. ♥
AND A CUTE GIRL.
YOU'RE SO LUCKY, TAKENAGA.
MOVED
MUMBLE MUMBLE
ブブブ ツツツ
BABBLE BABBLE
ブブブ ツツツ
HUH?
はっ

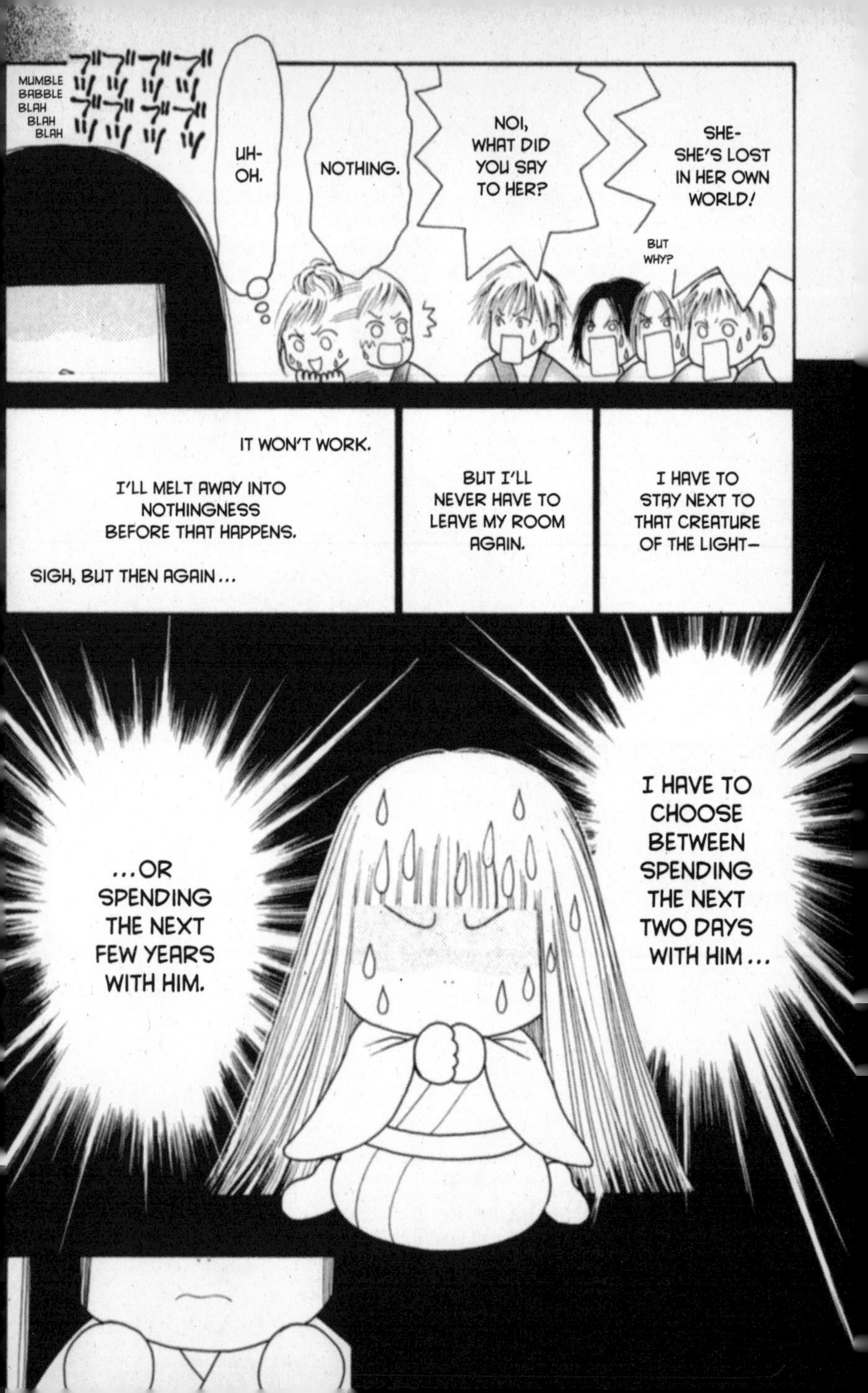
SHE- SHE'S LOST IN HER OWN WORLD!
BUT WHY?
NOI, WHAT DID YOU SAY TO HER?
NOTHING.
UH- OH.
ブツブツブツブツブツブツブツブツ
MUMBLE BABBLE BLAH BLAH BLAH
I HAVE TO STAY NEXT TO THAT CREATURE OF THE LIGHT—
BUT I'LL NEVER HAVE TO LEAVE MY ROOM AGAIN.
IT WON'T WORK.
I'LL MELT AWAY INTO NOTHINGNESS BEFORE THAT HAPPENS.
SIGH, BUT THEN AGAIN...
I HAVE TO CHOOSE BETWEEN SPENDING THE NEXT TWO DAYS WITH HIM...
...OR SPENDING THE NEXT FEW YEARS WITH HIM.

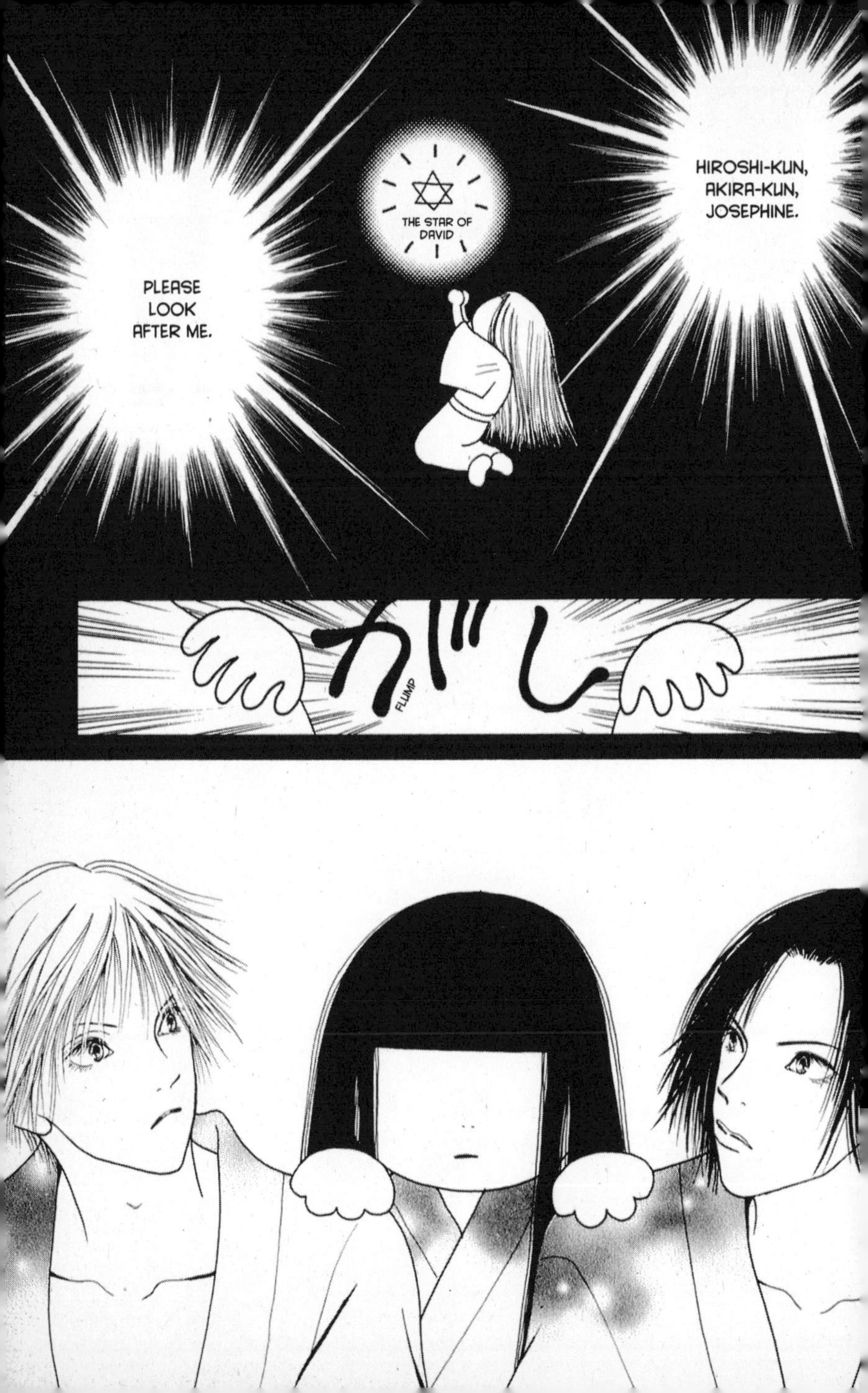
HIROSHI-KUN, AKIRA-KUN, JOSEPHINE.
THE STAR OF DAVID
PLEASE LOOK AFTER ME.
がし
FLUMP

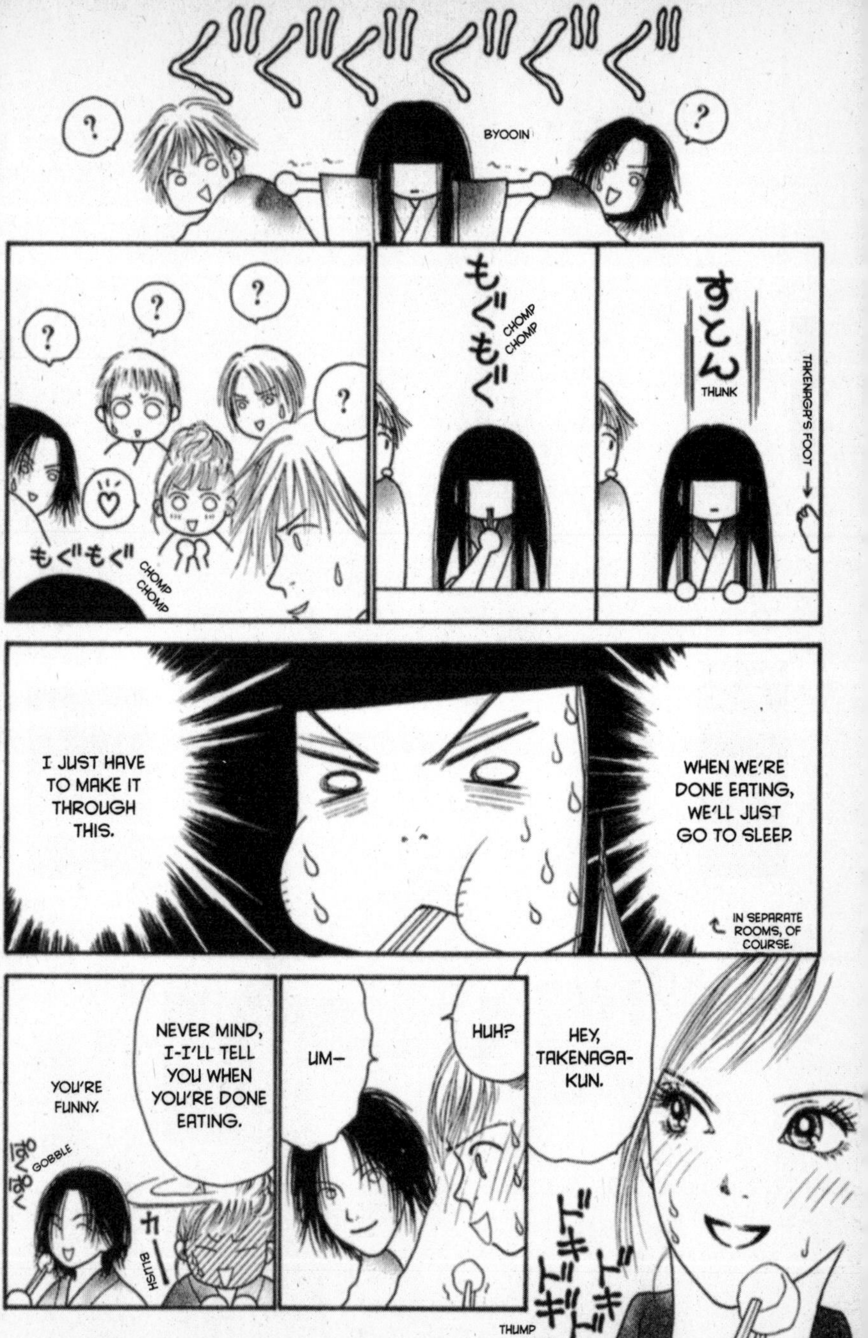
ぐぐぐぐぐぐ
BYOOIN
すとん
THUNK
TAKENAGA'S FOOT
もぐもぐ
CHOMP CHOMP
もぐもぐ
CHOMP CHOMP
WHEN WE'RE DONE EATING, WE'LL JUST GO TO SLEEP.
IN SEPARATE ROOMS, OF COURSE.
I JUST HAVE TO MAKE IT THROUGH THIS.
HEY, TAKENAGA-KUN.
ドキドキ
ドキドキ
THUMP THUMP
HUH?
UM—
NEVER MIND, I-I'LL TELL YOU WHEN YOU'RE DONE EATING.
YOU'RE FUNNY.
ぱくぱく
GOBBLE
カー
BLUSH

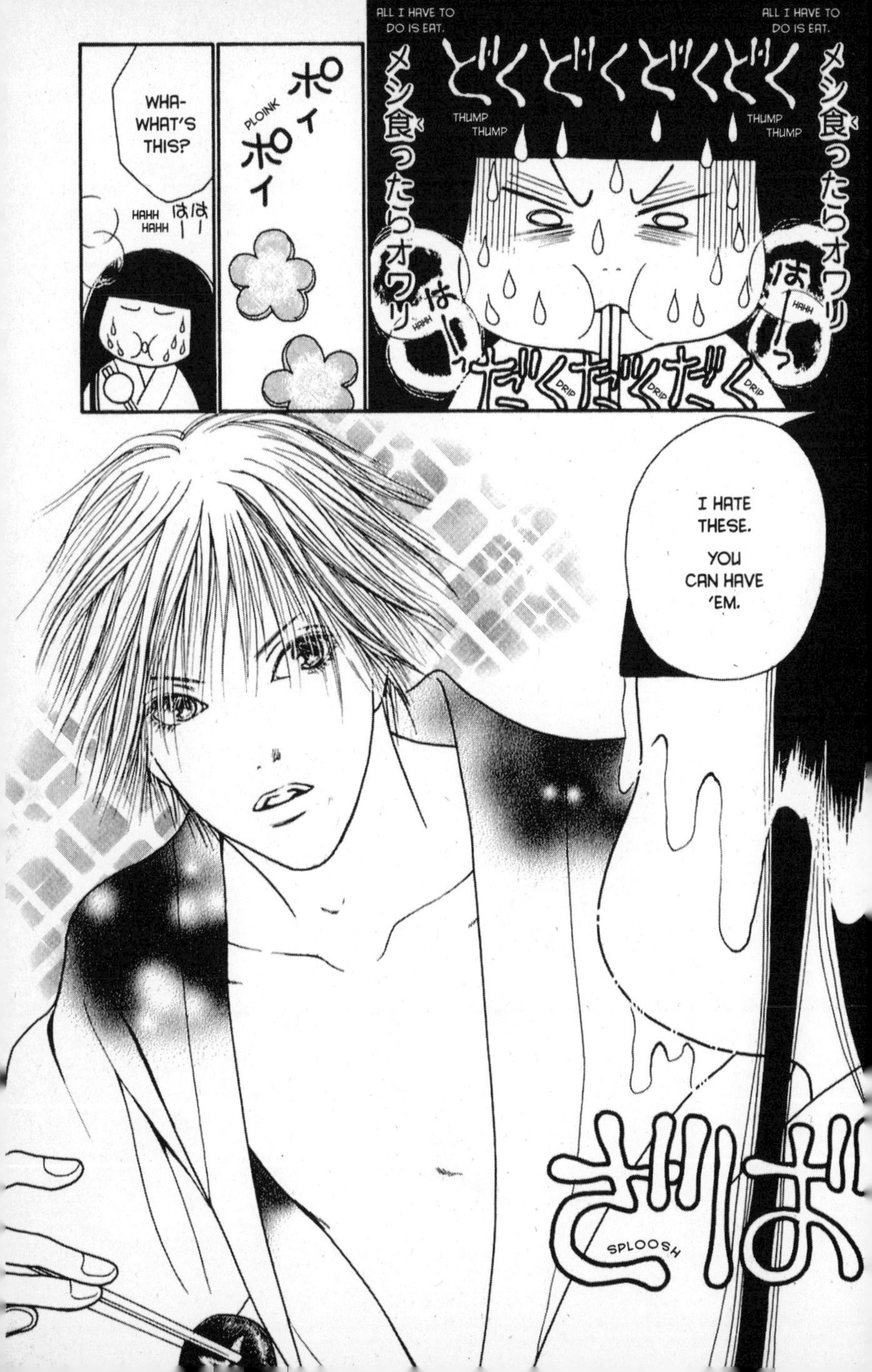
ALL I HAVE TO DO IS EAT.
メシ食ったらオワリ
どくどくどくどく
THUMP THUMP
THUMP THUMP
はっ
HAHH
だくだくだく
DRIP DRIP DRIP
はっ
HAHH
メシ食ったらオワリ
ALL I HAVE TO DO IS EAT.
ポイポイ
PLOINK
WHA-WHAT'S THIS?
はは
HAHH HAHH
I HATE THESE.
YOU CAN HAVE 'EM.
SPLOOSH

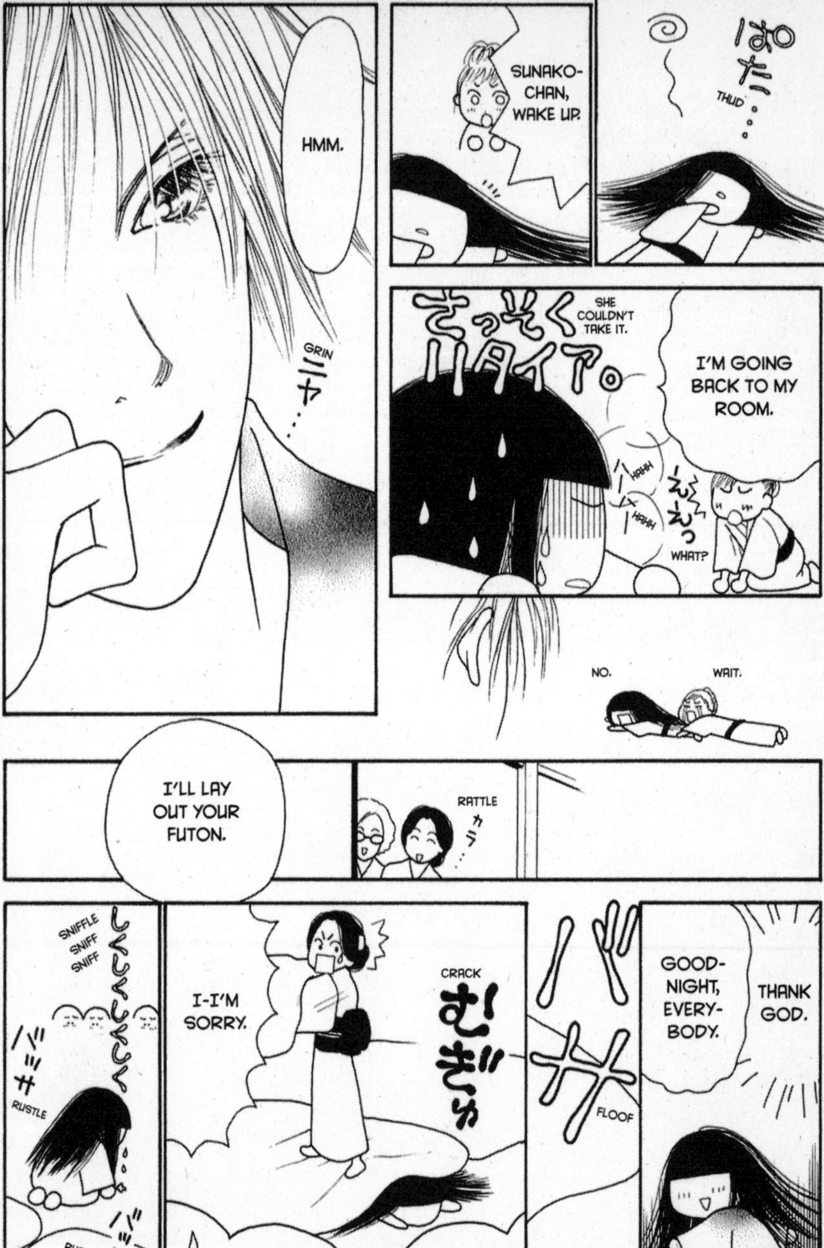
ぱた…
THUD
SUNAKO-CHAN, WAKE UP.
さっそくリタイア。
SHE COULDN'T TAKE IT.
I'M GOING BACK TO MY ROOM.
ハァハァ
HAHH HAHH
ええっ
WHAT?
NO.
WAIT.
HMM.
ニヤ…
GRIN
カラ…
RATTLE
I'LL LAY OUT YOUR FUTON.
THANK GOD.
GOOD-NIGHT, EVERY-BODY.
バサ
FLOOF
むぎゅ
CRACK
I-I'M SORRY.
しくしくしく
SNIFFLE SNIFF SNIFF
バサ
RUSTLE
バサ
RUSTLE

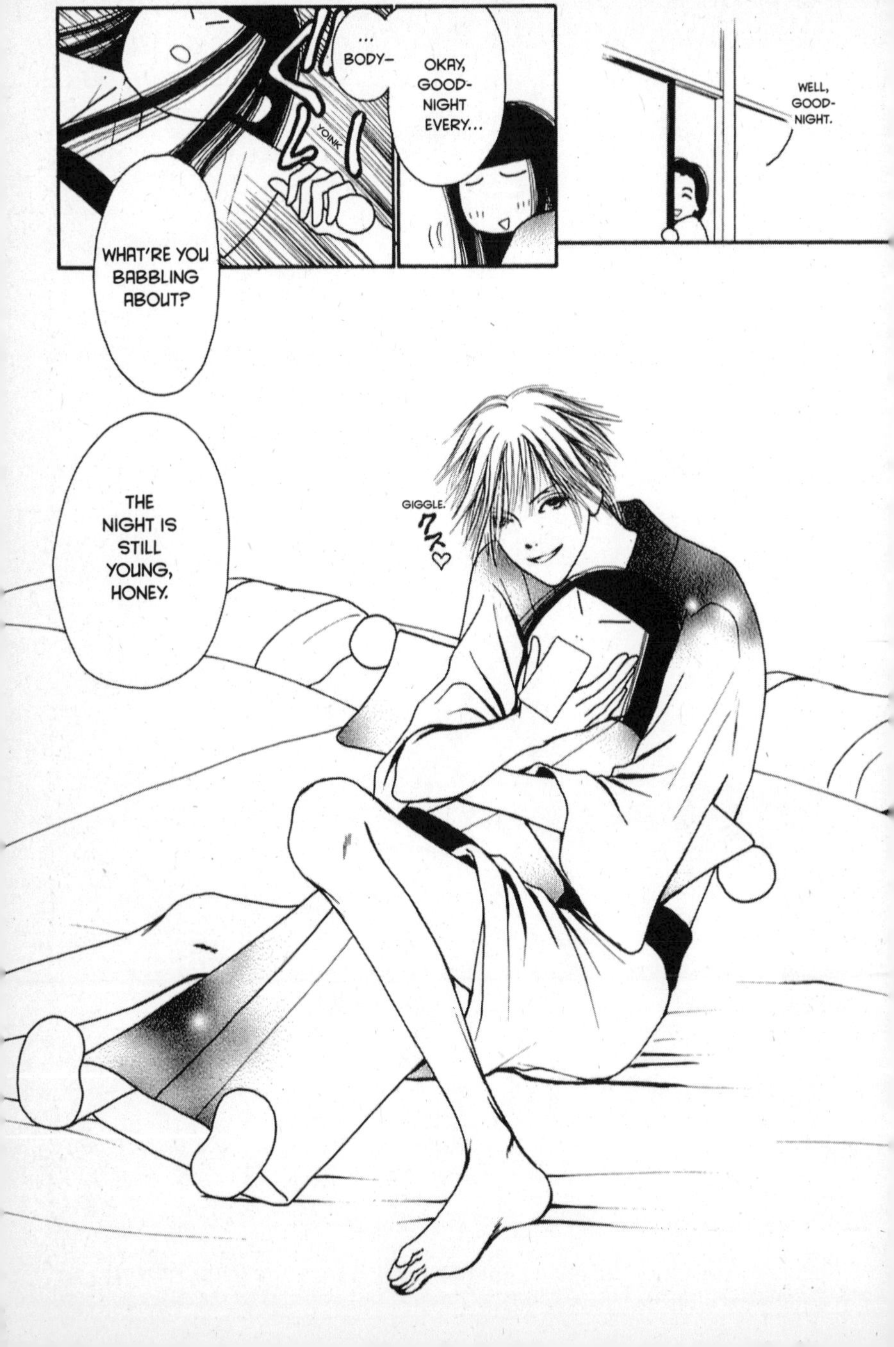
WELL, GOOD-NIGHT.
OKAY, GOOD-NIGHT EVERY...
...BODY-
YOINK
WHAT'RE YOU BABBLING ABOUT?
GIGGLE.
THE NIGHT IS STILL YOUNG, HONEY.

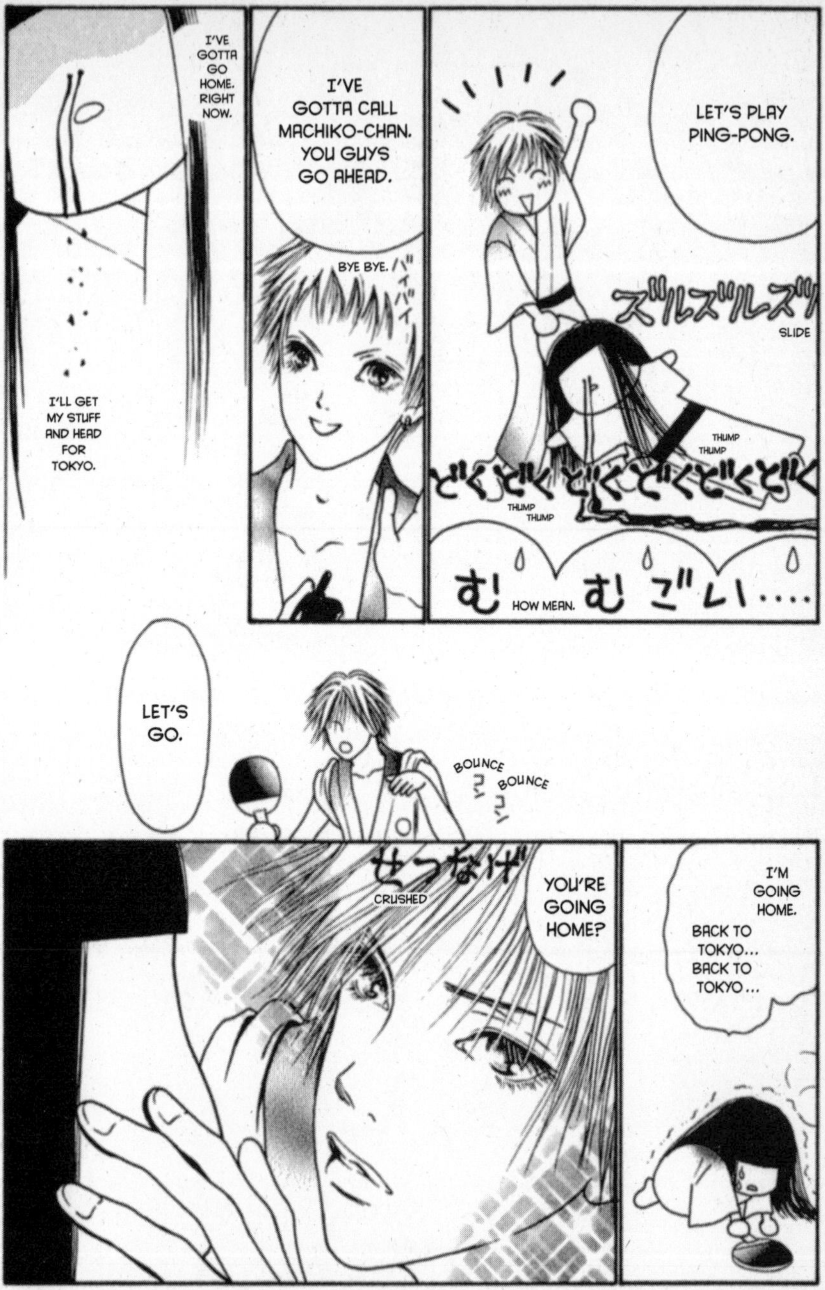

LET'S PLAY PING-PONG.
ズルズルズッ
SLIDE
どくどくどくどくどくどく
THUMP THUMP
THUMP THUMP
む! むごい....
HOW MEAN.
I'VE GOTTA CALL MACHIKO-CHAN. YOU GUYS GO AHEAD.
バイバイ
BYE BYE.
I'VE GOTTA GO HOME. RIGHT NOW.
I'LL GET MY STUFF AND HEAD FOR TOKYO.
LET'S GO.
BOUNCE
BOUNCE
I'M GOING HOME.
BACK TO TOKYO... BACK TO TOKYO...
YOU'RE GOING HOME?
せつなげ
CRUSHED

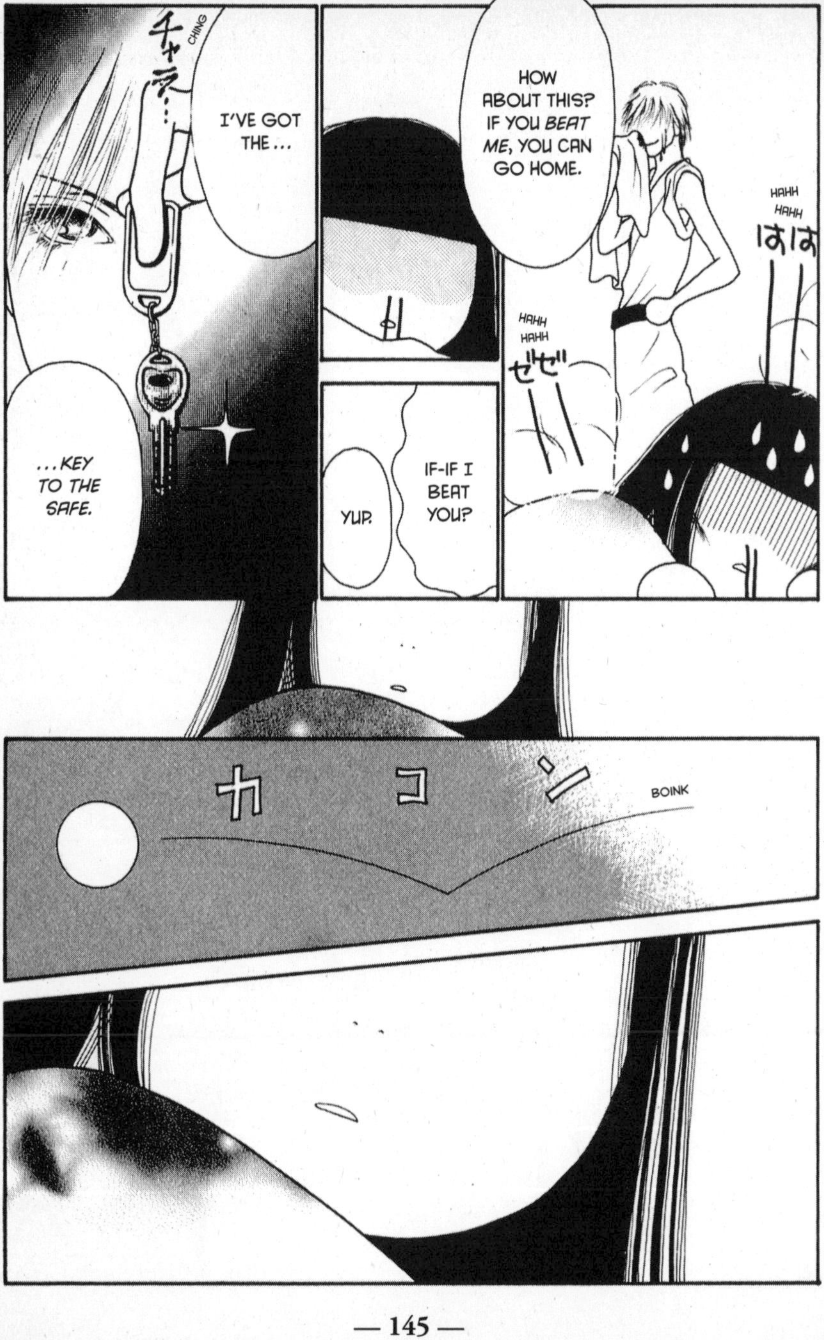
HOW ABOUT THIS? IF YOU *BEAT ME*, YOU CAN GO HOME.
HAHH HAHH
はは
HAHH HAHH
ぜぜ
IF-IF I BEAT YOU?
YUP.
チャラ…
CHING
I'VE GOT THE…
…KEY TO THE SAFE.
カコン
BOINK

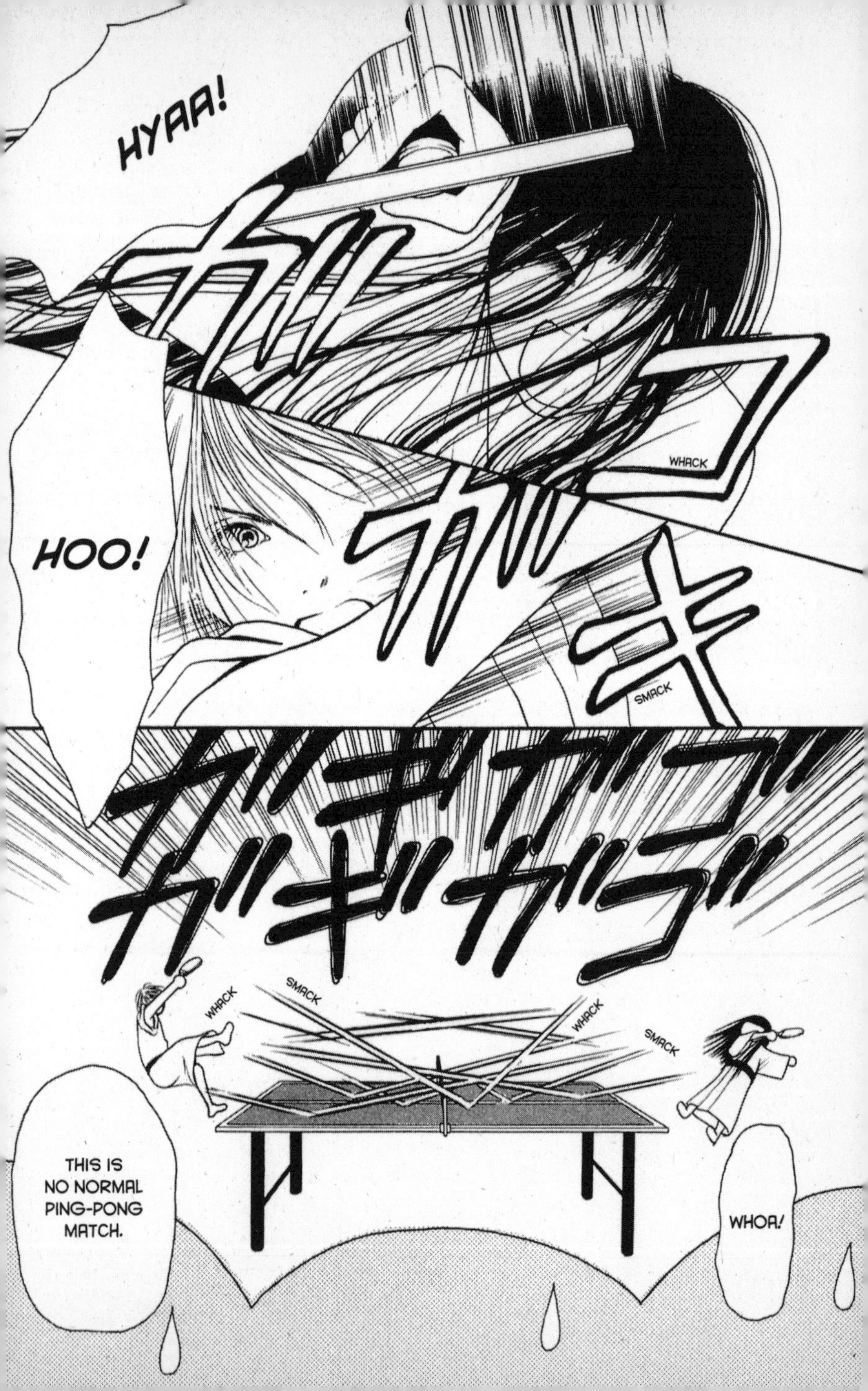
HYAA!
WHACK
HOO!
SMACK
SMACK
WHACK
SMACK
WHACK
WHOA!
THIS IS NO NORMAL PING-PONG MATCH.

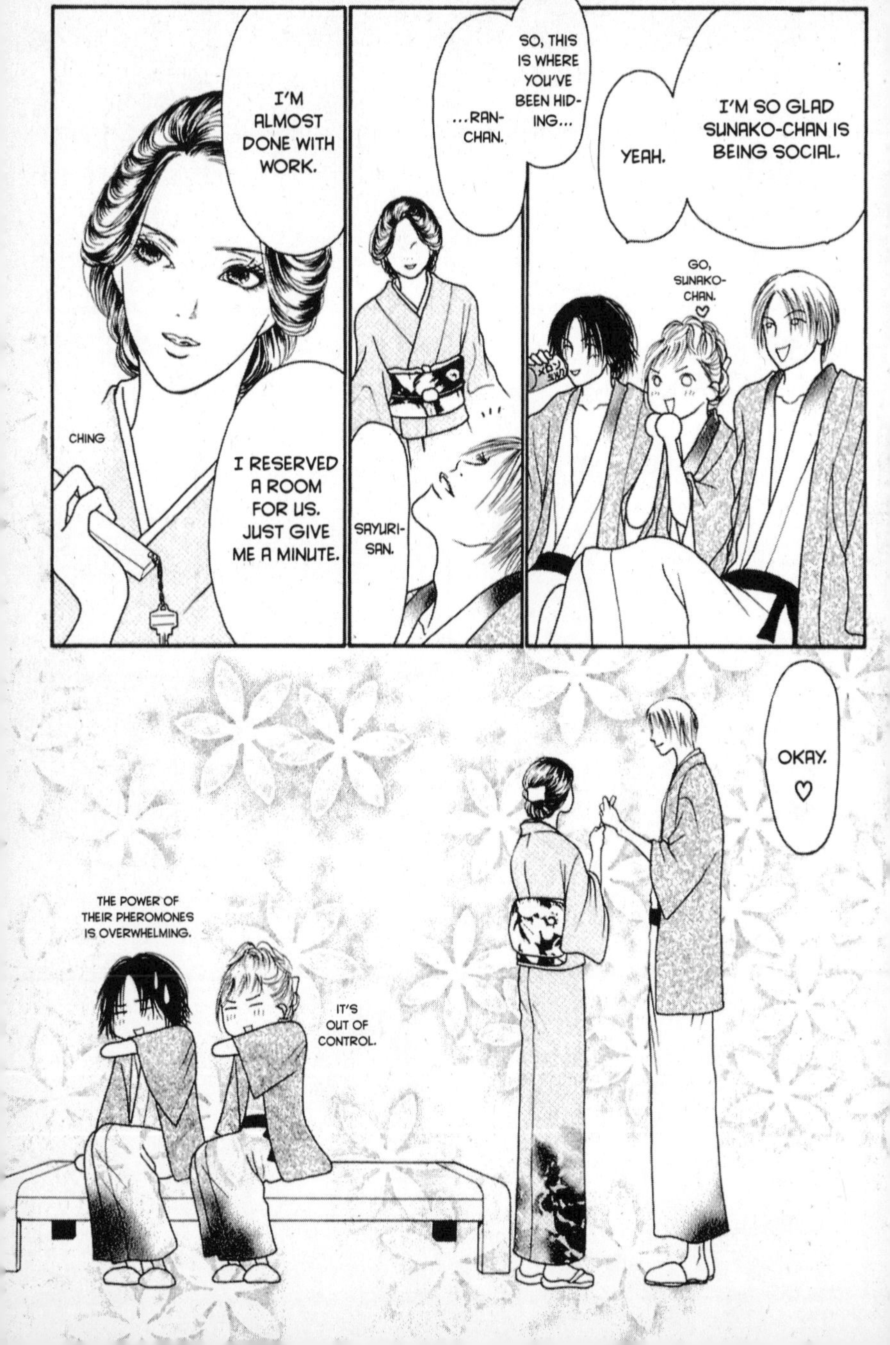
I'M SO GLAD SUNAKO-CHAN IS BEING SOCIAL.
YEAH.
GO, SUNAKO-CHAN. ♡
SO, THIS IS WHERE YOU'VE BEEN HID-ING...
...RAN-CHAN.
...
SAYURI-SAN.
I'M ALMOST DONE WITH WORK.
CHING
I RESERVED A ROOM FOR US. JUST GIVE ME A MINUTE.
OKAY. ♡
THE POWER OF THEIR PHEROMONES IS OVERWHELMING.
IT'S OUT OF CONTROL.

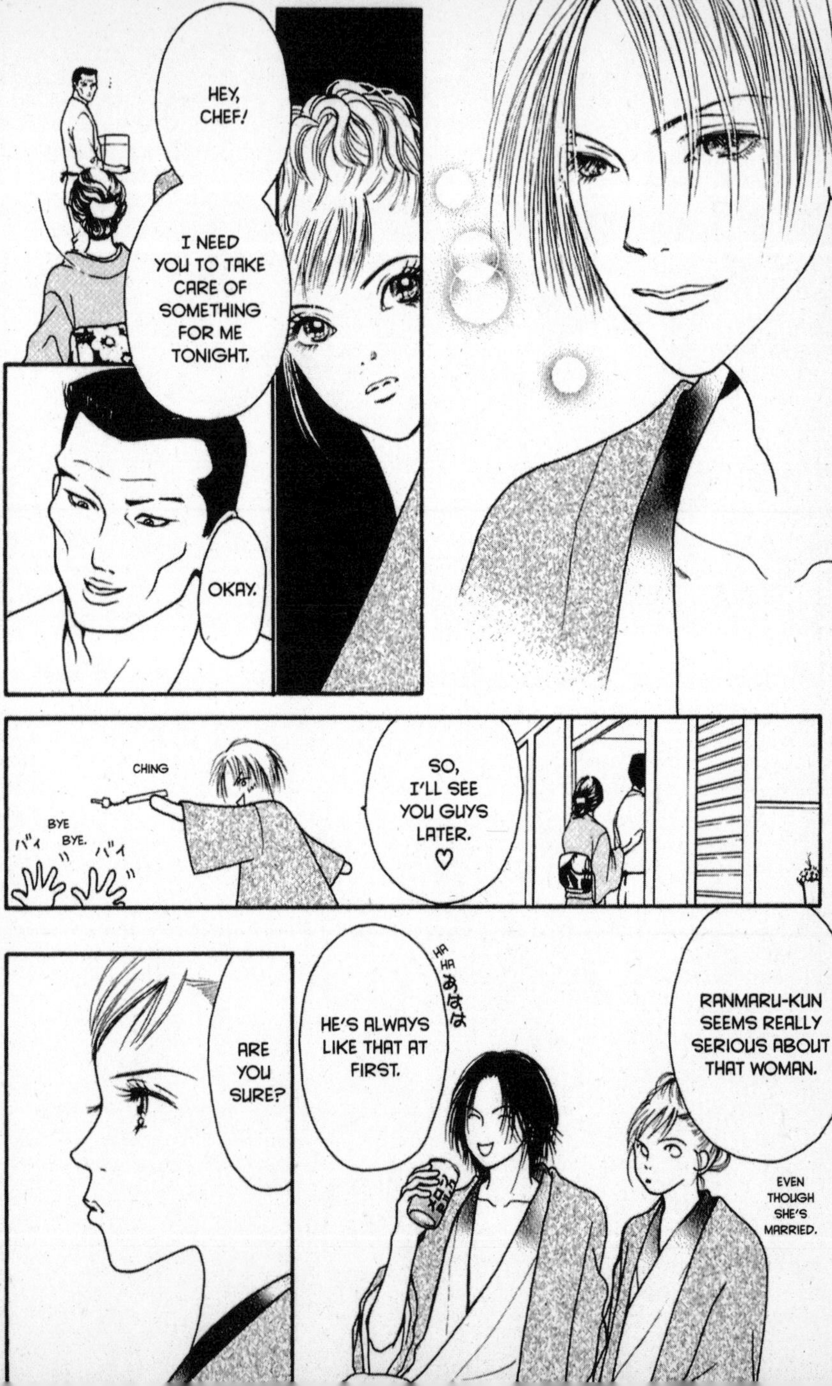
HEY, CHEF!
I NEED YOU TO TAKE CARE OF SOMETHING FOR ME TONIGHT.
OKAY.
SO, I'LL SEE YOU GUYS LATER. ♡
CHING
BYE バイ
BYE. バイ
RANMARU-KUN SEEMS REALLY SERIOUS ABOUT THAT WOMAN.
EVEN THOUGH SHE'S MARRIED.
HA HA あはは
HE'S ALWAYS LIKE THAT AT FIRST.
ARE YOU SURE?

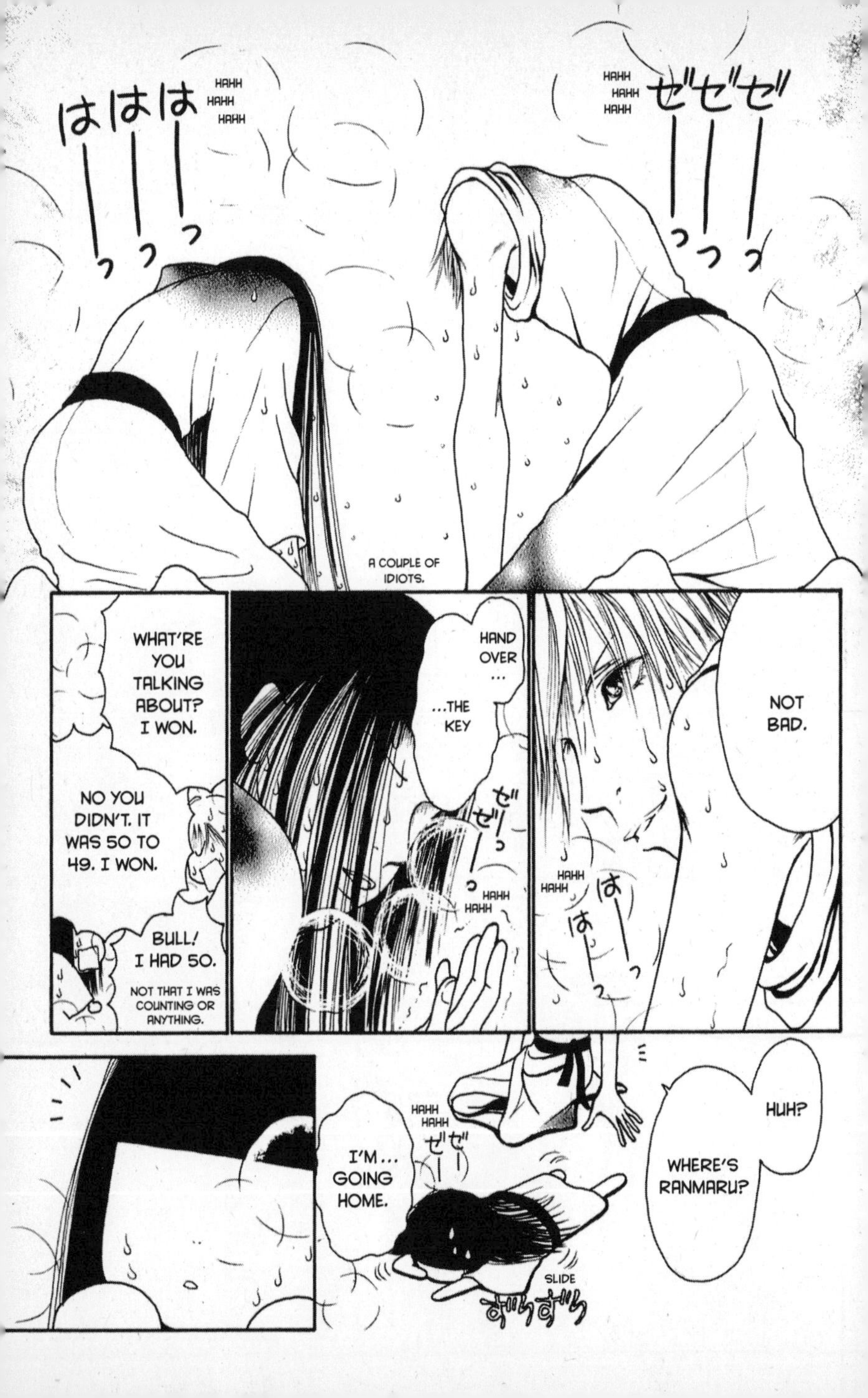
HAHH HAHH HAHH
ぜぜぜーっっっ
ははは―っっっ
HAHH HAHH HAHH
A COUPLE OF IDIOTS.
NOT BAD.
HAHH HAHH
はーっ はっ
HAND OVER ...
...THE KEY
ぜっ ぜっ
HAHH HAHH
WHAT'RE YOU TALKING ABOUT? I WON.
NO YOU DIDN'T. IT WAS 50 TO 49. I WON.
BULL! I HAD 50.
NOT THAT I WAS COUNTING OR ANYTHING.
HUH?
WHERE'S RANMARU?
HAHH HAHH
ぜーぜー
I'M... GOING HOME.
SLIDE

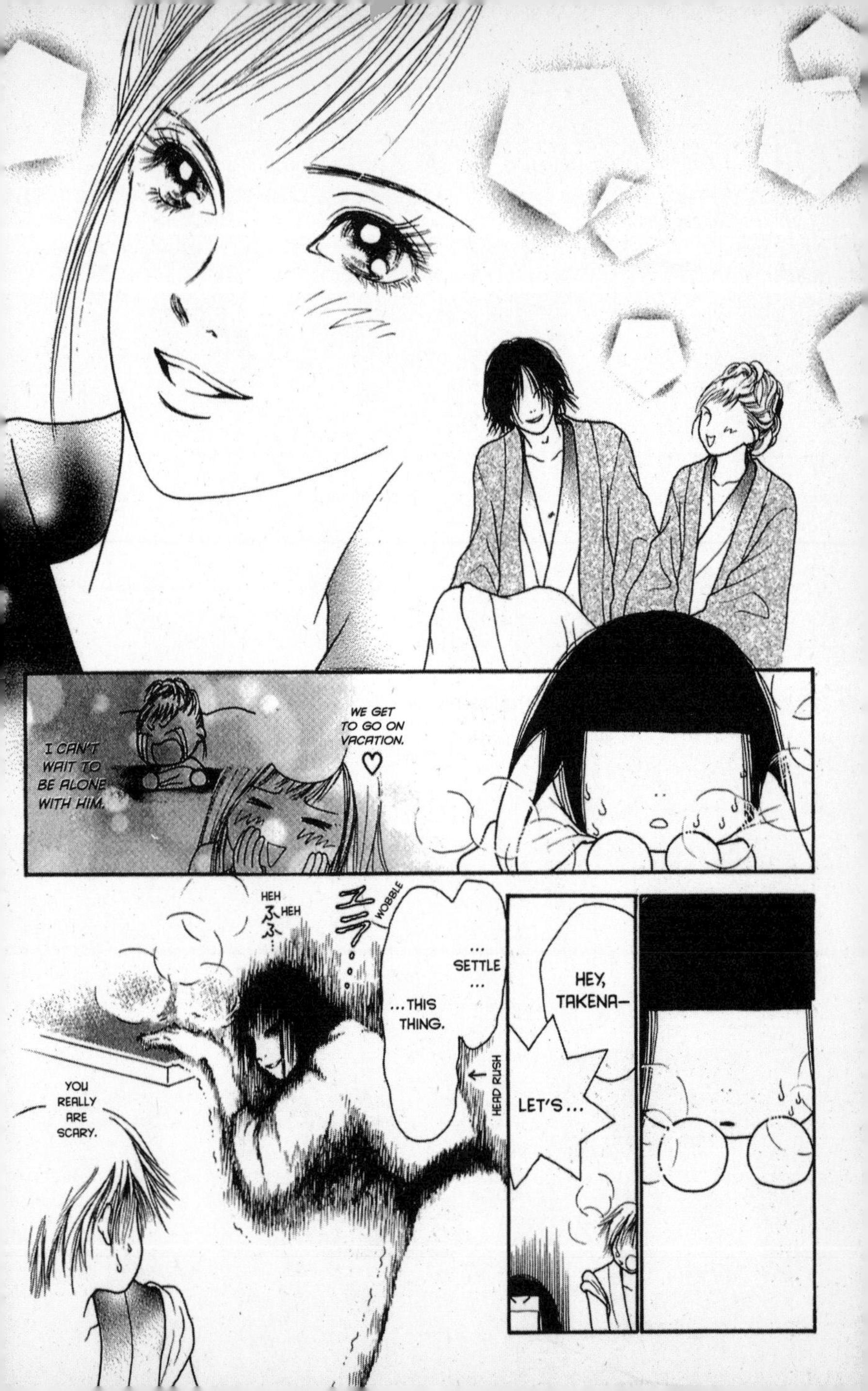
WE GET TO GO ON VACATION. ♥
I CAN'T WAIT TO BE ALONE WITH HIM.
HEY, TAKENA—
LET'S...
...SETTLE...
...THIS THING.
WOBBLE
HEAD RUSH
HEH HEH
ふふ...
YOU REALLY ARE SCARY.

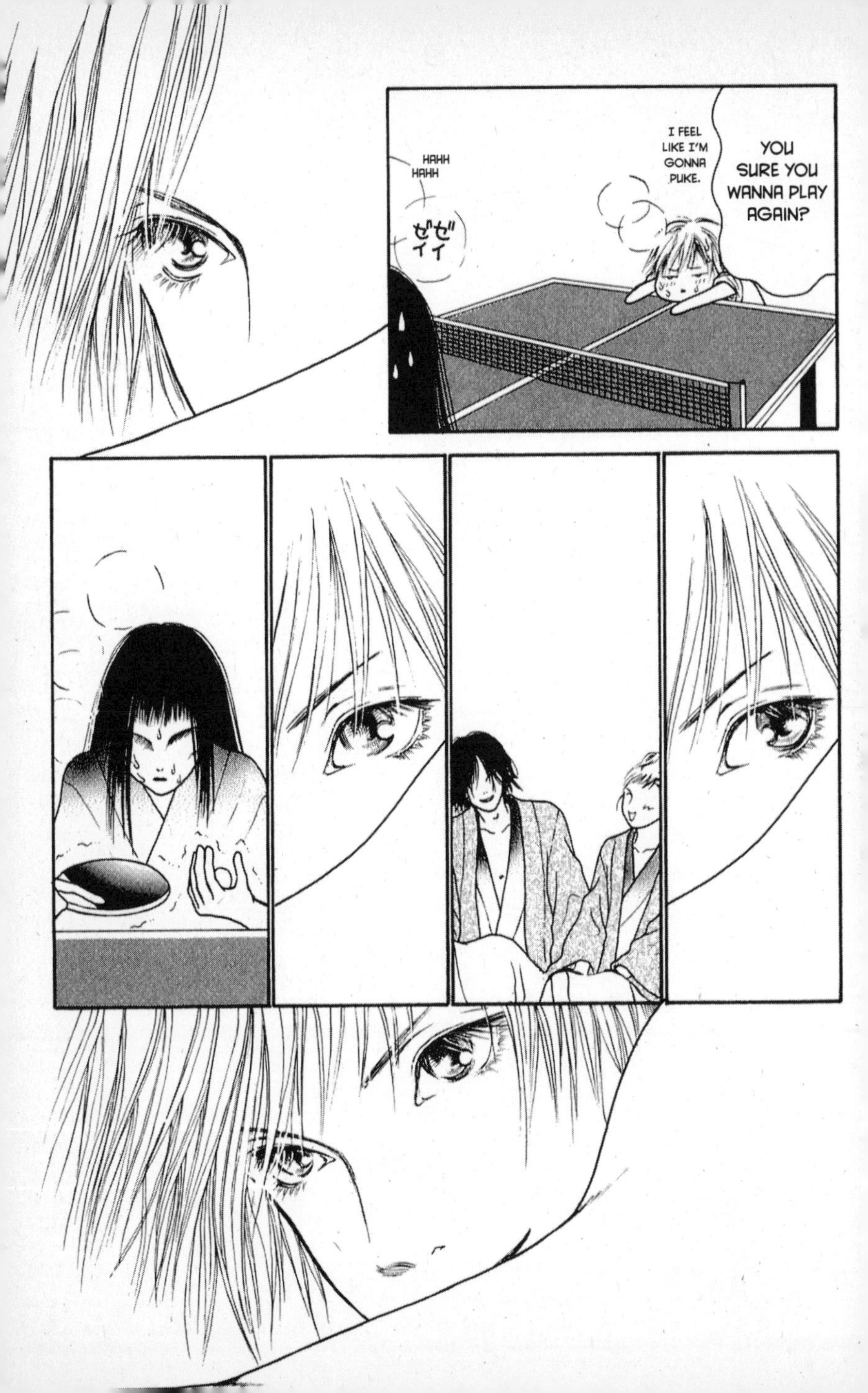
YOU SURE YOU WANNA PLAY AGAIN?
I FEEL LIKE I'M GONNA PUKE.
HAHH HAHH
ゼゼイイ

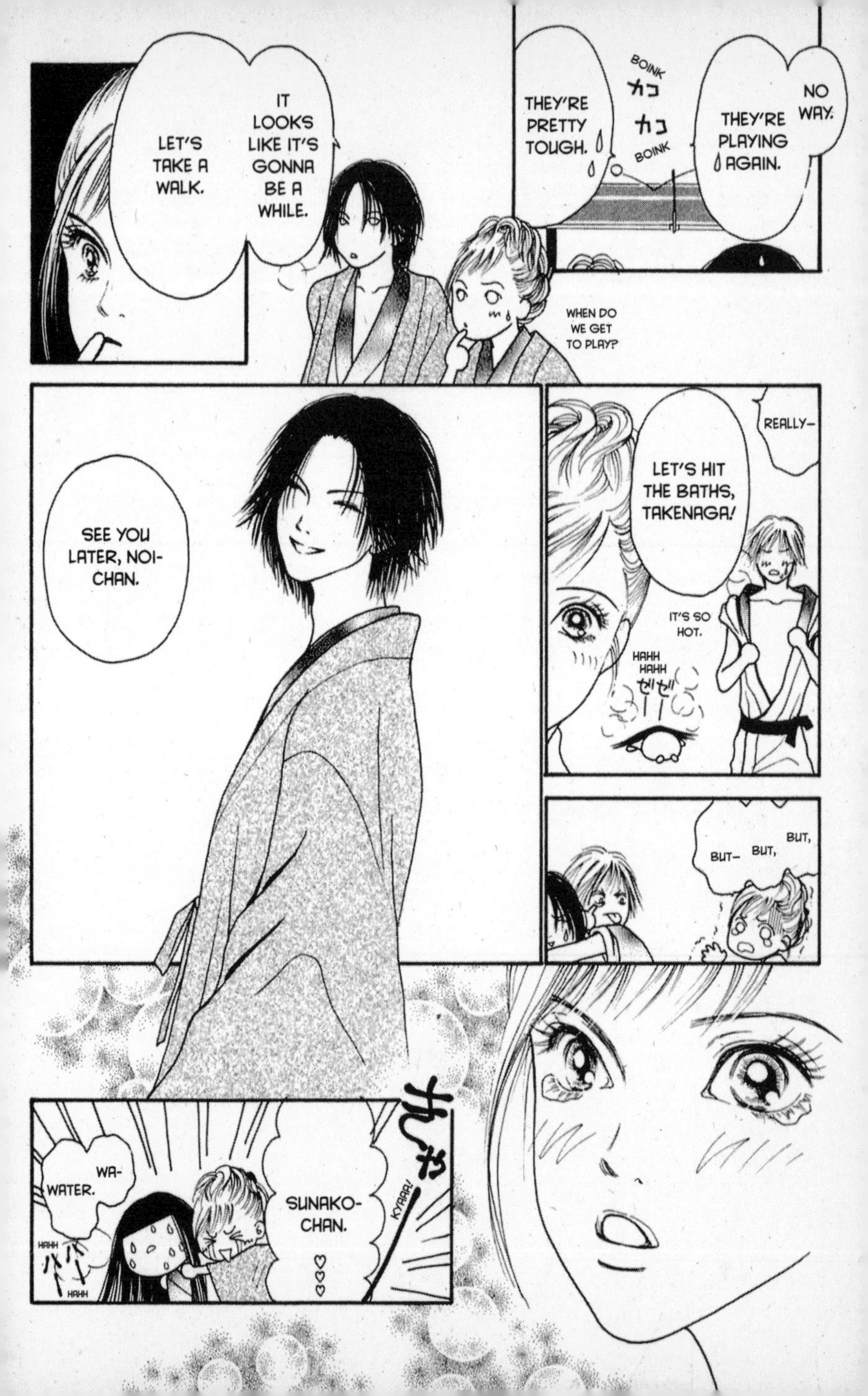
NO WAY.
THEY'RE PLAYING AGAIN.
BOINK
カコ
カコ
BOINK
THEY'RE PRETTY TOUGH.
IT LOOKS LIKE IT'S GONNA BE A WHILE.
LET'S TAKE A WALK.
WHEN DO WE GET TO PLAY?
REALLY—
LET'S HIT THE BATHS, TAKENAGA!
IT'S SO HOT.
HAHH HAHH
BUT, BUT, BUT—
SEE YOU LATER, NOI-CHAN.
KYAAA!
SUNAKO-CHAN.
♡♡♡
WA-WATER.
HAHH HAHH

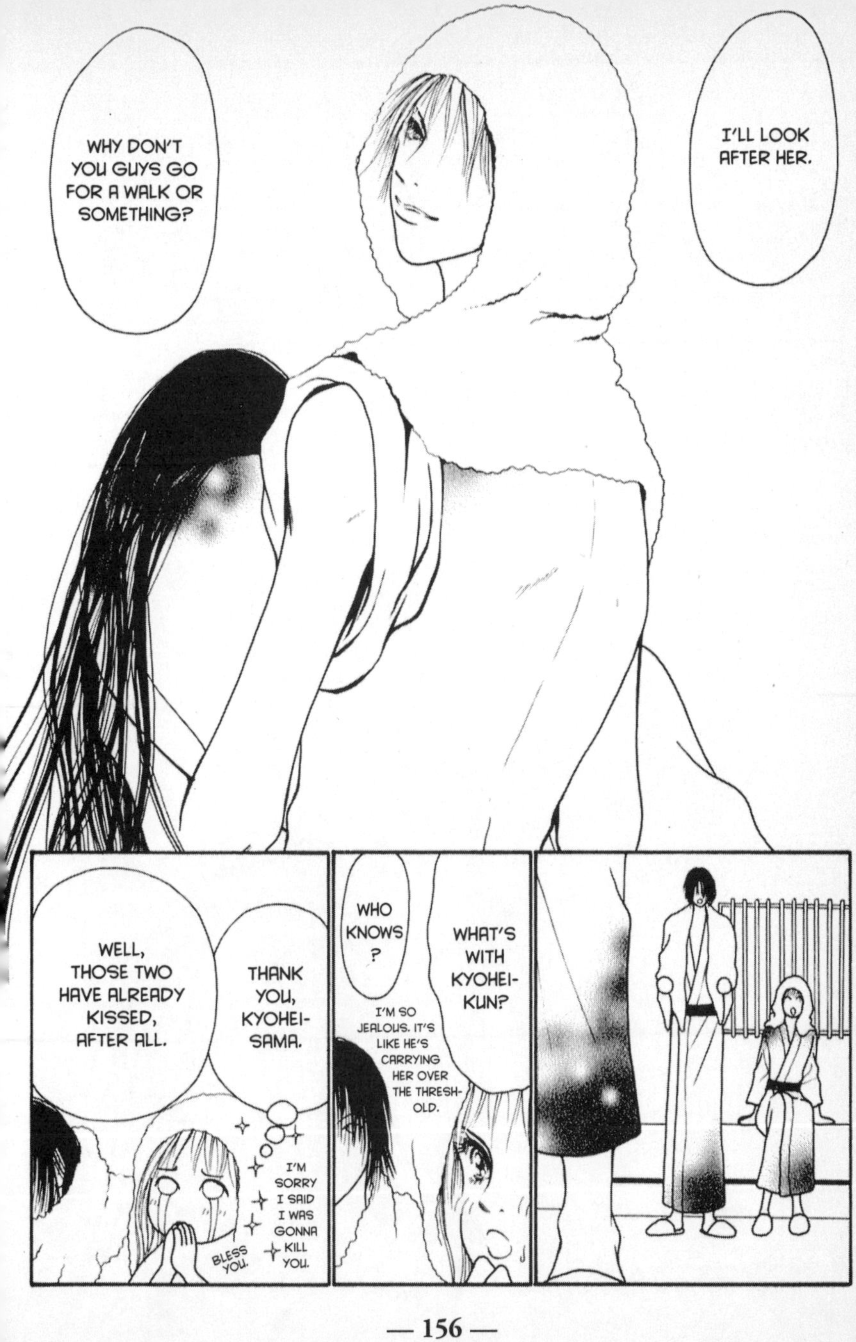
I'LL LOOK AFTER HER.
WHY DON'T YOU GUYS GO FOR A WALK OR SOMETHING?
WHAT'S WITH KYOHEI-KUN?
WHO KNOWS?
I'M SO JEALOUS. IT'S LIKE HE'S CARRYING HER OVER THE THRESH-OLD.
THANK YOU, KYOHEI-SAMA.
WELL, THOSE TWO HAVE ALREADY KISSED, AFTER ALL.
I'M SORRY I SAID I WAS GONNA KILL YOU.
BLESS YOU.

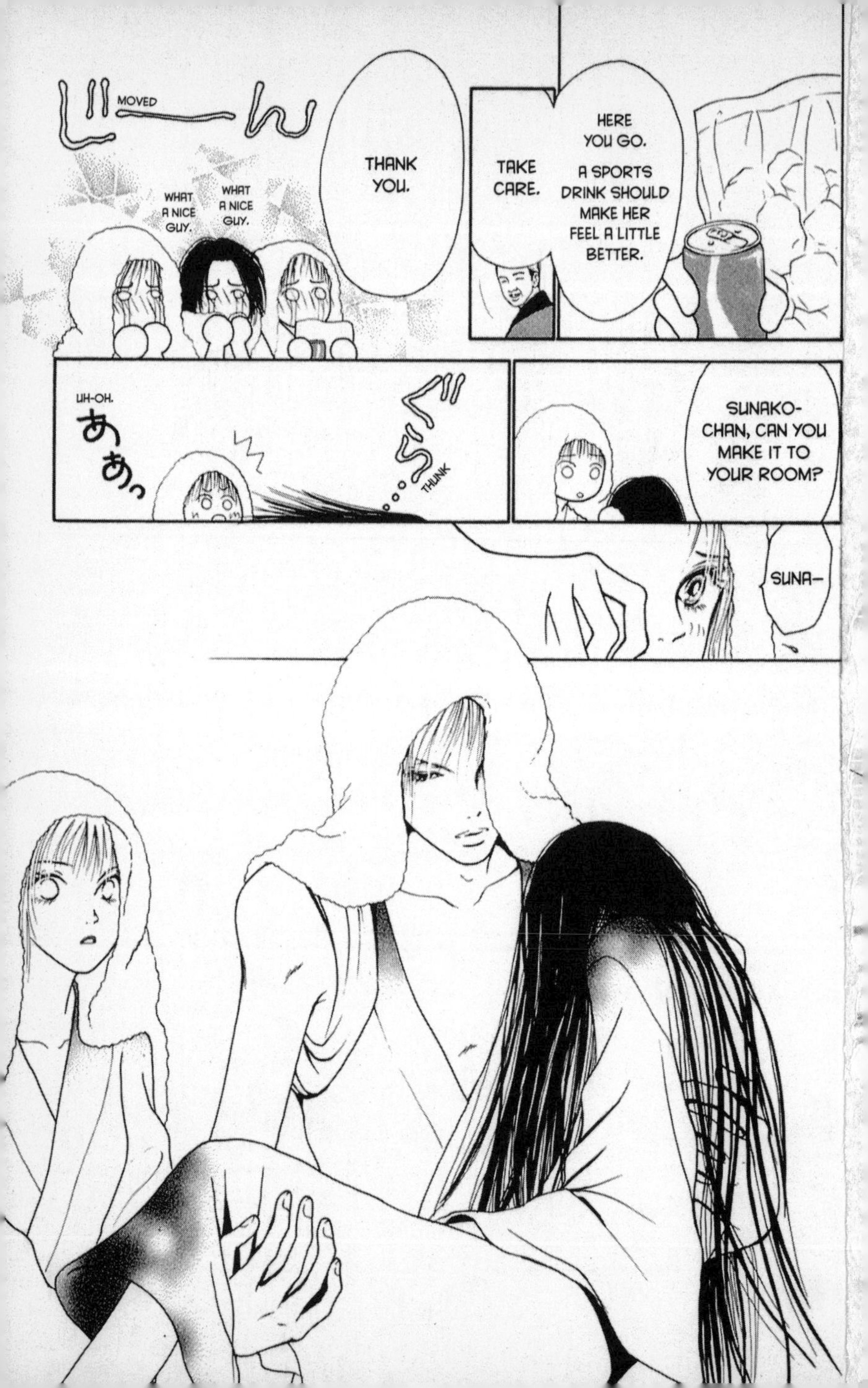
HERE YOU GO.
A SPORTS DRINK SHOULD MAKE HER FEEL A LITTLE BETTER.
TAKE CARE.
THANK YOU.
じーん
MOVED
WHAT A NICE GUY.
WHAT A NICE GUY.
SUNAKO-CHAN, CAN YOU MAKE IT TO YOUR ROOM?
ぐら
THUNK
ああっ
UH-OH.
SUNA—

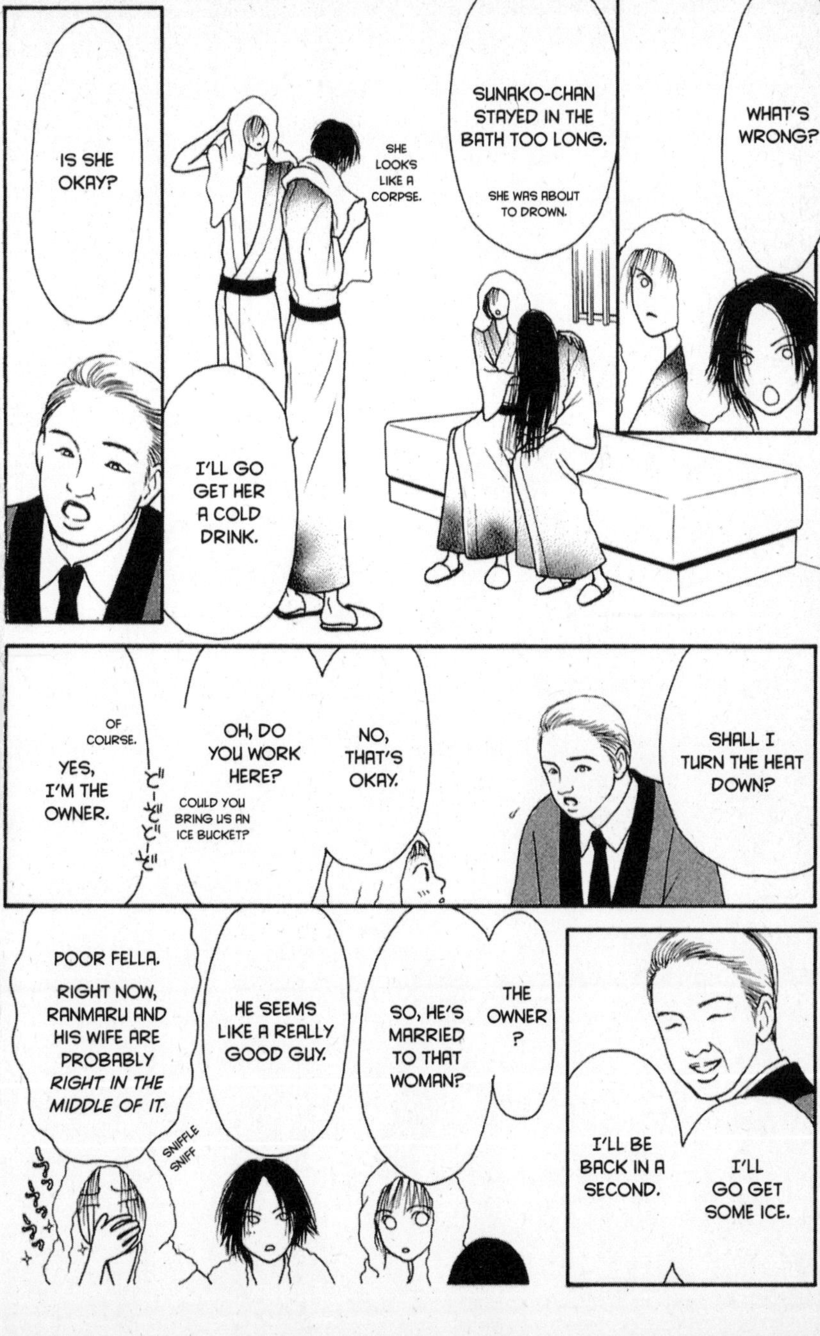
WHAT'S WRONG?
SUNAKO-CHAN STAYED IN THE BATH TOO LONG.
SHE WAS ABOUT TO DROWN.
SHE LOOKS LIKE A CORPSE.
I'LL GO GET HER A COLD DRINK.
IS SHE OKAY?
SHALL I TURN THE HEAT DOWN?
NO, THAT'S OKAY.
OH, DO YOU WORK HERE?
COULD YOU BRING US AN ICE BUCKET?
YES, I'M THE OWNER.
OF COURSE.
I'LL GO GET SOME ICE.
I'LL BE BACK IN A SECOND.
THE OWNER?
SO, HE'S MARRIED TO THAT WOMAN?
HE SEEMS LIKE A REALLY GOOD GUY.
SNIFFLE SNIFF
POOR FELLA.
RIGHT NOW, RANMARU AND HIS WIFE ARE PROBABLY *RIGHT IN THE MIDDLE OF IT.*

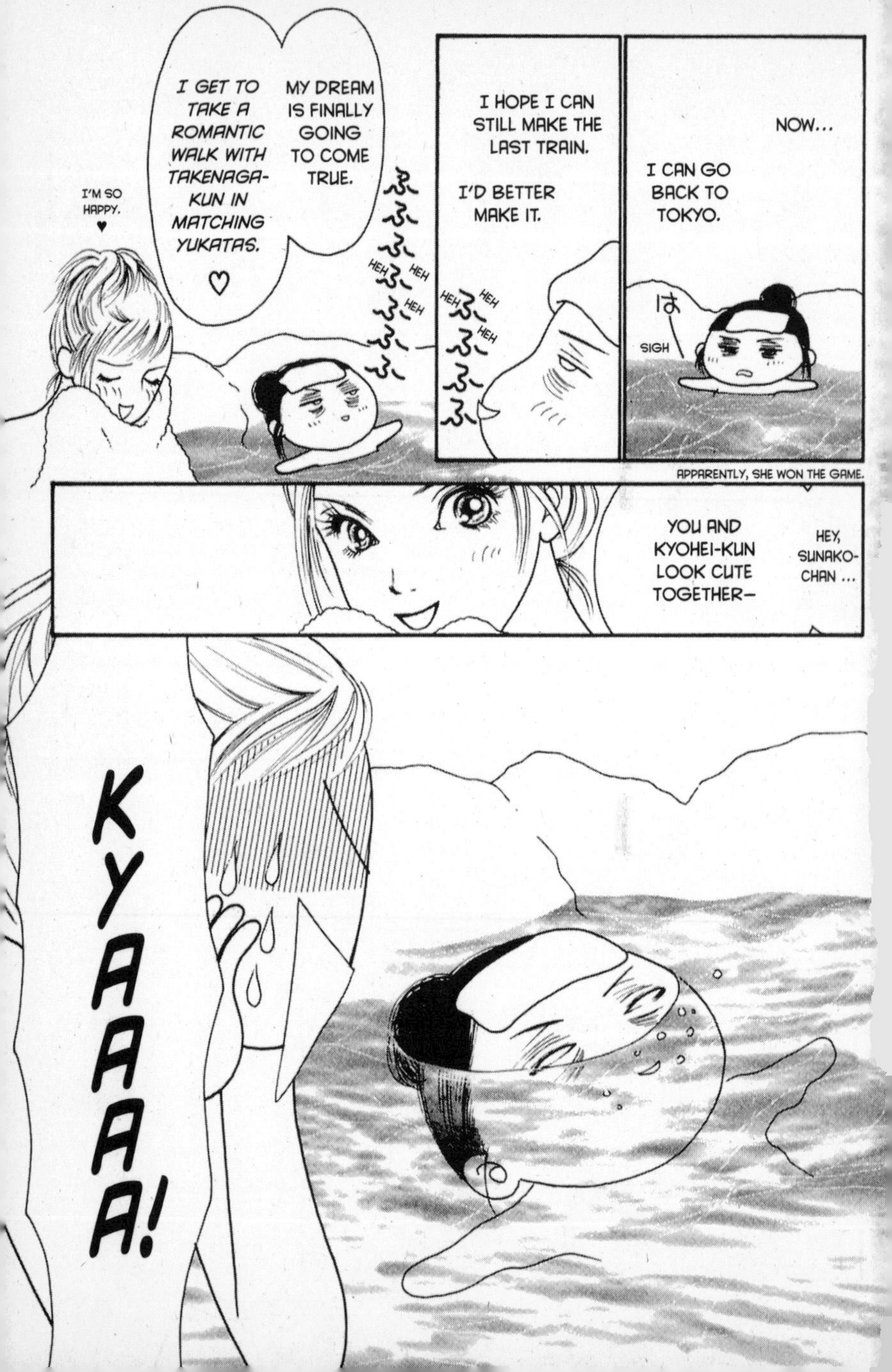
NOW...
I CAN GO BACK TO TOKYO.
は
SIGH
I HOPE I CAN STILL MAKE THE LAST TRAIN.
I'D BETTER MAKE IT.
ふふふふ
HEH HEH HEH
MY DREAM IS FINALLY GOING TO COME TRUE.
I GET TO TAKE A ROMANTIC WALK WITH TAKENAGA-KUN IN MATCHING YUKATAS. ♡
ふふふふふふふ
HEH HEH HEH
I'M SO HAPPY. ♥
APPARENTLY, SHE WON THE GAME.
HEY, SUNAKO-CHAN ...
YOU AND KYOHEI-KUN LOOK CUTE TOGETHER—
KYAAAAA!

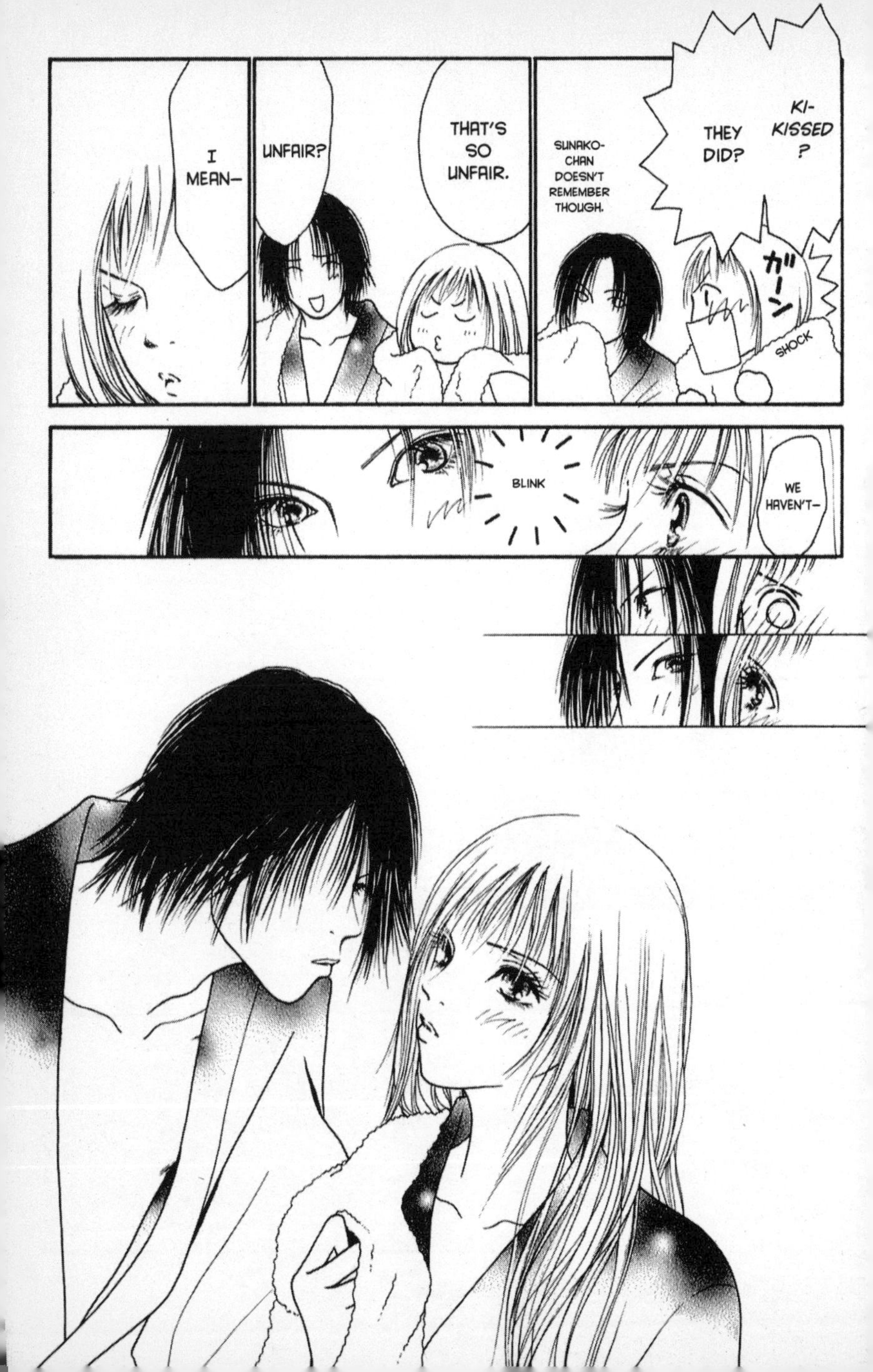
KI-KISSED?
THEY DID?
SUNAKO-CHAN DOESN'T REMEMBER THOUGH.
ガーン
SHOCK
THAT'S SO UNFAIR.
UNFAIR?
I MEAN—
WE HAVEN'T—
BLINK

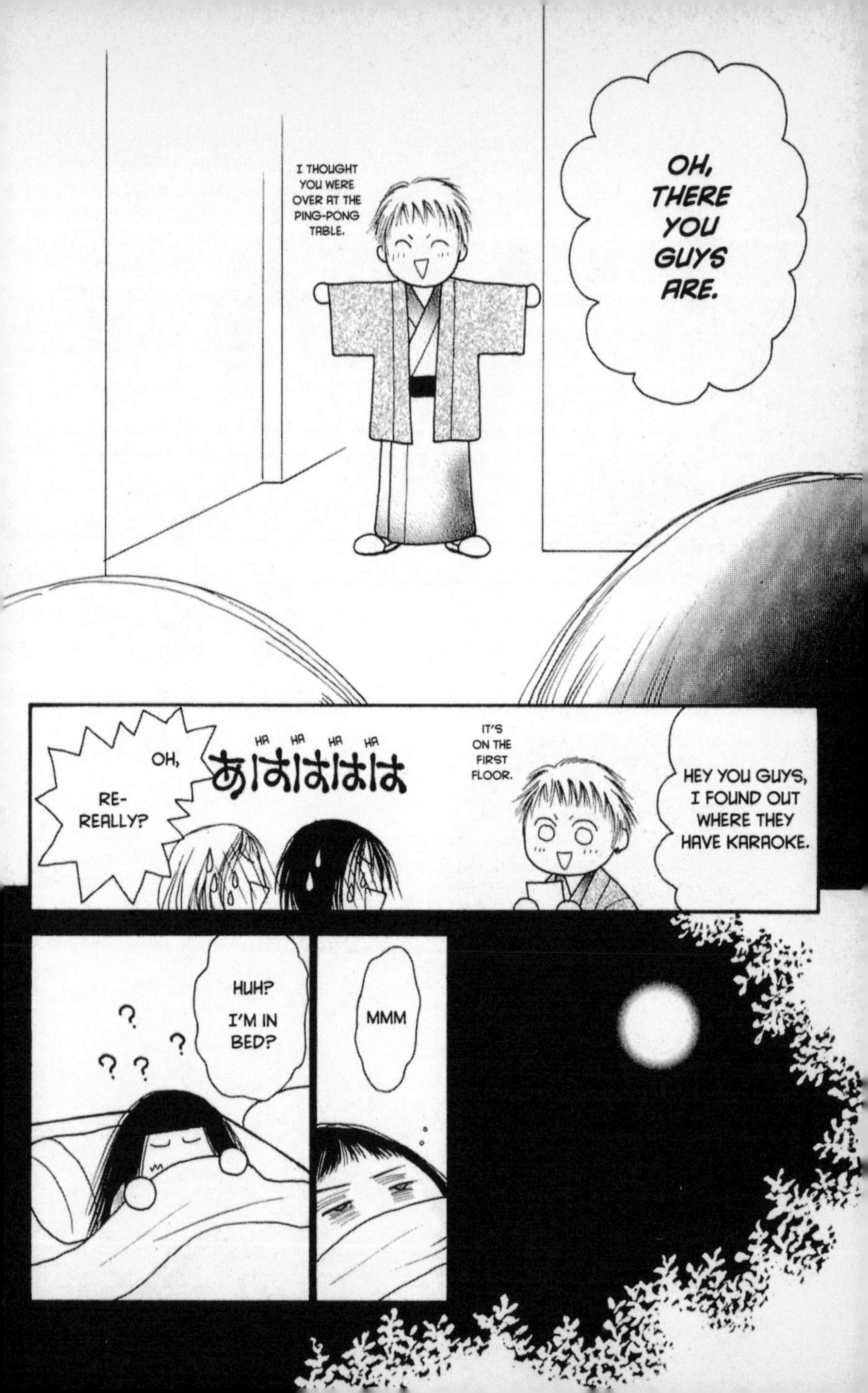
OH, THERE YOU GUYS ARE.
I THOUGHT YOU WERE OVER AT THE PING-PONG TABLE.
HEY YOU GUYS, I FOUND OUT WHERE THEY HAVE KARAOKE.
IT'S ON THE FIRST FLOOR.
HA HA HA HA
あはははは
OH, RE-REALLY?
MMM
HUH? I'M IN BED?
? ? ? ?

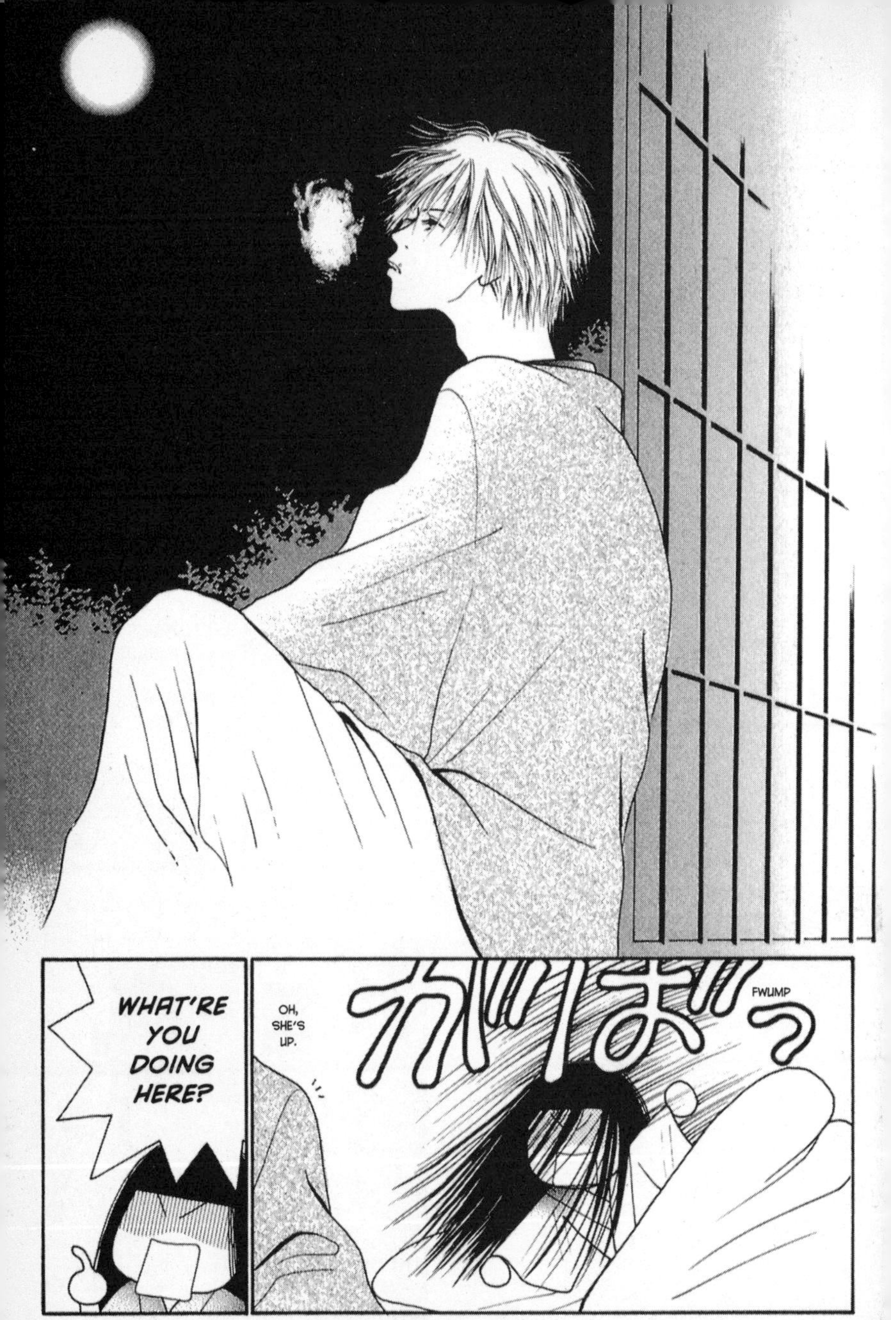
FWUMP
OH, SHE'S UP.
WHAT'RE YOU DOING HERE?

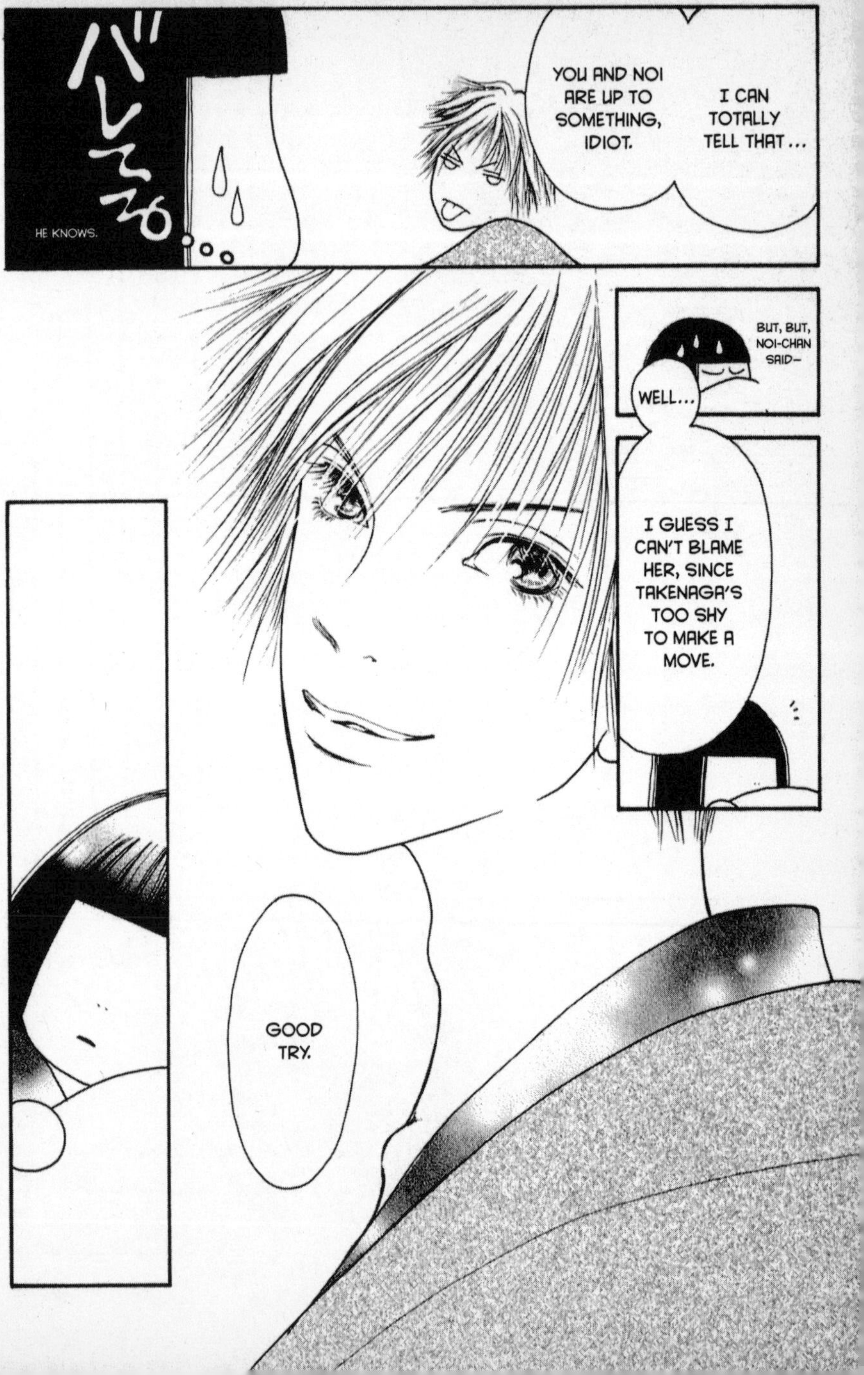
I CAN TOTALLY TELL THAT...
YOU AND NOI ARE UP TO SOMETHING, IDIOT.
バレてる
HE KNOWS.
BUT, BUT, NOI-CHAN SAID—
WELL...
I GUESS I CAN'T BLAME HER, SINCE TAKENAGA'S TOO SHY TO MAKE A MOVE.
GOOD TRY.

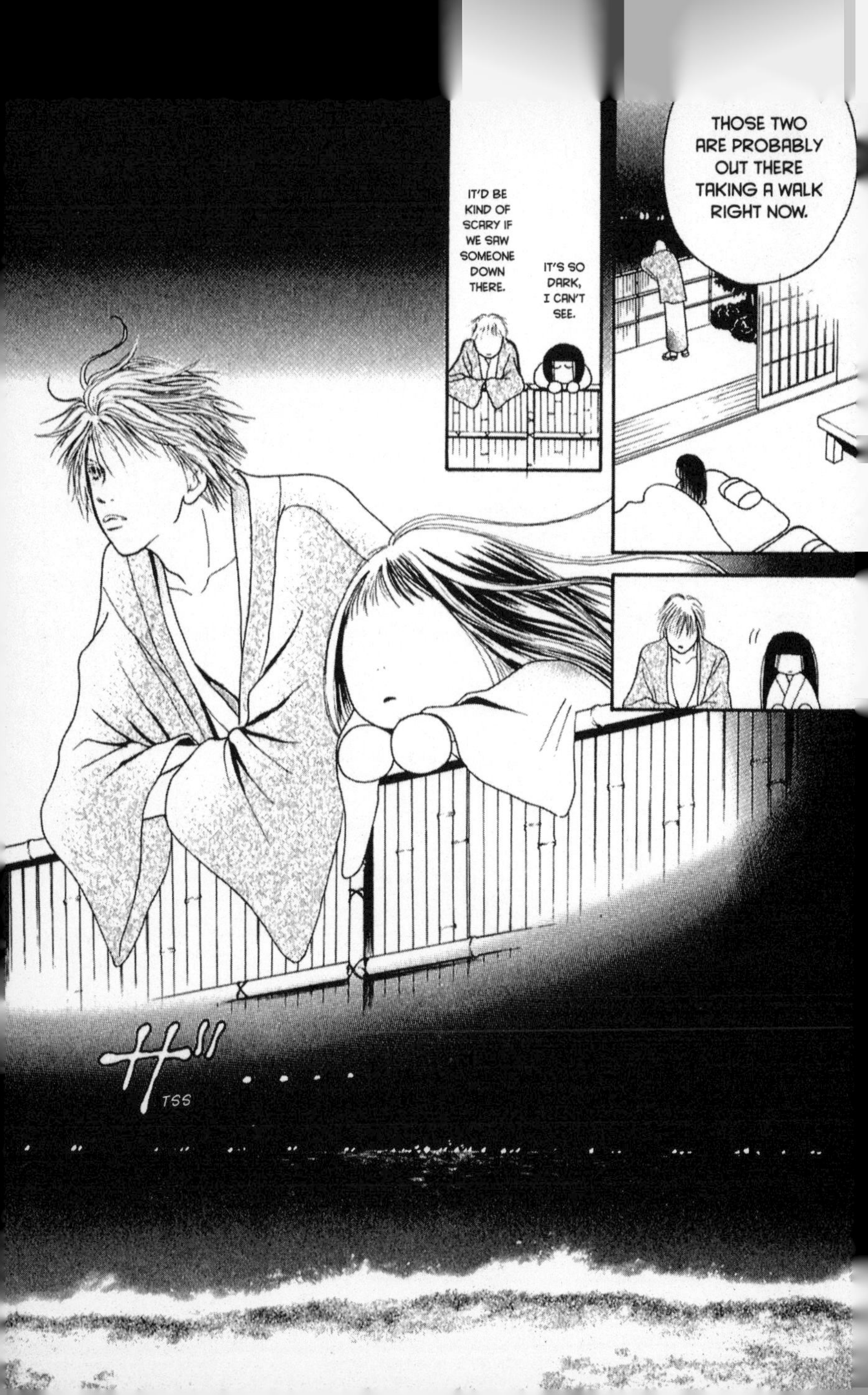
THOSE TWO ARE PROBABLY OUT THERE TAKING A WALK RIGHT NOW.
IT'S SO DARK, I CAN'T SEE.
IT'D BE KIND OF SCARY IF WE SAW SOMEONE DOWN THERE.
TSS

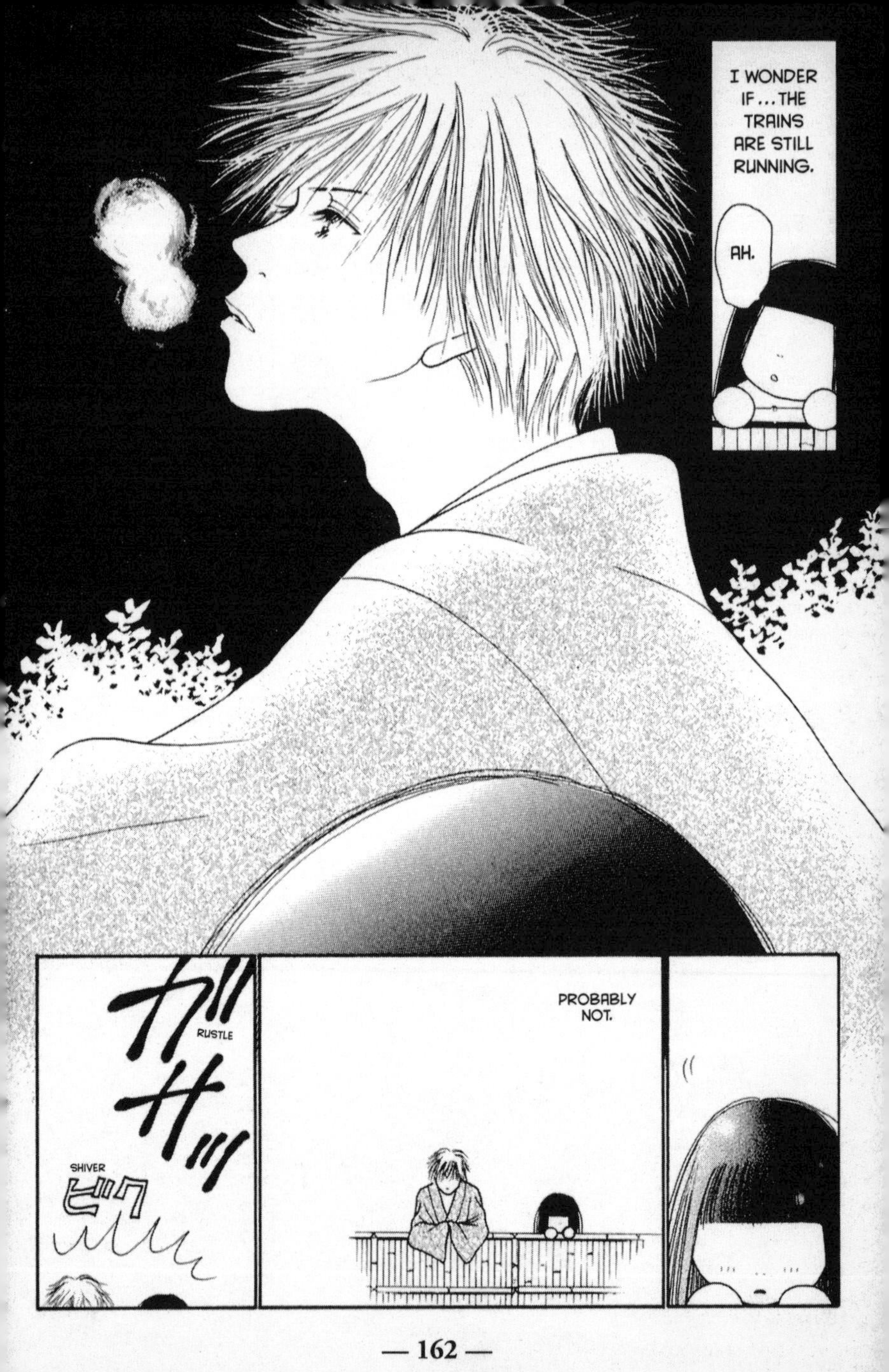
I WONDER IF... THE TRAINS ARE STILL RUNNING.
AH.
PROBABLY NOT.
RUSTLE
SHIVER

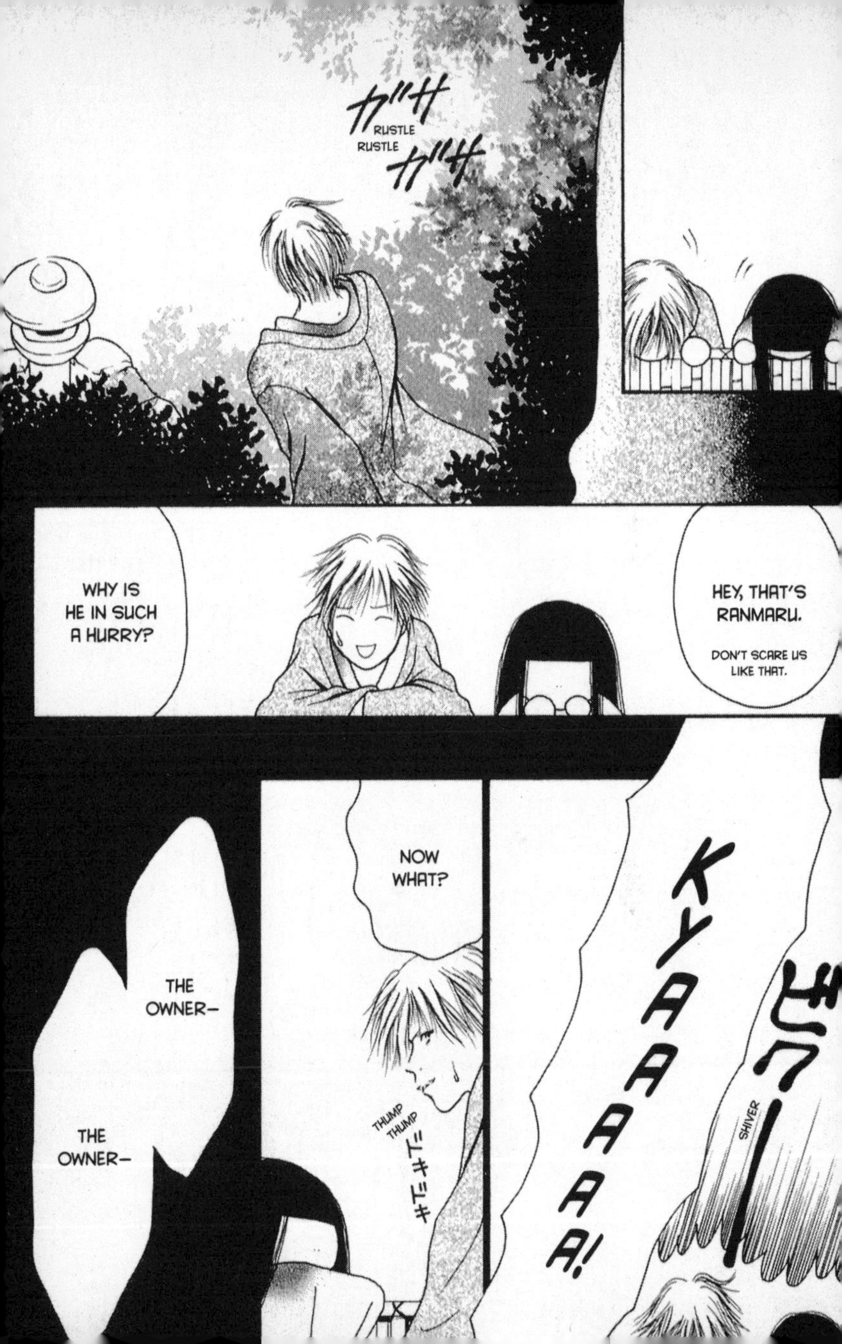
RUSTLE
RUSTLE
HEY, THAT'S RANMARU.
DON'T SCARE US LIKE THAT.
WHY IS HE IN SUCH A HURRY?
KYAAAAAAA!
SHIVER
NOW WHAT?
THUMP THUMP
THE OWNER–
THE OWNER–

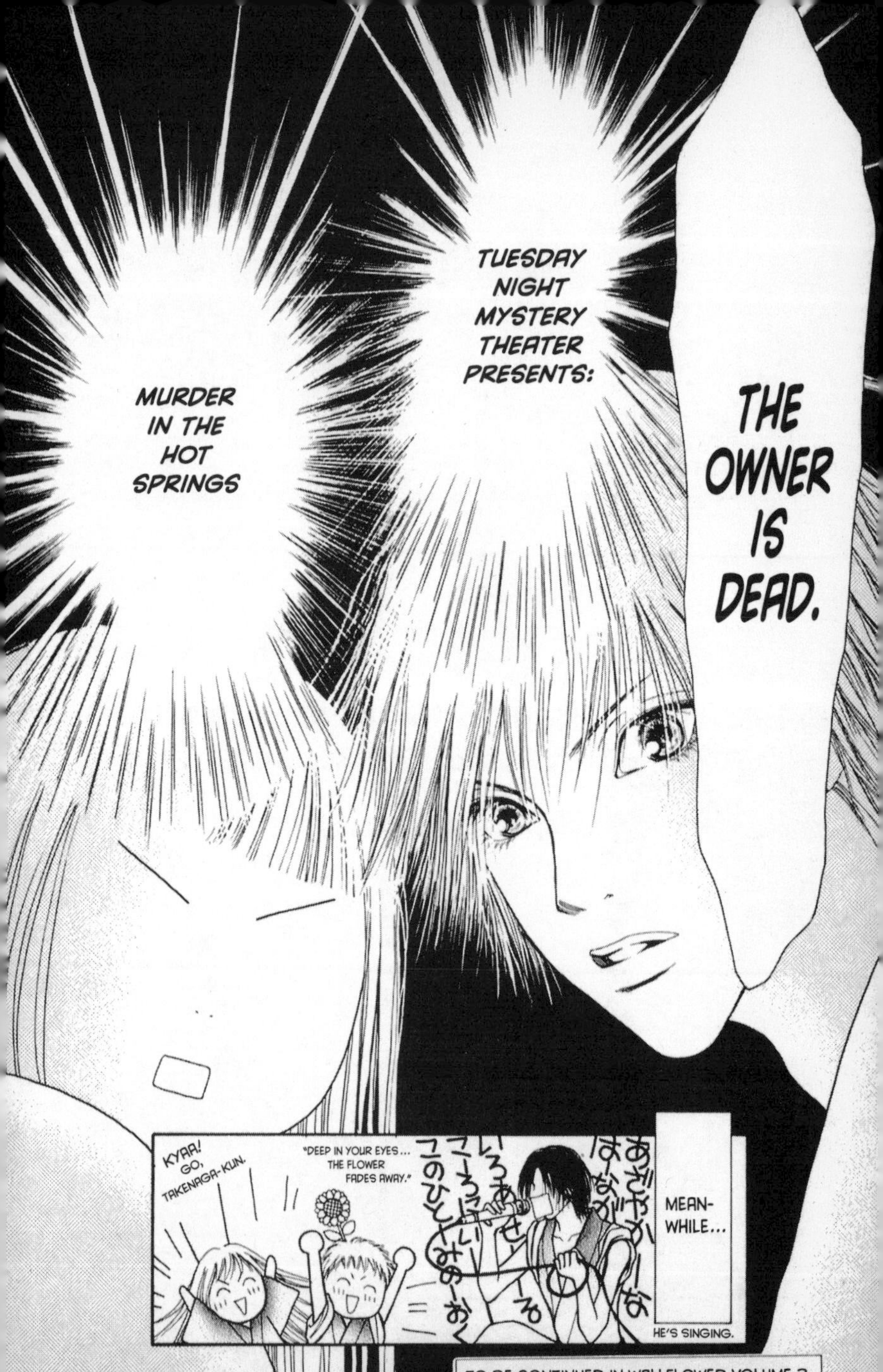
THE OWNER IS DEAD.
TUESDAY NIGHT MYSTERY THEATER PRESENTS:
MURDER IN THE HOT SPRINGS
MEAN-WHILE...
"DEEP IN YOUR EYES... THE FLOWER FADES AWAY."
KYAA! GO, TAKENAGA-KUN.
HE'S SINGING.

TO BE CONTINUED IN WALLFLOWER VOLUME 3.

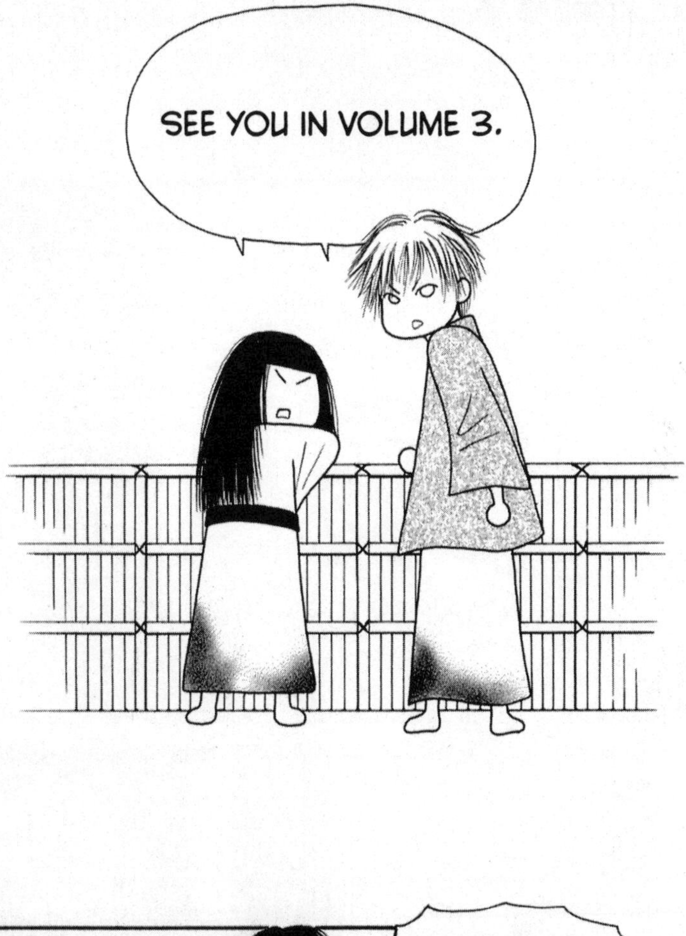
SEE YOU IN VOLUME 3.

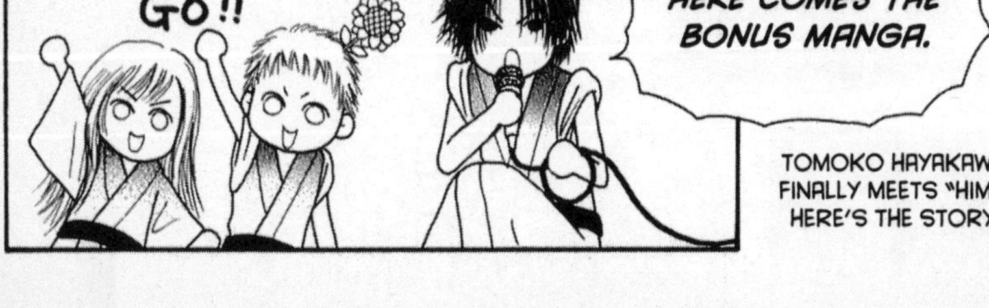
HERE COMES THE BONUS MANGA.
GO!!

TOMOKO HAYAKAWA FINALLY MEETS "HIM." HERE'S THE STORY.

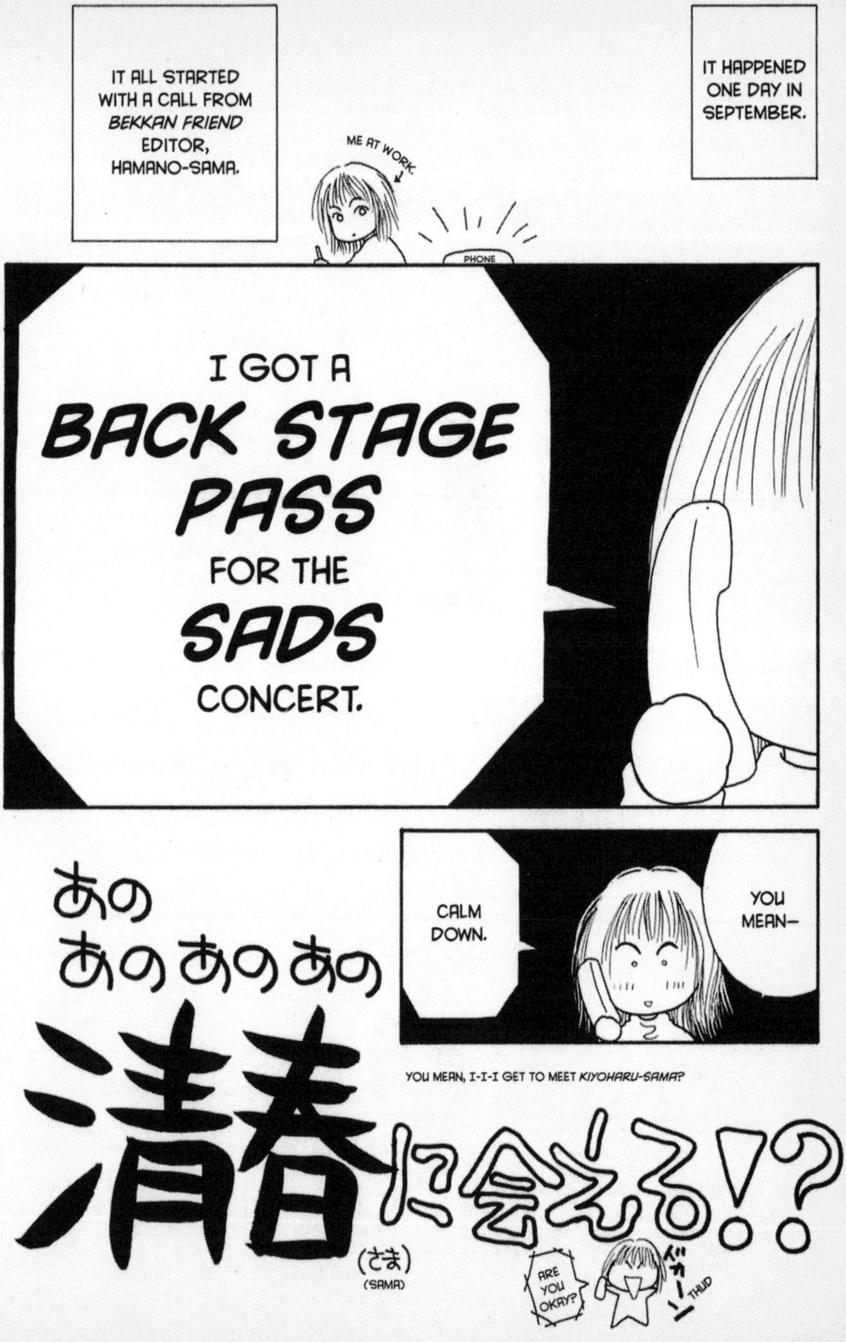
IT HAPPENED ONE DAY IN SEPTEMBER.
IT ALL STARTED WITH A CALL FROM *BEKKAN FRIEND* EDITOR, HAMANO-SAMA.
ME AT WORK.
PHONE
I GOT A **BACK STAGE PASS** FOR THE **SADS** CONCERT.
YOU MEAN—
CALM DOWN.
あの
あのあのあの
清春(さま)に会える!?
(SAMA)
YOU MEAN, I-I-I GET TO MEET *KIYOHARU-SAMA*?
ベガーン
THUD
ARE YOU OKAY?

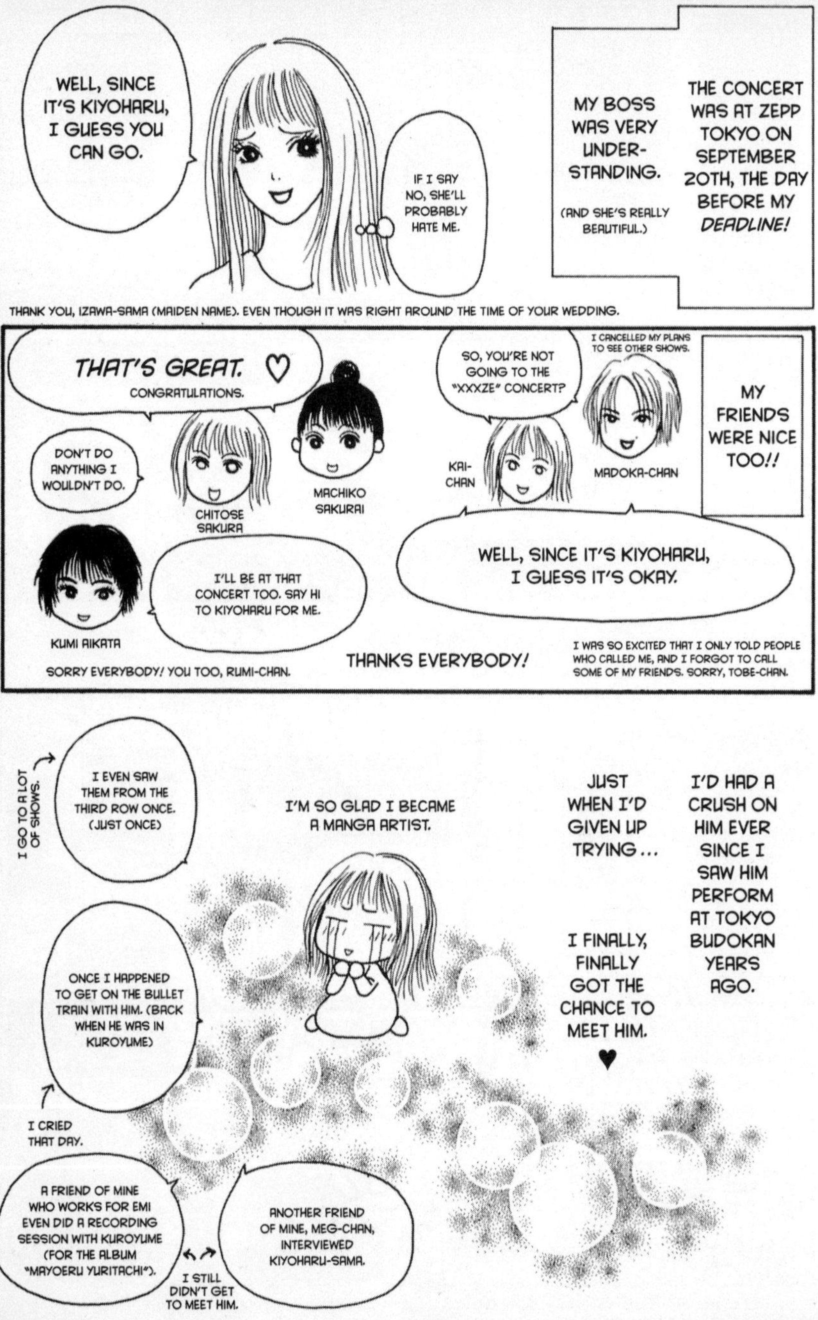
THE CONCERT WAS AT ZEPP TOKYO ON SEPTEMBER 20TH, THE DAY BEFORE MY *DEADLINE!*
MY BOSS WAS VERY UNDER-STANDING.
(AND SHE'S REALLY BEAUTIFUL.)
IF I SAY NO, SHE'LL PROBABLY HATE ME.
WELL, SINCE IT'S KIYOHARU, I GUESS YOU CAN GO.
THANK YOU, IZAWA-SAMA (MAIDEN NAME). EVEN THOUGH IT WAS RIGHT AROUND THE TIME OF YOUR WEDDING.
MY FRIENDS WERE NICE TOO!!
I CANCELLED MY PLANS TO SEE OTHER SHOWS.
SO, YOU'RE NOT GOING TO THE "XXXZE" CONCERT?
MADOKA-CHAN
KAI-CHAN
THAT'S GREAT. ♡
CONGRATULATIONS.
MACHIKO SAKURAI
DON'T DO ANYTHING I WOULDN'T DO.
CHITOSE SAKURA
WELL, SINCE IT'S KIYOHARU, I GUESS IT'S OKAY.
I'LL BE AT THAT CONCERT TOO. SAY HI TO KIYOHARU FOR ME.
KUMI AIKATA
I WAS SO EXCITED THAT I ONLY TOLD PEOPLE WHO CALLED ME, AND I FORGOT TO CALL SOME OF MY FRIENDS. SORRY, TOBE-CHAN.
THANKS EVERYBODY!
SORRY EVERYBODY! YOU TOO, RUMI-CHAN.
I'D HAD A CRUSH ON HIM EVER SINCE I SAW HIM PERFORM AT TOKYO BUDOKAN YEARS AGO.
JUST WHEN I'D GIVEN UP TRYING...
I FINALLY, FINALLY GOT THE CHANCE TO MEET HIM. ♥
I'M SO GLAD I BECAME A MANGA ARTIST.
I EVEN SAW THEM FROM THE THIRD ROW ONCE. (JUST ONCE)
I GO TO A LOT OF SHOWS.
ONCE I HAPPENED TO GET ON THE BULLET TRAIN WITH HIM. (BACK WHEN HE WAS IN KUROYUME)
I CRIED THAT DAY.
ANOTHER FRIEND OF MINE, MEG-CHAN, INTERVIEWED KIYOHARU-SAMA.
A FRIEND OF MINE WHO WORKS FOR EMI EVEN DID A RECORDING SESSION WITH KUROYUME (FOR THE ALBUM "MAYOERU YURITACHI").
I STILL DIDN'T GET TO MEET HIM.

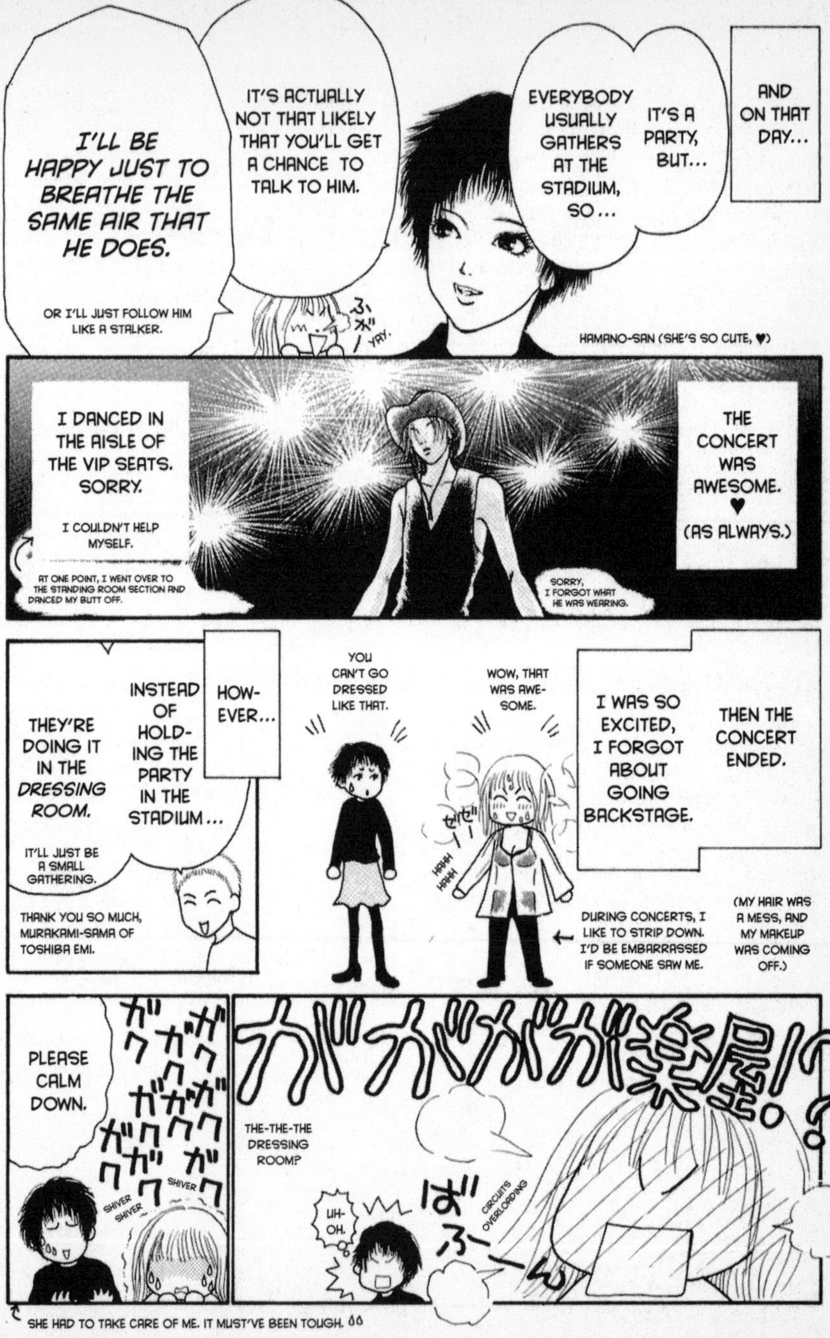
AND ON THAT DAY...
IT'S A PARTY, BUT...
EVERYBODY USUALLY GATHERS AT THE STADIUM, SO...
IT'S ACTUALLY NOT THAT LIKELY THAT YOU'LL GET A CHANCE TO TALK TO HIM.
I'LL BE HAPPY JUST TO BREATHE THE SAME AIR THAT HE DOES.
OR I'LL JUST FOLLOW HIM LIKE A STALKER.
YAY.
HAMANO-SAN (SHE'S SO CUTE, ♥)
THE CONCERT WAS AWESOME. ♥ (AS ALWAYS.)
SORRY, I FORGOT WHAT HE WAS WEARING.
I DANCED IN THE AISLE OF THE VIP SEATS. SORRY.
I COULDN'T HELP MYSELF.
AT ONE POINT, I WENT OVER TO THE STANDING ROOM SECTION AND DANCED MY BUTT OFF.
THEN THE CONCERT ENDED.
I WAS SO EXCITED, I FORGOT ABOUT GOING BACKSTAGE.
(MY HAIR WAS A MESS, AND MY MAKEUP WAS COMING OFF.)
WOW, THAT WAS AWE-SOME.
YOU CAN'T GO DRESSED LIKE THAT.
HAHH HAHH
DURING CONCERTS, I LIKE TO STRIP DOWN. I'D BE EMBARRASSED IF SOMEONE SAW ME.
HOW-EVER...
INSTEAD OF HOLD-ING THE PARTY IN THE STADIUM...
THEY'RE DOING IT IN THE *DRESSING ROOM.*
IT'LL JUST BE A SMALL GATHERING.
THANK YOU SO MUCH, MURAKAMI-SAMA OF TOSHIBA EMI.
ガガガガ楽屋!?
THE-THE-THE DRESSING ROOM?
ぼふーん
CIRCUITS OVERLOADING
UH-OH.
PLEASE CALM DOWN.
ガクガクガクガクガクガクガクガク
SHIVER SHIVER
SHIVER
SHE HAD TO TAKE CARE OF ME. IT MUST'VE BEEN TOUGH.

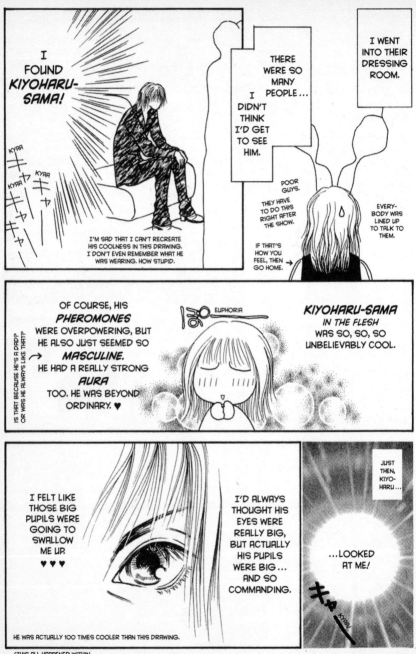

I WENT INTO THEIR DRESSING ROOM.
THERE WERE SO MANY PEOPLE...
I DIDN'T THINK I'D GET TO SEE HIM.
EVERY-BODY WAS LINED UP TO TALK TO THEM.
POOR GUYS.
THEY HAVE TO DO THIS RIGHT AFTER THE SHOW.
IF THAT'S HOW YOU FEEL, THEN GO HOME.
I FOUND KIYOHARU-SAMA!
KYAA
KYAA
KYAA
I'M SAD THAT I CAN'T RECREATE HIS COOLNESS IN THIS DRAWING. I DON'T EVEN REMEMBER WHAT HE WAS WEARING. HOW STUPID.
KIYOHARU-SAMA IN THE FLESH WAS SO, SO, SO UNBELIEVABLY COOL.
EUPHORIA
OF COURSE, HIS PHEROMONES WERE OVERPOWERING, BUT HE ALSO JUST SEEMED SO MASCULINE. HE HAD A REALLY STRONG AURA TOO. HE WAS BEYOND ORDINARY. ♥
IS THAT BECAUSE HE'S A DAD? OR WAS HE ALWAYS LIKE THAT?
JUST THEN, KIYO-HARU...
...LOOKED AT ME!
KYAA!
I'D ALWAYS THOUGHT HIS EYES WERE REALLY BIG, BUT ACTUALLY HIS PUPILS WERE BIG... AND SO COMMANDING.
I FELT LIKE THOSE BIG PUPILS WERE GOING TO SWALLOW ME UP. ♥♥♥
HE WAS ACTUALLY 100 TIMES COOLER THAN THIS DRAWING.

(THIS ALL HAPPENED WITHIN 1/10 OF A SECOND.)

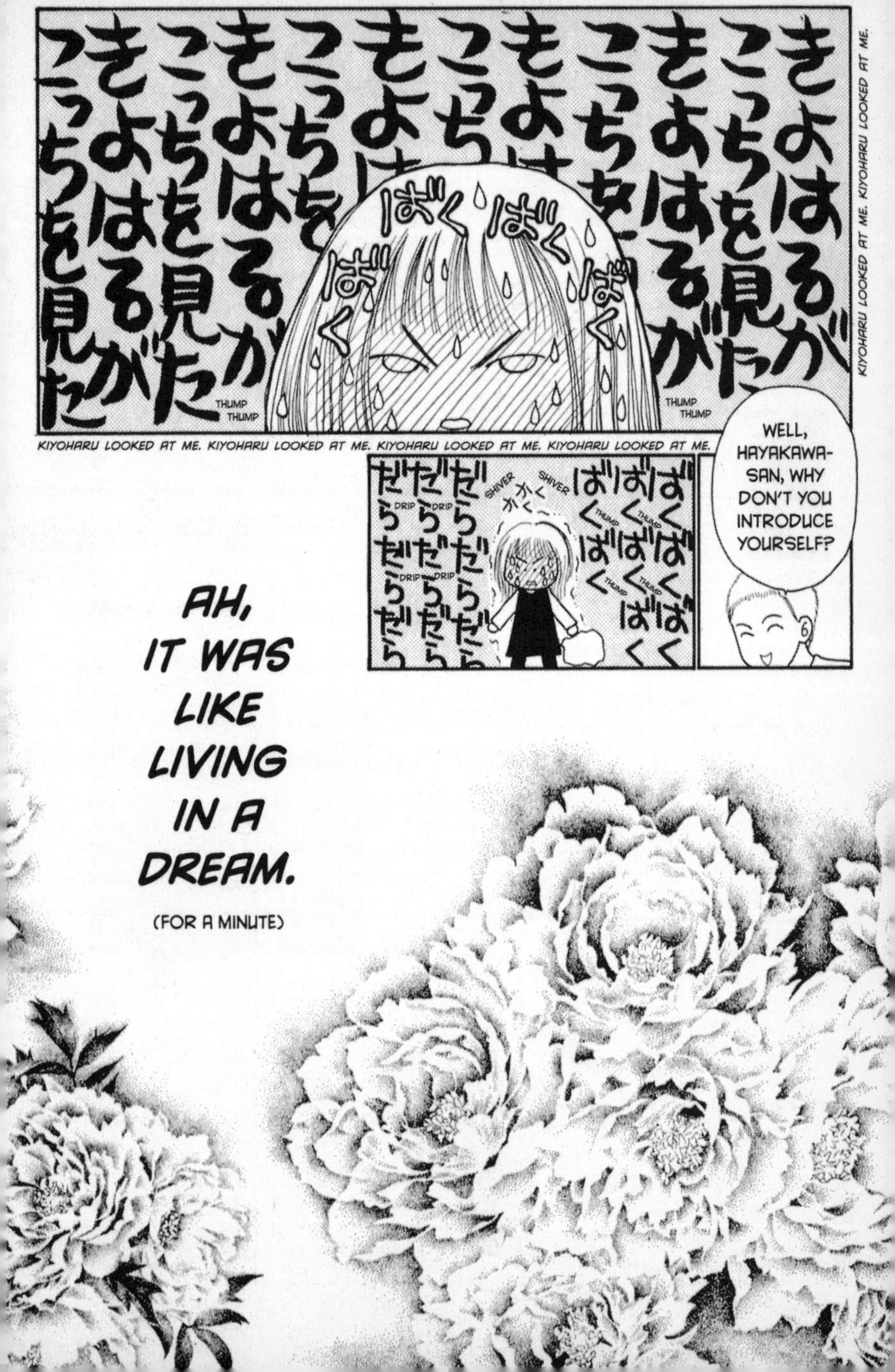

きよはるが
こっちを見た
きよはるが
こっちを見た
ばくばくばくばく
THUMP THUMP
THUMP THUMP
KIYOHARU LOOKED AT ME. KIYOHARU LOOKED AT ME.
KIYOHARU LOOKED AT ME. KIYOHARU LOOKED AT ME. KIYOHARU LOOKED AT ME. KIYOHARU LOOKED AT ME.
WELL, HAYAKAWA-SAN, WHY DON'T YOU INTRODUCE YOURSELF?
ばくばくばくばくばくばく
THUMP THUMP THUMP THUMP
かくかく
SHIVER SHIVER
だらだらだらだらだらだら
DRIP DRIP DRIP DRIP
AH, IT WAS LIKE LIVING IN A DREAM.
(FOR A MINUTE)

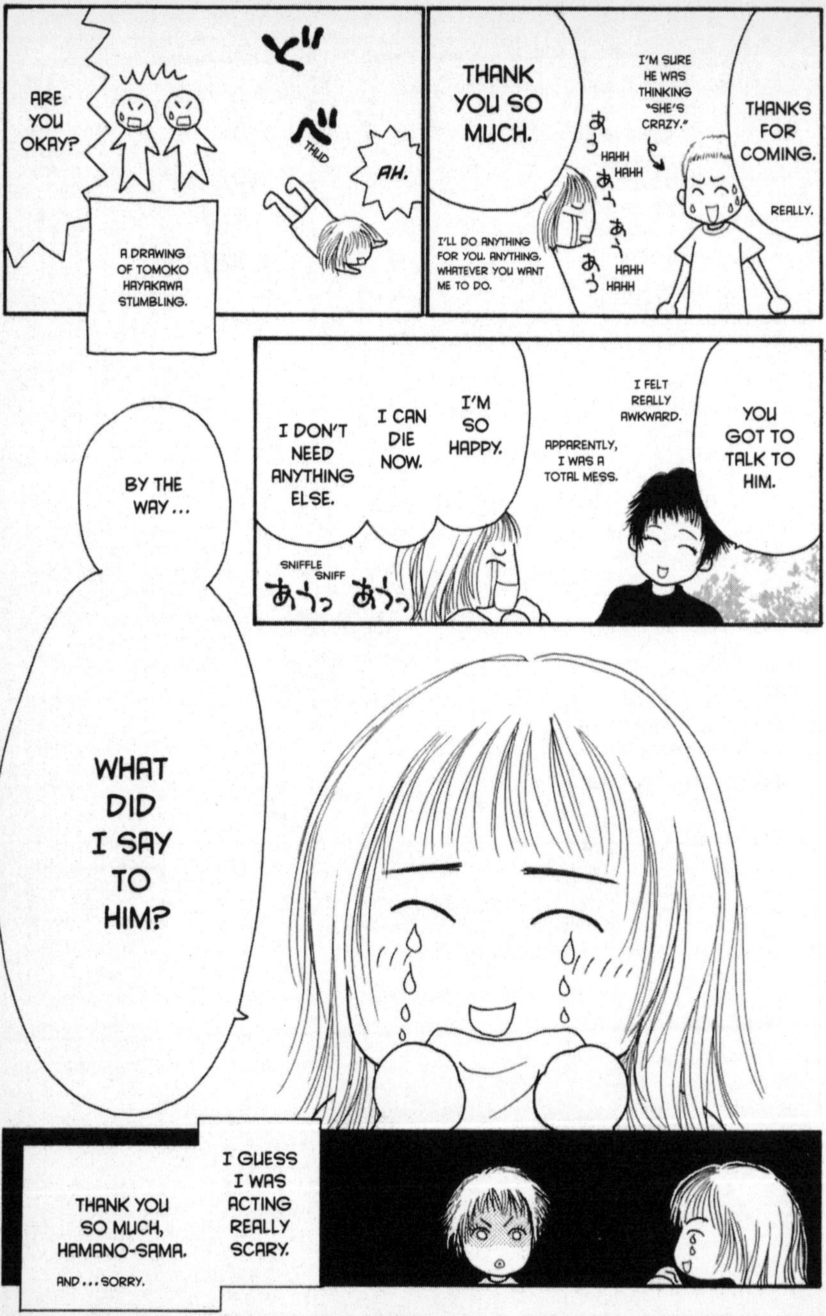
THANKS FOR COMING.
REALLY.
I'M SURE HE WAS THINKING "SHE'S CRAZY."
THANK YOU SO MUCH.
HAHH HAHH
HAHH HAHH
I'LL DO ANYTHING FOR YOU. ANYTHING. WHATEVER YOU WANT ME TO DO.
AH.
THUD
ARE YOU OKAY?
A DRAWING OF TOMOKO HAYAKAWA STUMBLING.
YOU GOT TO TALK TO HIM.
I FELT REALLY AWKWARD.
APPARENTLY, I WAS A TOTAL MESS.
I'M SO HAPPY.
I CAN DIE NOW.
I DON'T NEED ANYTHING ELSE.
SNIFFLE SNIFF
BY THE WAY...
WHAT DID I SAY TO HIM?
I GUESS I WAS ACTING REALLY SCARY.
THANK YOU SO MUCH, HAMANO-SAMA.
AND... SORRY.

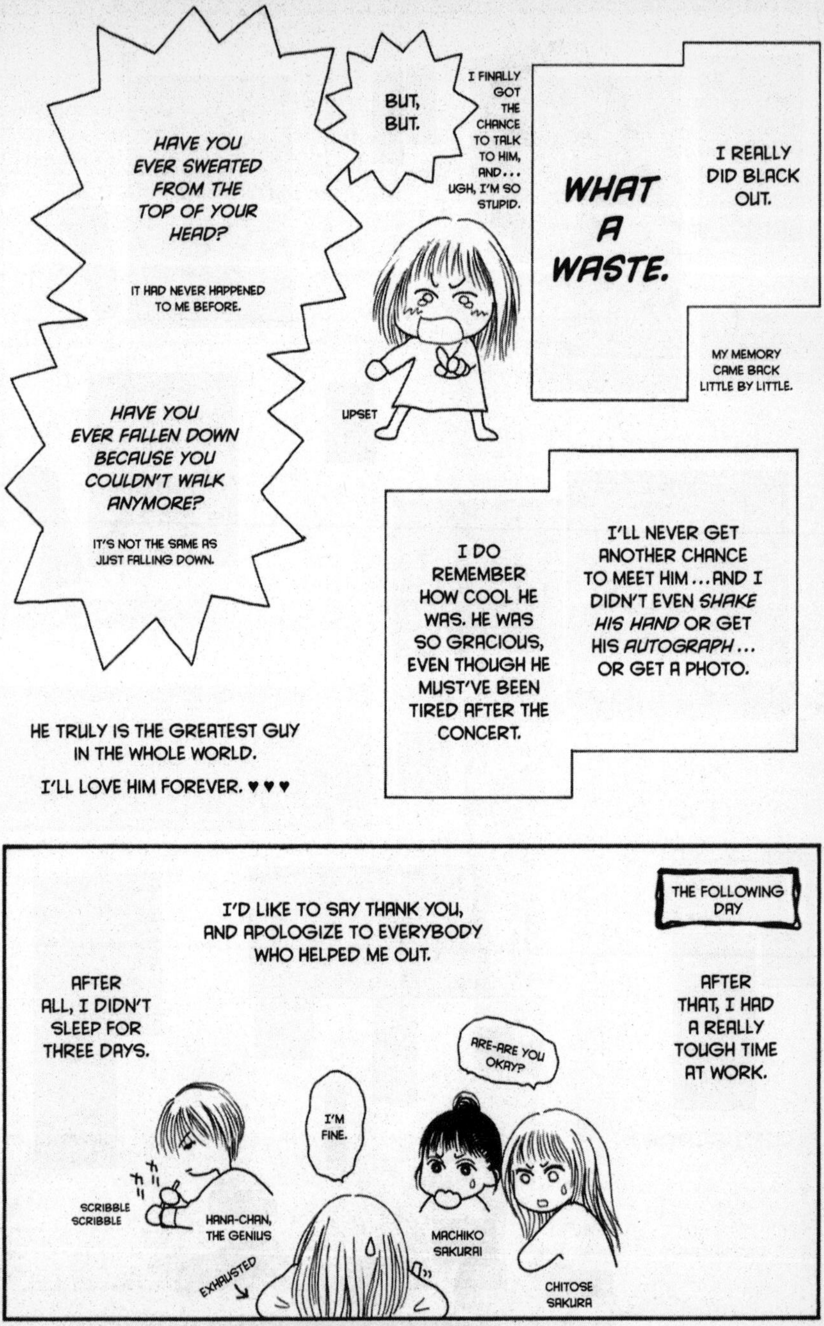
I REALLY DID BLACK OUT.
WHAT A WASTE.
MY MEMORY CAME BACK LITTLE BY LITTLE.
I FINALLY GOT THE CHANCE TO TALK TO HIM, AND... UGH, I'M SO STUPID.
BUT, BUT.
UPSET
HAVE YOU EVER SWEATED FROM THE TOP OF YOUR HEAD?
IT HAD NEVER HAPPENED TO ME BEFORE.
HAVE YOU EVER FALLEN DOWN BECAUSE YOU COULDN'T WALK ANYMORE?
IT'S NOT THE SAME AS JUST FALLING DOWN.
I'LL NEVER GET ANOTHER CHANCE TO MEET HIM... AND I DIDN'T EVEN *SHAKE HIS HAND* OR GET HIS *AUTOGRAPH*... OR GET A PHOTO.
I DO REMEMBER HOW COOL HE WAS. HE WAS SO GRACIOUS, EVEN THOUGH HE MUST'VE BEEN TIRED AFTER THE CONCERT.
HE TRULY IS THE GREATEST GUY IN THE WHOLE WORLD.
I'LL LOVE HIM FOREVER. ♥♥♥
THE FOLLOWING DAY
AFTER THAT, I HAD A REALLY TOUGH TIME AT WORK.
I'D LIKE TO SAY THANK YOU, AND APOLOGIZE TO EVERYBODY WHO HELPED ME OUT.
AFTER ALL, I DIDN'T SLEEP FOR THREE DAYS.
ARE-ARE YOU OKAY?
CHITOSE SAKURA
MACHIKO SAKURAI
I'M FINE.
EXHAUSTED
HANA-CHAN, THE GENIUS
SCRIBBLE SCRIBBLE

AS I WRITE THIS, MACHIKO SAKURAI IS AT MY HOUSE.

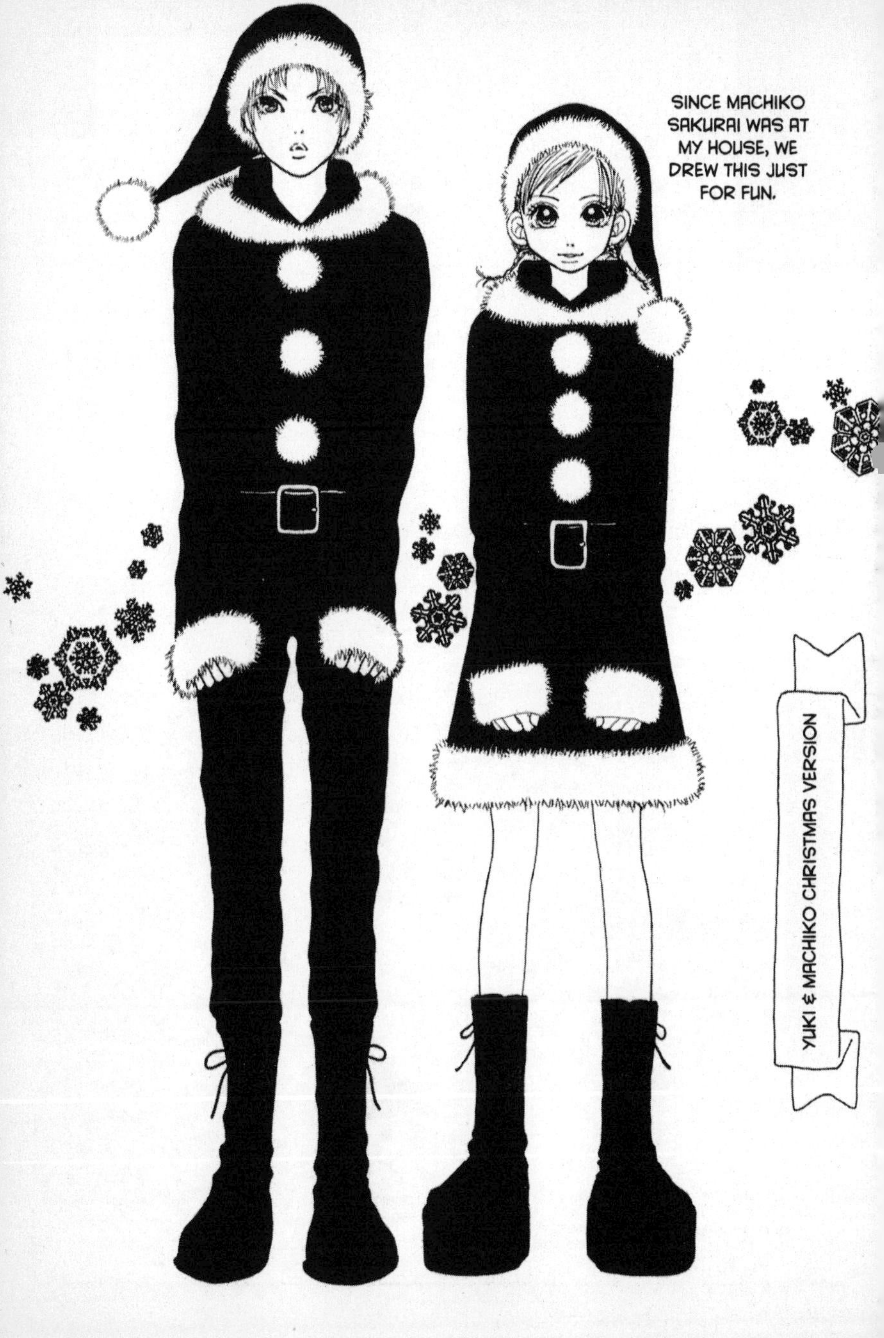
SINCE MACHIKO SAKURAI WAS AT MY HOUSE, WE DREW THIS JUST FOR FUN.
YUKI & MACHIKO CHRISTMAS VERSION

EXTRA BONUS

I GUESS IT'S BECAUSE I'M DRAWING A MANGA ABOUT "FOUR GUYS" THAT I KEEP GETTING LETTERS ASKING IF I BASED THEM ON THE "FOUR GUYS FROM THAT POPULAR BAND." PEOPLE KEEP COMPARING THE CHARACTERS TO THESE BAND MEMBERS.

LISTEN TO ME, THEY'RE NOT BASED ON THAT BAND. WHY WOULD A ***KIYOHARU MANIAC*** LIKE MYSELF BASE MY CHARACTERS ON SOME FAMOUS BAND?

I ALMOST WANT TO SAY THAT, OTHER THAN ***TAKENAGA***, THEY'RE ALL BASED ON ***KIYOHARU***. BUT OF COURSE, THEY LOOK NOTHING LIKE HIM.

HERE ARE SOME GUYS WHO *SLIGHTLY RESEMBLE* MY CHARACTERS. IF YOU WANT TO COMPARE THEM TO SOMEBODY, PLEASE COMPARE THEM TO THESE GUYS. (EXCEPT FOR TAKENAGA).

I'D BE HAPPY IF YOU'D COMPARE THEM TO BOY BANDS OR CELEBRITIES OR MOVIE STARS.

OH, OF COURSE I DESIGNED THEIR PERSONALITIES ALL BY MYSELF.

THEY'RE ALL MUSICIANS, EXCEPT FOR OGINO-KUN, WHO'S IN ADVERTISING. I GOT MOST OF THE PICTURES FROM FLYERS. THANKS FOR LETTING ME BORROW THE PICTURE, OGINO-KUN.

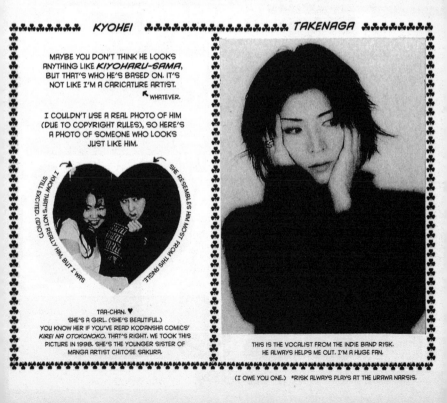

KYOHEI

MAYBE YOU DON'T THINK HE LOOKS ANYTHING LIKE ***KIYOHARU-SAMA***, BUT THAT'S WHO HE'S BASED ON. IT'S NOT LIKE I'M A CARICATURE ARTIST.

↖ WHATEVER.

I COULDN'T USE A REAL PHOTO OF HIM (DUE TO COPYRIGHT RULES), SO HERE'S A PHOTO OF SOMEONE WHO LOOKS JUST LIKE HIM.

I KNOW THAT'S NOT REALLY HIM, BUT I WAS STILL EXCITED. (IDIOT)

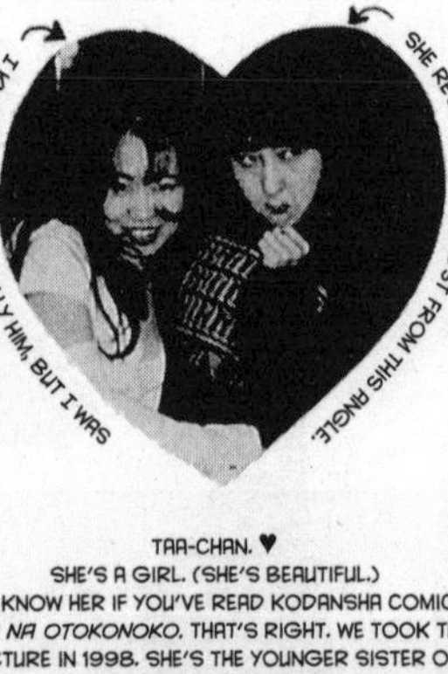

SHE RESEMBLES HIM MOST FROM THIS ANGLE.

TAA-CHAN. ♥
SHE'S A GIRL. (SHE'S BEAUTIFUL.)
YOU KNOW HER IF YOU'VE READ KODANSHA COMICS' *KIREI NA OTOKONOKO*. THAT'S RIGHT. WE TOOK THIS PICTURE IN 1998. SHE'S THE YOUNGER SISTER OF MANGA ARTIST CHITOSE SAKURA.

TAKENAGA

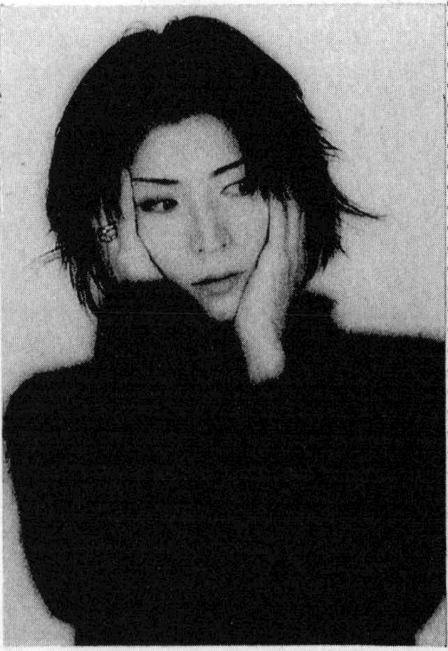

THIS IS THE VOCALIST FROM THE INDIE BAND RISK. HE ALWAYS HELPS ME OUT. I'M A HUGE FAN.

(I OWE YOU ONE.) *RISK ALWAYS PLAYS AT THE URAWA NARSIS.

RANMARU

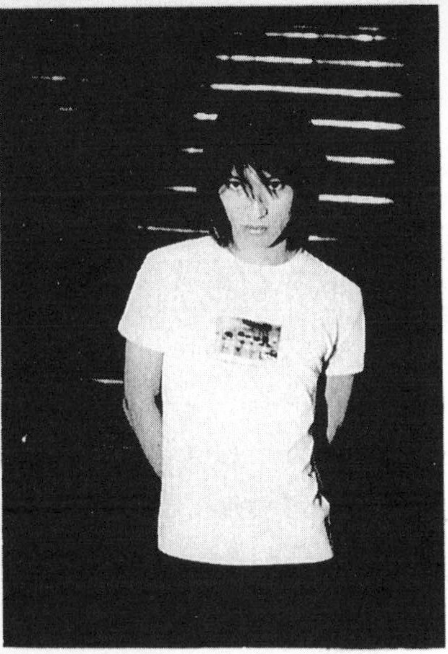

THIS IS OGIRI-KUN, THE VOCALIST FOR SHOCKING LEMON.
HE'S SO COOL. ♥ HE'S REALLY A GREAT GUY.
HE'S SO MANLY. HE'S NICE TOO.

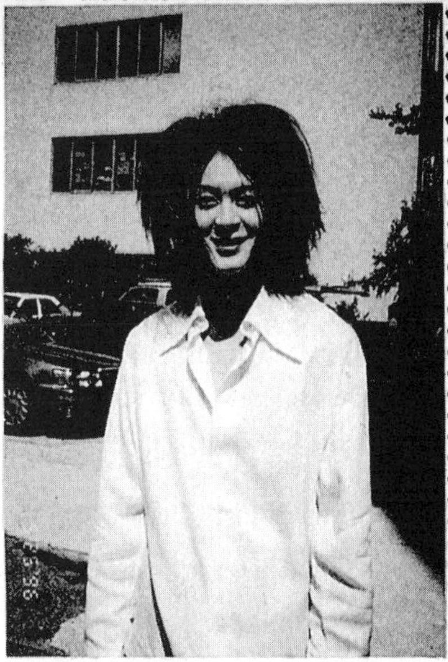

I'M SORRY, TSUKASA-KUN. I HAD TO USE A SNAPSHOT.
(BACK WHEN HE WAS A TEENAGER.) HE HAD BEAUTIFUL SKIN,
AND HE WAS SO THIN. I DIDN'T HAVE HIS FLYER.

YUKINOJO

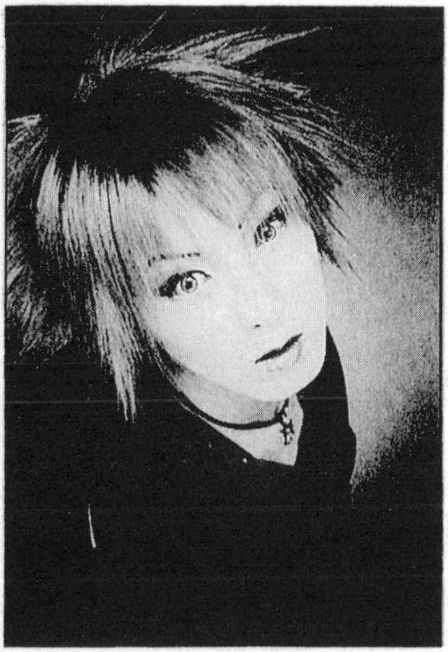

THIS IS BANSAKU-KUN.
HE'S SO CUTE. (BUT I THINK HE LOOKS
EVEN BETTER WITHOUT MAKEUP ON.)

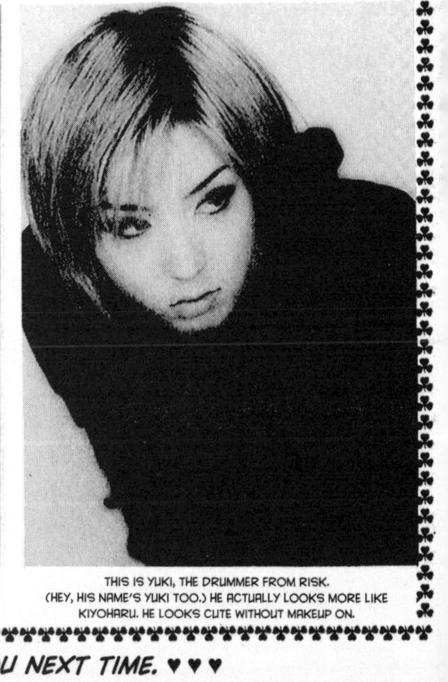

THIS IS YUKI, THE DRUMMER FROM RISK.
(HEY, HIS NAME'S YUKI TOO.) HE ACTUALLY LOOKS MORE LIKE
KIYOHARU. HE LOOKS CUTE WITHOUT MAKEUP ON.

THANKS FOR BEARING WITH ME. ♥

I'LL SEE YOU NEXT TIME. ♥♥♥

About the Creator

Tomoko Hayakawa was born on March 4.

   Since her debut as a manga creator, Tomoko Hayakawa has worked on many shojo titles with the theme of romantic love—only to realize that she could write about other subjects as well. She decided to pack her newest story with the things she likes most, which led to her current, enormously popular series, *The Wallflower*.

   Her favorite things are: Tim Burton's *The Nightmare Before Christmas*, Jean-Paul Gaultier, and samurai dramas on TV. Her hobbies are collecting items with skull designs and watching *bishonen* (beautiful boys). Her dream is to build a mansion like the one that the Addams family lives in. Her favorite pastime is to lie around at home with her cat, Ten (whose full name is Tennosuke).

   Her zodiac sign is Pisces, and her blood group is AB.

Translation Notes

Japanese is a tricky language for most Westerners, and translation is often more art than science. For your edification and reading pleasure, here are notes on some of the places where we could have gone in a different direction in our translation of the work, or where a Japanese cultural reference is used.

HOW CAN A GIRL LIKE THAT LIVE WITH SUCH HOT GUYS?
IT'S MORE LIKE SHE'S HAUNTING THEM.

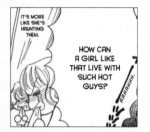

Haunting (page 8)

This is actually a pun that doesn't translate well into English. In Japanese, this girl literally says, "It's more like she's *living* with them." However, the character she uses for the word "living" is one that refers to unwelcome pests.

More Haunting (page 10)

Japanese high schools hold school festivals once a year. During the festival, each class sponsors an activity such as a dance or opens a food stall or a haunted house. Sometimes guests and visitors from other schools vote on the best project. A prize is often given to the winning class.

I HEARD THAT...
...THE CLASS THAT GETS THE MOST VOTES FOR THEIR SCHOOL FESTIVAL PROJECT...
...WINS 500,000 YEN. (APPROXIMATELY $5000)

MANGA CLUB

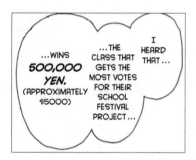

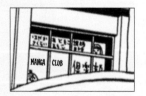

Manga Club (page 12)

During school festivals, sports teams and activity clubs usually put up signs and banners.

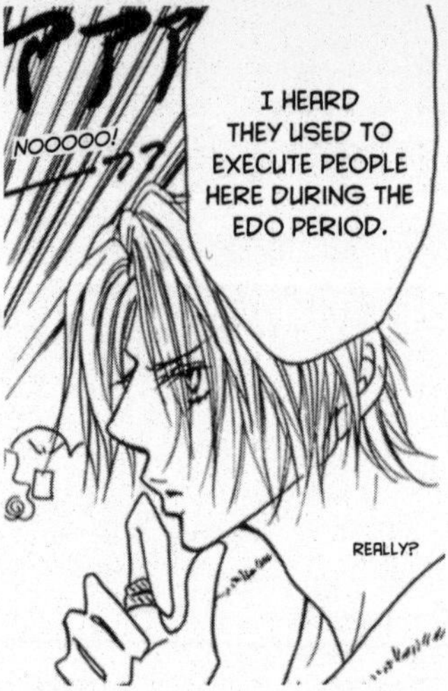
I HEARD THEY USED TO EXECUTE PEOPLE HERE DURING THE EDO PERIOD.
NOOOOO!
REALLY?

Edo (page 39)

The Edo period is a period in Japanese history that lasted through the mid 19th century. Edo is the old word for Tokyo.

Christmas (page 48)

In Japan, Christmas Eve is a holiday for lovers, much like Valentine's Day in the U.S. It's very important to have a date for Christmas Eve.

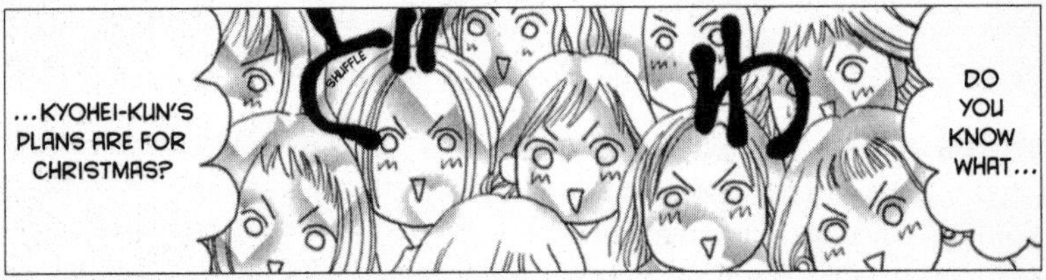
DO YOU KNOW WHAT...
SHUFFLE
...KYOHEI-KUN'S PLANS ARE FOR CHRISTMAS?

KFC for Everybody! (page 59)

For some reason, fried chicken is a celebratory Christmas food in Japan. KFC is always very busy on Christmas. Also, the "Sandy Claus" referenced here is a character from *Nightmare before Christmas*, one of Tomoko Hayakawa's favorite films.

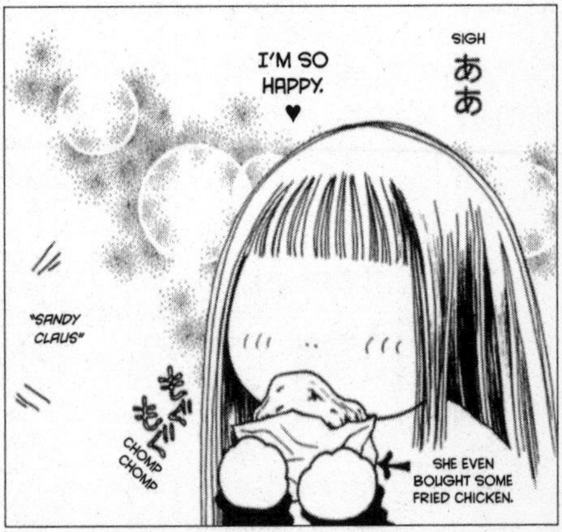
SIGH
ああ
I'M SO HAPPY. ♥
"SANDY CLAUS"
CHOMP CHOMP
SHE EVEN BOUGHT SOME FRIED CHICKEN.

Hahaa, My Lord (page 72)

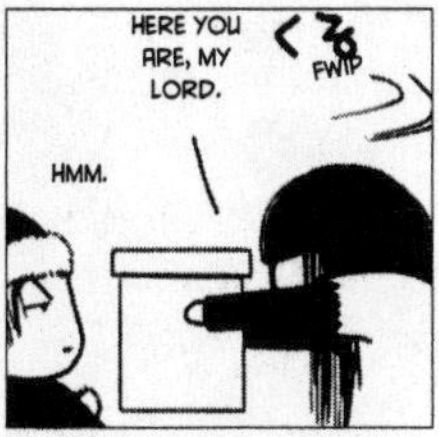
FWIP
HERE YOU ARE, MY LORD.
HMM.

When Sunako gives Kyohei the chicken, she says "hahaa." In samurai times, this is what people said when they presented a gift to someone of higher status. Here, we translated it as "here you are, my lord."

Soba Noodles (page 84)

Toshikoshi soba, translated as "New Year's Soba," is a traditional soba noodle dish eaten on New Year's Eve.

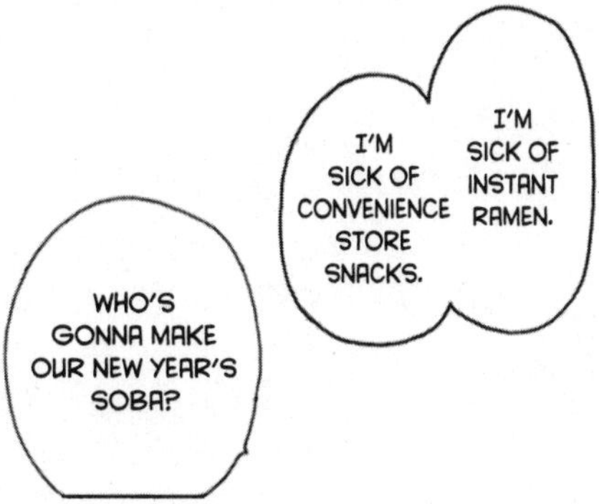
I'M SICK OF INSTANT RAMEN.
I'M SICK OF CONVENIENCE STORE SNACKS.
WHO'S GONNA MAKE OUR NEW YEAR'S SOBA?

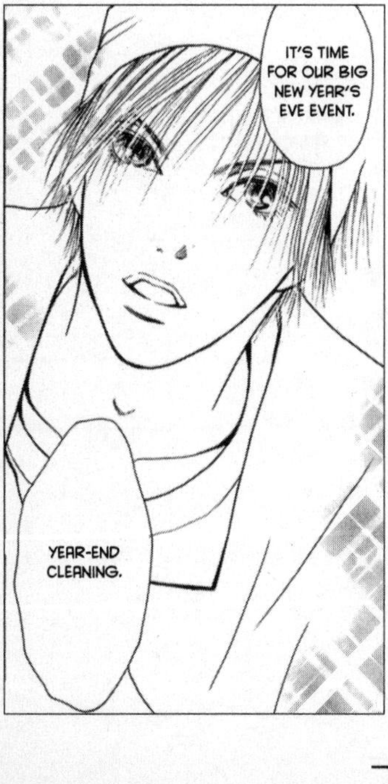
IT'S TIME FOR OUR BIG NEW YEAR'S EVE EVENT.
YEAR-END CLEANING.

Year-end Cleaning (page 86)

It's tradition to clean house before the New Year's festivities begin. It's the Japanese version of spring cleaning.

Smile, You're on Dorifu Camera (page 90)

Takenaga actually says "Are we in a *Dorifu* sketch or something?" *Dorifu* is an old sketch comedy group from the '80s.

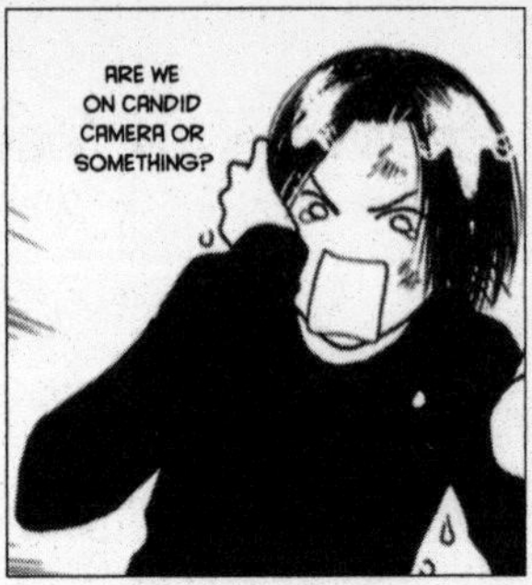
ARE WE ON CANDID CAMERA OR SOMETHING?

Love Songs (page 133)

Ranmaru actually says "It sounds like an *enka*." *Enka* is a popular style of Japanese music. The songs are often about lost or forbidden love.

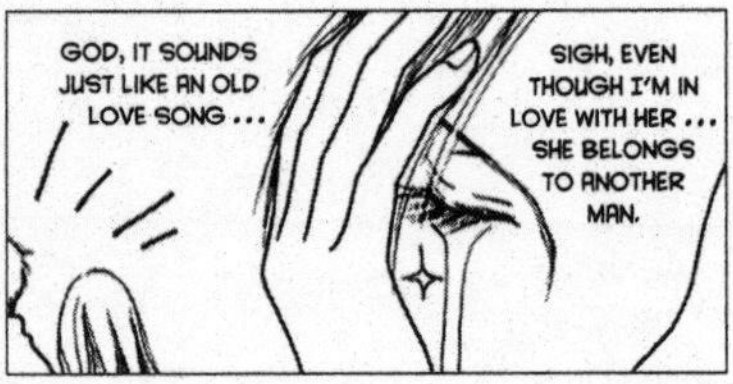
SIGH, EVEN THOUGH I'M IN LOVE WITH HER ... SHE BELONGS TO ANOTHER MAN.
GOD, IT SOUNDS JUST LIKE AN OLD LOVE SONG ...

Yukata (page 136)

A *yukata* is a casual kimono usually worn at a hot springs resort.

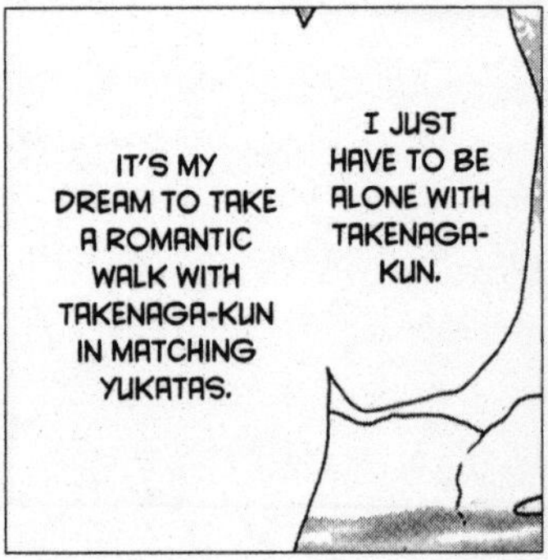
I JUST HAVE TO BE ALONE WITH TAKENAGA-KUN.
IT'S MY DREAM TO TAKE A ROMANTIC WALK WITH TAKENAGA-KUN IN MATCHING YUKATAS.

Preview of Volume 3

Here is an excerpt from Volume 3, on sale now in English.

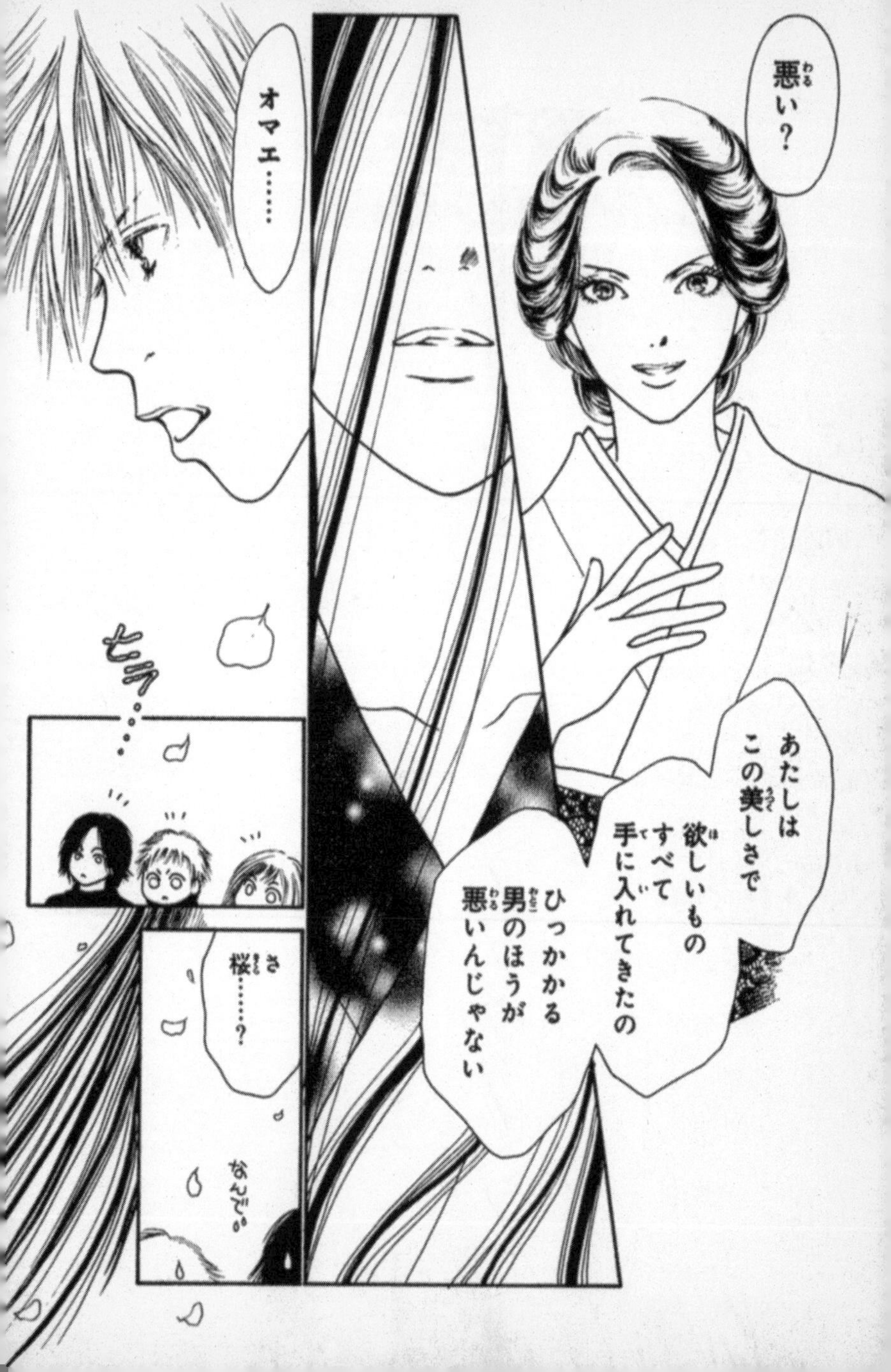
悪い？
あたしは この美しさで 欲しいもの すべて 手に入れてきたの
ひっかかる 男のほうが 悪いんじゃない
オマエ……
ヒラ……
桜……？
なんで。

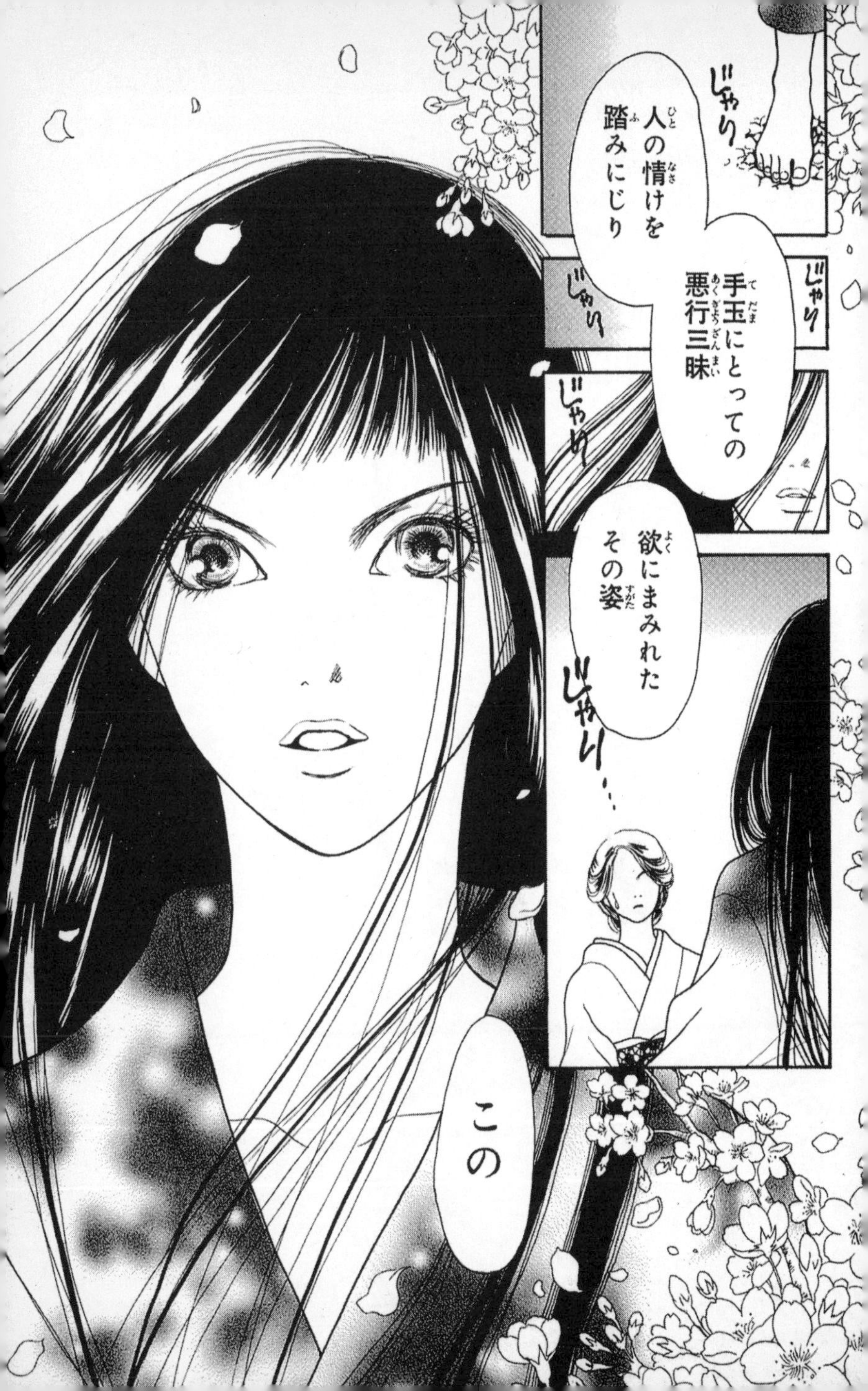
じゃり
人の情けを踏みにじり
じゃり
手玉にとっての悪行三昧
じゃり
じゃり
欲にまみれたその姿
じゃり…
この

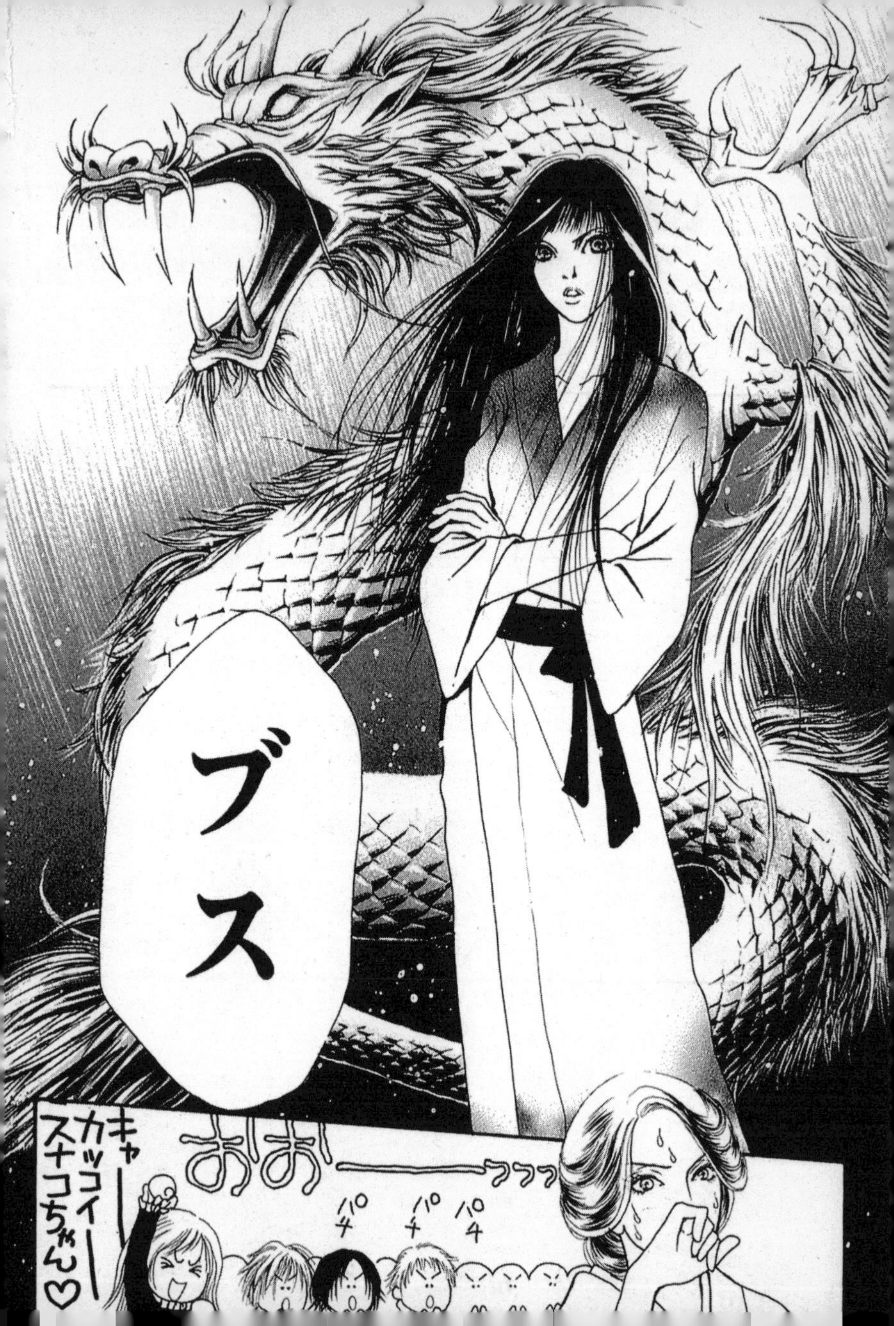
ブス
おお――っっっ
パチ パチ パチ
キャー カッコイー スナコちゃん♡

VOLUME 2
BY SATOMI IKEZAWA

Shy Yaya spends her time in awkward conversations with her handsome classmate, guitarist Moriyama; dressing up with fellow fans of the rock group Juliet; and avoiding her bitter, sadistic ex-friends. But whenever Yaya bumps her head or looks into a mirror, she changes into her other personality—boisterous, tough-as-nails Nana, who punishes the guilty and belts out Led Zeppelin tunes. Now Moriyama's mysterious adult friend, Shôhei, sets his sights on Nana. He is rumored to have close ties to the music industry, but instead harbors a secret agenda.

Volumes 1-7 are now available in bookstores.

 For more information and to sign up for Del Rey's manga e-newsletter, visit www.delreymanga.com

TOMARE!

止まれ

|STOP!|

You're going the wrong way!

Manga is a completely different type of reading experience.

To start at the *beginning*, go to the *end*!

That's right! Authentic manga is read the traditional Japanese way—from right to left. Exactly the *opposite* of how American books are read. It's easy to follow: Just go to the other end of the book, and read each page—and each panel—from right side to left side, starting at the top right. Now you're experiencing manga as it was meant to be!